D1558758

PLINY

NATURAL HISTORY

V

LIBRI XVII–XIX

371

PLINY

NATURAL HISTORY

WITH AN ENGLISH TRANSLATION
IN TEN VOLUMES

VOLUME V

LIBRI XVII–XIX

BY

H. RACKHAM, M.A.
FELLOW OF CHRIST'S COLLEGE, CAMBRIDGE

CAMBRIDGE, MASSACHUSETTS
HARVARD UNIVERSITY PRESS
LONDON
WILLIAM HEINEMANN LTD
MCMLXXI

American ISBN 0-674-99409-4
British ISBN 0 434 99371 9

First printed 1950
Reprinted 1961, 1971

Printed in Great Britain

CONTENTS

INTRODUCTION

This volume contains Books XVII, XVIII, XIX, of Pliny's *Naturalis Historia.* Book XVII continues the subject of arboriculture, begun in the preceding Books; Book XVIII deals with cereal agriculture; Book XIX with the cultivation of flax and other plants used for fabrics, and with vegetable gardening.

Pliny's own outline of the contents given in Book I will be found in Volume I, pp. 80–91.

At the time of his death Mr. Rackham was engaged in work on the galley proofs of this volume. With the exception of some parts which were re-written by Prof. E. H. Warmington the translation is Mr. Rackham's work. Note that there is an Index of plants at the end of Vol. VII.

PLINY:
NATURAL HISTORY
BOOK XVII

PLINII: NATURALIS HISTORIAE

LIBER XVII

I. NATURA arborum terra marique sponte sua provenientium dicta est; restat earum quae arte et humanis ingeniis fiunt verius quam nascuntur. sed prius mirari succurrit qua retulimus paenuria pro indiviso possessas a feris, depugnante cum his homine circa caducos fructus, circa pendentes vero et cum alitibus, in tanta deliciarum pretia venisse, clarissimo, ut equidem arbitror, exemplo L. Crassi atque Cn.
2 Domitii Ahenobarbi. Crassus orator fuit in primis nominis Romani; domus ei magnifica, sed aliquanto praestantior in eodem Palatio Q. Catuli qui Cimbros cum C. Mario fudit, multo vero pulcerrima consensu omnium aetate ea in colle Viminali C. Aquilii equitis Romani clarioris illa etiam quam iuris civilis scientia,

[a] The battle of the Raudine Plain, 101 B.C.

PLINY: NATURAL HISTORY

BOOK XVII

I. We have now stated the nature of the trees that grow of their own accord on land and in the sea; and there remain those which owe what is more truly described as their formation than their birth to art and to the ingenious devices of mankind. But it is in place first to express surprise at the way in which the trees that, under the niggardly system that we have recorded, were held in common ownership by the wild animals, with man doing battle with them for the fruit that fell to the ground and also with the birds for that which still hung on the tree, have come to command such high prices as articles of luxury—the most famous instance, in my judgement, being the affair of Lucius Crassus and Gnaeus Domitius Ahenobarbus. Crassus was one of the leading Roman orators; he owned a splendid mansion, but it was considerably surpassed by another that was also on the Palatine Hill, belonging to Quintus Catulus, the colleague of Gaius Marius in the defeat[a] of the Cimbrians; while by far the finest house of that period was by universal agreement the one on the Viminal Hill owned by Gaius Aquilius, Knight of Rome, who was even more celebrated for this property than he was for his knowledge of civil law, although nevertheless in the case of

Arboriculture. Valuable trees.

3 cum[1] tamen obiecta Crasso sua est. nobilissimarum gentium ambo censuram post consulatus simul gessere anno conditae urbis DCLXII frequentem iurgiis propter dissimilitudinem morum. tum Cn. Domitius, ut erat vehemens natura, praeterea accensus odio, quod ex aemulatione acidissimum[2] est, graviter increpuit tanti censorem habitare, $\overline{\text{M}}$ HS pro domo eius
4 identidem promittens; et Crassus, ut praesens ingenio semper et[3] faceto lepore sollers, addicere se respondit exceptis sex arboribus. ac ne uno quidem denario si adimerentur emptam volente Domitio Crassus 'Utrumne igitur ego sum,' inquit, 'quaeso, Domiti, exemplo gravis et ipsa mea censura notandus qui domo quae mihi hereditate obvenit comiter
5 habitem, an tu qui sex arbores $\overline{\text{M}}$ aestimes?' hae fuere lotoe patula ramorum opacitate lascivae, Caecina Largo e proceribus crebro iuventa nostra eas in domo sua ostentante, duraveruntque, quoniam et de longissimo aevo arborum diximus, ad Neronis principis incendia [quibus cremavit urbem annis postea][4] cultu virides iuvenesque, ni princeps
6 ille adcelerasset etiam arborum mortem. ac ne quis vilem de cetero Crassi domum nihilque in ea

[1] tum? *Mayhoff.*
[2] acidissimum? *Mayhoff*: avidissimum *aut* audissimum.
[3] *Rackham* (ita? *Warmington*): ut.
[4] *Secl. Detlefsen.*

Crassus his mansion was considered a reproach to him. Crassus and Domitius both belonged to families of high distinction, and they were colleagues as consuls and afterwards, in 92 B.C., as censors: owing to their dissimilarity of character their tenure of the censorship was filled with quarrels between them. On the occasion referred to, Gnaeus Domitius, being a man of hasty temper and moreover inflamed by that particularly sour kind of hatred which springs out of rivalry, gave Crassus a severe rebuke for living on so expensive a scale when holding the office of censor, and repeatedly declared that he would give a million sesterces for his mansion; and Crassus, who always had a ready wit and was good at clever repartees, replied that he accepted the bid, with the reservation of half a dozen trees. Domitius declined to buy the place even for a shilling without the timber. 'Well then,' said Crassus, 'tell me pray, Domitius, am I the one who is setting a bad example and who deserves a mark of censure from the very office which I am myself occupying—I, who live quite unpretentiously in the house that came to me by inheritance, or is it you, who price six trees at a million sesterces?' The trees referred to were nettle-trees, with an exuberance of spreading, shady branches; Caecina Largus, one of the great gentlemen of Rome, in our young days used frequently to point them out in the mansion, of which he was then the owner, and they lasted—as we have already also spoken of the limits of longevity in XVI. 234 ff.
trees—down to the Emperor Nero's conflagration, A.D. 64
thanks to careful tendance still verdant and vigorous, had not the emperor mentioned hastened the death even of trees. And let nobody suppose that Crassus's mansion was in other respects a poor affair, and that it

iurganti Domitio fuisse licendum[1] praeter arbores iudicet, iam columnas VI[2] Hymettii marmoris aedilitatis gratia ad scenam ornandam advectas in atrio eius domus statuerat, cum in publico nondum essent ullae marmoreae: tam recens est opulentia! tantoque tunc plus honoris arbores domibus adferebant ut sine illis ne inimicitiarum quidem pretium servaverit Domitius.

7 Fuere ab his et cognomina antiquis: Frondicio militi illi qui praeclara facinora Volturnum transnatans fronde inposita adversus Hannibalem edidit, Stolonum Liciniae genti: ita appellatur in ipsis arboribus fruticatio inutilis, unde et pampinatio inventa primo Stoloni dedit nomen. fuit et arborum cura legibus priscis, cautumque est XII tabulis ut qui iniuria cecidisset alienas lueret in singulas aeris XXV. quid existimamus, venturasne eas credidisse ad supra dictam aestimationem illos qui vel frugiferas

8 tanti taxaverant? nec minus miraculum in pomo est multarum circa suburbana fructu annuo addicto binis milibus nummum, maiore singularum reditu quam erat apud antiquos praediorum. ob hoc insita et arborum quoque adulteria excogitata sunt, ut nec

[1] *Mayhoff*: dicendum.
[2] *Urlichs* (*cf.* XXXVI. 7): IV.

contained nothing beside trees to attract this provoking bid from Domitius; on the contrary, he had already erected for decorative purposes in the court of the mansion six pillars of marble from Mt. Hymettus, which in view of his aedileship he had imported to embellish the stage of the theatre—and this although hitherto there were no marble pillars in any public place: of so recent a date is luxurious wealth! And at that date so much greater distinction was added to mansions by trees that Domitius actually would not keep to the price suggested by a quarrel without the timber in question being thrown in.

Men's names from trees.

In former generations people even got their surnames from trees: for instance Frondicius, the soldier who performed such remarkable exploits against Hannibal, swimming across the Volturno with a screen of foliage on his head, and the Licinian family of the Stolones—*stolo* being the word for the useless suckers growing on the actual trees, on account of which the first Stolo received the name from his invention of a process of trimming vines. In early days trees even were protected by the law, and the Twelve Tables provided that anybody wrongfully felling another man's trees should be fined 25 *asses* for each tree. What are we to think? That people of old who rated even fruit-trees so highly believed that trees would rise to the value mentioned above? And in the matter of fruit-trees no less marvellous are many of those in the districts surrounding the city, the produce of which is every year knocked down to bids of 2000 sesterces per tree, a single tree yielding a larger return than farms used to do in old days. It was on this account that grafting, and the practice of adultery even by trees, was devised, so that not even fruit

Valuable fruit-trees.

9 poma pauperibus nascerentur. nunc ergo dicemus quonam maxime modo tantum ex his vectigal contingat, veram colendi rationem absolutamque prodituri, et ideo non volgata tractabimus nec quae constare animo advertimus, sed incerta atque dubia in quibus maxime fallitur vita; nam diligentiam supervacuis adfectare non nostrum est. ante omnia autem [in universum et] [1] quae ad cuncta arborum genera pertinent in commune de caelo terraque dicemus.

10 II. Aquilone maxime gaudent, densiores ab adflatu
eius laetioresque et materie firmiores. qua in re
plerique falluntur, cum in vineis pedamenta non sint
a vento eo opponenda et id tantum a septentrione
servandum. quin immo tempestiva frigora plurimum arborum firmitati conferunt et sic optime
germinant, alioqui, si blandiantur austri, defeti-
11 scentes, ac magis etiam in flore. nam si cum defloruere protinus sequantur imbres, in totum poma
depereunt, adeo ut amygdalae et piri, etiam si
omnino nubilum fuit austrinusve flatus, amittant
fetus. circa vergilias quidem pluere inimicissimum
viti et oleae, quoniam tum coitus est earum; hoc
est illud quadriduum oleis decretorium, hic articulus
austrinus nubili spurci quod diximus. fruges quoque
peius maturescunt austrinis diebus, sed celerius.

[1] *Secl. Mayhoff.*

---

[a] This comes from Theophrastus and is applicable to Greece, not Italy.

[b] At the end of spring.

should grow for the poor. We will now therefore state in what manner it chiefly comes about that such a large revenue is derived from these trees, going on to set forth the genuine and perfect method of cultivation, and for that purpose we shall not treat of the commonly known facts and those which we observe to be established, but of uncertain and doubtful points on which practical conduct chiefly goes wrong; as it is not our plan to give careful attention to superfluities. But first of all we will speak about matters of climate and soil that concern all kinds of trees in common.

Effect of aspect and weather.

II. Trees are specially fond of a north-east [a] aspect, wind in that quarter rendering their foliage denser and more abundant and their timber stronger. This is a point on which most people make a mistake, as the props in a vineyard ought not to be placed so as to shelter the stems from wind in that quarter, and this precaution should only be taken against a north wind. What is more, exposure to cold at the proper season contributes very greatly to the strength of the trees, and they bud best under those circumstances, as otherwise, if exposed to the caresses of the winds from the south-west, they languish, and especially when in blossom. In fact if the fall of the blossom is followed immediately by rain, the fruit is entirely ruined—so much so that almonds and pears lose their crop of fruit if the weather should be only cloudy or a south-west wind prevail. Rain at the rising of the Pleiads [b] indeed is extremely unfavourable for the vine and the olive, because that is their fertilizing season; this is the four-day period that decides the fate of the olives, this is the critical point when a south wind brings the dirty clouds
we spoke of. Also cereals ripen worse on days when XVI. 109.
the wind is in the south-west, though they ripen faster.

12 illa sunt noxia frigora quae septentrionibus aut praeposteris fiunt horis; hiemem quidem aquiloniam esse omnibus satis utilissimum. imbres vero tum expetendi evidens causa est, quoniam arbores fetu exinanitas et foliorum quoque amissione [1] languidas naturale est avide esurire, cibus autem earum imber.
13 quare tepidam esse hiemem, ut absumpto partu arborum sequatur protinus conceptus, id est germinatio, ac deinde alia florescendi exinanitio, inutilissimum experimentis creditur. quin immo si plures ita continuentur anni, etiam ipsae moriantur [2] arbores, quando nemini dubia poena est in fame laborantium; ergo qui dixit hiemes serenas optandas non pro
14 arboribus vota fecit. nec per solstitia imbres vitibus conducunt. hiberno quidem pulvere laetiores fieri messes luxuriantis ingenii fertilitate dictum est; alioqui vota arborum frugumque communia sunt nives diutinas sedere. causa non solum quia animam terrae evanescentem exhalatione includunt et conprimunt retroque agunt in vires frugum atque radices, verum quod et liquorem sensim praebent, purum praeterea levissimumque, quando aquarum
15 caelestium spuma pruina est.[3] ergo umor ex his non universus ingurgitans diluensque, sed quomodo sititur

[1] *Edd.*: emissione.
[2] moriuntur *edd.*
[3] *Rackham*: spuma est (pruina est *cd. Par. Lat.* 6795).

---

[a] Virgil, *Georgics* I. 100 hiemes orate serenas.

[b] A fragment of primitive verse preserved by Macrobius *Saturn.* v. 20 runs:

Hiberno pulvere, verno luto
Grandia farra, Camille, metes.

[c] Perhaps: 'thanks to a natural tendency to abundant growth'.

Cold weather only does damage when it comes with northerly winds, or not at the proper seasons; indeed for a north-east wind to prevail in winter is most beneficial for all crops. But there is an obvious reason for desiring rain in that season, because it is natural for the trees when exhausted by bearing fruit and also by the loss of their leaves to be famished with hunger, and rain is a food for them. Consequently experience inspires the belief that a mild winter, causing the trees the moment they have finished bearing to conceive, that is to bud, again, this being followed by another exhausting period of blossoming, is an extremely detrimental thing. Indeed if several years in succession should take this course, even the trees themselves may die, since no one can doubt the punishment they suffer from putting forth their strength when in a hungry condition; consequently the poet who told us to pray for finer winters [a] was not framing a litany for the benefit of trees. Nor yet is wet weather over midsummer good for vines. It has indeed been said,[b] thanks to the fertility of a vivid imagination,[c] that dust in winter makes more abundant harvests; but, quite apart from this, it is the prayer of trees and crops in common that snow may lie a long time. The reason is not only because snow shuts in and imprisons the earth's breath when it is disappearing by evaporation, and drives it back into the roots of the vegetation to make strength, but because it also affords a gradual supply of moisture, and this moreover of a pure and extremely light quality, owing to the fact that rime is the foam of the waters of heaven. Consequently the moisture from snow, not inundating and drenching everything all at once, but shedding drops as from a breast in proportion to the thirst felt, nourishes all

Trees benefited by snow.

destillans velut ex ubere, alit omnia quia[1] non inundat. tellus quoque illo modo fermentescit, et sui plena,[2] lactescentibus satis non effeta, cum tempus aperiit[3] tepidis adridet horis. ita maxime frumenta pinguescunt, praeterquam ubi calidus semper aer est, ut in Aegypto: continuatio enim et ipsa consuetudo idem quod modus aliubi efficit; plurimumque
16 prodest ubicumque non esse quod noceat. in maiore parte orbis, cum praecoces excurrere germinationes evocatae indulgentia caeli, secutis frigoribus exuruntur. qua de causa serotinae hiemes noxiae, silvestribus quoque, quae magis etiam dolent urguente umbra sua nec adiuvante medicina, quando vestire teneras intorto stramento in silvestribus non est.
17 ergo tempestivae aquae hibernis primum imbribus, dein germinationem antecedentibus; tertium tempus est cum educant poma, nec protinus sed iam valido fetu. quae fructus suos diutius continent longioresque desiderant cibos, his et serotinae aquae utiles, ut viti, oleae, punicis. hae tamen[4] pluviae generis cuiusque arboribus diverso modo desiderantur, aliis alio tempore maturantibus; quapropter eisdem imbribus aliqua laedi videas, aliqua iuvari etiam in

[1] *Mayhoff*: quae. [2] *Detlefsen*: plena a.
[3] *Rackham*: aperit. [4] *Mayhoff*: iam.

vegetation for the very reason that it does not deluge it. In this way the earth also is made to ferment, and is filled with her own substance, not exhausted by seeds sown in her trying to suck her milk, and when lapse of time has removed her covering she greets the mild hours with a smile. This is the method to make corn crops fatten most abundantly—except in countries where the atmosphere is always warm, for instance Egypt: for there the unvarying temperature and the mere force of habit produce the same effect as management produces elsewhere; and in any place it is of the greatest benefit for there to be nothing to cause harm. In the greater part of the world, when at the summons of heaven's indulgence the buds have hurried out too early, if cold weather follows they are shrivelled up. This is why late winters are injurious, even to forest trees as well, which actually suffer worse, because they are weighed down by their own shade, and because remedial measures cannot help them, to clothe the tender plants with wisps of straw not being possible in the case of forest trees. Consequently rain is favourable first at the period of the winter storms, and next with the wet weather coming before the budding period; and a third season is when the trees are forming their fruit, though not at the first stage but when the growth has become strong and healthy. Trees that hold back their fruit later and need more prolonged nourishment also receive benefit from late rains, for instance the vine, the olive and the pomegranate. These rains, however, are required in a different manner for each kind of tree, as they come to maturity at different times; consequently you may see the same storm of rain causing damage to some trees and benefiting others even

Effects of rain.

eodem genere, sicut in piris alio die hiberna quaerunt pluvias, alio vero praecocia, ut pariter quidem omnia desiderent hibernum tempus [1] ante germinationem.
18 quae aquilonem austro utiliorem facit ratio eadem mediterranea maritimis praefert—sunt enim plerumque frigidiora—et montuosa planis et nocturnos imbres diurnis: magis fruuntur aquis sata non statim auferente eas sole.

19 Conexa et situs vinearum arbustorumque ratio est, quas in horas debeant spectare. Vergilius ad occasus seri damnavit, aliqui sic maluere quam in exortu, a pluribus meridiem probari adverto; nec arbitror perpetuum quicquam in hoc praecipi posse—ad soli naturam, ad loci ingenium, ad caeli cuiusque mores
20 dirigenda sollertia est. in Africa meridiem vinaes spectare et viti inutile et colono insalubre est, quoniam ipsa meridianae subiacet plagae, quapropter ibi qui in occasum aut septentriones conseret optime miscebit solum caelo. cum Vergilius occasus improbet, nec de septentrione relinqui dubitatio videtur; atqui in subalpina [2] Italia magna ex parte vineis ita positis compertum est nullas esse fertiliores.
21 multum rationis optinent et venti. in Narbonensi provincia atque Liguria et parte Etruriae contra

[1] *Ian*: tempus est (tempus set *Mayhoff*).
[2] subalpina? *Mayhoff*: cisalpina (cisalpina Gallia *Strack*).

---

[a] *I.e.* the trees up which the vines are trained.

in the same class of trees, as for example among pears, winter varieties require rain on one day and early pears on another, although they all alike need a period of wintry weather before budding. The same cause that makes a north-west wind more beneficial than a south-west wind also renders inland regions superior to places on the coast—the reason being that they are usually cooler—and mountain districts superior to plains, and rain in the night preferable to rain by day, vegetation getting more enjoyment from the water when the sun does not immediately make it evaporate.

Effects of aspect on vines.

Connected with this subject is also the theory of the situation for vineyards and trees [a]—what aspect they should face. Virgil condemned their being planted looking west, but some have preferred that aspect to an easterly position, while most authorities, I notice, approve the south; and I do not think that any hard and fast rule can be laid down on this point—skilled attention must be paid to the nature of the soil, the character of the locality and the features of the particular climate. In Africa for vineyards to face south is bad for the vine and also unhealthy for the grower, because the country itself lies under the southern quarter of the sky, and consequently he who there chooses a westerly or northern aspect for planting will achieve the best blending of soil with climate. When Virgil condemns a western aspect, there seems no doubt that he condemns a northern aspect also, although in Italy below the Alps it has generally been experienced that no vineyards bear better than those so situated. The wind also forms a great consideration. In the province of Narbonne and in Liguria and part of Tuscany it is thought to be a mistake to plant vines

Georg. II. 298.

circium serere imperitia existimatur, eundemque oblicum accipere providentia; is namque aestates ibi temperat, sed tanta plerumque violentia ut
22 auferat tecta. quidam caelum terrae parere cogunt ut quae in siccis serantur orientem ac septentriones spectent, quae in umidis meridiem. nec non ex ipsis vitibus[1] causas mutuantur, in frigidis praecoces serendo, ut maturitas antecedat algorem, quae poma vitesque rorem oderint, contra ortus, ut statim auferat sol, quae ament, ad occasus vel etiam
23 ad septentriones, ut diutius eo fruantur. ceteri fere rationem naturae secuti in aquilonem obversas vites et arbores poni suasere: odoratiorem etiam fieri talem fructum Democritus putat. Aquilonis situm ventorumque reliquorum diximus secundo volumine, dicemusque proximo plura caelestia. interim manifestum videtur salubritatis argumentum quoniam in meridiem etiam spectantium semper ante decidant folia. similis et in maritimis causa:
24 quibusdam locis adflatus maris noxii, in plurimis idem alunt, quibusdam satis e longinquo aspicere maria iucundum, propius admoveri salis halitum inutile. similis et fluminum stagnorumque ratio: nebulis adurunt aut aestuantia refrigerant. opacitate atque

[1] vitis *Detlefsen.*

in a position directly facing a west-north-west wind, but at the same time to be a wise arrangement to let them catch the wind from that quarter sideways, because it moderates the heat of summer in those regions, although it usually blows with such violence as to carry away the roofs of houses. Some people make the question of aspect depend on the nature of the soil, letting vines planted in dry situations face east and north and those in a damp one south. Moreover, they borrow rules from the vines themselves, by planting early varieties in cold situations, so that their ripening may come before the cold weather, and fruit-trees and vines that dislike dew, with an eastern aspect, so that the sun may carry off the moisture at once, but those that like dew, facing west or even north, so that they may enjoy it for a longer time. But the rest, virtually following Nature's system, have recommended that vines and trees should be placed so as to face north-east; and Democritus is of opinion that the fruit so grown also has more scent. We have dealt in Book Two with positions facing north-east and II. 119. the other quarters, and we shall give more meteorological details in the next Book. In the meantime XVIII. 321 ff. a clear test of the healthiness of the aspect seems to lie in the fact that trees facing south are always the first to shed their leaves. A similar influence also operates in maritime districts: sea breezes are injurious in some places, while at the same time in most places they encourage growth; and some plants like having a distant view of the sea but are not benefited by being moved nearer to its saline exhalations. A similar principle applies also to rivers and marshes: they shrivel up vegetation by their mists or else they serve to cool excessively hot districts. The trees

etiam rigore gaudent quae diximus. quare experimentis optime creditur.
25 III. A caelo proximum est terrae dixisse rationem,
haud faciliore tractatu, quippe non eadem arboribus
convenit et frugibus plerumque, nec pulla qualem
habet Campania ubique optima vitibus, aut quae
tenues exhalat nebulas, nec rubrica multis laudata.
cretam in Albensium Pompeianorum agro et argillam
cunctis ad vineas generibus anteponunt, quamquam
praepingues,[1] quod excipitur in eo genere. invicem
sabulum album in Ticiniensi multisque in locis
nigrum itemque rubrum, etiam pingui terrae per-
26 mixtum, infecundum est. argumenta quoque iudi-
cantium saepe fallunt. non utique laetum solum
est in quo procerae arbores nitent praeterquam illis
arboribus; quid enim abiete procerius? at quae
vixisse possit alia in loco eodem? nec luxuriosa
pabula pinguis soli semper indicium habent: nam
quid laudatius Germaniae pabulis? at [2] statim subest
27 harena tenuissimo caespitum corio. nec semper
aquosa est terra cui proceritas herbarum, non, Hercules, magis quam pinguis adhaerens digitis, quod in
argillis arguitur. scrobes quidem regesta in eosdem [3]
nulla [4] conplet, ut densa atque rara ad hunc modum
deprehendi possit; ferroque omnis rubiginem obducit.

[1] praepingue est *Detlefsen.* [2] *Mayhoff*: et.
[3] *Rackham*: eos. [4] nulla⟨non⟩? *Warmington.*

[a] The writer is here contradicting Virgil, who says in *Georgics* II. 217–237 that a steamy soil which sucks up moisture and is always covered with grass, and which does not make iron rust, is good for vines trained up elm-trees, for olives, and for grazing and ploughland; and as a method of testing the quality of the soil he suggests digging a hole and then filling it in again, when if the earth does not completely fill the hole

that we have specified like shade and even cold. Consequently the best course is to rely on experiment.

Soils favourable for trees, vines, and crops. XVI. 74.

III. It comes next after the heavens to give an account of the earth, a subject no easier to deal with, inasmuch as the same land is not as a rule suited for trees and for crops, and the black earth of the kind that exists in Campania is not the best soil for vines everywhere, nor is a soil that emits thin clouds of vapour, nor the red earth that many writers have praised. The chalky soil in the territory of Alba Pompeia and a clay soil are preferred to all the other kinds for vines, although they are very rich, a quality to which exception is made in the case of that class of plants. Conversely the white sand in the Ticino district, and the black sand found in many places, and likewise red sand, even when intermingled with rich soil, are unproductive. The signs adduced in judging soil are often misleading. A soil in which lofty trees do brilliantly is not invariably favourable except for those trees: for what grows higher than a silver fir? yet what other tree could have lived in the same place? Nor do luxuriant pastures always indicate a rich soil: for what is more famous than the pastures of Germany? but immediately underneath a very thin skin of turf there is sand. And land where plants grow high is not always damp, any more, I protest, than soil that sticks to the fingers is always rich—a fact that is proved in the case of clay soils. In point of fact no soil when put back into the holes out of which it is dug completely fills them, so as to make it possible to detect a close soil and a loose soil in this manner; and all soil covers iron with rust.[a] Nor can a heavy

the land will be suitable for grazing and for vineyards, but if it more than fills it the soil will do for heavy arable land.

nec gravis aut levior iusto deprehenditur pondere: quod enim pondus terrae iustum intellegi potest? neque fluminibus adgesta semper laudabilis, quando
28 senescant sata quaedam aquosa sede [1]; neque illa quae laudatur diu praeterquam salici utilis sentitur. inter argumenta stipulae crassitudo est, tanta alioqui in Leborino Campaniae nobili campo ut ligni vice utantur; sed id solum ubicumque arduum opere, difficili cultu [2] bonis suis acrius paene quam vitiis
29 posset adfligit agricolam. et carbunculus, quae terra ita vocatur,[3] emendari marga [4] videtur; nam tofus naturae [5] friabilis expetitur quoque ab auctoribus. Vergilius et quae filicem ferat non inprobat vitibus; salsaeque terrae multa melius creduntur, tutiora a vitiis innascentium animalium. nec colles opere nudantur si quis perite fodiat, nec campi omnes minus solis atque perflatus quam opus sit accipiunt; et quasdam pruinis ac nebulis pasci diximus vites. omnium rerum sunt quaedam in alto secreta et suo
30 cuique corde pervidenda. quid quod mutantur saepe iudicata quoque et diu conperta? [6] in Thessalia circa Larisam emisso lacu frigidior facta ea regio est, oleaeque desierunt quae prius fuerant,

[1] *Rackham*: aqua sed (aquae sede? *Mayhoff*).
[2] [difficili cultu]? *Rackham*
[3] [quae . . . vocatur]? *Rackham*.
[4] marga *Usener*: videmacra *et alia* (intenta cura *Mayhoff*).
[5] *Mayhoff*: natura *Detlefsen*: scaber natura *edd. vett.*: scaber ac *Sillig*: satura ac *aut* satur ac.
[6] *Gelen.*: compressa.

[a] Red sandstone.

or a light soil be detected by a standard of weight, for what can be understood to be the standard weight of earth? Nor is alluvial soil deposited by rivers always to be recommended, seeing that some plants do not flourish in a damp situation; nor does that much praised alluvial soil prove in experience to be beneficial for a long period, except for a willow. One of the signs of a good soil is the thickness of the stalk in corn, which incidentally in the famous Leborine plain in Campania is so large that they use it as a substitute for wood; but this class of soil is everywhere hard to work, and owing to this difficulty of cultivation puts almost a heavier burden on the farmer because of its merits than it could possibly inflict by reason of defects. Also the soil designated glowing-coal earth[a] appears to be improved by marl; and in fact tufa of a pliable consistency is actually held by the authorities to be a desideratum. For vines Virgil actually does not disapprove of a soil in which ferns grow; and many *Georg.* II. 189.
plants are improved by being entrusted to salt land, as they are better protected against damage from creatures breeding in the ground. Hillsides are not denuded of their soil by cultivation if the digging is done skilfully, and not all level ground gets less than the necessary amount of sun and air; and some varieties of vine, as we have said, draw nourishment XIV. 23.
from frosts and clouds. All matters contain some deeply hidden mysteries, which each person must use his own intelligence to penetrate. What of the fact that changes often occur even in things that have been investigated and ascertained long ago? In the district of Larisa in Thessaly the emptying of a lake has lowered the temperature of the district, and olives which used to grow there before have disappeared,

item vites aduri, quod non antea, . . .[1] Aenos sensit admoto Hebro, et circa Philippos cultura siccata regio mutavit caeli habitum. at in Syracusano agro advena cultor elapidato solo perdidit fruges luto, donec regessit lapides. in Syria levem tenui sulco inprimunt vomerem, quia subest saxum exurens aestate semina.

31 Iam in quibusdam locis similis aestus inmodici et frigorum effectus. est fertilis frugum Thracia[2] rigore, aestibus Africa et Aegyptus. in Chalcia Rhodiorum insula locus quidam est in tantum fecundus ut suo tempore satum demetant hordeum sublatoque[3] protinus serant et cum aliis frugibus metant. glareosum oleis solum aptissimum in Venafrano, pinguissimum in Baetica. Pucina vina in saxo cocuntur, Caecubae vites in Pomtinis paludibus madent. tanta est argumentorum ac soli
32 varietas ac differentia. Caesar Vopiscus cum causam apud censores ageret campos Rosiae dixit Italiae sumen esse, in quibus perticas pridie relictas gramen operiret; sed non nisi ad pabulum probantur. non tamen indociles natura nos esse voluit, et vitia confessa

[1] *Pintianus*: ⟨coeperunt, contra calorem augeri⟩ *Urlichs.*
[2] frugum Thracia? *Mayhoff*: Thracia frugum.
[3] *Rackham*: sublatumque.

---

[a] The MS. text seems to give 'olives . . . have disappeared; also the city of Aenos has seen its vines nipped, which did not occur before, since the river Maritza . . .' The passage has been conjecturally expanded to conform with Theophrastus on which it is based.

[b] East of Aquileia.

also the vines have begun to be nipped, which did not occur before; while on the other hand the city of Aenos, since the river Maritza was brought near to it, has experienced an increase of warmth [a] and the district round Philippi altered its climate when its land under cultivation was drained. On the other hand on land belonging to Syracuse a farmer who was a newcomer to the district by removing the stones from the soil caused his crops to be ruined by mud, until he carried the stones back again. In Syria they use a light ploughshare that cuts a narrow furrow, because the subsoil is rock which causes the seeds to be scorched in summer.

Soil and climate.

Again, immoderate heat and cold have a similar effect in certain places. Thrace owes its fertility in corn to cold, Africa and Egypt to heat. There is one place in the island of Chalcia belonging to Rhodes which is so fertile that they reap barley sown at its proper time and after carrying it at once sow the field again and reap a second crop of barley with the other harvest. In the district of Venafrum a gravel soil is found to be most suitable for olives, but in Baetica a very rich soil. The vines of Pucinum [b] are scorched on rock, whereas those of Caecubum grow in the damp ground of the Pontine Marshes. So much variety and diversity obtains in the evidence of experience and in soil. Vopiscus Caesar when appearing in a case before the Censors spoke of the plains of Rosia as 'the paps of Italy', where stakes left lying on the ground the day before were hidden with grass; but these plains are only valued for pasture. Nevertheless Nature did not wish that we should be uninstructed, and has caused errors to be fully admitted even where she had not given clear

fecit etiam ubi bona certa non fecerat: quamobrem primum crimina dicemus.

33 Terram amaram [probaverim][1] demonstrant eius[2] atrae degeneresque herbae, frigidam autem retorride nata, item uliginosam tristia, rubricam oculi argillamque, operi difficillimas quaeque rastros aut vomeres ingentibus glaebis onerent, quamquam non quod operi hoc et fructui adversum; item e contrario cineraceam et sabulum album; nam sterilis denso callo facile deprehenditur vel uno ictu cuspidis.
34 Cato breviter atque ex suo more vitia determinat: 'Terram cariosam cave neve plaustro neve pecore inpellas.' quid putamus hac appellatione ab eo tantopere reformidari ut paene vestigiis quoque interdicat? redigamus ad ligni cariem, et inveniemus illa quae in tantum abominatur vitia aridae, fistulosae, scabrae, canentis, exesae, pumicosae.
35 plus dixit una significatione quam possit ulla copia sermonis enarrari. est enim interpretatione vitiorum quaedam non aetate, quae nulla in ea intellegi potest, sed natura sua anilis,[3] terra, et ideo infecunda
36 ad omnia atque inbecilla. idem agrum optimum iudicat ab radice montium planitie in meridiem excurrentem,[4] qui est totius Italiae situs, terram vero teneram quae vocetur pulla; erit igitur haec optima

[1] *Secl. Mayhoff* (*vel* probaturis).
[2] *Mayhoff*: eas.
[3] *Mayhoff*: anus.
[4] *Rackham*: excurrente.

[a] *De Agri Cultura* (in early printed editions *De Re Rustica*) V. 6.
[b] *Ibid.*, I. 3, CLI. 2.

information as to the good points; and accordingly we will first speak about soil defects.

A bitter soil is indicated by its black undergrown plants; shrivelled shoots indicate a cold soil, and drooping growths show a damp soil; red earth and damp clay are noted by the eye—they are very difficult to work, and liable to burden the rakes or ploughshares with huge clods—although what is an obstacle to working the soil is not also a handicap to its productivity; and similarly the eye can discern the opposite, an ash-coloured soil and a white sand; while a barren soil with its hard surface is easily detected by even a single stroke of a prong. Cato [a] defines defects of soil briefly and in his customary style: 'Take care when the soil is rotten not to dent it either with a waggon or by driving cattle over it'. What do we infer from this designation to have been the thing that so much alarmed him that he almost prohibits even setting foot on it? Let us compare it with rottenness in wood, and we shall find that the faults of soil which he holds in such aversion consist in being dry, porous, rough, white, full of holes and like pumice-stone. He has said more by one striking word than could be fully recounted by any quantity of talk. For some soil exists which analysis of its vices shows to be not old in age, a term which conveys no meaning in the case of earth, but old in its own nature, and consequently infertile and powerless for every purpose. The same authority [b] gives the view that the best land is that extending in a level plain from the base of a mountain range in a southerly direction, this being the conformation of the whole of Italy, and that the soil called 'dark' is 'tender'; consequently this will be the best land both for

Varieties of soil.

et operi et satis. intellegere modo libeat dictam mira significatione teneram, et quidquid optari debet
37 in eo vocabulo invenietur. illa temperatae ubertatis, illa mollis facilisque culturae, nec madida nec sitiens, illa post vomerem nitescens, qualem fons ingeniorum Homerus in armis a deo[1] caelatam dixit addiditque miraculum nigrescentis, quamvis fieret ex auro; illa quam recentem exquirunt inprobae alites vomerem comitantes corvique aratoris vestigia ipsa rodentes.

38 Reddatur hoc in loco luxuriae quoque sententia aliqua et[2] in propositum certe. Cicero,[3] lux doctrinarum altera, 'Meliora,' inquit, 'unguenta sunt quae terram quam quae crocum sapiunt'—hoc enim maluit dixisse quam 'redolent.' ita est pro-
39 fecto, illa erit optima quae unguenta sapiet. quod si admonendi sumus qualis sit terrae odor ille qui quaeritur, contingit saepe etiam quiescente ea sub occasum solis, in quo loco arcus caelestes deiecere capita sua, et cum a siccitate continua immaduit imbre. tunc emittit illum suum halitum divinum ex sole conceptum, cui conparari suavitas nulla possit. is edi[4] commota debebit, repertusque neminem fallet; ac de terra odor optime iudicabit.

[1] *Hermolaus*: ab eo.
[2] *Warmington*: et alioqui? *Mayhoff*: et aliqua (Italica *Sillig*).
[3] propositum. Certe Cicero *vel* propositum certe citanda. Cicero *coni. Warmington.*
[4] *Warmington*: esse.

[a] *Iliad* XVIII. 541 ff.
[b] *De Oratore* III. 99.

working and for the crops. We need only try to see the meaning of this remarkably significant expression 'tender', and we shall discover that the term comprises every desideratum. 'Tender' soil is soil of moderate richness, a soft and easily worked soil, neither damp nor parched; it is soil that shines behind the ploughshare, like the field which Homer, the fountain-head of all genius, has described[a] as represented by a divine artist in a carving on a shield, and he has added the marvellous touch about the furrow showing black although the material used to represent it was gold; it is the soil that when freshly turned attracts the rascally birds which accompany the ploughshare and the tribe of crows which peck the very footprints of the ploughman.

Soils distinguished by taste or smell.

In this place moreover may be quoted a dictum as to luxury that is also undoubtedly to the point. Cicero, that other luminary of learning, says[b] 'Unguents with an earthy taste are better than those with the flavour of saffron'—he preferred the word 'taste' to 'smell'. It is certainly the case that a soil which has a taste of perfume will be the best soil. And if we need an explanation as to what is the nature of this odour of the soil that is desiderated, it is that which often occurs even when the ground is not being turned up, just towards sunset, at the place where the ends of rainbows have come down to earth, and when the soil has been drenched with rain following a long period of drought. The earth then sends out that divine breath of hers, of quite incomparable sweetness, which she has conceived from the sun. This is the odour which ought to be emitted when the earth is turned up, and when found it will deceive no one; and the scent of the soil will be the best criterion of its

talis fere est in novalibus caesa vetere silva, quae
40 consensu laudatur. et in frugibus quidem ferendis eadem terra utilior intellegitur quotiens intermissa cultura quievit, quod in vineis non fit; eoque est diligentius eligenda, ne vera existat opinio eorum qui
41 iam Italiae terram existimavere lassam. operis quidem facultas[1] in aliis generibus constat et caelo, nec potest arari post imbres aliqua, ubertatis vitio lentescens: contra in Byzacio Africae illum centena quinquagena fruge fertilem campum nullis, cum siccum est, arabilem tauris, post imbres vili asello et a parte altera iugi anu vomerem trahente vidimus scindi. terram enim terra emendandi,[2] ut aliqui praecipiunt, super tenuem pingui iniecta aut gracili bibulaque super umidam ac praepinguem, dementis[3] operae est: quid potest sperare qui colit talem?

42 IV. Alia est ratio, quam Britanniae et Galliae invenere, alendi eam ipsa, genusque quod[4] vocant margam: spissior ubertas in ea intellegitur et quidam terrae adipes ac velut glandia in corporibus, ibi densante se pinguitudinis nucleo. non omisere et hoc Graeci—quid enim intemptatum illis? leuc-

[1] facilitas *Mayhoff*.

[2] emendandi ⟨ratio⟩? *Warmington, sed cf.* Tac. *Ann.* XIII. 26, XV. 5.

[3] *Ian* (*cf.* II. 85): dementia.

[4] [quod]? *Mayhoff*.

quality. This is the kind of earth usually found in land newly ploughed where an old forest has been felled, earth that is unanimously spoken highly of. And in the matter of bearing cereals the same earth is understood to be more fertile the more often cultivation has been suspended and it has lain fallow; but this is not done in the case of vineyards, and consequently the greater care must be exercised in the selection of their site, so as not to justify the opinion of those who have formed the view that the land of Italy has by this time been exhausted. In other kinds of soil, it is true, ease of cultivation depends also on the weather, and some land cannot be ploughed after rain, as owing to excessive richness it becomes sticky; but on the other hand in the African district of Byzacium, that fertile plain which yields an increase of one hundred and fifty fold, land which in dry weather no bulls can plough, after a spell of rain we have seen being broken by a plough drawn by a wretched little donkey and an old woman at the other end of the yoke. The plan of improving one soil by means of another, as some prescribe, throwing a rich earth on the top of a poor one or a light porous soil on one that is moist and too lush, is an insane procedure: what can a man possibly hope for who farms land of that sort?

Use of marls for manure.

IV. There is another method, discovered by the provinces of Britain and those of Gaul, the method of feeding the earth by means of itself, and the kind of soil called marl: this is understood to contain a more closely packed quality of richness and a kind of earthy fatness, and growths corresponding to the glands in the body, in which a kernel of fat solidifies. This also has not been overlooked by the Greeks—indeed what have they left untested? They give the

argillon vocant candidam argillam qua in Megarico agro utuntur, sed tantum in umida frigidaque terra.
43 illam Gallias Britanniasque locupletantem cum cura dici convenit.

Duo genera fuerant, plura nuper exerceri coepta proficientibus ingeniis: est enim alba, rufa, columbina, argillacea, tofacea, harenacea. natura duplex, aspera aut pinguis: experimenta utriusque in manu. usus aeque [1] geminus, ut fruges tantum alant aut
44 eaedem et pabulum. fruges alit tofacea, albaque si inter fontes reperta est, ad infinitum fertilis, verum aspera tractatu; si nimia iniecta est, exurit solum. proxima est rufa, quae vocatur acaunumarga, intermixto lapide terrae minutae, harenosae. lapis contunditur in ipso campo, primisque annis stipula difficulter caeditur propter lapides. inpendio tamen minima levitate dimidio minoris quam ceterae invehitur. inspergitur rara; sale eam misceri putant. utrumque hoc genus semel iniectum in L annos valet et frugum et pabuli ubertate.

45 Quae pingues esse sentiuntur, ex his praecipua alba. plura eius genera: mordacissimum quod supra diximus. alterum genus albae creta argentaria est; petitur ex alto, in centenos pedes actis plerumque

[1] *Detlefsen*: manus usaeque *aut sim.*

---

[a] Celtic *agaunum*, 'stone'.

name of *leucargillum* to a white clay that they use on the land at Megara, but only where the soil is damp and chilly. The other substance brings wealth to the provinces of Gaul and Britain, and may suitably receive a careful description.

There had previously been two kinds of marl, but recently with the progress of discoveries a larger number have begun to be worked: there is white marl, red marl, dove-coloured marl, argillaceous marl, tufa marl and sand marl. It has a two-fold consistency, rough or greasy, each of which can be detected by its feel in the hand. Its use is correspondingly double, to feed cereals only or to feed pasture-land as well. Tufa marl nourishes grain, and white marl, if it is found where springs rise, has unlimited fertilizing properties, but it is rough to handle, and if it is scattered in excessive quantities it scorches up the soil. The next kind is the red marl, which is known as *acaunumarga*,[a] consisting of stone mingled with a thin, sandy earth. The stone is crushed on the land itself, and in the earliest years of its employment the fragments make the cornstalks difficult to cut; however, as it is extremely light it can be carried for only half of the cost charged for the other varieties. It is scattered on the land thinly; it is thought to contain a mixture of salt. With both of these kinds a single scattering serves for fifty years to fertilize either crops or pasture.

Of the marls that are greasy to the touch the chief one is the white. It has several varieties, the most pungent being the one mentioned above. Another §§ 43–44.
variety of white marl is the chalk used for cleaning silver; this is obtained from a considerable depth in the ground, usually from pits made 100 feet deep, with

puteis, ore angustiore,[1] intus ut in metallis spatiante vena. hac maxime Britannia utitur. durat annis LXXX, neque est exemplum ullius qui bis in vita hanc
46 eidem iniecerit. tertium genus candidae glisomargam vocant; est autem creta fullonia mixta pingui terra, pabuli quam frugum fertilior, ita ut messe sublata ante sementem alteram laetissimum secetur; dum fruges,[2] nullum aliud gramen emittit. durat XXX annis; densior iusto Signini modo strangulat solum. columbinam Galliae suo nomine eglecopalam appellant; glaebis excitatur lapidum modo, sole et gelatione ita solvitur ut tenuissimas bratteas faciat.
47 haec ex aequo fertilis. harenacea utuntur si alia non sit, in uliginosis vero et si alia sit. Ubios gentium solos novimus qui fertilissimum agrum colentes quacumque terra infra pedes tres effossa et pedali crassitudine iniecta laetificent; sed ea non diutius annis X prodest. Aedui et Pictones calce uberrimos fecere agros, quae sane et oleis vitibusque utilissima
48 reperitur. omnis autem marga arato inicienda est, ut medicamentum rapiatur; et fimum desiderat quantulumcumque, primo plus aspera et quae in herbas non effunditur: alioquin novitate quaecumque

[1] angusto (angustiore?) *Mayhoff*: angustur *cd. Vat. Lat.* 3861, *m.* 1: angustatur *rell.*

[2] *Mayhoff*: dum in fruge est (in frugem exit *J. Mueller*).

a narrower mouth but with the shaft expanding in the interior, as is the practice in mines. This chalk is chiefly used in Britain. Its effect lasts for 80 years, and there is no case of anybody having scattered it on the same land twice in his lifetime. A third kind of white marl is called *glisomarga* ; this is fullers' chalk intermixed with a greasy earth, and it is a more effective dressing for pasture than for corn, so that, when a crop of corn has been carried, before the next sowing a very abundant crop of hay can be cut, although while growing corn the land does not produce any other plant. Its effect lasts 30 years; but if it is scattered too thickly it chokes the soil just as Segni plaster does. For dove-coloured marl the Gallic provinces have a name in their own language, *eglecopala* ; it is taken up in blocks like stone, and is split by the action of sun and frost so as to form extremely thin plates. This kind of marl is equally beneficial for corn and grass. Farmers use sandy marl if no other is available ; but they use it on damp soils even if another sort is available. The Ubii are the only race known to us who while cultivating extremely fertile land enrich it by digging up any sort of earth below three feet and throwing it on the land in a layer a foot thick; but the benefit of this top-dressing does not last longer than ten years. The Aedui and the Pictones have made their arable land extremely fertile by means of chalk, which is indeed also found most useful for olives and vines. But all marl should be thrown on the land after it has been ploughed, in order that its medicinal properties may be absorbed at once ; and it requires a moderate amount of dung, as at first it is too rough and is not diffused into vegetation; otherwise whatever

fuerit solum laedet, ne sic quidem primo anno fertilis. interest et quali solo quaeratur; sicca enim umido melior, arido pinguis; temperato alterutra, creta vel columbina, convenit.

49 V. Transpadanis cineris usus adeo placet ut anteponant fimo, iumentorumque, quod levissimum est, ob id exurant. utroque tamen pariter non utuntur in eodem arvo, nec in arbustis cinere, nec quasdam ad fruges, ut dicemus. sunt qui pulvere quoque uvas ali iudicent pubescentesque pulverent et vitium arborumque radicibus adspergant. quod certum est, Narbonensi provinciae et vindemias circius sic coquit, plusque [1] pulvis ibi quam sol confert.

50 VI. Fimi plures differentiae, ipsa res antiqua: iam apud Homerum regius senex agrum ita laetificans suis manibus reperitur. Augeas rex in Graecia excogitasse traditur, divulgasse vero Hercules in Italia, quae regi suo Stercuto Fauni filio ob hoc inventum inmortalitatem tribuit. M. Varro principatum dat turdorum fimo ex aviariis, quod etiam pabulo boum suumque magnificat, neque alio cibo celerius pinguescere adseverat. de nostris moribus bene sperare est si tanta apud maiores fuere

[1] plus quia *Detlefsen*.

---

[a] The trees on which the vines are trained.
[b] *Od.* XXIV. 225.
[c] From *stercus*, 'dung'.
[d] *De Re Rustica* I. 38. 2.

sort of marl is used it will injure the soil by its novelty, as even with dung it does not promote fertility in the first year. It also makes a difference what sort of soil the marl is required for, as the dry kind is better for a damp soil and the greasy kind for a dry soil, while either sort suits land of medium quality, either chalk-marl or dove-marl.

V. Farmers north of the Po are so fond of employing ash that they prefer it to dung, and they burn stable dung, which is the lightest kind, in order to get the ash. Nevertheless they do not use both kinds of manure indifferently in the same field, and do not use ashes in plantations of shrubs, nor for some kinds of crops, as we shall explain later. Some are of the opinion that dust helps the growth of grapes, and they sprinkle it on the fruit when it is forming and scatter it on the roots of the vines and the trees.[a] It is certainly the case that in the Province of Narbonne a wind from west-north-west ripens vintage grapes, and in that district dust contributes more than sunshine. *Other manures.*

VI. There are several varieties of dung, and its actual employment dates a long way back; as far back as Homer,[b] an aged king in the poem is found thus enriching his land with his own hands. The invention of this procedure is traditionally ascribed to King Augeas in Greece, and its introduction in Italy to Hercules, though Italy has immortalized Stercutus[c] son of Faunus on account of this invention. Marcus Varro[d] gives the first rank to thrushes' droppings from aviaries, which he also extols for fodder of cattle and swine, declaring that no other fodder fattens them more quickly. If our ancestors had such large aviaries that they supplied manure for the fields, it is *Dung.*

51 aviaria ut ex his agri stercorarentur. primum[1] Columella e[2] columbariis, mox ex[3] gallinariis facit, natantium alitum damnato. ceteri auctores consensu humanas dapes ad hoc inprimis advocant; alii ex his praeferunt potus hominum in coriariorum officinis pilo madefacto, alii per sese aqua iterum largiusque etiam quam cum bibitur admixta: quippe plus ibi mali domandum est cum ad virus illud vini homo accesserit. haec sunt certamina; invicemque ad tellurem quoque
52 alendam utuntur[4] homine.[5] proxime spurcitias suum laudant, Columella solus damnat. alii cuiuscumque quadripedis ex cytiso, aliqui columbaria praeferunt. proximum deinde caprarum est, ab hoc ovium, dein boum, novissimum iumentorum.

53 Hae fuere apud priscos differentiae, simulque praecepta non invenio recentia[6] utendi, quando et hic vetustas utilior; visumque iam est apud quosdam provincialium in tantum abundante geniali copia pecudum farinae vice cribris superinici, faetore aspectuque temporis viribus in quandam etiam gratiam mutato. (Nuper repertum oleas gaudere
54 maxime cinere e calcariis fornacibus.) Varro prae-

[1] *Pintianus e Colum.*: proximum.
[2] e (ex *Pintianus*): *v.l. om.*
[3] ex *add. Rackham.*
[4] aluntur: *Mayhoff.*
[5] *Urlichs*: homines.
[6] *Rackham* (recenti *Mayhoff*): rettuli (non invenio *secl. Urlichs*).

---

[a] *I.e.* the present-day supply of poultry is not a sign of extreme luxury.
[b] II. 14. 1.
[c] The Romans always drank their wine mixed with water.
[d] II. 14. 4.
[e] This remark seems to belong to the middle of § 49.

possible to be hopeful about our own morals.[a] But Columella[b] puts manure from dovecots first, and next manure from the poultry-yard, condemning the droppings of water birds entirely. The rest of the authorities advocate the residue of human banquets as one of the best manures, and some of them place even higher the residue of men's drink, with hair found in curriers' shops soaked in it, while others recommend this liquor by itself, after water has been again mixed with it and even in larger quantity than when the wine is being drunk[c]; the fact being that a larger amount of badness has to be overcome in the liquor when to the original poison of the wine the human factor has been added. These are contested questions; and they use man even for nourishing soil. Next to this kind of manure the dung of swine is highly commended Columella[d] alone condemning it. Others recommend the dung of any quadruped that feeds on cytisus, but some prefer pigeons' droppings. Next comes the dung of goats, after that sheeps' dung, then cow-dung and last of all that of beasts of burden.

These distinctions were recognized in early days, and at the same time I do not find modern rules for the use of dung, since in this matter also old times are more serviceable; and before now in some parts of the provinces there has been so large and valuable a supply of beasts that the practice has been seen of passing dung through a sieve, like flour, the stench and look of it being transformed by the action of time into something actually attractive. (It has lately been found that olives particularly thrive on ashes from a lime kiln.)[e] To the rules given Varro[f]

I. xxxviii. 3.

ceptis adicit equino quod sit levissimum segetes alendi, prata vero graviore[1] quod ex hordeo fiat multasque gignat herbas. quidam etiam bubulo iumentorum praeferunt ovillumque caprino, omnibus vero asininum, quoniam lentissime mandant; e contrario usus adversus utrumque pronuntiat. inter omnes autem constat nihil esse utilius lupini segete priusquam siliquetur aratro vel bidentibus versa manipulisve desectae circa radices arborum ac vitium obrutis; et ubi non sit pecus, culmo ipso vel etiam filice stercorare arbitrantur.

55 Cato: 'Stercus unde facias, stramenta, lupinum, paleas, fabalia ac frondis iligneam, querneam. ex segete evellito ebulum, cicutam, et circum salicta herbam altam ulvamque; eam substernito ovibus, bubusque frondem putidam.'—'Vinea si macra erit, sarmenta sua comburito et indidem inarato.' idemque: 'Ubi saturus eris frumentum, oves ibi delectato.'

56 VII. Nec non et satis quibusdam ipsis pasci terram dicit: 'Segetem stercorant fruges, lupinum, faba, vicia'; sicut e contrario: 'Cicer, quia vellitur et quia salsum est, hordeum, fenum Graecum, ervum, haec omnia segetem exurunt[2] et omnia quae velluntur. nucleos in segetem ne indideris.'—Vergilius et lino segetem exuri et avena et papavere arbitratur.

[1] *Rackham*: graviore et.
[2] exsugunt *Cato*.

---

[a] XXXVII. 2. XXX.
[b] XXXVII. 2. 1.
[c] Cato has 'suck up' or 'drain'.
[d] Especially olives.

adds the employment of the lightest kind of horse-dung for manuring cornfields, but for meadowland the heavier manure produced by feeding barley to horses, which produces an abundant growth of grass. Some people even prefer stable-manure to cowdung and sheeps' droppings to goats', but they rate asses' dung above all other manures, because asses chew their fodder very slowly; but experience on the contrary pronounces against each of these. It is however universally agreed that no manure is more beneficial than a crop of lupine turned in by the plough or with forks before the plants form pods, or else bundles of lupine after it has been cut, dug in round the roots of trees and vines; and in places where there are no cattle they believe in using the stubble itself or even bracken for manure.

Cato says [a]: 'You can make manure of stable-litter, lupines, chaff, bean-stalks and holm-oak or oak leaves. Pull up the dane-wort and hemlock out of the crop, and the high grass and sedge growing round osier beds; use this as litter for sheep, and rotten leaves for oxen.'—' If a vine is making poor growth, make a bonfire of its shoots and plough in the ashes therefrom.' He also says: ' Where you are going to sow corn, give your sheep a free run on the land.'

Crops that fertilize.

VII. Moreover Cato also says [b] that there are certain crops which themselves nourish the land: ' Cornland is manured by grain, lupine, beans and vetches'; just as on the contrary: ' Chick-pea, because it is pulled up by the roots and because it is salt, barley, fenugreek, bitter vetch,—these all scorch up [c] a cornland, as do all plants that are pulled up by the roots. Do not plant stone-fruit [d] in corn-land.'—Virgil holds the opinion that cornland is also scorched by flax, oats and poppies. *Georg.* I. 77.

57 VIII. Fimeta sub diu concavo loco et qui umorem colligat, stramento intecta ne in sole arescant, palo e robore depacto fieri iubent: ita fore ne innascantur his serpentes. fimum inicere terrae plurimum refert favonio flante ac luna sitiente[1]; id plerique prave intellegunt a favonii ortu faciendum ac Februario mense tantum, cum id pleraque sata et[2] aliis postulent mensibus. quocumque tempore facere libeat, curandum ut ab occasu aequinoctiali flante vento fiat lunaque decrescente ac sicca. mirum in modum augetur ubertas effectusque eius observatione tali.

58 IX. Et abunde praedicta ratione caeli ac terrae nunc de iis arboribus dicemus quae cura hominum atque arte proveniunt. nec pauciora prope sunt genera, tam benigne naturae gratiam retulimus; aut enim semine proveniunt aut plantis radicis aut propagine aut avolsione aut surculo aut insito in[3] consecto arboris trunco. nam folia palmarum apud Babylonios seri atque ita arborem provenire Trogum credidisse demiror. quaedam autem pluribus generibus seruntur, quaedam omnibus.

59 X. Ac pleraque ex his natura ipsa docuit et in primis semen serere, cum decidens exceptumque terra

[1] silente *Pintianus e Catone* XXIX.
[2] et *add. Rackham.*
[3] *V.l.* aut.

[a] Palms can be propagated by shoots from the leaves.

VIII. They recommend making dung-heaps in the open air in a hole in the ground made so as to collect moisture, and covering the heaps with straw to prevent their drying up in the sun, after driving a hard-oak stake into the ground, which will keep snakes from breeding in the dung. It pays extremely well to throw the manure on the ground when a west wind is blowing and during a dry moon; most people misunderstand this and think that it should be done when the west wind is just setting in, and only in February, whereas most crops require manuring in other months also. Whatever time is chosen for the operation, care must be taken to do it when the wind is due west and the moon on the wane and accompanied by dry weather. Such precautions increase the fertilizing effect of manure to a surprising degree.

Season for manuring.

IX. Having begun by stating at considerable length the principles of climate and soil, we will now describe the trees that are produced by the care and skill of mankind. There are almost as many varieties of these as there are of those that grow wild, so bountifully have we repaid our debt of gratitude to Nature; for they are produced either from seed or from root-cuttings or by layering or tearing off a slip or from a cutting or by grafting in an incision in the trunk of a tree. As for the story that at Babylon they plant palm-leaves and produce a tree in that way, I am surprised that Trogus believed it.[a] Some trees however can be grown by several of the above methods, and some by all of them.

Propagation of trees, various methods.

X. And the majority of these methods were taught us by Nature herself, in particular that of sowing a seed, because when a seed fell from a tree and was received into the earth it came to life again. Indeed

Growing trees from seed.

revivesceret.[1] sed quaedam non aliter proveniunt, ut castaneae, iuglandes, caeduis dumtaxat exceptis; et semine autem, quamquam dissimili,[2] ea quoque quae aliis modis seruntur, ut vites et mala atque pira; namque his pro semine nucleus, non ut supra dictis fructus ipse. et mespila semine nasci possunt. omnia haec tarda proventu ac degenerantia et insito restituenda, interdumque etiam castaneae.

60 XI. Quibusdam contra natura[3] omnino non degene-
randi quoquo modo seruntur, ut cupressis, palmae,
lauris—namque et laurus pluribus modis seritur.
genera eius diximus. ex his Augusta et bacalis et
tinus simili modo seruntur: bacae mense Ianuario
aquilonis adflatu siccatae leguntur expandunturque
rarae, ne calefiant acervo; postea quidam fimo ad
61 satum praeparatas urina madefaciunt; alii in qualo
pedibus in profluente deculcant donec auferatur cutis,
quae alioqui uligine infestatur nec patitur partum.[4]
in sulco repastinato palmi altitudine vicenae fere
acervatim seruntur,[5] mense Martio. eaedem et
62 propagine, triumphalis talea tantum. myrti genera
omnia in Campania bacis seruntur, Romae propagine.

[1] *Warmington*: vivesceret.
[2] dissimilia *Detlefsen*.
[3] contra natura? *Mayhoff*: natura contra.
[4] partum (*an* parturire?) *add. Mayhoff*.
[5] seruntur *hic Mayhoff*: *post* propagine.

there are some trees that are not grown in any other way, for instance chestnuts and walnuts, with the exception, that is, of those intended for felling; but also some grown in other ways are grown from seed as well, though a different kind of seed—for instance vines and apples and pears—as with these a pip serves as a seed, and not the actual fruit, as in the case of the trees mentioned above. Also medlars can be grown from seed. All of these trees are slow in coming on, and liable to degenerate so as to have to be restored by grafting; and sometimes this happens even with chestnuts.

XI. Some trees on the other hand have the property of not degenerating at all in whatever way they are propagated, for instance cypresses, the palm and laurels—for the laurel also can be propagated in a variety of ways. We have stated the various kinds XV. 127 ff.
of laurel. Of these the Augusta, the berry laurel and the laurustinus are propagated in a similar manner: their berries are picked in January, after they have been dried by a spell of north-east wind, and are spread out separately, so as not to ferment by lying in a heap; afterwards some people treat them with dung in preparation for sowing and soak them with urine, but others put them in running water in a wicker basket, and stamp on them till the skin is washed away, which otherwise is attacked by stagnant moisture and does not allow them to bear. They are planted in a freshly dug trench a hand's breadth deep, about twenty in a cluster; this is done in March. These laurels can also be propagated by layering, but the laurel worn in triumphal processions can only be grown from a cutting. Myrtles of all varieties are grown from berries in Campania, but at Rome

Tarentinam Democritus et alio modo seri docet, grandissimis bacarum tusis leviter, ne grana frangantur . . .[1] eaque intrita restem[2] circumlini atque ita seri; parietem fore mirae[3] densitatis, ex quo virgulae differantur. sic et spinas saepis causa serunt tomice moris spinarum circumlita. pilas autem laurus et myrti inopia[4] a trimatu tempestivom est transferre.

63 Inter ea quae semine seruntur Mago in nucibus operosus est. amygdalam in argilla molli meridiem spectante seri iubet; gaudere et dura calidaque terra, in pingui aut umida mori aut sterilescere; serendas quam maxime falcatas et e novella fimoque diluto maceratas per triduum aut pridie quam serantur aqua mulsa; mucrone defigi, aciem lateris in aquilonem spectare; ternas simul serendas triangula ratione palmam inter se distantes; denis diebus adaquari
64 donec grandescant. iuglandes nuces porrectae seruntur commissuris iacentibus, pineae nucleis septenis fere in ollas perforatas abditis aut ut laurus quae bacis seritur. citrea grano et propagine, sorba semine et

[1] *Lacunam* (⟨ex aqua farinam misceri⟩ ?) *Mayhoff.*
[2] *Erasmus* (*ed. Bas.*) : reste.
[3] mirae *add. Dalec.*
[4] myrti in sua loca *vel* in suum solum *coll.* 66, 75 *Warmington.*

---

[a] A gap in the Latin text may perhaps be filled up thus.
[b] But possibly the meaning is 'laurels and myrtles are ready for transplanting with a ball of soil round the roots at the end of three years'. The sentence would then belong rather to § 75 or 77 or §§ 79–83.

by layering. Democritus tells us that the Taranto myrtle is also grown in another way: the largest berries are taken, and after being crushed lightly so as not to break the pips ⟨are mixed into a paste with water⟩[a] and this is pounded up and smeared on a rope, which is then put in the ground; from this, he says, will grow up a remarkably thick hedge, from which slips can be transplanted. They also grow brambles for hedges in the same way, by smearing a rope of rushes with blackberries. In case of scarcity,[b] laurel and myrtle seeds are ready for transfer at the end of three years.

Among the trees that are grown from seed, Mago deals elaborately with those of the nut class. He says that the almond should be sown in soft clay soil with a south aspect, but that it also does well in hard warm ground, but in a rich or damp soil it dies or does not bear. He recommends choosing for sowing almonds shaped as much as possible like a sickle, and picked from a young tree, and says they should be soaked for three days in diluted manure, or else on the day before sowing in water sweetened with honey; and that they should be put in the ground with their point downward and with their sharp edge facing north-east; that they should be sown in groups of three, placed four inches apart from each other in a triangular formation; and that they should be watered every ten days, until they begin to swell. Walnuts are sown lying on their sides with the join of the shell downward; and pine-cones are planted in groups of about seven, contained in pots with a hole in the bottom, or else in the same way as a laurel that is being grown from berries. The citron is grown from pips and from layers, and the sorb from seed or

a radice planta et avolsione proveniunt, sed illa in calidis, sorba in frigidis et umidis.

65 XII. Natura et plantaria demonstravit multarum arborum[1] radicibus pullulante subole densa et pariente matre quas necet: eius quippe umbra turba indigesta premitur, ut in lauris, punicis, platanis, cerasis, prunis; paucarum in hoc genere rami parcunt suboli, ut ulmorum palmarumque. nullis vero tales pulluli proveniunt nisi quarum radices amore solis atque
66 imbris in summa tellure spatiantur. omnia ea non statim moris est in suo solo[2] locari sed prius nutrici dari atque in seminariis adolescere iterumque migrare, qui transitus mirum in modum mitigat etiam silvestres, sive arborum quoque ut hominum natura novitatis ac peregrinationis avida est, sive discedentes virus relincunt dum radici avellitur planta,[3] mansuescuntque tractatu ceu ferae.

XIII. Et aliud genus simile monstravit, avolsique
67 arboribus stolones vixere; quo in genere et cum perna sua avelluntur partemque aliquam e matris quoque corpore auferunt secum fimbriato corpore. hoc modo plantantur punicae, coryli, mali, sorbi, mespilae, fraxini, fici in primisque vites; cotoneum ita satum degenerat. ex eodem inventum est

[1] arborum *add. Rackham.*
[2] suo ⟨solo⟩ ? *Mayhoff*: suo *aut* sua.
[3] dum . . . planta *hic* ? *Mayhoff*: *post* ferae.

from a cutting from the root or from a slip; but the citron needs a warm situation, whereas the sorb requires a cool and damp one.

XII. Nature has also taught the art of making nurseries, as from the roots of many trees there shoots up a teeming cluster of progeny, and the mother tree bears offspring destined to be killed by herself, inasmuch as her shadow stifles the disorderly throng—as in the case of laurels, pomegranates, planes, cherries and plums; although with a few trees in this class, for instance elms and palms, the branches spare the young suckers. But young shoots of this nature are only produced by trees whose roots are led by their love of sun and rain to move about on the surface of the ground. All of these it is customary not to put in their own ground at once, but first to give them to a foster-mother and let them grow up in seed-plots, and then change their habitation again, this removal having a marvellously civilizing effect even on wild trees, whether it be the case that, like human beings, trees also have a nature that is greedy for novelty and travel, or whether on going away they leave their venom behind when the plant is torn up from the root, and like animals are tamed by handling.

Tree nurseries.

XIII. Also Nature demonstrated another kind of propagation resembling the previous one, and suckers torn away from trees continued to live; in this procedure the slips are torn away with their haunch as well, and carry off with them some portion also from their mother's body with its fibrous substance. This is a method used in striking pomegranates, hazels, apples, sorbs, medlars, ash plants, figs, and above all vines; but the quince if struck in this way deteriorates in quality. From the same method a way was

Growing from slips and suckers.

68 surculos abscisos serere: hoc primo saepis causa factum sabucis, cotoneis,[1] rubis depactis, mox et culturae, ut populis, alnis, salici, quae vel inverso surculo seritur. iam hae ibi disponuntur ubi libeat esse eas. quamquam[2] seminarii curam ante convenit dici quam transeatur ad alia genera.

69 XIV. Namque ad id praecipuum eligi solum refert, quoniam nutricem indulgentiorem esse quam matrem saepe convenit. sit ergo siccum sucosumque, bipalio subactum, advenis hospitale, et quam simillimum terrae ei[3] in quam transferendae sint, ante omnia elapidatum munitumque ab incursu etiam gallinacei generis, quam minime rimosum, ne penetrans sol
70 exurat fibras. intervallo sesquipedum seri—nam si inter se contingant, praeter alia vitia etiam verminosa fiunt[4]—, sariri convenit saepius herbasque evelli, praeterea semina ipsa fruticantia supputare ac falcem
71 pati consuescere. Cato et furcis crates inponi iubet altitudine hominis ad solem recipiendum atque integi culmo ad frigora arcenda; sic pirorum malorumque semina nutriri, sic pineas nuces, sic cupressos semine
72 satas et ipsas. minimis id granis constat, vix ut

[1] *Rackham*: cotoneo et.
[2] quamobrem *edd.*
[3] ei *add. Mayhoff.*
[4] *V.l.* fiunt, ideo.

discovered of cutting off slips and planting these, a plan first adopted with elders, quinces and brambles, which were planted for the purpose of making a hedge, but later it was also introduced as a way of growing trees, for instance poplars, alders, and willow, which last is even planted with the cutting upside down. Suckers are planted out at once in the place chosen for them to occupy; however, before going on to other classes of plants it is desirable to speak of the management of a nursery.

XIV. For, with a view to a nursery it pays to chose soil of the highest quality, since it often comes about that a nurse is more ready to humour young things than a mother. Consequently the soil should be dry and sappy, and well worked with a double mattock so as to be hospitable to the new arrivals, and it should resemble as closely as possible the earth into which they are to be transplanted; and before all the plot must be cleared of stones, and fenced in well enough to protect it even from the inroads of poultry; and it should be as free from cracks as possible, so that the sun may not penetrate into it and scorch the roots. The seeds should be sown eighteen inches apart, as if the plants touch one another, besides other defects they get worm-eaten; and it pays to hoe them and weed them fairly often, and also to prune the seedlings themselves when they branch and accustom them to endure the knife. Cato also recommends erecting hurdles supported on forked sticks, the height of a man, to catch the sun, and thatching these with straw to keep off the cold; and he says that this is the method for rearing pear and apple seeds, and pine cones, and also cypresses, as even they can be grown from seed. Cypress seed consists of very small grains, some of

Management of nurseries, Growing from seed.

XLVIII. 2, 3.

perspici quaedam possint, non omittendo naturae miraculo e tam parvo gigni arbores tanto maiore tritici et hordei grano, ne quis fabam reputet. quid simile origini suae habent malorum pirorumque semina? his principiis respuentem secures materiem nasci, indomita ponderibus inmensis prela, arbores velis, turribus murisque inpellendis arietes! haec est naturae vis,[1] haec potentia. super omnia erit e lacrima nasci aliquid, ut suo loco dicemus.

73 Ergo e cupresso femina—mas enim, ut diximus, non gignit—pilulae collectae quibus docuimus[2] mensibus siccàntur sole, ruptaeque emittunt semen formicis mire expetitum, ampliato etiam miraculo tantuli animalis cibo absumi natalem tantarum arborum. seritur Aprili mense, area aequata cylindris aut paviculis,[3] densum, terraque cribris
74 superincernitur pollicis crassitudine: contra maius pondus attollere se non valet torqueturque sub terram;[4] ob hoc et pavitur vestigiis. leniter[5] rigatur a solis occasu in trinis diebus, ut aequaliter bibat, donec erumpant. differuntur post annum dodrantali filo, custodita temperie ut viridi caelo serantur ac sine aura. mirumque dictu, periculum eo tantum

[1] *Caesarius*: natura eius.
[2] docuimus? *Mayhoff*: docui.
[3] *Urlichs*: volviculis *Mayhoff*: uuluoalis *aut* uulgo alis *aut* uulgiualis.
[4] *Rackham*: terra.
[5] *Edd.*: leviter.

them scarcely perceptible, and we must not fail to remark on Nature's miracle of producing trees from so small a seed when a grain of wheat or barley is so much larger, not to reckon a bean. What resemblance have apple seeds and pear seeds to their source of origin? To think that from these beginnings is born the timber that contemptuously rebuffs the axe, presses that are not overcome by immense weights, masts for sails, battering rams for demolishing towers and walls! Such is the force and such the potency of Nature. But the crowning marvel will be that there is something that derives its origin from a tear-drop, as we shall XIX. 162,
mention in the proper place. XXI. 24.

Well then, in the months that we have specified, the § 60.
tiny seed-balls are gathered from the female cypress—
for the male tree, as we have said, is barren—and are XVI. 211.
put to dry in the sun; and they burst open and emit their seed, which has a remarkable attraction for ants, a fact that actually increases the marvel, for the germ of such huge trees to be consumed for the food of such a small animal! The seed is sown in April, after the earth has been levelled by means of rollers or rammers; it is scattered thickly and a layer of earth a thumb deep is sprinkled upon it from sieves: it is not strong enough to rise up against a greater weight, and it twists back under the ground; on this account another method is merely to tread it into the earth. Every three days it is given a light watering, after sunset so as to soak in the moisture even, until the plants break out from the earth. They are transplanted after a year, when the seedling is nine inches long, regard being paid to the weather so that they may be planted under a bright sky and when there is no wind. And wonderful to say, on

die est si roravit quantulumcumque imbrem aut si adflavit; de reliquo tutae sunt perpetua securitate,
75 aquasque postea odere. et zizipha grano seruntur Aprili mense. tuberes melius inseruntur in pruno silvestri et malo cotoneo et in calabrice: ea est spina silvestris. quaecumque optime et myxas recipit, utiliter et sorbos.

Plantas ex seminario transferre in aliud priusquam suo loco ponantur operose praecipi arbitror, licet translatione folia latiora fieri spondeant.

76 XV. Ulmorum, priusquam foliis vestiantur, samara colligenda est circa Martias kalendas, cum flavescere incipit. dein biduo in umbra siccata serenda densa in refracto, terra super minuta incribrata, crassitudine qua in cupressis; pluviae si non adiuvent, rigandum. differendae ex arearum venis post annum in ulmaria
77 intervallo pedali in quamque partem. Atinias[1] ulmos autumno serere utilius, quia carentes semine[2] plantis seruntur. in arbustum quinquennes sub urbe transferantur[3] aut, ut quibusdam placet, quae vicenum pedum esse coeperunt. serantur[4] sulco qui novenarius dicitur altitudine pedum trium, pari

[1] Atinias *coll.* XVI 108 *Mayhoff*: maritas.
[2] *Mayhoff*: semine nam (*aut* non) ut e (semine nemut *Warmington*).
[3] *Rackham*: transferunt (-untur *cd. Chiffl.*).
[4] serantur *add. Rackham.*

---

[a] Identification uncertain.
[b] A tall variety.

that day and that day only it is dangerous for them if there is the smallest sprinkle of rain or a breath of wind; whereas for the future the plants are continually safe and secure, and later on they have a dislike for humidity. Jujube-trees are also grown from seed sown in April. Tuber-apples are better grafted on the wild plum, the quince or the buckthorn bush,[a] the last being a wild thorn. Any thorn also takes grafts of the sebesten-plum extremely well, and also takes the sorb-plum satisfactorily.

As for the recommendation to transfer plants from the nursery to some other place before they are planted out in the place assigned to them, I consider that this causes unnecessary trouble, albeit this process does guarantee the growth of leaves of a larger size.

Growing and planting elms, poplars and ash-trees.

XV. Elm-seed should be collected about the first of March, before the tree is clothed with foliage, when the seed is beginning to turn yellow. Then it should be left in the shade to dry for two days, and afterwards thickly sown in ground that has been broken up, and a layer of earth sifted fine in a sieve should be sprinkled on it, of the thickness recommended in the § 73.
case of cypresses; and if no rain comes to your assistance, it must be watered. A year afterwards the plants should be removed from the rows of the beds to the elm-grounds and planted at a distance of a foot apart each way. Atinian elms[b] it pays better to plant in autumn, because they are grown from cuttings, having no seed. For a grove in the neighbourhood of the city they should be transplanted when they are five years old, or, as some hold, when they have reached a height of twenty feet. They should be set in what is called a 'nine-square-foot' trench, 3 ft. deep and

latitudine et eo amplius. circa positas pedes terni undique e solido adaggerantur: arulas id vocant in Campania. intervalla ex loci natura sumantur[1]: rariores serendas in campestribus convenit. populos
78 et fraxinos, quia festinantius germinant, disponi quoque maturius convenit, hoc est ab idibus Februariis, plantis et ipsas nascentes. in disponendis arboribus arbustisque ac vineis quincuncialis ordinum ratio vulgata et necessaria, non perflatu modo utilis verum et aspectu grata, quoquo modo intueare in ordinem se porrigente versu. populos eadem ratio semine quae ulmos serendi, transferendi quoque e seminariis eadem et silvis.

79 XVI. Ante omnia igitur in similem transferri terram aut meliorem oportet, nec ex tepidis aut praecocibus in frigidos aut serotinos situs, ut neque ex his in illos, et[2] praefodere scrobes ante aliquanto[3] —si fieri possit, tanto prius donec pingui caespite
80 obducantur. Mago ante annum iubet, ut solem pluviasque conbibant, aut, si id condicio largita non sit, ignes in mediis fieri ante menses duos, nec nisi post imbres in his seri, altitudinem eorum in argilloso aut duro solo trium cubitorum esse in quamque partem, in pronis palmo amplius, iubetque[4] caminata

[1] *Rackham*: sumuntur.
[2] et *add. Rackham.*
[3] aliquanto *add.* ? *Mayhoff.*
[4] *Mayhoff*: et ubique.

[a] Thus:—

3 ft. broad and even larger. When they have been planted, mounds 3 ft. high from the ground level should be heaped round them—the name for these mounds in Campania is 'little altars'. The spacing must be settled according to the nature of the place: in level country it is suitable to plant the young trees wider apart. It is also proper to plant out poplars and ashes earlier, because they bud more quickly—that is, planting should start on the 13th of February: these trees also growing from cuttings. In spacing out trees and plantations and planning vineyards the diagonal arrangement[a] of rows is commonly adopted and is essential, being not only advantageous in allowing the passage of air, but also agreeable in appearance, as in whatever direction you look at the plantation a row of trees stretches out in a straight line. In the case of poplars the same method of growing them from seed is used as with elms, and also the same method of transplanting them from nurseries or forests.

Transplanting.

XVI. It is consequently of the first importance for shoots to be transplanted into similar or better soil, and not moved from warm or early ripening positions into cold or backward ones, nor yet from the latter to the former either; and to dig the trenches some time in advance—if possible, long enough before to allow the holes to get covered over with thick turf. Mago advises a year in advance, so as to let the holes absorb the sunshine and rain, or, if circumstances do not allow of this, he recommends making fires in the middle of the holes two months before, and only planting the seedlings in the holes so prepared just after rain has fallen. He says that in a clay soil or a hard soil the pits should measure 4 ft. 6 in. each way, or 4 inches more on sloping sites, and he prescribes

fossura ore conpressiore esse; in [1] nigra vero terra duo cubita et palmum quadratis angulis eadem mensura. Graeci auctores consentiunt non altiores quino semipede esse debere nec latiores duobus pedibus, nusquam vero semisquipede minus altos. quoniam in umido solo ad vicina aquae perveniatur,[2] Cato, si locus aquosus sit, latos pedes ternos in faucibus
81 imosque palmum et pedem, altitudine quattuor pedum, eos lapide consterni aut, si non sit, perticis salignis viridibus, si neque hae sint, sarmentis, ita ut in altitudinem semipes detrahatur. nobis adiciendum videtur ex praedicta arborum natura ut altius demittantur ea quae summa tellure gaudent, tamquam fraxinus, olea; haec et similia quaternos pedes oportet demitti: ceteris altitudinis pedes terni suffecerint. et est innoxium adradi partes quae se nudaverint. 'Excide radicem,' inquit, 'istam,' Papirius Cursor imperator, ad terrorem Praenestinorum
82 praetoris destringi securi iussa. testas aliqui, alii [3] lapides rotundos subici malunt qui et contineant umorem et transmittant, non item planos facere et a terreno arcere radicem existimantes. glarea substrata inter utramque sententiam fuerit.

83 Arborem nec minorem bima nec maiorem trima transferre quidam praecipiunt, alii cum manum

[1] *Mayhoff*: compressiores sint.
[2] *Mayhoff*: perveniat.
[3] alii *add. Rackham* (aliqui *Ian*).

---

[a] XLIII. 1.
[b] To take it out of the *fascis* or bundle of rods in which it was carried.

their being dug like an oven, narrower at the orifice; while in black earth he advises a hole 3 ft. 4 in. deep, in the form of a square of the same dimensions. The Greek authorities agree that the holes ought not to be more than 2½ ft. deep or 2 ft. wide, but nowhere less than 18 in. deep. Because of the fact that in damp ground one gets through to the neighbourhood of water, Cato[a] advises that if the place is damp the holes should be a yard wide at the orifice and 16 inches wide at the bottom, and 4 ft. deep, and that they should be floored with stones, or, if stones are not available, with stakes of green willow, or, if these are also not available, with brushwood, so as to reduce their depth by six inches. To us, after what has been said as to the nature of trees, it appears proper to add that those which are fond of the surface of the ground, for instance the ash and the olive, must be sunk deeper in; these and similar trees should be sunk four feet down, but for the others a depth of three feet will be enough. And there is no harm in trimming the parts that have become exposed: 'Lop clear that root there,' said General Papirius Cursor when to intimidate the chief magistrate of Palestrina he ordered the lictor to draw his axe.[b] Some persons recommend putting at the bottom a layer of potsherds—others prefer round stones—in order to hold in the moisture and also let some through, thinking that flat stones do not act in the same way and prevent the root from reaching the earth. A middle course between the two opinions would be to pave the bottom with a layer of gravel.

Precautions in transplanting. Choice of aspect.

Some people recommend transplanting a tree when it is not less than two years old and not more than three, others when it is large enough round to fill the

conpleat, Cato crassiorem quinque digitis. non omisisset idem, si attineret, meridianam caeli partem signare in cortice, ut translatae isdem et adsuetis statuerentur horis, ne aquiloniae meridianis oppositae solibus finderentur et algerent meridianae aquilonibus.
84 quod e diverso adfectant etiam quidam in vite ficoque, permutantes in contrarium; densiores enim folio ita fieri magisque protegere fructum et minus amittere, ficumque sic etiam scansilem fieri. plerique id demum cavent ut plaga deputati cacuminis meridiem
85 spectet, ignari fissuris nimii vaporis opponi; id quidem in horam diei quintam vel octavam spectare maluerim. aeque latet non neglegendum ne radices mora inarescant neve a septentrionibus aut ab ea parte caeli usque ad exortum brumalem vento flante effodiantur arbores, aut certe non adversae his ventis radices praebeantur, propter quod emoriuntur ignaris
86 causae agricolis. Cato omnes ventos et imbrem quoque in tota translatione damnat. et ad haec proderit quam plurimum terrae in qua vixerint radicibus cohaerere ac totas caespite[1] circumligari,

[1] totas cum caespite (*vel* totos caespites?) *Mayhoff*.

---

[a] XXVIII. 2.
[b] *I.e.* for the purpose of picking the figs.
[c] XXVIII. 1.

hand; Cato's view[a] is that it ought to be more than five inches thick. The same authority would not have omitted, if it were important, to recommend making a mark in the bark on the south side, so that when trees were transplanted they might be set in the same directions as regards the seasons as those to which they were accustomed, to prevent their north sides from being split if set facing the midday sun and their south sides from being nipped if facing the north wind. Some people also follow the contrary plan in the case of a vine or a fig, replanting them turned the other way round, from the view that this makes them grow thicker foliage and afford better shelter to their fruit and be less liable to lose it, and that a fig-tree so treated also becomes strong enough to be climbed.[b] Most people only take care to make the wound left where the end of a branch has been lopped face south, not being aware that this exposes it to cracks caused by excessive heat; I should prefer to let a lopped end point somewhat east of south or somewhat west of south. It is equally little known that care should be taken not to let the roots become dry owing to delay in replanting, and not to dig up trees when the wind is in the north or in any quarter between north and south-east, or at all events not to leave the roots exposed to the wind in these quarters; such exposure causes trees to die without the growers knowing the cause. Cato[c] disapproves of wind in any quarter and of rain also during all the time while transplantation is going on. It will be a good precaution against wind and rain to leave as much as possible of the earth in which the trees have been living clinging to their roots, and to bind them all round with turf, though for this purpose

cum ob id Cato in corbibus transferri iubeat, procul dubio utilissime, qui idem[1] summam terram contentus est subdi. quidam punicis malis substrato lapide non rumpi pomum in arboribus tradunt. radices inflexas poni melius; arborem ipsam ita locari ut media sit
87 totius scrobis necessarium. ficus si in scilla—bulborum hoc genus est—seratur, ocissime ferre traditur pomum neque vermiculationi obnoxium, quo vitio carent reliqua poma similiter sata. radicum filis[2] magnam adhibendam curam, ut exemptas appareat, non evolsas, quis dubitet? qua ratione et reliqua confessa omittimus, sicuti terram circa radices festuca conspissandam, quod Cato primum in ea re esse censet, plagam quoque a trunco oblini fimo et foliis praeligari praecipiens.

88 XVII. Huius loci pars est ad intervalla pertinens. quidam punicas et myrtos et lauros densiores seri iusserunt, in pedibus tantum[3] novenis, malos amplius paulo, vel magis etiam piros magisque amygdalas et ficos; quamquam[4] optime id[5] diiudicabit ramorum amplitudinis ratio locorumque, et umbrae cuiusque arboris, quoniam has quoque observari oportet: breves sunt quamvis magnarum arborum cum[6] ramos in

[1] *Pintianus*: (qui quidem *Mayhoff*): quidem.
[2] filis *Mayhoff*: eius.
[3] tantum? *Mayhoff*: tamen.
[4] *Mayhoff*: q$\overline{m}$ *aut* qu$\overline{o}$.
[5] id *add.*? *Mayhoff*.
[6] cum *add. Mayhoff*.

---

[a] XXVIII. 1, 2.
[b] XXVIII. 2. Cato advises that trees more than 5 fingers thick should be lopped before being transplanted, and the tops plastered over and bandaged.

Cato[a] directs conveying the trees to the fresh place in baskets, no doubt most useful advice; and moreover he thinks it satisfactory for the top layer of soil to be put at the bottom of the hole. Some writers say that with pomegranates to lay stones at the bottom of the hole will prevent the fruit from bursting open on the tree. It is better to plant the roots in a bent position; and it is essential for the tree itself to be so placed as to be exactly in the middle of the hole. It is said that if a fig-tree is planted stuck in a squill—this is a kind of bulb—it bears fruit very quickly, and is not liable to attacks of worm, a defect from which all other kinds of fruit trees planted in a similar way are exempt. Who can doubt that great care ought to be taken with the fibres of the roots, so that they may appear to have been taken, not torn, out of the ground? On this account we omit the remaining rules that are admitted, for instance that the earth round the roots should be rammed tight with a light mallet, which Cato[b] thinks of primary importance in this matter, also advising that a wound made on the trunk should be plastered over with dung and bandaged with leaves.

XVII. A part of this topic is the question of the spaces between the trees. Some people have advised planting pomegranates, myrtles, and laurels rather close together, only three yards apart, apples a little wider apart, pears still wider, and almonds and figs wider again; although this matter will best be decided by taking account of the length of the branches and the dimensions of the places concerned, as well as of the shadow of each particular tree, since these too must be considered: even large trees throw only small shadows when their branches curve round into

Spacing of trees.

orbem circinant, ut in malis pirisque, eaedem enormes cerasis, lauris.

89 XVIII. Iam quaedam umbrarum proprietas. iuglandum gravis et noxia etiam capiti humano omnibusque iuxta satis; necat gramina et pinus; sed ventis utraque resistit, quoniam et proiecta [1] vinearum ratione tegunt.[2] stilicidia pinus, quercus, ilicis ponderosissima, nullum cupressi, umbra minima et in se convoluta; ficorum levis, quamvis sparsa,
90 ideoque inter vineas seri non vetentur. ulmorum lenis, etiam nutriens quaecumque [3] opacat: Attico haec quoque videtur e gravissimis, nec dubito si emittantur in ramos: constrictae quidem illius noxiam esse non arbitror. iucunda et platani, quamquam crassa: licet gramini credere non sub [4] alia laetius operienti toros. populo nulla ludentibus
91 foliis; pinguis alno, sed pascens sata. vitis sibi sufficit, mobili folio iactatuque crebro solem umbra temperans, eodem gravi protegens in imbre. omnium fere levis umbra quorum pediculi longi.

[1] *Dalec.*: protecta (*cf.* XVI 35).
[2] *Rackham*: aegent (egent *cd. Par. Lat.* 6797).
[3] *Rackham*: quacumque.
[4] *Mayhoff*: non soli.

[a] Especially the aspen.

a circular shape, as in the case of apples and pears, whereas cherries and laurels throw exceptionally wide shadows.

Considerations of shade.

XVIII. We turn now to certain special properties of the shade of different trees. That of walnut is heavy, and even causes headache in man and injury to anything planted in its vicinity; and that of the pine-tree also kills grass; but both the pine and the walnut withstand wind, as also their projecting branches shield them like pent-houses. Very heavy raindrops fall from the pine, oak and holm-oak, but none at all from the cypress, which throws a very small compact shadow around it; and fig-trees give only a light shadow, however much spread out, and consequently it is not necessary to make it a rule not to plant them between vines. Elms give a gentle shade which actually promotes the growth of any plants that it falls on, although Atticus holds the view that also the shade of elms is one of the most oppressive, nor do I doubt that it is so if they are allowed to shoot out into branches, although I do not think that the shade of the elm does any harm when the tree is kept within bounds. The shade of the plane also though dense is agreeable, as we may learn from the evidence of grass, which under no other tree covers the banks more luxuriantly. The poplar[a] with its gaily quivering leaves gives no shade at all; the shade of the alder is dense but permits the growth of plants. The vine gives enough shade for itself, as its quivering foliage and constant tossing tempers the sunshine with shadow, while by the same means it affords shelter in a heavy shower of rain. Nearly all trees of which the leaves have long stalks afford only light shade.

Non fastidienda haec quoque scientia, atque non in ultimis ponenda, quando satis quibusque umbra aut nutrix aut noverca est: iuglandum quidem pinorumque et picearum et abietis quaecumque attingere non dubie venenum.

92 XIX. Stilicidii brevis definitio est. omnium quae proiectu frondis ita defenduntur ut per ipsas non defluant imbres, stilla saeva est. ergo plurimum intererit hac in quaestione, terra in qua seremus in quantum[1] arbores quasque alat. iam per se colles minora quaerunt intervalla. ventosis locis crebriores
93 seri conducit, oleam tamen maximo intervallo, de qua Catonis Italica sententia est in XXV pedibus, plurimum XXX seri; sed hoc variatur locorum natura. non alia maior in Baetica arbor; in Africa vero—fides penes auctores erit—miliarias vocari multas narrant a pondere olei quod ferant annuo proventu. ideo LXXV pedes Mago intervallo dedit undique aut in macro solo ac duro atque ventoso, cum minimum,
94 XLV. Baetica quidem uberrimas messes inter oleas metit. illam inscientiam pudendam esse conveniet adultas interlucare iusto plus et in senectam praecipitare aut, ut plerumque ipsis qui posuere coarguentibus

[1] quantum ⟨intervallum⟩? *Mayhoff.*

[a] VI. 1.

Even this department of knowledge is not to be despised, nor put in the last class, inasmuch as to each kind of plant shade is either a nurse or else a stepmother—at all events for the shadow of a walnut tree or a stone pine or a spruce or a silver fir to touch any plant whatever is undoubtedly poison.

Spacing of trees.

XIX. The question of raindrops falling from trees can be settled briefly. With all the trees which are so shielded by the spread of their foliage that the rain-water does not flow down over the tree itself the drip does cruel injury. Consequently in this enquiry it will make a great deal of difference over what space the soil in which we are going to plant causes the various trees to grow. In the first place, hillsides in themselves require smaller intervals between the trees. In places exposed to the wind, it pays to plant trees closer together, but nevertheless to give the olive very wide spacing, Cato's opinion[a] for Italy being that olives should be planted 25 or at most 30 feet apart; but this varies with the nature of the sites. The olive is the largest of all the trees in Andalusia; in Africa, however, so it is stated—the guarantee for this statement will rest with the authorities who make it—there are a number of trees called 'thousand-pounders', from the weight of oil that they produce in a year's crop. Consequently Mago has prescribed a space of 75 feet all round, or in thin, hard soil exposed to the wind, 45 feet at least. Andalusia however reaps most abundant crops of corn grown between the olives. It will be agreed that it shows shameful ignorance to thin full-grown trees more than a proper amount and hasten them into old age, or to cut them down altogether, by doing which the persons who planted them frequently manifest

imperitiam suam, totas excidere. nihil est foedius agricolis quam gestae rei poenitentia, multo iam ut praestet laxitate delinquere.

95 XX. Quaedam autem natura tarde crescunt, et in primis semine tantum nascentia et longo aevo durantia. at quae cito occidunt velocia sunt, ut ficus punica, prunus, malus, pirus, myrtus, salix, et tamen antecedunt divitiis: in trimatu enim ferre incipiunt ostendentes et ante. ex his lentissima est pirus, ocissima omnium cypirus et pseudocypirus frutex; protinus enim floret semenque perfert. omnia vero celerius adolescunt stolonibus ablatis unamque in stirpem redactis alimentis.

96 XXI. Eadem natura et propagines docuit. rubi namque curvati gracilitate et simul proceritate nimia defigunt rursus in terram capita iterumque nascuntur ex sese repleturi omnia ni resistat cultura, prorsus ut possint videri homines terrae causa geniti. ita pessima atque execranda res propaginem tamen docuit ac viviradicem. eadem autem natura et hederis. Cato propagari praeter vitem tradit ficum, oleam, punicam, malorum genera omnia, laurus, pruna, myrtum, nuces abellanas et Praenestinas, platanum.

---

[a] *Cypirus* is galingale, with of course no connection with *pirus*, pear.

their own incompetence. Nothing is more disgraceful for farmers than to do a thing and then have to be sorry for it, so that in fact it pays much better to err by leaving too much space between the trees.

XX. Some trees are by nature slow growers, and in particular those that only grow from seed and that live a long time. Those on the other hand that are short-lived, for instance the fig, pomegranate, plum, apple, pear, myrtle and willow, grow quickly, and nevertheless they lead the way in producing their riches, for they begin to bear at three years old, making some show even before. Among these the pear is the slowest of all to bear, and the cypirus [a] and the false cypirus bush the quickest, for this group flowers straight away and goes on to produce its seed. But all trees mature more quickly if the suckers are removed and the nourishing juices brought back into a single stem. *Pace of growth of trees.*

XXI. Nature has likewise also taught the art of reproducing from layers. Brambles curving over with their slender and also excessively long shoots plant their ends in the earth again and sprout afresh out of themselves, in a manner that would fill up the whole place if resistance were not offered by cultivation, so that it would be positively possible to imagine that mankind was created for the service of the earth. Thus a most evil and execrable circumstance has nevertheless taught the use of the layer and the quickset. Ivies also have the same property. Beside the vine, Cato gives instructions for layering the fig, olive, pomegranate, all kinds of apples, laurels, plums, myrtle, hazel and Palestrina nuts, and the plane. *Layering.* CXXXIII. 2 f., LI, LII

97 Propaginum duo genera: ramo ab arbore depresso in scrobem quattuor pedum quoquo versus[1] et post biennium amputato flexu plantaque translata post trimatum, quas si longius ferre libeat, in qualis statim aut vasis fictilibus defodere propagines aptissimum,
98 ut in his transferantur. alterum genus luxuriosius, in ipsa arbore radices sollicitando traiectis per vasa fictilia vel qualos ramis terraque circumfartis, atque hoc blandimento inpetratis radicibus inter poma ipsa et cacumina—in summa etenim cacumina hoc modo petuntur audaci ingenio[2] arborem aliam longe a tellure faciendi—eodem quo supra biennii spatio abscisa propagine et cum quasillo[3] sata. Sabina herba propagine seritur et avolsione; tradunt faece vini aut e parietibus latere tuso mire ali; iisdem modis rosmarinum seritur et ramo, quoniam neutri semen, rhododendrum propagine et semine.

99 XXII. Semine quoque inserere natura docuit, raptim avium fame devorato solidoque et alvi tepore madido cum fecundo fimi medicamine abiecto in mollibus arborum lecticis aut[4] ventis saepe translato in aliquas corticum rimas; unde vidimus cerasum in salice, platanum in lauru, laurum in ceraso et bacas

[1] versus (*vel* undique) *add.* ? *Mayhoff.*
[2] invento ? (*sed cf.* XV 49) *Mayhoff.*
[3] *Rackham* (quasillis *Sillig*: qualis illis *edd. vett.*): qua illis (quas illis *cd. Par. Lat.* 6795).
[4] *Rackham*: et.

There are two kinds of layer. A branch is bent down from the tree into a hole measuring four feet each way, and after two years is cut off at the bend, and three years later the growth is transplanted to another place; if it is desired to carry layers so struck a considerable distance, it is most suitable to plant them at once in baskets or earthenware pots, so that they may be carried to the fresh site in these. The other method is more elaborate; it is effected by inducing roots to grow on the tree itself by passing branches through earthenware pots or baskets and packing them round with earth, and so enticing roots to grow right among the fruit and at the ends of the branches—as branch-ends to form roots in this way are obtained at the top of the tree, by the daring device of creating another tree a long way off the ground—and after the same interval of two years as in the previous method cutting off the layer and planting it together with the basket. Savine is grown from a layer and also from a slip; it is said that wine-lees or crushed brick from walls make it grow marvellously; and rosemary is reproduced by the same methods and also from a branch, since neither savine nor rosemary has a seed; the oleander is grown both by layering and from seed.

Grafting with seed

XXII. Nature has also taught the method of grafting by means of seed; a seed that has been hurriedly swallowed whole by a hungry bird and has become sodden by the warmth of its belly is deposited together with a fertilizing manure of dung in a soft bed in the fork of a tree, or else, as often happens, is carried by the wind into some crevice or other in the bark; as a result of this we have seen a cherry tree growing on a willow, a plane on a laurel, a laurel on a cherry,

simul discolores. tradunt et monedulam condentem semina in thensauros cavernarum eiusdem rei praebere causas.

100 XXIII. Hinc nata inoculatio sutoriae simili fistula aperiendi in arbore oculum cortice exciso semenque includendi eadem fistula sublatum ex alia. in ficis et malis haec fuit inoculatio antiqua; Vergiliana quaerit sinum in nodo germine expulsi corticis gemmamque ex alia arbore includit.

101 XXIV. Et hactenus natura ipsa docuit, insitionem autem casus, magister alius et paene numerosior, ad hunc modum: agricola sedulus casam saepis munimento cingens, quo minus putrescerent sudes limen subdidit ex hedera; at illae vivaci morsu adprehensae suam ex aliena[1] fecere vitam apparuitque truncum esse pro terra. aufertur ergo serra aequaliter super-
102 ficies, levigatur falce truncus. ratio postea duplex, et prima inter corticem lignumque inserendi: timebant prisci truncum findere, mox inforare ausi medio ipsique in eo medullae calamum inprimebant, unum

[1] *Ed. Hack.*: alieno.

[a] *Georgics* II. 74 ff. [b] In the microscopic layer now called cambium.

and berries of different colours growing together. It is also reported that the same thing may be caused by a jackdaw when it hides seeds in the holes that are its storehouses.

XXIII. From this has been derived the process of inoculation, consisting in opening an eye in a tree by cutting away the bark with a tool resembling a shoemaker's punch and enclosing in it a seed that has been removed from another tree by means of the same tool. This was the method of inoculation used in old days in the case of figs and apples; but the method described by Virgil[a] is to find a recess in a knot of bark burst open by a shoot and to enclose in this a bud obtained from another tree. *Inoculation.*

XXIV. And so far Nature has herself been our instructor; but grafting was taught us by Chance, another tutor and one who gives us perhaps more frequent lessons, and this was how he did it: a careful farmer, making a fence round his house to protect it, put under the posts a base made of ivy-wood, so as to prevent them from rotting; but the posts when nipped by the bite of the still living ivy created life of their own from another's vitality, and it was found that the trunk of a tree was serving instead of earth. Continuing, the surface of the wood is levelled off with a saw and the trunk smoothed with a pruning-knife. Afterwards there is a two-fold method of procedure; and the first method consists of inserting the graft between[b] the bark and the wood, as people in former days were afraid of making a cleft in the trunk; although subsequently they ventured to bore right into the middle and adopted the plan of forcing the graft into the pith itself inside it, inserting only one graft as the *Grafting; elaborate rules for.*

inserentes, neque enim plures capiebat medulla. subtilior postea ratio vel senos addi[1] mortalitati eorum et numero, per media trunco leniter fisso cuneoque tenui fissuram custodiente, donec cuspidatim decisus descendat in rimam calamus.

103 Multa in hoc servanda: primum omnium, quae patiatur coitum talem arbor et cuius arboris. varie quoque et non isdem in partibus subest omnibus sucus: vitibus ficisque media sicciora[2] et e summa parte conceptus, ideo illinc surculi petuntur; oleis circa media sucus, inde et surculi: cacumina sitiunt.
104 facillime coalescunt quibus eadem corticis natura quaeque pariter florentia eiusdem horae cognationem sucorumque societatem habent; lenta res est quotiens umidis repugnant sicca, mollibus corticum duri. reliqua observatio ne fissura in nodo fiat—repudiat quippe advenam inhospitalis duritia, ut in parte nitidissima, ne longior multo tribus digitis, ne obliqua,
105 ne tralucens. Vergilius e cacumine inseri vetat, certumque est ab umeris arborum orientem aestivum spectantibus surculos petendos, et a feracibus et e germine novello, nisi vetustae arbori inserantur—ii

[1] *Mayhoff*: adici.
[2] *Edd.*: sicciore.

---

[a] *I.e.* if the text is correct, both to replace any grafts that died and to make a larger total number of living grafts.
[b] *Georgics* II. 78.

pith would not take more. But subsequently a more elaborate method is for as many as six grafts to be added to reinforce their liability to die and their number,[a] a cleft being carefully made through the middle of the trunk and being kept open by means of a thin wedge until the graft, the end of which has been pared into a point, goes right down into the crack.

In this process a great many precautions have to be observed. First of all we must notice what kind of tree will stand grafting of this nature, and what tree it will take a graft from. Also the sap is variously distributed, and does not lie under the bark in the same parts with all trees: in vines and figs the middle is drier, and generation starts from the top, shoots for grafting being consequently taken from the top of the tree, whereas in olives the sap is round the middle and grafts are also taken from there, the tops being parched up. Grafts and trunk grow together most easily when they have the same kind of bark and when they flower at the same time, so that they have the affinity of the same season and a partnership of juices; whereas it is a slow business when there is incompatibility between dry tissues and damp ones, and between hard and soft barks. The other points to be observed are not to make the cleft at a knot, as the inhospitable hardness repudiates a new-comer; to make it at the shiniest place; not to make it much more than three inches long, nor on a slant, nor so as to be transparent. Virgil[b] says that grafts must not be taken from the top, and it is certain that the slips should be obtained from the shoulders of the tree that look north-east, and from trees that are good bearers and from a young shoot, unless the tree on which they are to be grafted

enim robustiores esse debent; praeterea ut praegnates, hoc est gemmatione turgentes et qui parere illo speraverint anno, bimi utique nec tenuiores digito
106 minimo. inseruntur autem et inversi cum id agitur ut minor altitudo in latitudinem se fundat. ante omnia gemmantes nitere conveniet: nihil usquam ulcerosum aut retorridum spei favebit.[1] medulla calami commissurae in matre ligni corticisque iungatur, id enim satius quam foris cortici aequari. calami exacutio medullam ne nudet, tantum tenui[2] fistula detegat; fastigatio levi descendat cuneo tribus non ampliore digitis, quod facillime contingit tinctum
107 aqua radentibus. ne exacuatur in vento. ne cortex a ligno decedat alterutri. calamus ad corticem usque suum deprimatur; ne luxetur dum deprimitur neve cortex replicetur in rugas. ideo lacrimantes calamos inseri non oportet, non, Hercules, magis quam aridos, quia illo modo labat umore nimio cortex, hoc vitali
108 defectu non umescit neque concorporatur. id etiam religionis servant, ut luna crescente, ut calamus

[1] *Rackham*: favet.
[2] tantum tenui? *Mayhoff*: tamen tenui *aut* tenui tamen.

---

[a] *I.e.* upside down, the top of the slip being put in the hole, not the cut end. [b] The cambium-layer.

is an old one, as in that case the slip must be stouter. A further point is that slips that are going to be grafted must be pregnant, that is, swelling with bud-formations, and in expectation of giving birth in that year, and they must be at all events two years old, and not thinner than the little finger. But grafts are also inserted the other way round [a] when the intention is for them not to grow so long but to spread out. Before all things it will be serviceable for them to have buds and to be glossy, as nothing shabby or shrivelled anywhere will gratify one's hopes. The pith of the slip grafted should be put touching the place [b] in the mother tree where the wood and the bark meet, for that is more satisfactory than to place it level with the bark outside. The process of giving a point to the slip for grafting must not strip the pith quite bare, but only make it visible through a narrow aperture; the point must slope off in an even wedge not more than three inches long, which is most easily achieved by dipping the slip in water when paring it. It must not be exposed to wind while it is being pointed. The bark must not be allowed to become separated from the wood in either the graft or the trunk. The graft must be pressed right down to where its bark begins, but it must not be forced out of shape while it is being pressed home, nor have its bark folded back in wrinkles. Consequently shoots dripping with sap should not be used for grafting, no more, I swear, than ones that are dry, because in the former case excess of moisture causes the bark to slip, while in the latter owing to defective vitality it makes no moisture and does not incorporate with the trunk. Moreover there is a religious rule that a graft must be inserted while the moon is

utraque deprimatur manu; et alioqui hoc in opere duae simul manus minus nituntur, necessario temperamento. validius demissi tardius ferunt, fortius durant, contrarie[1] ex diverso. ne hiscat nimium rima laxeque capiat, aut ne parum, ut[2] exprimat aut conpressum necet; hoc maxime cavendum in praevalide accipientis
109 trunco. ut[3] media[4] fissura relinquatur,[5] quidam vestigio fissurae falce in truncis facto salice praeligant marginem ipsum, postea cuneo findunt continente vinculo libertatem dehiscendi. quaedam in plantario insita eodem die transferuntur. si crassior truncus inseratur, inter corticem et lignum inseri melius, cuneo optime osseo cortice ne[6] rumpatur laxato.
110 cerasi libro dempto finduntur. hae solae et post brumam inseruntur. dempto libro habent veluti lanuginem, quae si conprehendit insitum putrefacit. vinculum[7] cuneo adacto[8] utilissime adstringitur; inserere aptissimum quam proxime terrae patiatur nodorum truncique ratio. eminere calami sex digitorum longitudine non amplius debent.

111 Cato argillae vel cretae harenam fimumque bubulum admisceri[9] atque ita usque ad lentorem

[1] *Rackham*: contraria.
[2] *Detlefsen*: et.
[3] ut *Mayhoff*: in.
[4] modica? *Mayhoff*.
[5] *Edd.*: relinquant.
[6] ne *add. Rackham* (cortex ne *Mayhoff*).
[7] *Schneider*: incolume.
[8] *Schneider*: adactum.
[9] *Rackham*: admiscet.

[a] XL. 2 f.

waxing, and that both hands must be used in pressing it home; and apart from that, to use both hands at once in this job requires less effort, as it involves combining their forces. Grafts pressed in too forcibly are slower in bearing but last more stoutly, while the contrary procedure has the opposite results. The crack must not gape too wide and afford a loose hold, nor yet not wide enough, so as to squeeze the graft out or to kill it by pressure; special care must be taken to avoid the latter in the trunk of a tree that takes the graft with an excessively powerful hold. In order that a cleft may be left in the middle, some people make a line of cleavage in the trunk with a pruning-hook and bandage the actual edge of the incision with a withe, and afterwards force it apart with a wedge, the bandage keeping it from gaping open too freely. Some slips are grafted on plants in a seed-plot and then are transplanted on the same day. If a rather thick stock is used for grafting, it is better to insert it between the bark and the wood, after using a wedge, preferably of bone, to loosen the bark, so as not to break it. Cherry-trees have their inner rind removed before the incision is made. They are the only trees that are grafted even after midwinter. After the bark has been removed they have a layer of a sort of down, and if this gets a hold on the graft it makes it decay. The most effective way of tightening the bandage is by driving a wedge into it; it suits best to insert it as close to the ground as the formation of the tree and the knots allows. Grafts ought not to project to a length of more than six inches.

Cato [a] recommends making a mixture of pounded white clay or chalk and cowdung and so working it to a sticky consistency, and putting this into the fissure

subigi iubet idque interponi et circumlini. ex iis quae commentatus est facile apparet illa aetate inter lignum et corticem nec alio modo inserere solitos aut ultra latitudinem duum digitorum calamos demittere. inseri autem praecipit pira ac mala per ver et post
112 solstitium diebus L et[1] post vindemiam, oleas autem et ficos per ver tantum, luna sitiente,[2] praeterea post meridiem ac sine vento austro. mirum quod non contentus insitum munisse ut dictum est, et caespite ab imbre frigoribusque protexisse ac mollibus bifidorum viminum fasciis, lingua bubula—herbae id genus est—insuper optegi iubet eamque inligari opertam stramentis: nunc abunde arbitrantur paleato luto fasciari[3] libro duos digitos insito exstante.

113 Verno inserentes tempus urguet, incitantibus se gemmis praeterquam in olea, cuius diutissime oculi parturiunt, minimumque suci habet sub cortice, qui nimius insitis nocet. punica vero et ficum quaeque
114 alia sicca sunt recrastinare minime utile. pirum vel florentem inserere licet et in Maium quoque mensem protendere insitiones. quod si longius adferantur pomorum calami, rapo infixos optime custodire sucum arbitrantur, servari inter duos imbrices iuxta rivos vel

[1] et *add. Hardouin.*
[2] *Detlefsen*: sitiente, hoc est sicca.
[3] *Rackham* (fasciare *Ian*); farcire.

and smearing it round it. From his remarks on the subject it is easily seen that at that period they used to insert the graft between the wood and the bark and not otherwise, nor used they to put the slips more than two inches in. He advises grafting pear and apples during the spring and fifty days after midsummer and after the vintage, but olives and figs only in the spring and when a cloudless moon is shining, and moreover in the afternoon and not if there is a south wind blowing. It is remarkable that he is not content to have safeguarded the graft in the manner described, and to have protected it against rain and frost by means of turf and soft bundles of split osiers, but he says it must be covered with a layer of bugloss—a species of plant—as well, and that this should be tied on with a layer of straw; whereas nowadays they think it is very adequately packed with a wrapping of mud and chaff, the graft projecting two inches from the bark.

Seasons for grafting.

Those who do their grafting in spring are pressed for time, as the buds are just shooting, except in the case of the olive, the eyes of which are pregnant for a very long time, and it has a very small amount of sap under the bark, which when too abundant is injurious to the grafts. But with pomegranates and the fig and other trees of a dry nature it is far from beneficial to put off grafting till a late season. A pear-tree however may be grafted when actually in blossom, and the process may be carried forward even into May. If however cuttings of fruit trees have to be brought from a considerable distance, it is believed that they best preserve their sap if they are inserted in a turnip, and it is best to store them near a stream or a pond, packed between two hollow

piscinas utrimque terra obstructos; vitium vero in scrobibus siccis stramento opertos ac deinde terra obrutos ut cacumine exstent.

115 XXV. Cato vitem tribus modis inserit: praesectam findi iubet per medullam, in eam surculos, exacutos ut dictum est, addi, medullas iungi; altero, si inter se vites contingant, utriusque in obliquum latere contrario adraso iunctis medullis colligari; tertium genus est terebrare vitem in obliquum ad medullam calamosque addere longos pedes binos atque ita ligatum insitum intritaque inlitum operire terra
116 calamis subrectis. nostra aetas correxit ut Gallica uteretur terebra quae excavat nec urit, quoniam adustio omnis hebetat, atque ut gemmascere incipiens eligeretur calamus, nec plus quam binis ab insito emineret oculis, ulmi . . .[1] vimine alligato . . .[1] bina circumdarentur, . . .[1] acie a duabus partibus, ut inde potius destillaret mucor qui maxime vites infestat, dein cum evaluissent flagella pedes binos, vinculum insiti incideretur, ubertati crassitudine permissa.
117 vitibus inserendis tempus dedere ab aequinoctio autumno ad germinationis initia. sativae plantae silvestrium radicibus inseruntur natura spissioribus[2]; si sativae silvestribus[3] inserantur, degenerant in

[1] *Lacunas Mayhoff.*
[2] spissioribus? *Mayhoff coll.* § 121: siccioribus.
[3] silvestrium truncis *coni. Warmington, vel* si sativae . . . feritatem *gloss. Cf. Varr. R.R.* I. 40.

[a] XLI. 2 ff. [b] *Medulla* includes the unrecognised cambium-layer.
[c] The apparent lacunae in the text of this sentence have evaded conjectural restoration.

tiles blocked up at each end with earth; but it is thought that vine-cuttings are best stored in dry ditches, under a covering of straw, with earth then piled over them so as to let their tops protrude.

Grafting vines.

XXV. Cato[a] has three ways of grafting a vine: he advises cutting the stock short and splitting it through the pith, and then inserting into it the shoots after sharpening them at the end in the manner stated above, and making the cambium[b] of the two meet; the second method is, in case the vines are contiguous with one another, to pare down on a slant the side of each that faces the other and to tie them together with the cambiums joined; and the third is to bore a slanting hole in the vine down to the pith and insert slips a couple of feet long, and to tie the graft in that position and cover it up with a plaster of pounded earth, with the shoots upright. Our generation has improved on this method, so as to employ a Gallic auger which makes a hole in the tree without scorching it, because all scorching weakens it, and to select a slip that is beginning to bud, and not to let it protrude from the stock by more than two eyes, . . . of an elm . . . tied on with a withe . . . put two round . . . on two sides with a knife,[c] so that the slime which is the greatest enemy of vines may chiefly exude through them, and then when the whips have made two feet of growth, to cut the tie of the graft, allowing its growth to make thickness. They have fixed the time for grafting vines from the autumn equinox till the beginning of budding. Cultivated plants are grafted on roots of wild ones, which are of a closer texture, whereas if slips of cultivated plants are grafted on the trunks of wild ones they degenerate to the wild variety.

§ 106.

feritatem. reliqua caelo constant: aptissima insitis siccitas; huius enim remedium adpositis fictilibus vasis modicus umor per cinerem destillans[1]; inoculatio rores amat lenes.

118 XXVI. Emplastratio[2] et ipsa ex inoculatione nata videri potest, crasso autem maxime cortici convenit, sicut est ficis. ergo amputatis omnibus ramis ne sucum avocent, nitidissima in parte quaque praecipua cernatur hilaritas exempta scutula ita ne descendat ultra corticem ferrum, imprimitur ex alia[3] cortex par cum sui germinis mamma, sic conpage densata ut cicatrici locus non sit et statim fiat unitas, nec umorem nec adflatum recipiens; nihilominus tamen et luto
119 munire et vinculo melius. hoc genus non pridem repertum volunt qui novis moribus favent, sed iam et[4] apud veteres Graecos invenitur et apud Catonem, qui oleam ficumque sic inseri iussit mensura etiam praefinita secundum reliquam diligentiam suam, corticis scalpro excidi quattuor digitorum longitudinem et trium latitudinem atque ita coagmentari et illa sua intrita oblini, eadem ratione ut in malo. quidam huic generi miscuere fissuram in vitibus,

[1] *Ed. Hack.*: destillat.
[2] *Huet*: emplastri ratio.
[3] alia ⟨arbore⟩? *Rackham.*
[4] *Mayhoff*: etiam *aut* etiam et.

The rest depends on the weather: dry weather is most favourable for grafts, because a remedy for its ill effects is to place earthenware pots of ashes on the stock and let a small amount of water filter through the ashes; but grafting by inoculation likes a light fall of dew.

XXVI. Scutcheon grafting may itself also be thought to have sprung from grafting by inoculation, but it is most suited to a thick bark, such as that of fig-trees. The procedure is to prune all the branches so that they may not attract the sap, and then, at the most flourishing part of the tree and where it displays exceptional luxuriance, to remove a scutcheon, without allowing the knife to penetrate below the bark; and then to take a piece of bark of equal size from another tree, together with a protuberant bud, and press it into the place, fitting the join so closely that there is no room for a scar to form and a single substance is produced straight away, impervious to damp and to air—though all the same it is better to protect the splice by plastering it with mud and tying it with a bandage. People in favour of modern fashions make out that this kind of grafting was only recently invented, but it is found already in the old Greek writers and in Cato, who prescribed this method of grafting for the olive and the fig, in conformity with his invariable precision actually defining the proper measurement: he says that a piece of bark four inches long and three wide should be cut out with a knife, and so fitted to its place and smeared with that pounded mixture of his described above, in the same way as in grafting an apple. In the case of vines some people have combined with this kind of grafting the fissure method, removing a

Scutcheon grafting.

XLII.

§ 111.

120 exempta cortici tessella a latere calamo adigendo. tot modis insitam arborem vidimus iuxta Tiburtes tullios omni genere pomorum onustam, alio ramo nucibus, alio bacis, aliunde vite, piris, ficis, punicis malorumque generibus; sed huic brevis fuit vita. nec tamen omnia experimentis adsequi in natura[1] possumus; quaedam enim nasci nisi sponte nullo modo queunt, eaque inmitibus tantum et desertis locis proveniunt.
121 capacissima insitorum omnium ducitur platanus, postea robur, verum utraque sapores corrumpit. quaedam omni genere inseruntur, ut ficus, punicae[2]; vitis non recipit emplastra, nec quibus tenuis aut caducus rimosusque cortex, neque inoculationem siccae aut umoris exigui. fertilissima omnium inoculatio, postea emplastratio, sed utraque infirmissima; et quae cortice tantum nituntur vel levi aura ocissime deplantantur. inserere firmissimum et fecundius quam serere.

122 Non est omittenda raritas unius exempli. Corellius eques Romanus Ateste genitus insevit castaneam suomet ipsam surculo in Neapolitano agro; sic facta est castanea quae ab eo nomen accepit inter laudatas. postea Tereus eiusdem libertus Corellianam iterum

[1] *Mayhoff*: adsequi naturam.
[2] *Sic*? *Mayhoff*: ut ficus, ut punicae.

little square of bark on the side and then forcing in the shoot. We have seen beside the Falls of Tivoli a tree that has been grafted in all these ways and was laden with fruit of every kind, nuts on one branch, berries on another, while in other places hung grapes, pears, figs, pomegranates and various sorts of apples; but the tree did not live long. And nevertheless it is impossible for us by our experiments to attain to all the things found in Nature, as some cannot possibly come into existence except spontaneously, and these only occur in wild and uninhabited places. The tree most receptive of every kind of graft is believed to be the plane, and next to it the hard-oak, but both of these spoil the flavours of the fruit. Some trees, for instance the fig and the pomegranate, can be grafted in all the different methods, but the vine does not admit scutcheons, nor do trees that have a thin bark or one that peels off and cracks; nor do trees which are dry or contain only a little sap admit of inoculation. Inoculation is the most prolific of all methods of grafting, and grafting by scutcheon comes next, but both are very subject to displacement; and a graft that relies on the support of the bark only is very speedily dislodged by even a light breeze. Grafting by insertion is the firmest, and produces more fruit than a tree grown from planting.

Various graftings.

We must not omit one extremely exceptional case. In the territory of Naples a Knight of Rome named Corellius, a native of Este, grafted a chestnut with a slip cut from the tree itself, and this is how the celebrated variety of chestnut tree named after him was produced. Subsequently his freedman Tereus grafted a Corellius chestnut again. The

Graft taken from same tree.

insevit. haec est inter eas differentia: illa copiosior, haec Tereiana melior.

123 XXVII. Reliqua genera casus ingenio suo excogitavit ac defractos serere ramos docuit cum pali defixi radices cepissent. multa sic seruntur inprimisque ficus omnibus aliis modis nascens praeterquam talea, optime quidem vastiore ramo pali modo exacuto si[1] adigatur alte, exiguo super terram relicto capite eoque ipso harena cooperto. ramo seruntur et punica, palis laxato prius meatu,[2] item myrtus, omnium horum longitudine trium pedum, crassitudine minus bracchiali, cortice diligenter servato, trunco exacuto.

124 XXVIII. Myrtus et taleis seritur, morus talea tantum, quoniam in ulmo eam inseri religio fulgurum prohibet. quapropter de talearum satu nunc dicendum est. servandum in eo ante omnia ut taleae ex feracibus fiant arboribus, ne curvae neve scabrae aut bifurcae, ne[3] tenuiores quam ut manum impleant, ne minores pedalibus, ut inlibato cortice atque ut sectura inferior ponatur semper et quod fuerit[4] ab radice, adcumuleturque germinatio terra donec robur planta capiat.

[1] *Rackham*: si vastiore . . . exacuto.
[2] hiatu? *Rackham.*
[3] ne *add. edd.*
[4] *J. Mueller*: erit.

---

[a] *I.e.* the branch that is being planted so as to strike root and form the trunk of a new tree.

difference between the two varieties is this: the former is more prolific but the latter, the Tereus chestnut, of better quality.

Propagation by planting branches.

XXVII. It is mere accident that by its own ingenuity has devised the remaining kinds of reproduction; it taught us to break off branches from trees and plant them because stakes driven into the earth had taken root. This method is used to grow many trees, especially the fig, which can be grown in all the other ways except from a cutting; the best plan indeed is to take a comparatively large branch and point it at the end like a stake and drive it deep into the earth, leaving a small head above ground and covering up even this with sand. Pomegranates also are grown from a branch, the passage into the hole having first been widened with stakes; and so also the myrtle; in all of these a branch is used that is three feet long and not so thick as a man's arm, and the bark is carefully preserved and the trunk[a] sharpened to a point at the end.

Planting cuttings.

XXVIII. The myrtle is grown from cuttings as well as in other ways, and that is the only way used for the mulberry, because superstitious fear of lightning forbids its being grafted on an elm. Consequently we must now speak about the planting of cuttings. In this care must be taken above all that the cuttings are made from trees that bear well, that they are not bent in shape nor scabbed or forked, that they are thick enough to fill the hand and not less than a foot long, that they are planted without injury to the bark and always with the cut end and the part that was nearest the root downward, and during the process of budding the plant is kept heaped over with earth until it attains strength.

125 XXIX. Quae custodienda in olearum cura Cato iudicaverit, ipsius verbis optime praecipiemus: Taleas oleagineas quas in scrobe saturus eris tripedaneas facito, diligenterque tractato ne liber laboret cum dolabis aut secabis. quas in seminario saturus eris pedales facito. eas sic inserito: locus bipalio subactus sit beneque glutus; cum taleam demittes, pede taleam opprimito; si parum descendat, malleo aut mateola adigito, cavetoque ne librum scindas cum adiges. palo prius locum ne feceris quo taleam demittas, ita melius vivet. taleae ubi trimae sunt,
126 tum denique maturae sunt,[1] ubi liber se vertet. si in scrobibus aut in sulcis seres, ternas taleas ponito easque divaricato. supra terram ne plus quattuor digitos traversos emineant,[2] vel oculo servato.—Diligenter eximere oleam oportet et radices quam plurima [3] cum terra ferre; ubi radices bene operueris, calcare bene, ne quid [4] noceat. si quis quaerat quod tempus oleae serendae sit, agro sicco per sementem,
127 agro laeto per ver.—XXX. Olivetum diebus xv ante aequinoctium vernum incipito putare, ex eo die dies XL recte putabis. id hoc modo putato: qua locus recte ferax erit, quae arida erunt et si quid ventus interfregerit, inde ea omnia eximito; qua locus ferax non erit, id plus concidito artatoque [5] bene enodatoque stirpesque leves facito.—Circum oleas autumnitate

[1] *Cato*: tum denique curae sunt *aut* sint.
[2] *Cato*: traverso semine aut.
[3] plurima? *Mayhoff*: plurimas.
[4] ne aqua *Cato*.
[5] *Pontedera*: aratoque.

XXIX. We shall best convey in Cato's own words the rules that he judged necessary to keep in looking after olives: 'Make the olive slips that you are going to plant in the hole a yard long, and handle them carefully so as not to damage the bark when cutting or trimming them. Make those you are going to plant in the nursery a foot long. Plant them thus: the place must be first dug over with a mattock and have the soil well loosened; when you put the slip in, press down the slip with your foot; if it does not go down far enough, drive it in with a mallet or a beetle, and be careful not to break the bark while you are driving it in. Do not make a hole beforehand with a dibble into which to put the slip: if you do not, it will live better. The slips do not mature till three years old, when the bark will turn. If you plant them in holes or in furrows, put them in groups of three and keep these apart. Check just by the eye that they do not project more than four fingers' breadth above the earth.—In taking up an olive tree you should use great care and carry the roots with as much earth as possible; when you have well covered up the roots, tread them down well, so that nothing may injure them. If anyone asks what is the time for planting an olive, the answer is, where there is a dry soil, at seed-time, but where it is rich, in the spring.—XXX. Begin to prune an olive-yard a fortnight before the spring equinox; the six weeks from then onward will be the right time for pruning. Prune it in this way: in a really fertile place, remove all the parts that are dry and any branches broken by the wind; in a place that is not fertile, trim away more and reduce well and disentangle out and make the stocks smooth.—In the autumn season turn up

Cato, XLV.

Treatment of olive cuttings.

Cato, LXI. 2.

Cato, XLIV. LXI. 1.

oblaqueato et stercus addito.—Qui oletum saepissime et altissime miscebit, is tenuissimas radices exarabit. si male arabit,[1] radices susum abibunt, crassiores fient eo[2] et vires oleae abibunt.

128 Quae genera olearum et in quo genere terrae iuberet seri quoque spectare oliveta, diximus in ratione olei. Mago in colle et siccis et argilla inter autumnum et brumam seri iussit, in crasso aut umido aut subriguo solo a messe ad brumam; quod praecepisse eum Africae intellegatur.[3] Italia quidem nunc vere maxime serit; sed si et autumno libeat, post aequinoctium XL diebus ad Vergiliarum occasum IIII

129 soli dies sunt quibus seri noceat. Africae peculiare quod in oleastro eas[4] inserit quadam aeternitate, cum senescant proxima adoptioni virga immissa[5] atque ita alia arbore ex eadem iuvenescente iterumque et quotiens opus sit, ut aevis eadem oliveta constent. inseritur autem oleaster calamo et inoculatione.

130 Olea ubi quercus effossa est[6] male ponitur, quoniam vermes qui raucae vocantur in radice quercus nascuntur et transeunt. non inhumare taleas aut siccare prius quam serantur utilius conpertum. vetus

[1] si . . . arabit *Cato*: *om. codd.*
[2] *Rackham*: et eo in radices *codd.*, et in radices *Cato.*
[3] *Rackham*: intellegitur.
[4] *J. Mueller*: oleastro est.
[5] *Rackham*: emissa.
[6] *Mayhoff*: sit.

the earth round the olive-trees and add dung.—The man who stirs over his olive-yard most often and deepest, will plough up the thinnest roots. If he ploughs badly, the roots will spread out on the top of the ground and will become thicker, and the strength of the olive-trees will go away into them.'

Seasons for planting trees.

We have already stated, in treating of olive-oil, what kinds of olive trees Cato tells us to plant and in what kind of soil, and what aspect he advises for olive-yards. XV. 20 ff. Mago recommends that on sloping ground and in dry positions and in a clay soil they should be planted between autumn and the middle of winter, but in heavy or damp or watery soil between harvest and the middle of winter—though it must be understood that he gave this advice for Africa. Italy at any rate, at the present time, does its planting chiefly in spring, but if one chooses to plant in autumn as well, there are only four days of the forty between the equinox and the setting of the Pleiads on which it injures olives to be planted. It is peculiar to Africa that it grafts them on a wild olive, in a sort of everlasting sequence, as when they begin to get old the shoot next for engrafting is put in and so another young tree grows out of the same one and the process is repeated as often as is necessary, so that the same olive-yards go on for generations. The wild olive however is propagated both by grafting and by inoculation.

It is bad to plant an olive where an oak-tree has been dug up, because the worms called *raucae* breed in oak roots and go over to olives. It has been ascertained to pay better not to bury the cuttings in the ground or to dry them before they are planted. It has been found better for an old olive-yard to be

olivetum ab aequinoctio verno intra vergiliarum exortum interradi alternis annis melius inventum, item muscum radi,[1] circumfodi autem omnibus annis a solstitio duum cubitorum scrobe pedali altitudine, stercorari tertio anno.

Mago idem amygdalas ab occasu Arcturi ad bru-
131 mam seri iubet, pira non eodem tempore omnia, quoniam neque floreant eodem, oblonga aut rotunda ab occasu Vergiliarum ad brumam, reliqua genera media hieme ab occasu Sagittae, subsolanum aut septentriones spectantia, laurum ab occasu Aquilae ad
132 occasum Sagittae. conexa enim de tempore serendi inserendique[2] ratio est: vere et autumno id magna ex parte fieri decrevere; est et alia hora circa Canis ortus, paucioribus nota quoniam non omnibus locis pariter utilis intellegitur, sed haud omittenda nobis non tractus alicuius rationem verum naturae totius
133 indagantibus. in Cyrenaica regione sub etesiarum flatu conserunt, nec non et in Graecia, oleam maxime in Laconia. Coos insula et vites tunc serit, ceteri apud Graecos inoculare et inserere non dubitant, sed arbores non serunt. plurimumque in eo locorum natura pollet; namque in Aegypto omni serunt

[1] *Mayhoff e Colum.*: radici (circumdare radici *edd.*).
[2] inserendi *add. J. Mueller.*

raked over every other year between the spring equinox and the rising of the Pleiads, and also to have the moss scraped off the trees, but for them to be dug round every year just after midsummer with a hole a yard across and a foot deep, and to be manured with dung every third year.

Mago also tells us to plant almonds between the rising of Arcturus and the shortest day, and not to plant all kinds of pears at the same time, as they do not blossom at the same time either; he says that those with oblong or round fruit should be planted between the setting of the Pleiads and the shortest day, but the remaining kinds in midwinter after the setting of the Arrow, with an eastern or northerly aspect; and a laurel between the setting of the Eagle and the setting of the Arrow. For the rule as to the time for planting and that for grafting are connected: the authorities have decided that for the greater part grafting should be done in spring and autumn, but there is also another suitable season, about the rising of the Dogstar, known to fewer people because it is understood not to be equally advantageous for all localities, but as we are enquiring into the proper method not for a particular region but for the whole of nature we must not omit it. In the district of Cyrene they plant when the yearly winds are blowing, as they also do in Greece, and particularly the olive in Laconia. The island of Cos also plants vines at that season, but the rest of the farmers in Greece, though they do not hesitate to inoculate and to graft trees at that season, do not plant trees then. And the natural qualities of the localities carry very great weight in this matter; for in Egypt they plant in every month, and so in

mense et ubicumque imbres aestivi sunt,[1] at[2] in India et Aethiopia nescessario post haec autumno
134 seruntur arbores. ergo tria tempora eadem germinationis, ver et Canis Arcturique ortus. neque enim animalium tantum est ad coitus aviditas, sed multo maior est terrae ac satorum omnium libido, qua tempestive uti plurimum interest conceptus peculiariterque[3] in insitis, cum sit mutua cupiditas utrique
135 coeundi. qui ver probant ab aequinoctio statim admittunt, praedicantes germina parturire, ideo faciles corticum esse conplexus; qui praeferunt autumnum ab arcturi ortu, quoniam statim radicem quandam capiant et ad ver parata veniant atque non protinus germinatio auferat vires. quaedam tamen statutum tempus anni habent ubique, ut cerasi et amygdalae circa brumam serendi vel inserendi; de pluribus locorum situs optime iudicabit: frigida enim et aquosa verno conseri oportet, sicca et calida autumno.
136 communis quidem Italiae ratio tempora ad hunc modum distribuit: moro ab idibus Februariis in aequinoctium, piro autumnum ita ut brumam xv ne minus diebus antecedat,[4] malis aestivis et cotoneis, item sorbis, prunis, post mediam hiemem in idus Februarias, siliquae Graecae et persicis ante brumam per autumnum, nucibus iuglandi et pineae et abellanae

[1] ⟨non⟩ sunt *Hardouin.*
[2] at *Ian*: et.
[3] *Rackham*: peculiare utique.
[4] *Rackham*: antecedant.

every country that has a summer rainfall, but in India and Ethiopia trees are necessarily planted later, in autumn. Consequently there are three regular periods for germination, spring and the rise of the Dogstar and that of Arcturus. For in fact not only do animals possess a strong appetite for copulation, but the earth and all vegetable growths have a much greater desire, the indulgence of which at the proper season is of the greatest importance for conception, and peculiarly so in the case of grafts, as both graft and stock share a mutual eagerness to unite. Those who approve of spring for grafting begin it immediately after the equinox, stating that the buds are just coming out, which facilitates the joining of the barks; but those who prefer autumn begin at the rising of Arcturus, because the grafts at once so to speak take root and are prepared when they reach springtime, and do not have their strength taken away immediately by budding. Some kinds of trees however have a fixed time of year everywhere, for instance cherries and almonds, which have to be planted or grafted about midwinter; but as to the greater number of trees the lie of the land will make the best decision, as cold and damp lands must be planted in spring, but dry and warm sites in autumn. The system general in Italy at all events assigns the times for planting in the following manner: for a mulberry from February 13 to the spring equinox; for a pear the autumn, provided it is not less than a fortnight before the shortest day; for summer apples and quinces, and also sorbs and plums, from midwinter to February 13; for the Greek carob and for peaches, right through autumn till midwinter; for the nuts, walnut and pine-cone and hazel and almond

et Graecae atque castaneae a kal. Martiis ad idus easdem, salici et genistae circa Martias kal. hanc in siccis semine, illam in umidis virga seri diximus.

137 Est etiamnum nova inserendi ratio, ne quid sciens quidem praeteream quod usquam invenerim, Columellae excogitata, ut adfirmat ipse, qua vel diversae insociabilesque arborum naturae copulentur, ut fici atque oleae. iuxta hanc seri ficum iubet non ampliore intervallo quam ut contingi large possit ramo oleae quam maxime sequaci atque oboedituro, eumque omni interim tempore edomari meditatione
138 curvandi; postea fico adepta vires, quod evenire trimae aut utique quinquennii, detruncata superficie ipsum quoque deputatum et, ut dictum est, adraso cacumine defigi in crure fici, custoditum vinculis ne curvatura fugiat. ita quodam propaginum insitorumque temperamento triennio communem [1] inter duas matres coalescere, quarto anno abscisum totum adoptantis esse, nondum vulgata ratione aut mihi certe satis conperta.

139 XXXI. Cetero eadem illa de calidis frigidisque et umidis aut siccis supra dicta ratio et scrobes fodere monstravit. in aquosis enim neque amplos neque

[1] *Mayhoff*: communi *cd. Par. Lat.* 6797: commune *rell.*

[a] V. 11, 13; *de Arb.* xxvi, 2.

and chestnut, from March 1 to March 15; for the willow and broom about March 1. The broom is grown from seed in dry places and the willow from a slip in damp localities, as we have stated. XIV. 74, 77.

Grafting by layering. There is moreover a new method of grafting—so that I may not wittingly pass over anything that I have anywhere discovered—devised by Columella,[a] as he himself states, for the purpose of effecting a union even between trees of different natures and not easily combined, for example figs and olives. He gives instructions to plant a fig-tree near to an olive, with not too wide a space between for the fig at full spread to touch a branch of the olive, the most supple and pliant branch possible being chosen, and all the time during the process it must be trained by practice in curving; and afterwards, when the fig has gained full strength, which he says is a matter of three or at most five years, the top of it is cut off and the branch of the olive is itself also pruned and with its head shaved to a point in the way that has been stated is inserted in the shank of the fig, § 115. after having been secured with ties to prevent its escaping because of the bend in it. In this way, he says, by a sort of combination of layering and grafting, in three years the branch shared between the two mother trees grows together, and in the fourth year it is cut away and belongs entirely to the tree that has adopted it; this method however is not yet generally known, or at all events I have not yet obtained a complete account of it.

Trenching round trees. XXXI. For the rest, the same account that has been given above about warm and cold and damp and dry substances has also demonstrated the method § 135. of trenching. In watery soils it will be suitable to

altos facere expediet, aliter in aestivoso et sicco, ut quam maxime accipiant aquam contineantque. haec et veteres arbores colendi ratio est; ferventibus enim locis adcumulant aestate radices operiuntque, ne solis
140 ardor exurat. aliubi ablaqueant perflatusque admittunt, iidem hieme cumulis a gelu vindicant; contra illi hieme aperiunt umoremque sitientibus quaerunt. ubicumque circumfodiendi ratio [1] pedes in orbem ternos, neque id in pratis, quoniam amore solis umorisque in summa tellure oberrant.—Et de arboribus quidem fructus gratia serendis inserendisque in universum sint dicta haec.

141 XXXII. Restat earum ratio quae propter alias seruntur ac vineas maxime, caeduo ligno. principatum in his optinent salices, quas serunt [2] loco madido, tamen refosso pedes duos et semipedem, talea sesquipedali vel pertica, quae utilior quo plenior.
142 intervallo esse debent pedes seni. trimae pedibus binis a terra putatione coercentur, ut se in latitudinem fundant ac sine scalis tondeantur; salix enim fecundior quo terrae propior. has quoque omnibus annis
143 confodi iubent mense Aprili. haec est viminalium cultura. perticalis et virga et talea seritur, fossura

[1] *Mayhoff*: circumfodiendi arbores ratio in circuitum.
[2] *J. Mueller*: salices quarum.

make trenches neither broad nor deep, but the contrary in warm and dry ground, so that they may receive and retain water as much as possible. This is the method used in cultivating old trees as well, as in very warm localities growers heap earth over the roots in summer and cover them up, to prevent the heat of the sun from parching them. In other places they turn up the earth round them and give access to the air, but also in winter pile up earth to protect them from frost; whereas growers in hot climates open up the roots in winter and try to obtain moisture for the thirsty trees. Everywhere the rule is to dig a circular trench three feet in circumference round the tree, though this is not done in meadowland because the roots, owing to their love of sun and moisture, wander about on the surface of the ground.—And let these be our general observations in regard to planting and grafting trees for fruit.

Trees grown for supports and for timber: osier and white willow, white poplar, reed, chestnut and others.

XXXII. It remains to give an account of those which are grown as supports for other trees, particularly for vines, and which are felled for timber. Among these the first place is taken by willows, which are planted in a damp place, but in a hole dug two and a half feet deep, a truncheon or rod 18 inches long being used, the stouter the more serviceable. They should be set six feet apart. When three years old they are lopped off two feet from the ground to make them spread out wide and to enable them to be cut back without using ladders; for the willow is the more productive the nearer it is to the ground. It is advised that these trees also should be dug round every year, in April. This is the mode of cultivating the osier willow. The stake willow is grown both from a rod and from a truncheon, in a hole

eadem. perticas ex ea caedi iustum est quarto fere anno; et hae autem senescentium locum propagine sarciunt praecisa[1] post annum. salicis viminalis iugera singula sufficiunt xxv vineae iugeribus. eiusdem rei causa populus alba seritur bipedaneo pastinato, talea sesquipedali, biduo siccata, palmipedi intervallo, terra superiniecta duorum cubitorum crassitudine.

144 XXXIII. Harundo etiam dilutiore quam hae solo gaudet. seritur bulbo radicis, quod alii oculum vocant, dodrantali scrobe, intervallo duum pedum et semipedis; reficiturque ex sese vetere harundineto exstirpato, quod utilius repertum quam castrare, sicut antea; namque inter se radices serpunt mutuoque
145 decursu necantur. tempus conserendi priusquam oculi harundinum intumescant, ante kal. Martias. crescit ad brumam usque, desinitque cum durescere incipit: hoc signum tempestivam habet caesuram; et hanc autem quotiens et vineam fodiendam putant. seritur et traversa, non alte terra condita, erumpunt-
146 que e singulis oculis totidem plantae. seritur et deplantata pedali sulco, binis obrutis gemmis ut tertius nodus terram attingat, prono cacumine ne rores concipiat. caeditur decrescente luna. vineis fumo[2] siccata utilior quam viridis.

[1] *Mayhoff*: pertica. [2] *Schneider ex Geop.*: anno.

of the same depth. It is proper to cut rods from it in about three years; but these also fill up the place of trees that are growing old, by means of a layered new growth cut off after a year. A single acre of osier-willow will supply enough for 25 acres of vineyard. The white poplar is also grown for the same purpose, the hole being two feet deep and the cutting eighteen inches long and left two days to dry; the truncheons are planted one foot nine inches apart and a layer of earth a yard deep is thrown on the top of them.

XXXIII. The reed likes an even moister soil than osiers do. It is planted by putting the bulb of the root, which others call the 'eye', in a hole nine inches deep, two feet six inches apart; and it renews itself of its own accord when an old reed-bed has been rooted up, a method that has been found to pay better than thinning out, as used to be done previously, because the roots get twisted up together and are killed by their mutual inroads. The time to plant is before the eyes of the reeds swell up, which is before the first of March. It goes on growing till midwinter, and stops when it is beginning to get hard, which is the indication that it is ready for cutting; though it is thought that the reed also requires digging round as often as the vine does. It is also planted in a horizontal position, not buried deep in the ground, and as many shoots spring up as there are eyes. It is also grown by being planted out in a hole a foot deep, with two eyes buried so that the third knot is just touching the earth, and with the head bent down so as not to hold the dew. It is cut when the moon is on the wane. For propping vines a reed dried in smoke is more serviceable than one still green. *Reed.*

147 XXXIV. Castanea pedamentis omnibus praefertur facilitate tractatus, perdurandi pervicacia, regerminatione caedua vel salice laetior. quaerit solum facile nec tamen harenosum, maximeque sabulum umidum aut carbunculum vel tofi etiam farinam, quamlibet opaco septentrionalique et praefrigido situ, vel etiam declivi; recusat eadem glaream, rubricam,
148 cretam omnemque terrae fecunditatem. seri nuce diximus, sed nisi ex maximis non provenit, nec nisi quinis acervatim satis. refringi solum debet sub ea[1] ex Novembri mense in Februarium, quo solutae sponte cadunt ex arbore atque subnascuntur. intervalla sint pedalia, undique sulco dodrantali. ex hoc seminario transferuntur in aliud bipedali intervallo
149 post biennium. serunt et propagine, nulli quidem faciliore;[2] nudata enim radice tota in sulco prosternitur, tum ex cacumine supra terram relicto renascitur et alia ab radice. sed tralata nescit hospitari pavetque novitatem biennio fere; postea prosilit. ideo nucibus potius quam viviradicibus plantaria caedua implentur.
150 cultura non alia quam supra dictis, fodiendo supputandisque per biennium sequens. de cetero ipsa

[1] *Detlefsen*: debet supra.
[2] serunt et propagine . . . faciliore? *Mayhoff*: sunt et propagines . . . faciliores.

---

[a] The willow § 143 and the reed § 144.

XXXIV. The chestnut-tree is preferred to all other props because of the ease with which it is worked and its obstinate durability, and because when cut it buds again even more abundantly than the willow. It asks for a light yet not sandy soil, and especially a damp gravel or glowing-coal earth or even a powdery tufa, and it will grow in a site however shady, and facing north and extremely cold, or even in one on a slope; but at the same time it refuses dry gravel, red earth, chalk, and all rich fertile soils. We have said that it is grown from the nut, but it will only grow from very large ones, and only when they are planted five in a heap together. The soil underneath must be kept broken up from November to February, when the nuts detach themselves and fall from the tree and sprout in the ground underneath it. They should be planted in a hole measuring nine inches each way, with spaces of a foot between them. After two years they are transferred from this seed-plot to another and replanted two feet apart. People also grow them from a layer, which indeed is easier in their case than with any other tree: for the root is bared and the layer laid in the trench at full length, and then it throws out a new shoot from the top left above the earth and another from the root. When transplanted however it does not know how to make itself at home and dreads the novelty for almost two years, but afterwards it puts out shoots. Consequently plantations felled for timber are replenished by sowing nuts rather than by planting quicksets. The mode of cultivation is not different from that used for the trees[a] mentioned above: it is by loosening the soil and pruning the lower part for the next two years. For the rest the tree looks

Chestnut.

§ 59.

se colit umbra stolones supervacuos enecante. caeditur intra septimum annum. sufficiunt pedamenta iugeri vicenis vinearum iugeribus, quando etiam bifida ex stirpe fiunt, durantque ultra alteram silvae suae caesuram.

151 Aesculus similiter provenit, caesura triennio serior,[1] minus morosa nasci in quacumque terra seritur vere balano, sed non nisi aesculi, scrobe dodrantali, intervallis duorum pedum; saritur[2] leviter quater anno. hoc pedamentum minime putrescit caesumque maxime fruticat. praeter haec quae diximus sunt caedua[3] fraxinus, laurus, persica, corulus, malus, sed tardius nascuntur terramque defixa vix tolerant, non modo umorem. sabucus contra firmissima ad palum taleis seritur ut populus. nam de cupresso satis diximus.

152 XXXV. Et praedictis velut armamentis vinearum restat ipsarum natura praecipua tradenda cura.

Vitium surculis, et quarundam arborum quibus fungosior intus natura, geniculati scaporum nodi intersaepiunt medullam. ferulae ipsae breves et ad summa breviores articulis utrimque sua[4] internodia
153 includunt. medulla, sive illa vitalis anima est, ante

[1] *Caesarius*: senior.
[2] *Ian*: seritur.
[3] *Mayhoff*: sunt caedua quae diximus.
[4] *Mayhoff*: utique si in (*aut* his in).

after itself, as its shadow kills off superfluous suckers. It is lopped before the end of the sixth year. The props provided by one acre are enough for twenty acres of vines, as they even grow forked in two from the root, and they last till after the next lopping of the plantation they come from.

Other trees. The sessile-fruited oak is grown in a similar way, though later by three years in lopping, and less difficult to propagate in whatever soil it is sown; this is done in spring, with an acorn (but only a sessile-oak is grown from one) in a hole nine inches deep, with two foot spaces between the plants; the ground is lightly hoed four times a year. A sessile-oak grown as a prop is least liable to rot, and it makes new shoots when lopped most of any timber. Timber trees in addition to those we have mentioned are the ash, laurel, peach, hazel, apple, but these shoot more slowly and when fixed in the ground scarcely stand the action of the soil, not to mention the damp. The elder, on the contrary, which is very strong timber for a stake, is grown from cuttings like the poplar. About the cypress we have already said enough. XVI. 139 ff.

The vine, its structure and planting. XXXV. And now that a preliminary account has been given of what may be called the rigging that supports the vines, it remains to give a particularly careful description of the nature of the vines themselves.

The shoots of the vine, and of certain other trees that have a somewhat spongy inner substance, have stalks with knotted joints that make divisions across the pith. The actual lengths of cane are short, and get shorter towards the top, and they close up their pieces between the knots with joints at each end. The pith, or what is really the life-giving soul of the

se tendit longitudinem inplens [1] quamdiu nodi pervia patent fistula; cum vero concreti ademere transitum, repercussa erumpit ab ima sui parte iuxta priorem nodum alternis laterum semper inguinibus, ut dictum est in harundine ac ferula, quorum dexterum ab imo intellegitur articulo, laevum in proximo, atque ita per vices. hoc vocatur in vite gemma cum ibi caespitem fecit, ante vero quam faciat, in concavo oculus et in cacumine ipso germen. sic palmites, nepotes, uvae, folia, pampini gignuntur; mirumque firmiora esse in dextera parte genita.

154 Hos ergo in surculis nodos, cum seruntur, medios secare oportet ita ne profluat medulla. et in fico quidem dodrantales paxillis [2] solo patefacto seruntur sic ut descendant quae proxima arbori fuerint, duo oculi extra terram emineant (oculi autem in arborum
155 surculis proprie vocantur unde germinantur [3]). hac de causa et in plantariis aliquando eodem anno ferunt quos [4] fuere laturi fructus in arbore, cum tempestive sati praegnates inchoatos conceptus aliubi pariunt. ita satas ficos tertio anno transferre facile: hoc pro

[1] *Mayhoff*: inpellens.
[2] *Ian*: taxilli (paxilli *cd. Vat. Lat.* 3861, *m.* 2).
[3] [oculi . . . germinantur] *gloss. ? Warmington.*
[4] *Edd.*: quo.

tree, stretches forward filling up the length in front of it, so long as the knots are open, with a tube that allows a passage; but when they have become solidified and prevent passage, the pith is thrown back and bursts out at its lowest part close to the previous knot with a series of alternate lateral forks, as has been stated in the case of the reed and of the giant fennel; with these the swelling from the bottom knot can be observed on the right and that at the next one on the left, and so on alternately. In the case of a vine, when this swelling makes a knob at the knot it is called a 'gem', but before it makes a knob, in the hollow part it is called an 'eye' and at the actual top a 'germ'. This is the way in which the main shoots, side-shoots, grapes, leaves and tendrils are formed; and it is a remarkable fact that those growing on the right-hand side are the stronger.

XVI. 163, XIII. 122.

Propagation of figs.

Consequently when these slips are planted it is necessary to cut the knots in them across the middle, without letting the pith run out. And in the case of a fig nine-inch slips are planted in holes made in the ground with pegs, in such a way as to have the parts that were nearest to the tree sunk into the earth and two eyes projecting above the surface (the term 'eyes' in slips of trees properly denotes the points from which they send out shoots). It is because of this that even when bedded out the slips occasionally produce in the same year the fruit they were going to bear on the tree if they have been planted at the proper time when pregnant, and give birth in their other position to the progeny they had begun to conceive. Fig-trees struck in this way are easily transplanted two years later, as this tree

senescendi celeritate adtributum huic arbori, ut citissime proveniat.

156 Vitium numerosior satus est. primum omnium nihil seritur ex his nisi inutile et deputatum in sarmenta;opputatur autem quidquid proximo tulit fructum. solebat capitulatus utrimque e duro surculus seri, eoque argumento malleolus vocatur etiamnunc; postea avelli cum sua calce coeptus est, ut in fico; neque est aliud vivacius. tertium genus adiectum etiamnum expeditius sine calce, quod sagittae vocantur cum intorti panguntur, iidem[1] cum recisi nec intorti trigemmes. plures autem ex eodem
157 surculo hoc modo fiunt. serere e pampinariis sterile est, nec nisi e fecunda[2] oportet. quae raros habet nodos infecunda iudicatur, densitas gemmarum fertilitatis indicium est. quidam seri vetant nisi eos qui floruerint surculos. sagittas serere minus utile, quoniam in transferendo facile rumpitur quod intortum fuit. serantur[3] pedali non breviores longitudine, quinque sexve nodorum: pauciores tribus gemmis in hac mensura esse non poterunt.
158 inseri eodem die quo deputentur utilissimum, si multo postea necesse sit serere custoditos, uti praecepimus,

[1] *Gelen.*: id enim.
[2] e fecunda? *Mayhoff*: fecundo.
[3] *Rackham*: seruntur.

in compensation for the rapidity with which it grows old is endowed with the property of coming to maturity very rapidly.

Selection of vine-shoots for planting.

Vines give more numerous kinds of shoots for planting. The first point is that none of these are used for planting except useless growths lopped off for brushwood, whereas any branch that bore fruit last time is pruned away. It used to be the custom to plant the shoot with a knob of the hard wood on each side of it, and this explains why it is still called a 'mallet-shoot'; but afterwards the practice began of pulling it off with its own heel, as is done in the case of the fig; and there is no kind of slip that grows better. A third kind has been added that strikes even quicker, which has the heel removed; these slips are called 'arrows' when they are twisted before being set out, 'three-bud slips' when they are cut off and set without being twisted. By this method several can be obtained from the same shoot. To plant from young leafy shoots is unproductive, and a slip for planting must only be taken from a shoot that has already borne fruit. A shoot that has few knots in it is deemed unlikely to bear, whereas a crowd of buds is a sign of fertility. Some people say that only shoots that have flowered should be planted. It does not pay so well to plant arrow-slips, because anything that is twisted easily gets broken in being moved. Shoots chosen for planting should be not less than a foot long, with five or six knots; that length of shoot will not possibly have less than three buds. It pays best to plant them on the same day as they are cut off, or if a considerable postponement cannot be avoided, to keep them well protected, as we have instructed, or at all events to be careful § 114.

caveri utique ne extra terram positi sole inarescant, vento aut frigore hebetentur. qui diutius in sicco fuerint priusquam serantur in aqua pluribus diebus revirescant.

159 Solum apricum et quam mollissimum[1] in seminario sive in vinea bidente pastinari debet ternos pedes, bipalio aut[2] marra reici quaternum pedum fermento, ita ut in pedes binos fossa procedat, fossum purgari et extendi, ne crudum relinquatur, verum exigi mensura: male pastinatum deprendunt scamna inaequalia. metienda est et ea pars quae interiacet
160 pulvinis.[3] surculi seruntur et in scrobe et in sulco longiore, super quam tenerrima ingeritur terra, sed in gracili solo frustra nisi substrato pinguiore corio. gemmas non pauciores[4] quam duas integi oportet et proximam attingi, terram eodem[5] paxillo deprimi et spissari, interesse in plantario sesquipedes inter bina semina in latitudinem, in longitudinem semisses, ita satos malleolos XXIV mense recidere ad imum articulum, si[6] ipsi parcatur. oculorum inde materia emicat, cum qua XXXVI mense viviradix transfertur.

161 Est et luxuriosa ratio vites serendi ut quattuor malleoli vehementi vinculo colligentur ima parte

[1] mollissimum? *Mayhoff*: amplissimum.
[2] *Warmington*: alto. *Fortasse* pedes bipalio altum, marra.
[3] *Rackham*: pulvini.
[4] gemmas non pauciores *coll.* § 204 *add. Ian.*
[5] autem? *Mayhoff*.
[6] si *vel* sic, ut? *Mayhoff*: nisi.

not to lay them down on the surface of the earth and let them be dried up by the sun and nipped by wind or frost. Shoots that have been left too long in a dry place should be soaked in water for several days to restore their freshness.

Treatment of soil for vines.

The soil whether in a nursery or a vineyard should be exposed to the sun and should be as soft as possible, and it should be turned over with a two-pronged fork three feet down, and thrown back with a two-spit spade or mattock to swell naturally in ridges four feet high, so that each trench goes down two feet; and when dug the earth must be cleaned of weeds and spread out, so that no part may be left uncultivated, and it must be levelled accurately by measurement: unequal ridges show that the ground has been badly dug. The part of the ground lying between the banks must also be measured. Shoots are planted either in a hole or in a longer trench, and the finest possible layer of earth is heaped over them, although in a thin soil this is of no use unless a layer of richer soil is spread underneath. The earth should cover up not fewer than two buds and should just touch the third; it must be pressed down to the same level and compacted with the dibble; in the nursery plot there should be spaces eighteen inches broad and six inches longways between every two settings; and the mallet-shoots so planted should after two years be cut back to their bottom knot, if the knot itself is spared. From this point they throw out the substance of eyes, with which at the end of three years the quickset is planted.

Other methods of planting vines.

There is also a luxury method of growing vines—to tie four mallet-shoots together at the bottom with a tight string and so pass them through the shank

[luxuriosa][1] atque ita vel per ossa bubuli cruris vel per colla fictilia traiecti obruantur binis eminentibus gemmis. uniscunt hoc modo recisique palmitem emittunt. postea fistula fracta radix libere capit vires uvaque fert omnium corporum suorum acinos.
162 in alio genere invento[2] novicio finditur malleolus, medullaque erasa in se colligantur ipsi caules ita ut gemmis parcatur omni modo. tum malleolus in terra fimo mixta seritur, et cum spargere caules coepit, deciditur foditurque saepius. talis uvae acinos nihil intus ligni habituros Columella promittit, cum vivere semina ipsa perquam mirum sit medulla adempta.

163 Nasci surculis etiam quibus non sit articulatio arbores non omittendum videtur; namque buxi tenuissimis quinis senisve colligatis depacti proveniunt. quondam in observatione erat ut defringerentur ex inputata buxo, aliter vivere non crediti; detraxere hoc experimenta.

164 Seminarii curam sequitur vinearum ratio. quinque generum hae: sparsis per terram palmitibus, aut per se vite subrecta, vel cum amminiculo[3] sine iugo, aut pedatae simplici iugo, aut conpluviatae quadriplici.
165 quae pedatae ratio,[4] eadem intellegetur eius quoque

1 *Mayhoff.*
2 *Mayhoff*: inventu.
3 *Edd.*: anniculo.
4 *Ian*: pedata erat (p. erit *cd. Par. Lat.* 6795).

bones of an ox or else through earthenware pipes, and then bury them in the earth, leaving two buds protruding. This makes the shoots grow into one, and when they have been cut back they throw out a new shoot. Afterwards the pipe is broken and the root is left free to acquire strength and the vine bears grapes on all its constituent shoots. Under another method recently discovered a mallet-shoot is split down the middle and after the pith has been scraped out the actual lengths of stalk are tied together, every precaution being taken to avoid hurting the buds. The mallet-shoot is then planted in a mixture of earth and dung, and when it begins to throw out stalks, it is cut down and dug round several times. Columella guarantees that a vine so grown *de Arb.* 9. will bear grapes with no stones in them, although it is extremely surprising that the planted slips themselves will live after being deprived of their pith.

I think I ought not to omit to mention that trees will grow even from slips that have no joint in them; for instance box-trees come up if planted with five or six extremely slender slips tied together. It was formerly the practice to break off these slips from a box tree that had not been pruned, as it was believed that otherwise they would not live; but experience has done away with that notion.

Arrangement of vineyard. Trellises.

After the management of the nursery follows the arrangement of the vineyards. These are of five kinds—with the branches spreading about on the ground, or with the vine standing up of its own accord, or else with a stay but without a cross-bar, or propped with a single cross-bar, or trellised with four bars in a rectangle. It will be understood that the same system that belongs to a propped vine

in qua sine amminiculo vitis per se stabit; id enim non fit nisi pedamenti inopia. simplici iugo constat porrecto ordine quem canterium appellant; melior ea vino, quoniam sibi ipsa non obumbrat adsiduoque sole coquitur et adflatum magis sentit, celerius rorem dimittit, pampinationi quoque et occationi omnique
166 operi facilior; super cetera deflorescit utilius. iugum fit pertica aut harundine, aut crine funiculove ut in Hispania Brundisique. conpluviata copiosior vino est, [dicta a cavis aedium conpluviis][1]; dividitur in quaternas partes totidem iugis. huius serendi ratio dicetur, eadem valitura in omni genere, in hoc vero numerosior tantum.

III[2] vero seritur modis: optime in pastinato
167 proxime in sulco, novissime in scrobe. depastinatione, dictum est; sulco latitudo palae satis est, scrobibus ternorum pedum in quamque partem. altitudo in quocumque genere tripedalis, ideo nec vitis minor transferri debet, exstatura etiamnum duabus gemmis.
168 emolliri terram minutis in scrobe imo sulcis fimoque misceri necessarium. clivosa altiores scrobes poscunt,

[1] *Warmington.*
[2] III *add. Sillig.*

---

[a] This explanation looks like an interpolated note, belonging to the end of § 164.

is that of one in which the vine is left to stand by itself without a stay, for this is only done when there is a shortage of props. A vineyard with the single cross-bar is arranged in a straight row which is called a *canterius*; this is better for wine, as the vine so grown does not overshadow itself and is ripened by constant sunshine, and is more exposed to currents of air and so gets rid of dew more quickly, and also is easier for trimming and for harrowing the soil and all operations; and above all it sheds its blossoms in a more beneficial manner. The cross-bar is made of a stake or a reed, or else of a rope of hair or hemp, as in Spain and at Brindisi. More wine is produced by a rectangle-frame vineyard (the name is taken from the rectangular openings in the roofs of the courts of houses)[a]; this is divided into compartments of four by the same number of cross-bars. The method of growing vines with this frame will be described, and the same account will hold good in the case of every sort of frame, the only difference being that in this case it is more complicated.

Preparation of the ground Methods of planting.

There are in fact three ways of planting a vine; the best is to use ground that has been dug over, the next best to plant in a furrow, and the last to plant in a hole. The method of digging over has been described; for a furrow a spade's breadth is enough, § 159. and for holes the breadth of a yard each way. In each method the depth must be a yard, and consequently the vine transplanted must be not less than a yard long, even so allowing two buds to be above the surface. It is essential to soften the earth by making very small furrows at the bottom of the hole and to mix dung with it. Sloping ground requires deeper holes, with their edges on the lower

praeterea pulvinatis a devexitate labris. qui ex his longiores fient, ut vites binas accipiant e diverso, alvei vocabuntur. esse vitis radicem in medio scrobe oportet, sed ipsam innixam solido in orientem aequinoctialem spectare, adminicula prima e calamo
169 accipere; vineas limitari decumano XVIII pedum latitudinis ad contrarios vehiculorum transitus, aliisque traversis limitibus denum pedum distingui per media iugera, aut, si maior modus sit, totidem pedum cardine quot decumano limitari, semper vero quintanis semitari, hoc est ut quinto quoque palo singulae iugo paginae includantur; solo spisso non nisi repastinato nec nisi viviradicem seri, tenero et
170 soluto vel malleolum sulco vel scrobe. in colles sulcos agere traversos melius quam pastinare, ut defluvia transtris eorum contineantur; aquoso caelo vel sicco solo malleolos serere autumno, nisi si tractus ratio mutabit[1]: siccus enim et calidus autumno poscet, umidus frigidusque etiam veris exitu. in arido solo viviradix quoque frustra seritur, male et in siccis malleolus, nisi post imbrem, at in riguis vel frondens vitis et usque ad solstitium recte, ut in Hispania.

[1] *Detlefsen*: mutavit.

---

[a] *pagina*, the trade term for four rows of vines joined together in a square by their trellises.

[b] We should say 'every fourth'. Each *pagina* has four *pali*. To the Romans 5 was the fifth number after 1, 2 being *secundus*, 'the following number'.

side banked up as well. Some of these holes will be made longer, so as to take two vines at opposite ends, and these will be called beds. The root of the vine should be in the middle of the hole, but the slip itself, bedded in firm soil, should be pointing due east, and at first it should be given supports made of reed. Vineyards should be bisected by a main path running east and west, six yards wide so as to allow the passage of carts going in opposite directions; and they should be intersected by other cross-paths ten feet wide running through the middle of each acre, or, if the vineyard is a specially large one, it should have a main cross-path north and south as many feet wide as the one east and west, but always be divided up by fifth-row cross-paths—that is, so that each square [a] of vines may be enclosed by every fifth [b] stay. Where the soil is heavy it should only be planted after being dug over several times, and only quickset should be planted, but in a thin, loose soil even a mallet-shoot may be set in a hole or a furrow. On hill-sides it is better to drive furrows across the slope than to dig up the soil, so that the falling away of earth may be held up by the cross-banks formed by the furrows. In rainy conditions or dry soil when the weather is wet mallet-shoots are best planted in autumn, unless the character of the particular area requires otherwise: a dry and hot soil will call for autumn planting, but a damp and cold soil will need it as late as the end of spring. It is no good planting a quickset either in dry soil, nor is it much use to plant a mallet-shoot in dry soils either, except after rain, but in well watered soils a vine may properly be planted even when it is producing leaves, and right on to midsummer, as is the practice in Spain. It is

quiescere ventos sationis die utilissimum; plerique austros optant, Cato abdicat.

171 Interesse medio temperamento inter binas vites oportet pedes quinos, minimum autem laeto solo pedes quaternos, tenui plurimum octonos—Umbri et Marsi ad vicenos intermittunt arationis gratia in his quae vocant porculeta; pluvioso [1] et caliginoso

172 tractu rariores poni, sicco densiores. subtilitas parsimoniae conpendia invenit, cum vinea in pastinato seratur, obiter seminarium faciendi, ut et viviradix loco suo et malleolus qui transferatur inter et [2] vites et ordines seratur, quae ratio in iugero circiter $\overline{\text{XVI}}$ viviradicum donat; interest autem biennium fructus, quo tardius in sato provenit quam in tralato.

173 Viveradix posita in vinea post annum resecatur usque ad terram, ut unus tantum emineat oculus, adminiculo iuxta adfixo et fimo addito. simili modo et secundo anno reciditur viresque concipit et intra se pascit suffecturas oneri. alias festinatione pariendi gracilis atque eiuncida, ni cohibeatur castigatione tali, in fetum exeat tota. nihil avidius nascitur ac, nisi ad pariendum vires serventur, tota fit fetus.[3]

[1] *Rackham*: pluvio.
[2] et *add. Rackham.*
[3] [nihil . . . fetus] ? *Warmington.*

most advantageous if there is no wind on the day for planting, and though many growers like a south wind, Cato disapproves of this. XL. 1.

Spacing. The space between every two vines in a soil of medium density should be five feet, and in a rich soil four feet at least, and in a thin soil eight feet at most—growers in Umbria and Marsia leave a space of up to twenty feet to allow of ploughing between the rows, in the case of the vineyards for which the local name is 'ridged fields'; vines should be planted further apart in a rainy and misty district but closer together in a dry one. Elaborate economy has discovered a way of saving space, when planting a vineyard on ground that has been well dug over, by making a nursery-bed at the same time, so that while the quickset is planted in the place it is to occupy, the mallet-shoot is also planted, so that it may be transplanted between the vines as well as between the rows of props; this plan gives about 16,000 quicksets in an acre of ground, while it makes a difference of two years' fruit, as a planted quickset bears two years later than a transplanted mallet-shoot.

Quicksets. A quickset placed in a vineyard after two years is cut back right down to the ground, leaving only one eye above the surface; a stake is fixed close to the plant, and dung is added. In the following year also it is again lopped in a similar way, and it acquires and fosters within it sufficient strength to bear the burden of reproduction. Otherwise in its hurry to bear it would shoot up slim and meagre like a bulrush and unless it were restrained with the pruning described would spend itself entirely on growth. No tree sprouts more eagerly than the vine, and unless its strength is kept for bearing, it turns entirely into growth.

174 Pedamenta optuma quae diximus aut ridicae e robore oleaque, si non sint, pali e iunipero, cupresso, laburno,[1] sabuco. reliquorum generum sudes omnibus annis recidantur.[2] saluberrima in iugo harundo conexa fasciculis durat annis quinis. cum breviores palmites sarmento iunguntur inter se funium modo, ex hoc arcus [3] funeta dicuntur.

175 Tertius vineae annus palmitem velocem robustumque emittit et quem faciat aetas vitem; hic in iugum insilit. aliqui tum excaecant eum supina falce auferendo oculos, ut longius evocent, noxia iniuria: utilior enim consuetudo pariendi, satiusque pampinos adiugatae detergere usque quo placeat roborari eam.
176 sunt qui vetant tangi proximo anno quam tralata sit, neque ante LX mensem falce curari, tunc autem ad tres gemmas recidi. alii et proximo quidem anno recidunt, sed ut ternos quaternosve singulis annis adiciant articulos, quarto demum perducant ad iugum. fit [4] utrimque fructu tardum, praeterea retorridum et nodosum pumilionum incremento. optimum autem matrem esse firmam, postea fetum audacem. nec tutum est quod cicatricosum, magno imperitiae errore:
177 quidquid est tale plagis nascitur, non e matre. totas

[1] *Hermolaus* (lauru? *coll. Colum. Mayhoff*): alba populo *Warmington coll.* § 143: alburno.
[2] *Rackham*: reciduntur.
[3] arcus ⟨facti⟩? *Rackham*: ⟨fiunt⟩ qui *vel* ⟨f.⟩ quae *Warmington.*
[4] fit? *Mayhoff* (ideo *edd.*): id.

---

[a] Viz. especially chestnut wood, § 147 ff.
[b] A conjecture—or perhaps read 'laurel' or 'white poplar'.

The best props for vine are those of which we have spoken,[a] or else stakes from hard-oak and olive or if they are not available, props obtained from the juniper, cypress, laburnum [b] or elder. Staves of all other kinds must be cut back every year. For the cross-bar, reeds tied together in bundles are best for the growth of the vine, and they last five years. When shorter branches are tied together with brushwood so as to make a sort of rope, the arcades made of them are called rope-trellises. *Props and cross-bars.*

In its third year a vine sends out a quick-growing strong sprig (which in time becomes a tree); and this leaps up to the cross-bar. Thereupon some growers 'blind' it by removing the eyes with a pruning-knife turned upward, with the object of making it grow longer—a most damaging practice, as the tree's habit of putting out shoots is more profitable, and it is better to trim off leafy shoots from the plant tied to the cross-bar to the point where it is decided to let it make strength. Some people forbid touching it in the year after it is transplanted, and do not allow it to be trimmed with a pruning-knife till after 5 years, but then advise cutting it back to three buds. Others prune it back even the next year, but so as to let it add three or four new joints every year, and finally bring it up to the level of the cross-bar in the fourth year. Both methods make the tree slow to fruit, and also shrivelled and knotty, with the growth natural to dwarfs. But it is best for the mother to be strong and for the new growth to strike out boldly. Also there is no safety in a shoot covered with scars—that idea is a great mistake, due to inexperience: any growth of that sort arises from a blow, it is not due to the mother vine. She should *Pruning, trimming and tying.*

habeat illa vires dum roboratur, et annuos accipiet[1] tota fetus cum permissum fuerit nasci: nihil natura portionibus parit. quae excreverit satis firma protinus in iugo collocari debebit, si etiamnum infirmior erit,
178 sub ipso iugo hospitari recisa. viribus, non aetate decernitur: temerarium est ante crassitudinem pollicarem viti imperare. sequente anno palmites educentur[2] pro viribus matris singuli aut gemini; iidem et secuto si coget infirmitas nutriantur, tertioque demum duo adiciantur; nec sunt plures quaternis umquam permittendi, breviterque non indulgendum et semper inhibenda fecunditas. et ea est natura ut parere malit quam vivere—quidquid materiae adimitur fructui accedit; illa se mavult[3] quam fructum gigni, quoniam fructus caduca res est; sic perniciose luxuriat, nec ampliat se sed egerit.

179 Dabit consilium et soli natura: in macro, etiamsi vires habebit, recisa intra iugum moretur, ut omnis fetura sub eo exeat. minimum id esse debebit interllum, ut attingat iugum speretque,[4] non teneat, ideo[5] non recumbat in eo nec delicate se spargat. ita

[1] *Mayhoff*: accipit.
[2] *Mayhoff* (salventur *Hardouin*: *alii alia*): salutentur.
[3] *Detlefsen*: semina mavult *cd. Par. Lat.* 6797: s. vult *rell.*
[4] *Gelen.*: superetque.
[5] ideo? *Mayhoff*: adeo.

possess her full strength while the new shoot is growing sturdy, and she will welcome her yearly progeny with her whole substance when it is permitted to be born: Nature engenders nothing piecemeal. When the new growth has become strong enough it will have to be put in position on a cross-bar at once, but if it is still rather weak it must be pruned back and put in a sheltered position directly under the bar. It is the strength of the stem and not its age that decides; it is rash to put a vine under control before it has reached the thickness of one's thumb. In the following year one branch or two according to the strength of the parent vine should be brought on, and the same shoots must be nursed in the following year also if lack of strength makes this necessary, and only in the third year should two more be added; nor should more than four branches ever be allowed to grow—in short no indulgence should be shown, and fertility should always be kept in check. Also Nature is such that she wants to produce offspring more than she wants to live—all that is subtracted from a plant's wood is added to the fruit; the vine on the contrary prefers its own growth to the production of fruit, because fruit is a perishable article; thus it luxuriates ruinously, and does not fill itself out but exhausts itself.

The nature of the soil will also provide advice: in a thin soil, even if the vine possesses strength, it must be pruned back and kept within the cross-bar, so that all its young growth may shoot underneath the bar. The gaps between will have to be very small, so that the vine may just touch the bar and hope to grasp it but not actually do so, and consequently may not recline upon it and spread itself out luxuriously.

temperetur hic modus ut crescere etiamnum malit quam parere.

180 Palmes duas tresve gemmas habere sub iugo debet ex quibus materia nascatur, tunc per iugum erigi alligarique, ut sustineatur iugo, non pendeat, vinculo mox adstrictius a tertia gemma alligari, quoniam et sic coercetur impetus materiae densioresque citra pampini exultant; cacumen religari vetant. natura haec est: deiecta pars aut praeligata fructum dat, plurimumque ipsa curvatura; quod citra est materiem emittit[1] offensante, credo, spiritu et illa quam diximus medulla. quae ita emicuerit materia fructum
181 dabit anno sequente. sic duo genera palmitum: quod e duro exit materiamque in proximum annum promittit pampinarium vocatur aut ubi[2] supra cicatricem est fructuarium, alterum ex anniculo palmite semper fructuarium. relinquitur sub iugo et qui vocatur custos—hic est novellus palmes, non longior tribus gemmis, proximo anno materiam daturus si vitis luxuria se consumpserit—et alius iuxta eum, verrucae magnitudine, qui furunculus appellatur, si forte custos fallat.

182 Vitis antequam septumum annum a surculo conpleat evocata ad fructum eiuncescit ac moritur. nec

[1] *Mayhoff*: mittit.
[2] *V.ll.* aut si, aut uti.

[a] Or stock-branch.

This restriction must be so carefully managed that the vine may still want to grow rather than to bear.

The main branch should have two or three buds below the cross-bar from which wood may be produced, and then it should be stretched out along the bar and tied to it, so as to be held up by it, not to hang down from it, and then after the third bud it should be fastened more tightly to it by means of a tie, because that also has the effect of restraining the outgrowth of the wood and causing a more abundant outburst of shoots short of the tie; but it is forbidden to tie the end of the main branch. The nature of the vine is that the part hanging down or bound with a ligature yields fruit, and most of all the actual curve of the branch, but that which is short of the ligature makes wood, I suppose because the vital spirit and the pith mentioned above §§ 152–153.
meets an obstacle. The woody shoot so produced will bear fruit in the following year. Thus there are two kinds of main branches; the shoot which comes out of the hard timber and promises wood for the next year is called a leafy shoot[a] or else when it is above the scar a fruit-bearing shoot, whereas the other kind of shoot that springs from a year-old branch is always a fruit-bearer. There is also left underneath the cross-bar a shoot called the keeper—this is a young branch, not longer than three buds, which will provide wood next year if the vine's luxurious growth has used itself up—and another shoot next to it, the size of a wart, called the pilferer, is also left, in case the keeper-shoot should fail.

A vine called on to produce fruit before it completes seven years from being planted as a slip turns into a rush-like growth and dies. Nor is it

veterem placet palmitem in longum et ad quartum usque pedamentum emitti, ut quos [1] alii dracones alii funiculos vocant, ut faciat [2] quae masculeta appellant cum induruit vitis, pessimum in vinea traducere.
183 quinto anno et ipsi palmites intorquentur singulaeque singulis materiae emittuntur ac deinde proximis, prioresque amputantur. semper custodem relinqui melius, sed is proximus viti esse debet, nec longior quam dictum est, et si luxuriaverint palmites, intorqueri, ut quattuor materias, vel duas si uniiuga erit vinea, emittat.

184 Si per se vitis ordinabitur sine pedamento, qualecumque initio adminiculum desiderabit, dum stare condiscat et recta surgere, cetera a primordio eadem, dividi autem putatione pollices in aequali examine undique, ne praegravet fructus parte aliqua. obiter idem deprimens prohibebit in excelsum emicare. huic vineae trium pedum altitudo excelsior nutat, ceteris a quinto, dum ne excedat hominis longitudinem
185 iustam. iis quoque quae sparguntur in terra breves ad limitandum [3] caveas circumdant, scrobibus per ambitum factis, ne vagi palmites inter se pugnent occursantes; maiorque pars terrarum ita supinam in

[1] *Rackham*: ut quod *aut* quod (ut quod *cd. Vat. Lat.* 3861, *m.* 2).
[2] *Rackham*: faciant.
[3] *Ian*: imitandum.

thought proper to allow an old main branch to shoot out to a great length and as far as a fourth prop, like the old growths called by some 'snake-branches' and by others 'cables', so as to make what are named 'male growths'. When a vine has become hard, it is very bad to bring it across on a trellis. When a vine is four years old the main branches themselves also are twisted over, and each throws out one growth of wood, first one and then the next ones, and the earlier shoots are pruned away. It is always better to leave a keeper-shoot, but this should be one next the vine, and not longer than the length that was stated; and if the main branches shoot too § 181.
luxuriantly, to twist them back, so that the vine may produce only four growths of wood, or even only two if it is trained on a single cross-bar.

Vines grown without supports.

If the vine is to be trained by itself without a prop, at the beginning it will want some sort of support until it learns to stand and to rise up straight, while in all other respects it will need the same treatment from the start, except that it will need to have the pruned stumps distributed by pruning in a regular cluster all round, so that the fruit may not overload one side of the tree. Incidentally, the fruit weighing down the bough will prevent it from shooting right up high. With this vine a height of above a yard begins to bend over, but all the others start bending at five feet, only the height must not be allowed to exceed the average height of a man. Growers also put low cages round the vines that spread out on the ground, to restrict their spread, with trenches made round them, so that the straggling branches may not meet each other and fight; and the greater part of the world lets its vintage grapes lie on the

tellurem vindemiam mittit, siquidem et in Africa et in Aegypto Syriaque ac tota Asia et multis locis Europae
186 hic mos praevalet. ibi ergo iuxta terram conprimi debet vitis, eodem modo et tempore nutrita radice quo in iugata vinea, ut semper pollices tantum relinquantur, fertili solo cum ternis[1] gemmis, gracilioreque binis,[2] praestatque multos esse quam longos. quae de natura soli diximus tanto potentiora sentientur quanto propior fuerit uva terrae.

187 Genera separari ac singulis conseri tractus utilissimum—mixtura enim generum etiam in vino, non modo in musto discors—aut si misceantur, non alia quam pariter maturescentia iungi necessarium. iuga altiora quo laetior ager et quo planior, item roscido, nebuloso minusque ventoso conveniunt, contra humiliora gracili et arido et aestuoso ventisque exposito. iuga ad pedamentum quam artissimo nodo vinciri oportet, vitem leni[3] contineri. quae genera vitium et in quali solo caeloque essent conserenda cum enumeraremus naturas earum et vinorum docuimus.

188 De reliquo cultu vehementer ambigitur. plerique aestate tota post singulos rores confodi iubent vineam,

[1] ternis? *Mayhoff*: tribus.

[2] graciliore binis *e Colum. Pintianus* (-que *add.*? *Mayhoff*): graciliore quinis.

[3] leni? *Mayhoff*: leve (levi *cd. Par. Lat.* 6797).

ground in this manner, inasmuch as this custom prevails both in Africa and in Egypt and Syria and the whole of Asia and at many places in Europe. In these vineyards therefore the vine ought to be kept down close to the ground, nourishment being given to the root in the same way and at the same time as in the case of a vine trained on a cross-bar, care being always taken to leave merely the pruned stumps, with three buds on each in fertile land and two where the soil is thinner, and it pays better to have many of them than to have long ones. The properties of soil that we have spoken of will make themselves felt more powerfully the nearer the bunches of grapes are to the ground.

Distribution of varieties of vine.

It pays best to keep the different kinds of vine separate and plant each plot with only one sort, for a mixture of different varieties spoils the flavour even in the wine and not only in the must; or if they are mixed, it is essential not to combine any but those that ripen at the same time. The richer the soil and the more level the ground the greater the height of the cross-bars required, and high cross-bars also suit land liable to dew and fog and where there is comparatively little wind, whereas lower bars suit thin, dry and parched land and places exposed to the wind. The cross-bars should be tied to the prop as tightly as possible, but the vine should be kept together with an easy tie. We stated what kinds of vines should be grown and in what sort of soil and with what aspect when we were enumerating the natures of the various vines and wines. XIV. 20 ff.

Other points as to vine-growing: various views.

The remaining points connected with the cultivation of the vine are vehemently debated. The majority of writers recommend digging over the

alii vetant gemmantem, decuti enim oculos tractuque intrantium deteri, et ob id arcendum procul omne quidem pecus, sed maxime lanatum, quoniam facillime auferat gemmas; inimicos et pubescente uva rastros, satisque esse vineam ter anno confodi, ab aequinoctio verno ad vergiliarum exortum et canis ortu et
189 nigrescente acino. quidam ita determinant: veterem semel a vindemia ante brumam (cum alii ablaqueare et stercorare satis putent), iterum ab idibus Aprilibus, antequam concipiat, hoc est in VI idus Maias, dein prius quam florere incipiat, et cum defloruerit, et variante se uva; peritiores adfirmant, si iusto saepius fodiatur, in tantum tenerescere acinos ut rumpantur. quae fodiantur ante ferventes horas diei fodiendas convenit, sicuti lutum neque arare neque fodere, fossione pulverem excitatum contra soles nebulasque prodesse.

190 Pampinatio verna in confesso est ab idibus Maiis intra dies X, utique antequam florere incipiat, et ea[1] infra iugum debere fieri. de sequente variant sententiae: cum defloruerit aliqui pampinandum putant,

[1] eam *edd.*

vineyard after every fall of dew throughout the whole of the summer, but others forbid this while the vines are in bud, because the eyes get knocked off or rubbed by the drag of people going between the rows, and for this reason it is necessary to keep away all cattle, but especially sheep, as their fleeces most easily remove buds; they also say that raking does harm while bunches of grapes are forming; that it is enough for a vineyard to be dug over three times in a year, between the spring equinox and the rising of the Pleiads, at the rise of the Dogstar, and when the grapes are turning black. Some people give the following rules: to dig over an old vineyard once between vintage and midwinter (though others think it is enough to loosen the soil round the roots and manure it), a second time after April 13 but before the vines bud, that is before May 10, and then before the vine begins to blossom, and after it has shed its blossom, and when the bunch is changing colour; but more expert growers declare that if the ground is dug more often than necessary the grapes become so thin-skinned that they burst. It is agreed that when vineyards are dug it should be done before the hottest part of the day, and likewise that a mud-like wet soil ought not to be either ploughed or dug; and that the dust raised by digging is beneficial to the vine as a protection against sun and fog.

Hand-trimming.

It is agreed that the spring trimming of foliage should take place within ten days from May 15, at all events before the vine begins to blossom, and that it should be done below the level of the cross-bar. As to the subsequent trimming opinions vary: some people think that it should take place when the vine has shed its blossom, others when the grapes are

alii sub ipsa muturitate. sed de his Catonis praecepta decernent; namque et putationum tradenda ratio est.

191 Protinus hanc a vindemia, ubi caeli tepor indulget, adoriuntur; sed et[1] in hoc fieri numquam debet ratione naturae ante exortum aquilae, ut in siderum causis docebimus proximo volumine, immo vero favonio, quoniam anceps culpa est[2] praeproperae festinationis. si saucias recenti medicina mordeat quaedam hiemis ruminatio, certum est gemmas earum frigore hebetari plagasque findi et caeli vitio exuri oculos lacrima destillante; nam gelu fragiles fieri
192 quis nescit? operarum ista conputatio est in latifundiis, non legitima naturae festinatio. quo maturius putantur aptis diebus, eo plus materiae fundunt, quo serius, eo fructum uberiorem. quare macras prius conveniet putare, validas novissime, plagam omnem obliquam fieri ut facile decidant imbres, et ad terram verti quam levissima cicatrice acie falcis exacuta plagaque conlevata,[3] recidi autem semper inter duas
193 gemmas, ne sit vulnus oculis in recisa parte. nigram esse eam noxium[4] existimant et donec ad sincera veniatur recidendam, quoniam e vitioso materia utilis non exeat. si macra vitis idoneos palmites non ha-

[1] et *add. J. Mueller.*
[2] est ? *Mayhoff*: sit.
[3] *Pintianus*: convelata.
[4] noxium *add.* ? *Mayhoff.*

just beginning to ripen. But on this point the instructions of Cato shall decide; for we also have to describe the proper method of pruning. § 197.

This is set about directly after the vintage when *Pruning.* the warmth of the weather allows; but even in warm weather on natural principles it never ought to be done before the rise of the Eagle, as we shall show XVIII. 283. when dealing with astronomical considerations in the following volume, nor yet when the wind is in the west—inasmuch as excessive haste involves a double possibility of error. If a late snap of wintry weather should nip the vines while still suffering from wounds inflicted by recent treatment, it is certain that their buds will be benumbed by the cold and the wounds will open, and the eyes, owing to the juice dripping from them, will be nipped by the inclemency of the weather; for who does not know that frost makes them brittle? All this depends on calculations regarding labour on large estates, not on the legitimate acceleration of Nature's processes. Given suitable weather, the earlier vines are pruned, the larger amount of wood they make, and the later they are pruned, the more abundant supply of fruit. Consequently it will be proper to prune meagre vines earlier and strong ones last; and always to make the cut on a slant, so that rain may fall off easily, and turned towards the ground, with the lightest possible scar, using a pruning-knife with a well sharpened edge and giving a smooth cut; but always to prune between two buds, so as not to wound the eyes in the part of the shoot cut back. They think it a sign of damage for this to be black, and that it should be cut back till one comes to the sound part, since useful wood will not shoot from a bad stock. If a meagre vine has not

beat, ad terram recidi eam novosque elici utilissimum, in pampinatione non hos detrahere pampinos qui cum uva sint, id enim et uvas supplantat praeterquam in novella vinea. inutiles iudicantur in latere nati, non ab oculo, quippe etiam uva quae nascatur e duro
194 rigescente ut nisi ferro detrahi non possit. pedamentum quidam inter duas vites utilius putant statui, et facilius ablaqueantur ita, meliusque est uniiugae vineae, si tamen et ipsi iugo sint vires nec flatu infesta regio. in quadripertita quam proximum oneri adminiculum esse debet, ne tamen inpedimentum sentiat ablaqueatio, cubito abesse non amplius; ablaqueari autem prius quam putari iubent.

195 Cato de omni cultura vitium ita praecipit: 'Quam altissimam vineam facito alligatoque recte, dum ne nimium constringas. hoc modo eam curato: capita vitium per sementem ablaqueato; vineam [1] putatam circumfodito, arare incipito; ultro citroque sulcos perpetuos ducito; vites teneras quam primum propagato, sic occato.[2] veteres quam minimum castrato; potius, si opus erit, deicito biennioque post praecidito. vitem novellam resecari tum erit tempus
196 ubi valebit. si vinea ab vite calvata erit, sulcos

[1] per . . . vineam *add. e Cat. Pintianus.*
[2] sic occato *e Cat. Sillig*: cato.

[a] XXXIII. 4.

got suitable branches, it is a very good plan to cut it back to the ground and get it to put out new branches, and in trimming it pays not to remove the shoots growing with a cluster of grapes, for that dislodges the grapes also, except in a newly planted vine. Shoots springing on the side of the branch and not from an eye are judged to be of no use, since moreover a bunch of grapes that springs from a hard branch is so stiff that the bunch can only be removed with a knife. Some people consider that it pays better for a prop to be set between two vines, and that method does make it easier to turn up the earth round them, and it is better for a vine on a single cross-bar, provided, that is, that the trellis itself is a strong one and the locality is not exposed to high winds. In the case of a vine supported by four cross-rails the stay ought to be as close as possible to the load, although to avoid interfering with digging over the soil it ought to be 18 inches away, not more; but they advise digging over before pruning.

Cato on vine-growing.

The following are the instructions given by Cato[a] on the whole subject of vine growing: 'Make the vine grow as high as possible, and tie it up well, only not binding it too tight. Treat it in the following manner: turn over the earth round the base of the vines during seed-time; after pruning a vine dig round it and begin to plough; drive continuous furrows to and fro; plant layers of young vines as soon as possible, and then harrow the ground. Prune old vines as little as possible; preferably, if necessary, layer them on the ground and cut off the layers two years later. The time for cutting back a young vine will be when it has gained strength. If a vineyard has become bare of vines, make furrows between the

interponito ibique vivam radicem serito; umbram a sulcis removeto, crebroque fodito. in vinea vetere serito ocinum si macra erit—quod granum capit ni serito—et circum capita addito stercus, paleas,
197 vinaceas, aliquid horumce.[1] ubi vinea frondere coeperit, pampinato. vineas novellas alligato crebro, ne caules praefringantur;[2] et quae iam in perticam ibit eius pampinos teneros alligato leviter porrigitoque uti recte stent. ubi uva varia fieri coeperit, vites subli-
198 gato.[3] vitis insitio una est per ver, altera cum uva floret; ea optima est. vineam veterem si in alium locum transferre voles, dumtaxat bracchium crassam licebit. primum deputato; binas gemmas ne amplius relinquito. ex radicibus bene exfodito, et cave radices ne saucies. ita uti fuerit ponito in scrobe aut in sulco operitoque et bene occulcato; eodemque modo vineam statuito, alligato flexatoque uti fuerit; crebroque fodito.'—Ocinum, quod in vinea seri iubet, antiqui appellabant pabulum umbrae patiens, quod celerrime proveniat.

199 Sequitur arbusti ratio mirum in modum damnata Sasernae patri filioque, celebrata Scrofae, vetustissimis post Catonem peritissimisque, ac ne a Scrofa quidem nisi Italiae concessa, cum tam longo iudicetur aevo nobilia vina non nisi in arbustis gigni et in his

[1] horum quo rectius valeat e *Cat. Sillig.*
[2] *Cato*: caulis perfringatur.
[3] *lacunam hic Ian* (subligato, pampinato uvasque expellito, circum capita sarito *Cato*).

---

[a] From ὠκύς, 'swift'.

vines and plant a quickset in each; prevent any shade from falling on the furrows, and dig them over frequently. Plant *ocinum*[a] clover in an old vineyard if the soil is meagre—forbear to sow anything that makes seed—and put dung, chaff and grape husks or something of that sort round the feet. When a vine begins to show leaves, trim it. Fasten young vines with several ties, so that the stems may not get broken; and as soon as a vine begins to run out into a rod, tie down its young shoots lightly and stretch them out so as to be in the right position. When the grapes begin to become mottled, tie up the vines below. One season for grafting a vine is during spring, and another when the bunch blossoms: the latter is the best. If you want to transplant an old vine, you will only be able to do so if it is of the thickness of an arm. First prune it; do not leave more than two buds on the stem. Dig it well up from the roots, and be careful not to injure the roots. Place it in the hole or furrow just as it was before, and cover it up and tread it down well; and set up the vine and tie it and bend it over in the same direction as it was before; and dig the ground frequently.'—*Ocinum*, which Cato recommends planting in a vineyard, was the old name for a fodder-plant capable of standing shade, and refers to its rapid growth.

Growing vines on trees; selection of trees, and management.

There follows the method of growing vines on a tree, which was condemned in a remarkable way by Saserna the elder and by his son, but highly spoken of by Scrofa—these are the oldest writers on agriculture after Cato, and are very great authorities; and even Scrofa only allows it in Italy, although so long a period of time gives the verdict that high-class wines can only be produced from vines on trees, and

quoque laudatiora summis sicut uberiora imis: adeo
200 excelsitate proficitur. hac ratione et arbores eligun-
tur: prima omnium ulmus, excepta propter nimiam
frondem Atinia, dein populus nigra, eadem de causa,
minus densa folio; non spernunt plerique et fraxinum
ficumque, etiam oleam si non sit umbrosa ramis.
harum satus cultusque abunde tractatus est. ante
xxxvi mensem attingi falce vetantur; alterna servantur bracchia, alternis putantur annis, sexto anno
201 maritantur. Transpadana Italia praeter supra dictas
cornu, opulo, tilia, acere, orno, carpino, quercu
arbustat agros, Venetia salice propter uliginem soli.
et ulmus detruncata media in tria ramorum scamna
digeritur, nulla fere viginti pedum altiore arbore.
tabulata earum ab octavo pede altitudinis dilatantur
in collibus siccisque agris, a duodecumo in campestri-
202 bus et umidis. meridianum solem spectare palmae
debent, rami a proiectu digitorum modo subrigi,
tonsili in his tenuium quoque virgultorum barba, ne
obumbrent. intervallum iustum arborum, si aretur
solum, quadrageni pedes in terga frontemque, in latera
viceni; si non aretur, hoc in omnis partes. singulis
denas saepe adnutriunt vites, damnato agricola

that even so the choicer wines are made from the grapes at the top of the trees, while those lowest down give a large quantity: so beneficial is the effect of height. It is on this principle also that trees are selected: first of all the elm (excepting the Atinian variety because it has too many leaves), then the black poplar, for the same reason, it having less dense foliage; also the ash and the fig are not despised by most growers, and even the olive if it has not shady branches. The planting and cultivation of these trees has been abundantly treated. It is prohibited to touch them with the pruning-knife before they are three years old; alternate branches are kept, they are pruned every other year, and in their sixth year they are wedded to the vines. Italy north of the Po beside the trees mentioned above plants its vineyards with cornel, guelder rose, lime, maple, rowan, hornbeam, and oak, but the Venezia uses willow because of the dampness of the soil. Also the elm is lopped of its top and has its middle branches spread out on three levels, no tree as a rule being left more than twenty feet high. On hills and in dry lands the stages of the elms are spread out at a height of eight feet, and on plains and in damp localities at twelve feet. The branching of the trunk should face south, and the boughs should spread up from the fork like fingers on the hand, and also have their shaggy growth of thin twigs shaved off, so as not to give too much shade. The proper space between the trees, if the soil is to be ploughed, is forty feet behind and in front and twenty at the sides, but if it is not to be ploughed, twenty feet every way. Growers often grow ten vines against each tree, great fault being found with a

XII. 22 ff., XV. 1 ff., XVI. 62 ff.

203 minus ternis. maritare nisi validas inimicum, enecante veloci vitium incremento. serere tripedaneo scrobe necessarium distantes inter sese arboremque singulis pedibus; nihil ibi malleoli atque pastinationis,[1] nulla fodiendi inpendia, utpote cum arbusti ratio haec peculiari dote praestet quod ab eodem solo ferri[2] fruges et vitibus prodest, superque quod vindicans se altitudo non, ut in vinea, ad arcendas animalium iniurias pariete vel saepe vel fossarum utique inpendio muniri se cogit.

204 In arbusto e praedictis sola viveradicum ratio, item propaginum, et haec gemina, ut diximus: qualorum ex[3] ipso tabulato maxime probata, quoniam a pecore tutissima est, altera deflexa vite vel palmite iuxta suam arborem aut circa proximam caelibem. quod supra terram est a matre radi iubetur ne fruticet; in terra non pauciores quattuor gemmae obruuntur ad radicem capiendam, extra in capite binae relincuntur.

205 vitis in arbusto quattuor pedes longo constat[4] sulco, tres lato, alto duos cum semipede. post annum propago inciditur ad medullam, ut paulatim radicibus suis adsuescat, caulis a capite ad duas gemmas reciditur; tertio totus mergus absciditur repetiturque

[1] *Mayhoff*: pastinationi.
[2] *Mayhoff*: seri.
[3] *Mayhoff*: et.
[4] *Mayhoff*: in longo constat omnis.

farmer who trains less than three on each. It damages any but strong trees to wed vines to them, as the rapid growth of the vines kills them off. It is essential to plant the vines in a trench three feet deep, with a space of a foot between them and the tree; this saves the need of a mallet-shoot and of turning over the ground and the expense of digging, inasmuch as this method of using a tree has the special advantage that for the same ground to carry corn actually benefits the vines, and moreover that the height of the vine looks after itself, and does not make it necessary, as in a vineyard, to guard it with a wall or hedge, or at all events by going to the expense of ditches, so as to protect it from injury by animals.

Layering of vines grown on trees.

In growing vines on a tree the only method used among those already described is that of quicksets or of layers; and of layering there are two varieties, as we have said: that of using baskets projecting from § 97. the actual staging of the tree, the most approved method, as it is safest from cattle, and the other one by bending down a vine or a main branch at the side of its own tree or round the nearest to it not occupied. It is recommended that the part of the parent tree above the ground should be scraped, to prevent it from making shoots; and not less than four buds are covered up in the ground so as to take root, while two are left above ground on the head. A vine grown on a tree is set in a trench four feet long, three broad and two and a half deep. After a year a cut is made in the layer down to the cambium, so that it may gradually get used to its roots, and the stem is pruned back at its end down to two buds from the ground; and at the end of two years the layer is completely cut off from the stock and is put back deeper into the

altius in terram, ne ex reciso frondeat. tolli viveradix a vindemia protinus debet.

206 Nuper repertum draconem serere iuxta arborem—ita appellamus palmitem emeritum pluribusque induratum annis. hunc praecisum quam maxima amplitudine, tribus partibus longitudinis deraso cortice quatenus obruatur—unde et rasilem vocant—deprimere sulco, reliqua parte ad arborem erecta, ocissimum in vite est.[1] si gracilis sit vitis aut terra, usitatum est quam proxime solum decidi, donec firmetur radix, sicuti neque roscidam seri neque a septentrionis flatu; vites aquilonem spectare debent ipsae, palmites autem earum meridiem.

207 Non est festinandum ad putationem novellae, sed primo in circulos materies colligenda, nec nisi validae putatio admovenda, seriore anno fere ad fructum arbusta vite quam iugata; sunt qui omnino putari vetent priusquam arborem longitudine aequaverit. prima falce sex pedes a terra recidatur, flagello infra relicto et nasci coacto incurvatione materiae. tres ei
208 gemmae, non amplius, deputato supersint. ex his emissi palmites proximo anno imis digerantur scamnis

[1] est *add.* ? *Mayhoff.*

ground, so that it may not shoot from the place where it was cut off. As for a quickset, it should be removed immediately after the vintage.

A plan has recently been invented of planting a snake-branch near the tree—that is our name for a veteran main branch that has grown hard with many years' service. The quickest plan in the case of a vine is to cut this old branch off as long as possible and scrape the bark off three-quarters of its length, down to the point to which it is to be buried in the ground—for this reason it is also called a 'scraped' shoot—and then to press it down in the furrow, with the remaining part standing straight up against the tree. If the vine be meagre or the soil thin, it is customary to cut down the plant as close to the ground as possible, until the root gets strong, and likewise not to plant it when there is dew on it, nor in a place exposed to a north wind; the vines themselves ought to face north-east, but their young shoots should have a southerly aspect.

Pruning vines on trees.

There must be no hurry to prune a young vine, but at first the growth should be collected together into circular shapes, and no pruning should be applied except to a strong plant, a vine trained on a tree being about a year later in bearing fruit than one trained on a cross-bar. Some people forbid pruning altogether until the vine equals the tree in height. At the first pruning it should be cut back six feet from the ground, a shoot being left below and encouraged to grow by bending over the wood. It should have three buds and not more left when it has been pruned. In the following year the branches sent out from these should be spread out on the lowest stages of the trees and allowed to climb to

ac per singulos annos ad superiora scandant, relicto semper duramento in singulis tabulatis et emissario uno qui subeat usque quo placuerit. de cetero putatione omnia[1] flagella quae proxime tulerint recidantur, nova circumcisis undique capreolis spargantur in tabulatis. vernacula putatio deiectis per ramos vitium crinibus circumvestit arborem crinesque ipsos uvis, Gallica in traduces porrigitur, Aemiliae viae in ridicas Atiniarum ambitu, frondem earum fugiens.

209 Est quorundam inperitia sub ramo vitem vinculo suspendendi, suffocante iniuria: contineri debet vimine, non artari (quin immo etiam quibus salices supersunt molliore hoc vinculo facere malunt herbaque Siculi quam vocant ampelodesmon, Graecia vero universa iunco, cypero, ulva), liberata quoque vinculo[2] per aliquot dies vagari et incondita spargi atque in terra quam per totum annum spectaverit recumbere;
210 namque ut veterina a iugo et canis a cursu volutatio iuvat, ita tum et vitium porrigi lumbos; arbor quoque ipsa gaudet adsiduo levata onere, similis respiranti, nihilque est in opere Naturae quod non exemplo dierum noctiumque aliquas vices feriarum velit. ob id

[1] *Mayhoff e Colum.*: omni.
[2] vinculo ⟨volt⟩ ? *Mayhoff.*

the next higher level every year, one hard growth being always left at each stage, and one growing shoot left to mount up as high as it pleases. In addition, all the whips that have borne fruit last time should be cut back by pruning, and fresh shoots should have their tendrils cut away all round and be spread out on the stages. Our Italian method of pruning drapes the tree with tresses of vines festooned along the branches and clothes the tresses themselves with bunches of grapes, but the Gallic method spreads out into growths passing from tree to tree, while the method used on the Aemilian Road spreads over supports consisting of Atinian elms, twining round them but avoiding their foliage.

Instructions for tying vines.

An ignorant way of some growers is to suspend the vine by means of a tie beneath a bough of the tree, a damaging procedure which stifles it, as it ought to be held back with an osier withe, not tied tightly (indeed even people who have plenty of willows prefer to do it with a tie softer than the one which these supply, namely with the plant which the Sicilians call by the Greek name 'vine-tie', while the whole of Greece uses rush, galingale and sedge); also it ought to be released from its tie for some days and allowed to stray about and spread in disorder and lie down on the ground which it has been gazing at all the year through; for just as draft cattle when unyoked and dogs after a run like to roll on the ground, so even the vines' loins like a stretch when released; also the tree itself enjoys being relieved of the continual weight, like a man recovering his breath, and there is nothing in Nature's handiwork that does not desire some alternations of holiday, after the pattern of the days and nights. On this account pruning the

protinus a vindemia putari et lassas etiamnum fructu edito inprobatur. putatae rursus alligentur alio loco, namque orbitas vinculi sentiunt vexatione non dubia.

211 Traduces Gallicae culturae [1] bini utrimque e [2] lateribus, si par [3] quadrageno distet spatio, quaterni, si viceno, inter se obvii miscentur alliganturque una conciliati, virgultorum comitatu obiter rigorati qua deficiant, aut si brevitas non patiatur ipsorum, adalligato protenduntur in viduam arborem unco. traducem bimum praecidere solebant—onerat [4] enim vetustate; melius donare tempus ut rasilem [5] faciant, si [6] largiatur crassitudo; alias utile toros futuri draconis pasci.

212 Unum etiamnum genus est medium inter hoc et propaginem, totas supplantandi in terram vites cuneisque findendi et in sulcos plures simul ex una propagandi, gracilitate singularum firmata circumligatis hastilibus, nec recisis qui a lateribus excurrant pampinis. Novariensis agricola, traducum turba non contentus nec copia ramorum, inpositis etiamnum patibulis palmites circumvolvit; itaque praeter soli
213 vitia cultura quoque torva fiunt vina. alia culpa

[1] *Mayhoff* (Gallica e cultura *Sillig*): cultura.
[2] e *add. Mayhoff*.
[3] *Mayhoff*: pars.
[4] oneratur? *Warmington*.
[5] *Urlichs*: transilem.
[6] *Edd.*: ni.

vines directly after vintage and when they are still weary from producing fruit is disapproved of. When they have been pruned they must be tied to the tree again in another place, for unquestionably they feel annoyance at the marks made round them by the tie.

Treatment of cross-shoots.

The cross-shoots of the Gallic method of growing—two from each side if the pair of vines are forty feet apart, but four if twenty—when they meet are intertwined with each other and tied together in a single cluster, during the process being stiffened with the aid of wooden rods where they fail, or if the shoots themselves are too short to allow of this, they are stretched out to reach an unoccupied tree by means of a hook tied to them. It used to be the custom to prune these cross-shoots every two years, as they make too heavy a weight when they grow old; but it is better to give them time to make a 'scraped' shoot, if their thickness is sufficient; § 206. otherwise it pays to supply nourishment to the knobs of the snake-branch about to form.

Layering of shoots. Precautions for pruning.

There is still one other method intermediate between this one and propagation by layering—that of throwing down the whole vine on the earth and splitting it with wedges, and leading the shoots from a single vine into several trenches, reinforcing the slenderness of each shoot by tying it to a rod, and not lopping off the branches which run out from the sides. A farmer at Novara, not content with a multitude of shoots carried from tree to tree nor with an abundance of branches, also twines the main branches round forked props set in the ground; and thus beside the faults of the soil the wines are also made harsh by the method of cultivation. Another mistake is made with the vines near the city of

iuxta urbem Aricinis, quae alternis putantur annis, non quia id viti conducat sed quia vilitate reditum inpendia exuperent. medium temperamentum in Carsulano secuntur, cariosasque tantum vitis partes incipientesque inarescere deputando, ceteris ad uvam relictis detracto onere supervacuo, pro nutrimento omni est raritas volneris; sed nisi pingui solo talis cultura degenerat in labruscam.

214 Arbusta arari quam altissime desiderant, tametsi[1] frumenti ratio non exigit. pampinari ea non est moris, et hoc conpendium operae. deputantur cum vite pariter interlucata densitate ramorum qui sint supervacui et absumant alimenta. plagas ad septentriones aut ad meridiem spectare vetuimus; melius si neque in occasus solis; diu dolent talia quoque[2] ulcera et difficile sanescunt algendo nimis aestuandove; non eadem ut[3] in vite libertas, quoniam certa latera, sed facilius abscondere et detorquere quo velis vitis[4] plagas. in arborum tonsura supino ore[5] velut calices faciendi, ne consistat umor.

215 XXXVI. Viti adminicula addenda quae scandat adprehensa si maiora sint. vitium generosarum

[1] *Pintianus*: tanta est.
[2] [quoque] *Warmington.*
[3] ut *add. Mayhoff.*
[4] vitis *add. Warmington.*
[5] *Ian*: supiniore.

La Riccia, which are pruned every other year, not because that is beneficial for a vine but because owing to the low price at which the wine sells the expenses might exceed the return. In the Casigliano district they follow an intermediate compromise, and by the plan of pruning away only the decayed parts of the vine and those beginning to wither, and leaving the rest to bear grapes relieved of superfluous weight, the scantiness of the injury inflicted serves instead of all nutriment; but except in a rich soil this method of cultivation degenerates into a wild vine.

Treatment of trees used for vine-props.

The trees for training vines on require the ground to be ploughed as deep as possible, although the system of growing corn there does not need this. It is not customary for them to be trimmed of leaves, and this economizes labour. They are pruned together with the vine, light being let through the density of branches that are superfluous and consume nutriment. We have given the rule against leaving lopped ends § 84. facing north or south, and it is better not to let them face west either, as wounds facing in those directions too suffer for a long time and heal with difficulty, because of undergoing excessive cold or heat; there is not the same freedom as in the case of the vine, since trees have fixed aspects, but it is easier to hide away the wounds of a vine and twist them in any direction you like. In pruning trees cup-like hollows should be made with a mouth sloping downwards, to prevent water from lodging in them.

Seasons for pruning, etc.

XXXVI. Props should be placed against a vine which it may catch hold of and climb up if they are taller than it is. It is said that espaliers for vines of high quality should be cut about March 19th–23rd,

pergulas quinquatribus putandas et, quarum servare uvas libeat, decrescente luna tradunt, quae vero interlunio sint putatae nullis animalium obnoxias esse. alia ratione plena luna noctu tondendas, cum sit ea in leone, scorpione, sagittario, tauro, atque in totum serendas plena aut crescente utique censent. sufficiunt in Italia cultores deni in centena iugera vinearum.

216 XXXVII. Et abunde satu cultuque arborum tractato, quoniam de palmis et cytiso in peregrinis arboribus adfatim diximus, ne quid desit, indicanda reliqua natura est magno opere pertinens ad omnia ea. infestantur namque et arbores morbis—quid enim genitum caret his malis? set [1] silvestrium quidem perniciosos negant esse vexarique tantum grandine in germinatione aut flore, aduri quoque fervore aut flatu frigidiore praepostero die, nam [2] suo frigora
217 etiam prosunt, ut diximus. 'Quid ergo? non et vites algore intereunt?' hoc quidem est quo deprehendatur soli vitium, quoniam non evenit nisi in frigido. itaque per hiemes caeli rigorem probamus, non soli. nec infirmissimae arbores gelu periclitantur, sed maximae, vexatisque ita cacumina prima inarescunt, quoniam praestrictus non potuit eo pervenire umor.

[1] set? *Mayhoff*: et.
[2] *Mayhoff*: quoniam *Gelen.*: quam.

and, if it is intended to keep the grapes for raisins, when the moon is on the wane, but that those cut between the old moon and the new are immune from all kinds of insects. Another theory holds the opinion that vines should be pruned by night at full moon when the moon is in the Lion or Scorpion or Archer or Bull; and in general that they should be planted when the moon is at full, or at all events is waxing. In Italy a gang of ten farmhands is enough for a hundred acres of vineyard.

Diseases of trees. Effects of frost.

XXXVII. And having treated of the planting and cultivation of trees with sufficient fullness, since we have said enough about palms and tree-medick among foreign trees, in order that nothing may be lacking a statement must be given of the other natural features of great importance in relation to all these matters. For even trees are liable to attacks of disease—since what created object is exempt from these evils? But forest trees at all events are said not to have any deadly diseases and only to be liable to damage by hail when they are budding or in flower, and also to be nipped by heat or exceptionally cold wind coming out of season, for cold weather in its proper season actually does them good, as we have stated. 'What then?' it will be said. 'Does not frost kill even vines?' Well, that is how a fault of soil is detected, because it only happens on chilly ground. And consequently we approve of cold in winter time that is due to the climate and not to the soil. And it is not the weakest trees that are endangered by frost, but the largest ones, and when they are thus attacked it is their tops that dry away first, because the sap has been congealed and has not been able to get there.

XIII. 26, 130 ff.

§ 10.

218 Arborum quidam communes morbi, quidam privati generum. communis vermiculatio et sideratio ac dolor membrorum, unde partium debilitas, societate nominum quoque cum hominis miseriis: trunca dicimus certe corpora et oculos germinum exustos ac
219 multa simili sorte. itaque laborant et fame et cruditate, quae fiunt umoris quantitate, aliqua[1] vero et obesitate, ut omnia quae resinam ferunt nimia pinguitudine in taedam mutantur et, cum radices quoque pinguescere coepere, intereunt ut animalia nimio adipe, aliquando et pestilentia per genera, sicut inter homines nunc servitia nunc plebes urbana vel rustica.

220 Vermiculantur magis minusve quaedam, omnes tamen fere, idque aves cavi corticis sono experiuntur. iam quidem et hoc in luxuria esse coepit, praegrandesque roborum delicatiore sunt in cibo—cosses[2] vocant—atque etiam farina saginati hi[3] quoque altiles fiunt.
221 maxime autem arborum hoc sentiunt piri, mali, fici, minus quae amarae sunt et odoratae. eorum qui in ficis existunt alii nascuntur ex ipsis, alios parit qui vocatur cerastes, omnes tamen in cerasten figurantur sonumque edunt parvoli stridoris. et sorbus arbor

[1] *Mayhoff*: aliquae.
[2] cossos *vel* cossos eos *coni. Warmington coll.* XI. 113; cf XXX. 15.
[3] [hi] ? *Mayhoff*.

Some diseases are common to all trees and some are peculiar to special kinds. Common to all are damage by worms and star-blight and pain in the limbs, resulting in debility of the various parts —maladies sharing even their names with those of mankind: we certainly speak of trees being mutilated and having the eyes of their buds burnt out and many misfortunes of a kind resembling our own. Accordingly they suffer both from hunger and from indigestion, maladies due to the amount of moisture in them, and some even from obesity, for instance all which produce resin owing to excessive fatness are converted into torch-wood, and when the roots also have begun to get fat, die like animals from excessive adipose deposit; and sometimes also they die of epidemics prevailing in certain classes of tree, just as among mankind diseases sometimes attack the slaves and sometimes the urban or the rural lower classes.

Maladies common to all trees.

Particular trees are attacked by worm in a greater or smaller degree, but nearly all are liable, and birds detect worm-eaten wood by the hollow sound when they tap the bark. Nowadays indeed even this has begun to be classed as a luxury, and specially large wood-maggots found in oakwood—the name for these is *cosses*—figure in the menu as a special delicacy, and actually even these creatures are fed with flour to fatten them for the table. The trees most liable to be worm-eaten are pears, apples, and figs; those that have a bitter taste and a scent are less liable. Of the maggots found in fig-trees some breed in the trees themselves, but others are produced by the insect called in Greek the horned insect; all of them however assume the shape of that insect, and emit a little buzzing sound. Also the service-tree is

Damage by larvae of insects.

infestatur vermiculis rufis ac pilosis, atque ita emoritur; mespila quoque in senecta obnoxia ei morbo est.

222 Sideratio tota e caelo constat; quapropter et grando in his causis intellegi debet et carbunculatio et quod pruinarum iniuria evenit. haec enim verno tepore[1] invitatis et erumpere audentibus satis mollibus insidens adurit lactescentes germinum oculos, quod in flore carbunculum vocant. pruinae perniciosior natura, quoniam lapsa persidit gelatque ac ne aura quidem ulla depellitur, quia non fit nisi inmoto aere et sereno. proprium tamen siderationis est sub ortu canis siccitatum vapor, cum insita ac novellae arbores moriuntur, praecipue ficus et vitis.

223 Olea praeter vermiculationem, quam aeque ac ficus sentit, clavum etiam patitur, sive fungum placet dici vel patellam; haec est solis exustio. nocere tradit Cato et muscum rubrum. nocet plerumque vitibus atque oleis et nimia fertilitas. scabies communis omnium est. inpetigo et quae adgnasci solent cocleae peculiaria ficorum vitia, nec ubique—sunt enim quaedam aegritudines et locorum.

224 Verum ut homini nervorum cruciatus sic et arbori, ac duobus aeque modis: aut enim in pedes, hoc est radices, inrumpit vis morbi, aut in articulos, hoc est cacuminum digitos, qui longissime a toto corpore exeunt; sunt apud Graecos sua nomina utrique

[1] *Gelen.*: tempore.

infected with red, hairy caterpillars, which eventually kill it; and the medlar as well is liable to the same disease when it grows old.

Star-blight depends entirely on the heavens, and consequently we must include among these causes of injury hail and carbuncle-blight, and also damage due to frost. The former when the plants are tempted by the warmth of spring to venture to burst out settles on them while they are fairly soft and scorches the milky eyes of the buds, the part which in the flower is called the carbuncle. Frost is of a more damaging nature, because when it has fallen it settles down and freezes, and is not dispelled even by any slight breeze, because it only occurs when the air is motionless and calm. A peculiarity however of star-blight at the rising of the Dog-star is a parching heat, when grafts and saplings die, especially figs and vines. *Star-blight, frost and other maladies and causes of damage.*

The olive besides suffering from worm, to which it is as liable as is the fig, is also affected by wart, or, as some prefer to call it, fungus or 'platter'; this is a scorch caused by the sun. Cato states that red scale is also injurious to the olive. Excessive fertility also usually injures vines and olive. Scab is common to all trees. Eruption and epidermic growths on the bark called 'snails' are maladies peculiar to figs, and that not in all districts—for some diseases belong to particular localities. *de Agr. = R.R.* VI. 2.

But just as man is subject to affliction of the sinews, so also is a tree, and in two ways, as is the case with man: for the force of the disease either attacks its feet, that is the roots, or its knuckles, that is the fingers of the top branches, which project farthest from the whole body; with the Greeks there are

225 vitio.[1] nigrescunt[2] ergo, et undique primo dolor, mox et macies earum partium fragilis, postremo tabes morsque, non intrante suco aut non perveniente; maximeque id fici sentiunt, caprificus omnibus immunis est quae adhuc diximus. scabies gignitur roribus lentis post vergilias; nam si largiores[3] fuere, perfundunt bene[4] arborem, non scalpunt scabie at grossi[5] cadunt; si vero[6] imbres nimii fuere, alio modo ficus laborat radicibus madidis.

226 Vitibus praeter vermiculationem et siderationem morbus peculiaris articulatio tribus de causis: una vi tempestatium germinibus ablatis, altera, ut notavit Theophrastus, in supinum excisis, tertia culturae imperitia laesis; omnes enim earum iniuriae in articulis sentiuntur. siderationis genus est uvis[7] deflorescentibus roratio, aut cum acini priusquam crescant decocuntur in callum. aegrotant et cum alsere, laesis uredine attonsarum oculis. et calore hoc evenit intempestivo, quoniam omnia modo constant
227 certoque temperamento. fiunt et culpa colentium vitia,[8] cum praestringuntur, ut dictum est, aut circum-

[1] sunt . . . vitio *hic* ? *Mayhoff*: *infra post* ergo et.
[2] *E Theophr. Dalec.*: inarescunt.
[3] *Dalec.*: rariores.
[4] perfundunt bene *Rackham* (p. benigne ? *Mayhoff*): perfunduntne.
[5] et (at ? *Mayhoff*) grossi *ed. Hack.*: eteros si.
[6] si vero ? *Mayhoff*: sive.
[7] *C. F. W. Mueller*: et his *aut* in his.
[8] *Mayhoff*: vitium (vitia *cd. Par. Lat.* 6796) colentia.

special names for each of these diseases. Consequently they turn black, and first there is pain all over and then the parts mentioned also become emaciated and brittle, and lastly comes wasting consumption and death, the sap not entering or not permeating the parts affected. Figs are extremely liable to this disease, but the wild fig is immune from all the maladies we have so far specified. Scab is caused by gentle falls of dew occurring after the rising of the Pleiads; for if the dew has been more copious it gives the tree a good drenching, and does not streak it with scab, although the green figs fall off; but if there has been excessive rain a fig-tree is liable to another malady due to dampness of the roots.

In addition to worm-disease and star-blight vines suffer from a disease of the joints that is peculiar to them; it is due to three causes—first, loss of buds owing to stormy weather, second, as noted by Theophrastus, pruning done with an upward cut, and third, damage caused by lack of skill in their cultivation; for all injuries to which vines are liable are felt in their joints. One kind of star-blight is dew-disease, when the grape-vines shed their blossoms, or when the grapes shrivel up into a hard lump before they grow big. Vines are also sickly when they have been nipped by cold, the eyes being injured by frost-bite after the branches have been pruned. This also happens owing to unseasonable hot weather, since everything depends on measure and on a fixed proportion. Defects may also be caused by the fault of the vine-dressers, when the vines are tied too tight, as has been said, or else when the digger trenching round them has injured them with a damaging blow,

Cf. Theophr., *H.P.*, IV. 14. 6 ff.

§ 209.

fossor iniurioso ictu verberavit, vel etiam subarator inprudens luxavit radices corpusve desquamavit; est et quaedam contusio falcis hebetioris. quibus omnibus causis difficilius tolerant frigora aut aestus, quoniam in ulcus penetrat iniuria omnis a foris. infirmissima vero malus, maxime quaequae dulcis est.
228 quibusdam debilitas sterilitatem, non necem adfert, ut si quis pino cacumen auferat vel palmae; sterilescunt enim nec moriuntur. aegrotant aliquando et poma ipsa per se sine arbore, si necessariis temporibus imbres aut tepores vel adflatus defuere aut contra abundavere; decidunt enim aut deteriora fiunt. pessimum est inter omnia cum deflorescentem vitem et oleam percussit imber, quoniam simul defluit fructus.

229 Sunt ex eadem causa nascentes et urucae, dirum animal, eroduntque frondem, aliae florem quoque, olivarum,[1] ut in Mileto, ac depastam arborem turpi facie relinquunt. nascitur hoc malum tepore umido et lento; fit aliud ex eodem si sol acrior insecutus inussit ipsum vitium ideoque mutavit. est etiamnum peculiare olivis et vitibus—araneum vocant—cum
230 veluti telae involvunt fructum et absumunt. adurunt et flatus quidam eas maxime, sed et alios fructus. nam vermiculationem et poma ipsa per se quibusdam[2]

[1] *Urlichs*: olivarum quoque.
[2] *Mayhoff*: quibusdam annis.

or even when a careless person ploughing underneath them has displaced the roots or scaled the bark off the trunk; also a contusion may be caused by pruning with too blunt a knife. All of these causes make it more difficult for a vine to bear cold or hot weather, since every harmful influence from outside makes its way into the sore. But the most delicate of all trees is the apple, and particularly any kind that bears sweet fruit. With some trees weakness causes barrenness but does not kill them, as is the case with a pine or a palm if you lop off their top, as they cease to bear but do not die. Sometimes also the fruit by itself is attacked by disease but not the tree, if there has been a lack of rain or of warm weather or wind at the times when they are needed, or if on the contrary they have been too plentiful, for the fruit falls off or deteriorates. The worst among all kinds of damage is when a vine or olive has been struck by heavy rain when shedding its blossom, as the fruit is washed off at the same time.

Caterpillars and fungus and the weather.

Heavy rain also breeds caterpillars, noxious creatures that gnaw away the foliage of olives, and others the flower too, as at Miletus, and leave the half-eaten tree shamefully disfigured. This pestilence is bred by damp sticky heat; and another one due to the same cause occurs if too keen a sun follows, and burns in the damage done by the damp and so alters its nature. There is in addition a malady peculiar to olives and vines, called cobweb, when the fruit gets wrapped up in a sort of webbing which stifles it. There are also certain currents of air which are specially blighting to olives, though they dry up other fruit as well. As to worm, in some trees even the fruits of themselves suffer from it—apples, pears,

sentiunt, mala, pira, mespila, punica; in oliva ancipiti eventu, quando sub cute innati[1] fructum adimunt, augent si in ipso nucleo fuere erodentes eum. gigni illos prohibent pluviae quae fiunt post Arcturum; eaedem si austrinae fuere, generant druppis quoque,
231 quae maturescentes tum sunt praecipue caducae. id riguis magis evenit, etiamsi non cecidere fastidiendis. sunt et culicum genera aliquis molesta, ut glandibus, fico, qui videntur ex umore nasci tum dulci subdito corticibus; et aegrotatio quidem fere in his est.

232 Quaedam temporum causae aut locorum non proprie dicantur morbi quoniam protinus necant, sicut tabes cum invasit arborem aut uredo vel flatus alicuius regionis proprius, ut est in Apulia atabulus, in Euboea Olympias; hic enim si flavit circa brumam, frigore exurit arefaciens, ut nullis postea solibus recreari possint. hoc genere convalles et adposita fluminibus
233 laborant, praecipueque vitis, olea, ficus; quod cum evenit,[2] detegitur statim in germinatione, in oliva tardius. sed in omnibus signum est revivescendi si folia amisere; alioqui quas putes praevaluisse moriuntur. nonnumqum inarescunt folia eademque

[1] *Mayhoff*: subeunti nati. [2] *C. F. W. Mueller*: venit.

[a] Probably 'honey-dew' secreted by, not eaten by, aphides.

medlars and pomegranates; but in the case of the olive an attack of worm has a two-fold result, inasmuch as if they breed under the skin they destroy the fruit, while if they have been in the actual stone, gnawing it away, they make the fruit larger. Rain following the rising of Arcturus prevents their breeding; and also if this rain is accompanied by a south wind it breeds worms in half-ripe olives as well, which are then particularly liable to fall off when ripening. This happens particularly with olives in damp localities, making them very unattractive even if they do not drop off. There is also a kind of gnat troublesome to some fruits, for instance acorns and figs, which appears to be bred from the sweet juice[a] secreted underneath the bark at that season; and indeed these trees are usually sickly.

Some influences of seasons or localities cannot *Wind blight.* properly be called diseases, since they cause instantaneous death, for instance when a tree is attacked by wasting or blast, or by the effect of a special wind prevailing in a particular district, like the sirocco in Apulia or the Olympias wind in Euboea, which if it blows about midwinter shrivels up trees with dry cold so that no amount of subsequent sunshine can revive them. This kind of blight infests narrow valleys and trees growing by rivers, and particularly vines, olive and figs; and when this has occurred, it is at once detected at the budding season, though rather later in the case of olives. But it is a sign of recovery in all of them if they lose their leaves; failing that, the trees which one would suppose to have been strong enough to resist the attack die. Sometimes however the leaves dry on the tree and then come to life again. Other trees

revivescunt. alia in terris septentrionalibus, ut Ponto, Thracia, frigore aut gelu laborant si post brumam continuavere XL diebus; et ibi autem et in reliquis partibus, si protinus editis fructibus gelatio magna consecuta est, etiam paucis diebus necat.

234 Quae iniuria hominum constant secundum vim[1] habent causas. pix, oleum, adeps inimica praecipue novellis. cortice in orbem detracto necantur, excepto subere, quod sic etiam iuvatur, crassescens enim praestringit et strangulat; nec andrachle offenditur si non simul incidatur et corpus. alioqui et cerasus et tilia et vitis corticem amittunt,[2] sed non vitalem nec proximum corpori, verum eum qui subnascente alio
235 expellitur. quarundam natura rimosus cortex, ut platanis. tiliae renascitur paulo minus quam totus. ergo his quarum cicatricem trahit medentur luto fimoque et aliquando prosunt, si non vehementior frigorum aut calorum vis secuta est; quaedam tardius ita moriuntur, ut robora et quercus. refert et tempus anni; abieti enim et pino si quis detraxerit sole taurum vel geminos transeunte, cum germinant, statim moriuntur, eandem iniuriam hieme passae
236 diutius tolerant; similiter ilex et robur quercusque.

[1] vim *add. Detlefsen.* [2] amittunt? *Mayhoff*: mittunt.

[a] It would kill the cork-tree likewise.
[b] *Arbutus Andrachne.*

in the northern countries like the province of Pontus and Thrace suffer from cold or frost if they go on for six weeks after midwinter without a break; but both in that region and in the remaining parts of the world, a heavy frost coming immediately after the trees have produced their fruit kills them even in a few days.

Effects of damage especially to bark.

Kinds of damage due to injury done by man have effects proportionate to their violence. Pitch, oil and grease are particularly detrimental to young trees. To strip off the bark all round trees kills them, except [a] in the case of the cork tree, which is actually benefited by this treatment, because the bark thickening stifles and suffocates the tree; nor does it do any harm to andrachne [b] if care is taken not to cut into the body of the plant as well. Beside this, the cherry, the vine and the lime shed some bark, though not the layer next to the body which is essential to life, but the layer that is forced outward as another forms underneath it. The bark of some trees, for instance planes, is fissured by nature. That of the lime after it is stripped grows again almost in its entirety. Consequently with trees the bark of which forms a scar, the scars are treated with mud and dung, and sometimes they do the tree good, if the stripping is not followed by a period of exceptionally cold or hot weather. But some trees, for instance hard oaks and common oaks, die, but rather slowly, under this treatment. The time of year also matters; for instance if a fir or a pine is stripped of its bark while the sun is passing through the Bull or the Twins, when they are budding, they die at once, whereas if they undergo the same injury in winter they endure it longer; and similarly the holm oak,

si angusta decorticatio fuit, nihil nocet ut[1] supra dictis, infirmioribus quidem et in solo gracili vel ab una tantum parte detractus interemit. similem et decacuminatio rationem habet piceae, cedri, cupressi—hae enim detracto cacumine aut ignibus adusto
237 intereunt—similem et depastio animalium. oleam quidem etiam si lambat capra sterilescere auctor est Varro, ut diximus. quaedam hac iniuria moriuntur, aliqua deteriora tantum fiunt, ut amygdalae—ex dulcibus enim transfigurantur in amaras,—aliqua vero etiam utiliora, ut aput Chios pirus quam Phocida
238 appellant. nam detruncatio diximus quibus prodesset. intereunt pleraque et fissa stirpe, exceptis vite, malo, fico, punicis, quaedam vel ab ulcere tantum; pinus[2] hanc iniuriam spernit et omnia quae resinam gignunt. radicibus amputatis mori minime mirum est; pleraeque etiam[3] non omnibus sed maximis aut quae sunt inter illas vitales abscisis moriuntur.

239 Necant invicem inter sese umbra vel densitate atque alimenti rapina; necat et hedera vinciens, nec viscum prodest, et cytisus necat,[4] necantur[5] eo quod halimon vocant Graeci. quorundam natura non necat quidem sed laedit odorum aut suci mixtura, ut raphanus et laurus vitem; olfactatrix enim esse[6]

[1] *V.l.* nocetur.
[2] *Bodaeus*: ficus.
[3] *Mayhoff*: tamen.
[4] necat *add.* ? *Mayhoff*.
[5] *Rackham* (necatur *Hardouin*): nec aureo.
[6] esse *add. Rackham.*

the hard oak and the common oak. If only a narrow band of bark is removed, it causes no harm, as with the trees above mentioned, although with weaker § 234.
trees at all events and in a thin soil to remove the bark even from only one part kills the tree. A similar effect is also produced by lopping the top of a spruce, prickly cedar or cypress, for to remove the top or to scorch it with fire is fatal to these trees; and the effect of being gnawn by animals is also similar. Indeed, according to Varro, as we have stated, an VIII. 204,
olive goes barren if merely licked by a she-goat. XV. 34.
Certain trees die of this injury, but some only deteriorate, for instance almonds, the fruit of which is changed from sweet to bitter, but others are actually improved, for instance the pear called the Phocian pear in Chios. For we have mentioned trees that XIII. 36.
are actually benefited by having the top lopped off. XVII. 201.
Most trees die also when the trunk is split, excepting the vine, apple, fig and pomegranates, and some merely from a wound, though the pine and all the resinous trees despise this injury. For a tree to die when its roots are cut off is not at all surprising; most trees die even when deprived not of all their roots but of the largest ones or those among them that are essential to life.

Damage by other trees and by other plants.

Trees kill one another by their shade or the thickness of their foliage and by robbing each other of nutriment; they are also killed by ivy binding them round, and mistletoe does them no good, and cytisus kills them, and they are killed by the plant called *halimon* by the Greeks. The nature of some plants though not actually deadly is injurious owing to its blend of scents or of juice—for instance the radish and the laurel are harmful to the vine; for the vine

intellegitur et tingui odore mirum in modum, ideo,
cum iuxta sit, averti et recedere saporemque inimicum
240 fugere. hinc sumpsit Androcydes medicinam contra
ebrietates, raphanum mandi praecipiens. odit et caulem et olus omne, odit et corylum, ni procul absint,
tristis atque aegra; nitrum quidem et alumen, marina
aqua calida et fabae putamina vel ervi viti[1] ultima
venena sunt.

241 XXXVIII. Inter vitia arborum est et prodigiis
locus. invenimus ficos sub foliis natas, vitem et
malum punicam stirpe fructum tulisse, non palmite
aut ramis, vitem uvas sine foliis, oleas quoque amisisse
folia bacis haerentibus. sunt et[2] miracula fortuita:
nam et oliva in totum ambusta revixit, et in Boeotia
242 derosae locustis fici regerminavere. mutantur arbores
et colore fiuntque ex nigris candidae, non semper
prodigio, sed eae maxime quae ex semine nascuntur;
et populus alba in nigram transit. quidam et sorbum
si in calidiora loca venerit sterilescere putant. prodigio
autem fiunt ex dulcibus acerba poma aut dulcia ex
acerbis, e caprifico fici aut contra, gravi ostento cum
in deteriora mutantur, ex olea in oleastrum, ex

[1] viti *add. Rackham.*
[2] et *add. edd.*

can be inferred to possess a sense of smell, and to be affected by odours in a marvellous degree, and consequently when an evil-smelling plant is near it to turn away and withdraw, and to avoid an unfriendly tang. This supplied Androcydes with an antidote against intoxication, for which he recommended chewing a radish. The vine also abhors cabbage and all sorts of garden vegetables, as well as hazel, and these unless a long way off make it ailing and sickly; indeed nitre and alum and warm sea-water and the pods of beans or bitter vetch are to a vine the direst poisons.

XXXVIII. Among the maladies of trees it is in place to speak also of prodigies. We find that figs have grown underneath the leaves of the tree, a vine and a pomegranate have borne fruit on their trunk, not on a shoot or a branch, a vine has borne grapes without having any leaves, and also olives have lost their leaves while the fruit remained on the tree. There are also marvels connected with accident: an olive has come to life again after being completely burnt up, also fig-trees in Boeotia gnawed down by locusts have budded afresh. Trees also change their colour and turn from black to white, not always with portentous meaning, but chiefly those that grow from seed; and the white poplar turns into a black poplar. Some people also think that the service-tree goes barren if transplanted to warmer localities. But it is a portent when sour fruits grow on sweet fruit-trees and sweet on sour, and figs on a wild fig-tree or the contrary, and it is a serious manifestation when trees turn into other trees of an inferior kind, from an olive into a wild olive or from a white grape or green fig into a black grape or a

Portentous behaviour of trees.

candida uva et fico in nigras, aut ut Laodiciae Xerxis
243 adventu platano in oleam mutata. qualibus ostentis Aristandri apud Graecos volumen scatet, ne in infinitum abeamus, apud nos vero C. Epidii commentarii, in quibus arbores locutae quoque reperiuntur. subsedit in Cumano arbor gravi ostento paulo ante Pompei Magni bella civilia paucis ramis eminentibus; inventum Sibyllinis libris internicionem hominum fore, tantoque eam maiorem quanto propius ab urbe portentum factum[1] esset.

244 Sunt prodigia et cum alienis locis enascuntur, ut in capitibus statuarum vel aris, et cum in arboribus ipsis alienae. ficus in lauro nata est Cyzici ante obsidionem; simili modo Trallibus palma in basi Caesaris dictatoris circa bella civilia eius. nec non et Romae in Capitolio in ara Iovis[2] bello Persei enata palma victoriam triumphosque portendit; hac tempestatibus prostrata eodem loco ficus enata est M. Messalae C. Cassii censorum lustro, a quo tempore pudicitiam
245 subversam Piso gravis auctor prodidit. super omnia quae umquam audita sunt erit prodigium in nostro aevo Neronis principis ruina factum in agro Marrucino, Vettii Marcelli e primis equestris ordinis oliveto

[1] *Rackham*: urbe postea facta.
[2] in ara Iovis *cd. Vat. Lat.* 3861, *m.* 2: in capita bis *rell.*: in capite Iovis *quidam apud Dalec.*

---

[a] Presumably noisy flocks of starlings roosting in trees produced this impression, as they do even in London now.
[b] By Mithridates, 75 B.C.
[c] 171–168 B.C.
[d] 154 B.C.

black fig, or as when a plane-tree at Laodicea changed into an olive on the arrival of Xerxes. Not to launch out into an absolutely boundless subject, the volume by Aristander teems with portents of this nature in Greece, as do the Notes of Gaius Epidius in our own country, including cases of trees that talked.[a] An alarming portent occurred a little before the civil wars of Pompey the Great, when a tree in the territory of Cumae sank into the ground leaving a few branches projecting; and a statement was found in the Sibylline Books that this portended a slaughter of human beings, and that the nearer to the city the portent had occurred the greater the slaughter would be.

Another class of portent is when trees grow in the wrong places, as on the heads of statues or on altars, and when different kinds of trees grow on trees themselves. At Cyzicus before the siege[b] a fig-tree grew on a laurel; and similarly at Tralles about the time of Caesar's civil wars a palm grew up on the pedestal of the dictator's statue. Moreover at Rome during the war with Perseus[c] a palm-tree grew up on the altar of Jove on the Capitol, portending victory and triumphal processions; and after this tree had been brought down by storms, a fig-tree sprang up in the same place, this occurring during the censorship[d] of Marcus Messala and Gaius Cassius, a period which according to so weighty an authority as Piso dates the overthrow of the sense of honour. A portent that will eclipse all those ever heard of occurred in our own day in the territory of the Marrucini, at the fall of the emperor Nero: an olive grove belonging to a leading member of the equestrian order named Vettius Marcellus bodily crossed the public highway,

universo viam publicam transgresso arvisque inde e contrario in locum oliveti profectis.

246 XXXIX. Nunc expositis arborum morbis consentaneum est dicere et remedia. ex his quaedam sunt communia omnium, quaedam propria quarundam. communia ablaqueatio, adcumulatio, adflari radices aut cooperiri, riguus[1] dato potu vel ablato, fimum suco refectis, putatio levatis onere, item suco emisso quaedam veluti detractio sanguinis, circumrasio corticis, vitium extenuatio et domitura palmitum, gemmarum, si frigus retorridas hirtasque fecerit,

247 repumicatio et quaedam politura. arborum his aliae magis aliae minus gaudent, veluti cupressus et aquam aspernatur et fimum et circumfossuram amputationemque et omnia remedia odit, quin etiam necatur riguis, vitis et punicae praecipue aluntur. ficus arbor ipsa riguis alitur, pomum vero eius marcescit.

248 amygdalae si colantur fossione florem amittunt. nec insitas circumfodere oportet priusquam validae ferre coeperint poma. plurimae autem amputari sibi volunt onerosa ac supervacua, sicut nos ungues et capillum. reciduntur veteres totae ac rursus a stolone aliquo resurgunt, sed non omnes, nec nisi quarum naturam pati diximus.

[1] *Ian coll.* § 250 : riguas.

and the crops growing on the other side passed over in the opposite direction to take the place of the olive grove.

XXXIX. Now that we have set out the diseases of trees it is suitable also to state the remedies for them. Some of these are common to all trees and some peculiar to some of them. Remedies common to all are loosening the soil, banking it up, admitting air to the roots or covering them up, making a channel to give them water or to drain it away, dung refreshing them with its juice, pruning to relieve them of weight, also letting out the sap like a surgical blood-letting, scraping a ring of bark, stretching out the vine-sprays and checking the shoots, trimming off and as it were polishing up the buds if they have been shrivelled and roughened by cold weather. Some trees like these treatments more and others less, for example the cypress scorns both water and dung and hates being dug round and pruned and all kinds of nursing, in fact irrigation kills it, whereas it is exceptionally nourishing for vines and pomegranates. In the case of the fig irrigation nourishes the tree itself but makes the fruit decay. Almond-trees lose their blossom if the ground round them is made clean by being dug over. Also trees that have been grafted must not be dug round before they are strong and begin to bear fruit. Most trees however want to have their burdensome and superfluous growth pruned away, just as we have our nails and hair cut. Old trees are cut down entirely and spring up again from some sucker, but they will not all do this but only those whose nature we have stated to allow of it.

Remedies for diseases of trees. Dislikes of trees.

XVI. 128, 130, 173, 241.

249 XL. Rigua aestivis vaporibus utilia, hieme inimica, autumno varie et e natura soli, quippe cum vindemiator Hispaniarum stagnante solo uvas demetat, cetero maiore in parte orbis etiam pluvias autumni aquas derivare conveniat.[1] circa canis ortum rigua maxime prosunt, ac ne tum quidem nimia, quoniam inebriatis radicibus nocent. et aetas modum temperat; novellae enim minus sitiunt. desiderant autem maxime rigari quae adsuevere, contra siccis locis genita non expetunt umorem nisi necessarium.

250 XLI. Asperiora vina rigari utique cupiunt in Sulmonense Italiae agro, pago Fabiano, ubi et arva rigant; mirumque, herbae aqua illa necantur, fruges aluntur et riguus pro sarculo est. in eodem agro bruma, tanto magis si nives iaceant geletve, ne frigus vites adurat, circumfundunt riguis, quod ibi tepidare vocant, memorabili natura in amne solis, eodem aestate vix tolerandi rigoris.

251 XLII. Carbunculi ac robiginum remedia demonstrabimus volumine proximo. interim est et scariphatio quaedam in remediis, cum macie corticis ex aegritudine adstringente se iustoque plus vitalia

[1] *Rackham*: convenit.

---

[a] Sagrus, now the Sangro.

XL. Irrigation is good for trees in the heat of summer but bad for them in winter; in the autumn its effect varies and depends on the nature of the soil, inasmuch as in the Spanish provinces the vintager picks the grapes when the ground is under water, whereas in the greater part of the world it pays to drain off the rain water even in autumn. Irrigation is most beneficial about the rising of the Dogstar, and even then not too much of it, because it hurts the roots when they are soaked to the point of intoxication. The age of the tree also controls the due amount; young saplings are not so thirsty. But those that require most watering are those that have been used to it, whereas those which have sprung up in dry places only need a bare minimum of moisture.

Irrigation of trees.

XLI. The harsher vines need to be watered, at all events in the Fabii district of the territory of Sulmo in Italy, where they irrigate even the plough-land; and it is a remarkable fact that in that part of the country water kills herbaceous plants but nourishes corn, and irrigation takes the place of a hoe for weeding. In the same district they irrigate the land round the vines at midwinter to prevent their suffering from cold, the more so if snow is lying or there is a frost; this process is there called 'warming' the vines, owing to the remarkable influence of the sun on the river,[a] which in summer is almost unbearably cold.

XLII. We shall point out the remedies for glowing-coal-blight and mildew in the next Book. In the meantime the list of remedies includes a sort of scarification. The bark when rendered meagre by disease shrinks up and exerts an undue amount of compression on the vital parts of the tree; for this

XVIII. 279 ff.

Scarification and other remedies for trees.

arborum conprimente exacutam[1] falcis aciem utraque manu inprimentes perpetuis incisuris deducunt ac veluti cutem laxant. salutare id fuisse argumento sunt dilatatae cicatrices et internato corpore expletae;

252 XLIII. magnaque ex parte similis hominum medicina et arborum est, quando earum quoque terebrantur ossa. amygdalae ex amaris dulces fiunt si circumfosso stipite et ab ima parte circumforato defluens pituita abstergeatur. et ulmis detrahitur sucus inutilis supra terram foratis usque ad medullam, in senecta aut cum

253 alimento nimio abundare sentiuntur. idem et ficorum turgido cortice incisuris in oblicum levibus emittitur: ita fit ne decidant fructus. pomiferis quae germinant nec ferunt fructum fissa radice inditur lapis fertilesque fiunt, hoc idem in amygdalis e robore cuneo adacto, in piris sorbisque e taeda, ac cinere et terra cooperto.

254 etiam radices circumcidisse prodest vitium luxuriantium ficorumque et circumcisis cinerem addidisse. fici serotinae fiunt si primae grossi cum fabae magnitudinem excessere detrahantur; subnascuntur enim quae serius maturescunt. eaedem cum[2] frondere incipiunt si cacumina rami cuiusque detrahantur

[1] *Urlichs*: exactam.
[2] cum *add. edd.*

[a] The comparison is with the operation for removing carious bone in man.

the vine-dressers holding a pruning knife with a very sharp edge in both hands press it into the trunk and make long incisions downwards, and as it were loosen its skin. It proves that this treatment has been beneficial if the scars widen out and fill up with new wood growing between their edges; XLIII. and to a large extent the medical treatment of trees resembles that of human beings, as the bones of trees also are treated by perforation.[a] Bitter almonds are made into sweet ones if the stem of the tree has the earth dug away round it and a ring of holes pierced in it at the bottom, and then the gum exuding is wiped off. Also elms can be relieved of useless sap by having holes pierced in them above the level of the earth right into the cambium when they are getting old, or when they are observed to be receiving excessive nourishment. The sap is also discharged from the bark of figs when swollen by means of light cuts made on a slant; this treatment prevents the fruit from falling off. Fruit-trees that make buds but produce no fruit are treated by making a cleft in the root and inserting a stone in it, and this makes them bear; and the same result is produced in almonds by driving in a wedge of hard oak, and in pears and service-berries by means of a wedge of stone pine, and covering up the hole with ashes and earth. It also pays to cut round the roots of vines and figs when over-luxuriant and to put ashes on the cut parts. Late figs are produced if those of the first crop are picked off the tree still unripe, when they are a little larger than a bean, as a second crop grows which ripens later. Also fig-trees are made stronger and more productive if the tips of all the branches are docked when they begin to make

firmiores fertilioresque fiunt. nam caprificatio maturat.

255 XLIV. In ea culices nasci e grossis manifestum,
quoniam cum evolavere non inveniuntur intus grana,
quae in eos versa apparet; exeundi tanta est aviditas
ut plerique aut pede relicto aut pinnae parte erumpant. est et aliud genus culicum quos vocant
centrinas, fucis apium similes ignavia malitiaque cum
pernicie verorum et utilium; interemunt enim illos
256 atque ipsi commoriuntur. vexant et tineae semina
ficorum, contra quas remedium in eadem scrobe
defodere taleam lentisci inversa parte quae fuerit a
cacumine. uberrimas autem ficus rubrica amurca
diluta et cum fimo infusa radicibus frondere incipientium facit. caprificorum laudantur maxime nigrae
et in petrosis, quoniam frumenta plurima habeant,
caprificatio ipsa post imbrem.

257 XLV. In primis autem cavendum ne ex remediis
vitia fiant, quod evenit nimia aut intempestiva
medicina. interlucatio arboribus prodest, sed omnium annorum trucidatio inutilissima. vitis tantum
tonsuram annuam quaerit, alternam vero myrtus,
punicae, oleae, quia celeriter fruticescunt. ceterae

foliage. The object of the process that employs the gall-insect from the wild fig is to ripen the fruit. XV. 81.

Insects infesting figs.

XLIV. In the gall-insect process it is clear that the unripe figs give birth to gnats, since when these have flown away the fruit is found not to contain any seeds, which have obviously turned into the gnats; these are so eager to escape that most of them leave a foot or part of a wing behind them in forcing their way out. There is also another kind of gnat with a Greek name meaning 'sting-fly'; these resemble drone bees in their sloth and malice, and also in killing the genuine and serviceable insects; for the sting-flies kill the real gnats and themselves die with them. The seeds of figs are also infested by moths, a remedy against them being to bury a slip of mastich upside down in the same hole. But the way to make fig-trees bear very large crops is to dilute red earth with the lees from an olive-press, mix dung with it, and pour the mixture on the roots of the trees when they are beginning to make leaves. Of wild figs the black ones and those growing in rocky places are the most highly spoken of, because they contain the largest number of grains; the best times for the actual process of transference of the gall-insect from the wild fig is said to be just after rain has fallen.

Over-pruning.

XLV. But it is of the first importance to avoid allowing our remedies to produce other defects, which results from using remedial processes to excess or at the wrong time. To prune away branches is beneficial for trees, but to slaughter them every year without respite is extremely unprofitable. A vine only requires a yearly trimming, but myrtles, pomegranates and olives one every other year, because they produce shoots with great rapidity. All other

rarius tondeantur,[1] nulla autumno; ac ne radantur quidem nisi vere. putatio ne plaga sit[2]; vitalia sunt omnia quaecumque non supervacua.

258 XLVI. Similis fimi ratio.[3] gaudent eo, sed cavendum ne in fervore solis admoveatur, ne inmaturum, ne validius quam opus sit. urit vineas suillum nisi quinquennio interposito, praeterquam si riguis diluatur; et a coriariorum sordibus nisi admixta aqua, item largius: iustum existimant in denos pedes quadratos tres modios. id quidem soli natura decernet.

259 XLVII. Columbino ac suillo plagis quoque arborum medentur. si mala punica acida nascantur, ablaqueatis radicibus fimum suillum addi iubent; eo anno vinolenta, proximo dulcia futura. alii urina hominis aqua mixta riganda censent quater anno, singulis amphoris, aut cacumina spargi vino lasere diluto, si findantur in arbore, pediculum intorqueri, ficis utique amurcam adfundi, ceteris arboribus aegris faecem
260 vini, aut lupinum circum radices earum seri. aqua quoque lupini decocti circumfusa pomis prodest. fici cum Volcanalibus tonuit cadunt; remedium est ut ante stipula hordeacea areae stringantur.

[1] *Mayhoff*: tondentur.
[2] sit *add. Detlefsen* (fiat cavendum? *add. Mayhoff*).
[3] *Gelenius*: similis firmatio.

[a] August 23.

trees should be trimmed less frequently, and none in autumn; and they must not even have their trunks scraped except in spring. Pruning must not be assault and battery: every part of the tree that is not actually superfluous is conducive to its vitality.

XLVI. A similar method belongs to dung. Trees delight in it, but care must be taken not to apply it while the sun is hot, or while it is too fresh, or stronger than is necessary. Swine dung burns the vines unless used at intervals of five years, except if it is diluted by being drenched with water; and so will manure made from tanners' refuse unless water is mixed with it, and also if it is used too plentifully: the proper amount is considered to be three *modii* for every ten square feet. Anyhow that will be decided by the nature of the soil.

Care in manuring.

XLVII. Pigeon and swine manure are also used for dressing wounds in trees. If pomegranates produce sour fruit, it is advised to dig round the roots and apply swine's dung; then in that year the fruit will have a flavour of wine, but next year it will be sweet. Others are of opinion that pomegranates should be watered four times a year with human urine mixed with water, an *amphora* to each tree, or that the ends of the branches should be sprinkled with silphium diluted with wine; and that if the fruit splits on the tree, its stalk should be twisted; and that figs in any case should have dregs of olive oil poured on them, and other trees when ailing wine-lees, or else lupines should be sown round their roots. It is also good for the fruit to pour round the tree water in which lupines have been boiled. Figs are liable to fall off when it thunders at the Feast of Vulcan[a]; a remedy is to have the ground round the trees covered with

Manuring with dung and urine.

cerasos praecoces facit cogitque maturescere calx admota radicibus; et haec autem ut[1] omnia poma intervelli melius est ut quae relicta sint grandescant.

261 Quaedam poena emendantur aut morsu excitantur, ut palmae ac lentisci; salsis enim aquis aluntur. salis vim et cineres sed leniorem habent, ideo ficis adsperguntur rutaeque,[2] ne fiant verminosae neve radices putrescant. quin et vitium radicibus aquam salsam iubent adfundi si sint lacrimosae, si vero fructus earum decidant, cinerem aceto conspergi ipsasque inlini, aut sandaraca si putrescat uva, si vero fertiles non sint, aceto acri subacto cinere rigari atque oblini;

262 quod si fructum non maturent prius inarescentem, praecisarum ad radices plagam fibrasque aceto acri et urina vetusta madefacere atque eo luto obruere, saepe fodere. olearum, si parum promisere fructus, nudatas radices hiberno frigori opponunt eaque castigatione proficiunt. omnia haec annua caeli ratione constant et aliquando serius poscuntur, aliquando celerius. nec non ignis aliquis prodest, ut harundini; ambusta namque densior mitiorque

263 resurgit.[3] Cato et medicamenta quaedam conponit, mensurae quoque distinctione, ad maiorum arborum radices amphoram, ad minorum urnam, amurcae et

[1] ut (*an* et ?) *add. Mayhoff.*
[2] *Dalec.* : rutaque.
[3] resurgit ? *coll.* § 248, XVI. 163 *Mayhoff* : surgit.

barley straw in advance. Cherries are brought on and made to ripen by applying lime to the roots; but with cherries also, as with all fruit, it is better to thin the crop, in order to make the fruit left on grow bigger.

Medicinal treatment of vines and trees.

Some trees are improved by severe treatment or stimulated by a pungent application—for instance the palm and the mastich, which get nutriment from salt water. Ashes also have the effect of salt, but it acts more gently; consequently they are sprinkled on figs and on rue, to prevent their getting maggotty or rotting at the roots. It is also advised to pour salt water on the roots of vines if they are too full of moisture, but if their fruit falls off, to sprinkle ashes with vinegar and smear them on the vines themselves, or ashes with sandarach if the grapes rot; but if the vines do not bear, to sprinkle and smear them with ashes mixed with strong vinegar; and if they do not ripen their fruit but let it dry up first, the vines should be lopped down to the roots and the wound and fibres of the wood drenched with strong vinegar and stale urine and covered up with the mud so produced, and repeatedly dug round. If olives give too little promise of fruit, growers bare their roots and expose them to the winter cold, and the trees profit by this drastic treatment. All these methods depend on the state of the weather in each year and sometimes are required later and sometimes more speedily. Also fire is beneficial for some plants, for instance reeds, which when burnt off grow up again thicker and more pliable. Cato moreover gives prescriptions for certain medicaments, also specifying quantity—for the roots of the bigger trees an *amphora*, for those of the smaller ones half that XCIII–XCV.

aquae portione aequa, ablaqueatis prius radicibus paulatim adfundi iubens, in olea hoc amplius stramentis ante circumpositis, item fico; huius praecipue vere terram adaggerari radicibus, ita futurum ut non decidant grossi maiorque fecunditas nec scabra
264 proveniat. simili modo ne convolvolus fiat in vinea amurcae congios duos decoqui in crassitudinem mellis, rursusque cum bituminis tertia parte et sulpuris quarta sub diu coqui, quoniam exardescat sub tecto; hoc vites circa capita ac sub bracchiis ungui: ita non fore convolvolum. quidam contenti sunt fumo huius mixturae suffire vineas secundo flatu continuo triduo.
265 plerique non minus auxilii et alimenti arbitrantur in urina quam Cato in amurca, addita modo pari aquae portione, quoniam per se noceat.[1] aliqui volucre appellant animal praerodens pubescentes uvas; quod ne accidat, falces cum sint exacutae fibrina pelle detergent atque ita putant, aut sanguine ursino linunt post putationem easdem. sunt arborum pestes et
266 formicae; has abigunt rubrica ac pice liquida peruncticaudicibus, nec non et pisce suspenso iuxta in unum locum congregant, aut lupino trito cum oleo radices

[1] plerique . . . noceat *transponenda in* § 262 *post* saepe fodere? *Warmington.*

measure of olive-lees and water in equal amounts, and his instructions are first to dig round the roots and then to pour the liquid on them gradually. In the case of an olive it should be used more copiously, straw having first been put round the stem, and the same with a fig; with a fig, especially in spring, earth should be heaped up round the roots, and this will ensure that the unripe fruit will not fall off and the tree will bear a larger crop and will not develop roughness of the bark. In a similar manner to prevent a vine from breeding leaf-rolling caterpillar he advises boiling down two gallons of lees of olive-oil to the thickness of honey, and boiling it again mixed with a third part of bitumen and a fourth part of sulphur, this second boiling being done in the open air because the mixture may catch fire indoors; and he says this preparation is to be smeared round the bases and under the arms of the vines, and that will prevent caterpillar. Some growers are content with submitting the vines for three days on end to the smoke from this concoction boiled to the windward of them. Most people think there is as much food value for the plants in urine as Cato assigns to wine-lees, provided it is mixed with an equal quantity of water, because it is injurious if used by itself. Some give the name of the ' fly ' to a creature that gnaws away the young grapes; to prevent this they wipe the pruning-knives on a beaver skin after they have been sharpened and then use them for pruning, or smear them with bear's blood after pruning. Ants also are pests to trees; these are kept away by smearing the trunks with a mixture of red earth and tar, and also people get the ants to collect in one place by hanging up a fish close by, or they smear the roots

linunt. multi et has et talpas amurca necant, contraque urucas et mala putrescentia[1] lacerti viridis felle tangi cacumina iubent, privatim autem contra urucas ambiri arbores singulas a muliere initiante
267 menses, nudis pedibus, recincta. item ne quod animal pastu malefico decerpat frondem, fimo boum diluto spargi folia quotiens imber interveniat, quoniam oblinatur ita virus medicaminis, mira quaedam excogitante sollertia humana, quippe cum averti grandines carmine credant plerique, cuius verba inserere non equidem serio ausim, quamquam a Catone proditis contra luxata membra iungenda harundinum fissurae. idem arbores religiosas lucosque succidi permisit sacrificio prius facto, cuius rationem precationemque eodem volumine tradidit.

[1] putrescentia? *Mayhoff*: putrescant (mala ne putrescant *edd.*).

of the tree with lupin pounded with oil. Many people kill ants and also moles with the dregs of olive oil, and to protect the tops of the trees against caterpillars and pests productive of decay they advise touching them with the gall of a green lizard, but as a protection against caterpillars in particular they say that a woman just beginning her monthly courses should walk round each of the trees with bare feet and her girdle undone. Also to prevent any creature from injuring the foliage by noxious nibbling they recommend sprinkling the leaves with cow-dung mixed with water every time there is a shower of rain, as the rain smears the poison of the mixture over the tree: so remarkable are some of the devices invented by human skill, inasmuch as most people believe that hailstorms can be averted by means of a charm, the words of which I would not for my own part venture seriously to introduce into my book, although Cato has published the words CLX, CXXXIX.
of a charm for sprained limbs which have to be bandaged to reed splints. The same author has allowed the felling of consecrated trees and groves after a preliminary sacrifice has been performed, the ritual of which and the accompanying prayer he has reported in the same volume.

BOOK XVIII

LIBER XVIII

1 I. Sequitur natura frugum hortorumque ac florum quaeque alia praeter arbores aut frutices benigna tellure proveniunt, vel per se tantum herbarum inmensa contemplatione, si quis aestimet varietatem, numerum, flores, odores coloresque et sucos ac vires earum quas salutis aut voluptatis hominum gratia gignit. qua in parte primum omnium patrocinari terrae et adesse cunctorum parenti iuvat, quam-
2 quam inter initia operis defensae. quoniam tamen ipsa materia accedimus[1] ad reputationem eiusdem parientis et noxia, nostris eam criminibus urguemus nostramque culpam illi inputamus. genuit venena, set quis invenit illa praeter hominem? cavere ac refugere alitibus ferisque satis est. atque cum arbore exacuant limentque cornua elephanti et uri, saxo rhinocerotes, utroque apri dentium sicas, sciantque ad nocendum praeparare se animalia, quod tamen eorum excepto homine et tela sua venenis
3 tinguit? nos et sagittas unguimus ac ferro ipsi nocen-

[1] *Mayhoff* (inducti accedimus? *Rackham*): accedit intus.

BOOK XVIII

I. Our next subject is the nature of the various kinds of grain and of gardens and flowers and the other products of Earth's bounty beside trees or shrubs, the study of herbaceous plants being itself of boundless scope, if one considers the variety and number, the blossoms, scents and colours, and the juices and properties of the plants that she engenders for the health or the gratification of men. And in this section it is our pleasant duty first of all to champion Earth's cause and to support her as the parent of all things, although we have already pleaded her defence in the opening part of this treatise. Nevertheless, now that our subject itself brings us to consider her also as the producer of noxious objects, they are our own crimes with which we charge her and our own faults which we impute to her. She has engendered poisons—but who discovered them except man? Birds and beasts are content merely to avoid them and keep away from them. And although the elephant and the ure-ox sharpen and whet their horns on a tree and the rhinoceros on a rock, and boars point the poniards of their tusks upon both trees and rocks, and even animals know how to prepare themselves for inflicting injury, yet which of them excepting man also dips its weapons in poison? As for us, we even poison our arrows

Cereal agriculture. Earth's bounteous products and man's abuse of them.

II. 154 ff.

tius aliquid damus, nos et flumina inficimus et rerum naturae elementa, ipsumque quo vivitur in perniciem vertimus. neque est ut putemus ignorari ea ab animalibus; quae praeparent enim[1] contra serpentium dimicationes, quae post proelium ad medendum excogitarint, indicavimus. nec ab ullo praeter
4 hominem veneno pugnatur alieno. fateamur ergo culpam ne iis quidem quae nascuntur contenti; etenim quanto[2] plura eorum genera humana manu fiunt! quid? non et hominis quidem vi[3] venena nascuntur? atra ceu serpentium lingua vibrat tabesque animi contacta adurit culpantium omnia ac dirarum alitum modo tenebris quoque suis et ipsarum noctium quieti invidentium gemitu, quae sola vox eorum est, ut inauspicatarum animantium vice obvii quoque
5 vetent agere aut prodesse vitae. nec ullum aliud abominati spiritus praemium novere quam odisse omnia. verum et in hoc eadem naturae maiestas: quanto plures bonos genuit ut fruges! quanto fertilior in his quae iuvent alantque! quorum aestimatione et gaudio nos quoque relictis exustioni suae istis hominum rubis pergemus excolere vitam, eoque constantius quo operae nobis maior quam famae gratia expetitur. quippe sermo circa rura est

[1] enim *add. Detlefsen.*
[2] *Huet*: quando.
[3] *Detlefsen.*: ut.

---

[a] *I.e.* the air.

and add to the destructive properties of iron itself; we dye even the rivers and the elemental substances of Nature, and turn the very means[a] of life into a bane. Nor is it possible for us to suppose that animals do not know of these things; for we have indicated the preparations that they make to guard against encounters with serpents and the remedies that they have devised to employ after the battle. Nor does any creature save man fight with poison borrowed from another. Let us therefore confess our guilt, we who are not content even with natural products, inasmuch as how far more numerous are the varieties of them made by the human hand! Why, are not even poisons actually the product of man's violence? Their livid tongue flickers like the serpent's, and the corruption of their mind scorches the things it touches, maligning all things as they do and like birds of evil omen violating even the darkness that is their own element and the quiet of the night itself with their groaning, the only sound they utter, so that like animals of evil omen when they even cross our path they forbid us to act or to be of service to life. And they know no other reward for their abhorred vitality than to hate all things. But in this matter also Nature's grandeur is the same: how many more good men has she engendered as her harvest! How much more fertile is she in products that give aid and nourishment! We too then will continue to enrich life with the value we set on these things and the delight they give us, leaving those brambles of the human race to the consuming fire that is theirs, and all the more resolutely because we achieve greater gratification from industry than we do from renown. The subject

VIII. 88, 96 ff.

agrestesque usus, sed quibus vita constet honosque apud priscos maximus fuerit.

6 II. Arvorum sacerdotes Romulus in primis instituit seque duodecimum fratrem appellavit inter illos Acca Larentia nutrice sua genitos, spicea corona quae vitta alba colligaretur sacerdotio ei pro religiosissimo insigni data, quae prima apud Romanos fuit corona; honosque is non nisi vita finitur et exules etiam
7 captosque comitatur. bina tunc iugera p. R. satis erant, nullique maiorem modum adtribuit, quo servorum paulo ante principis Neronis contento huius spatii viridiariis? piscinas iuvat maiores habere, gratumque si non aliquem culinas. Numa instituit deos fruge colere et mola salsa supplicare atque, ut auctor est Hemina, far torrere, quoniam tostum cibo salubrius esset, id uno modo consecutus, statuendo
8 non esse purum ad rem divinam ni tostum. is et Fornacalia instituit farris torrendi ferias et aeque religiosas Terminis agrorum; hos enim deos tum maxime noverant, Seiamque a serendo, Segestam a segetibus appellabant, quarum simulacra in

---

[a] The twelve Fratres Arvales who offered a yearly sacrifice to the Lares of the fields in order to secure good harvests.

[b] Properly *far* = *ador* = ζειὰ δίκοκκος was *Triticum dicoccum* two-grained or 'emmer-wheat', not 'spelt'. *Far* was beardless (§ 92), but most 'emmers' now have beards.

of our discourse is indeed the countryside and rustic practices, but it is on these that life depends and that the highest honour was bestowed in early days.

Early Roman agriculture.

II. Romulus at the outset instituted the Priests of the Fields,[a] and nominated himself as the twelfth brother among them, the others being the sons of his foster-mother Acca Larentia; it was to this priesthood that was assigned as a most sacred emblem the first crown ever worn at Rome, a wreath of ears of corn tied together with a white fillet; and this dignity only ends with life, and accompanies its holders even into exile or captivity. In those days two acres of land each was enough for the Roman people, who assigned to no one a larger amount—which of the persons who but a little time before were the slaves of the Emperor Nero would have been satisfied with an ornamental garden of that extent? They like to have fishponds larger than that, and it is a thing to be thankful for if someone does not insist on kitchens covering a greater area. Numa established worship of the gods with an offering of corn and winning their favour with a salted cake, and, according to Hemina, of roasting emmer wheat[b] because it was more wholesome for food when roasted—though he could attain this only in one way, by establishing that emmer was not in a pure condition for a religious offering unless it had been roasted. It was also Numa who established the Feast of Ovens, the holiday when emmer is roasted, and the equally solemn holiday dedicated to the Boundary-marks of estates, these bounds being in those days particularly recognized as gods, with the goddesses Seia named from sowing the seed and Segesta from reaping the harvest, whose statues we see in the

circo videmus—tertiam ex his nominare sub tecto
religio est—ac ne degustabant quidem novas fruges
aut vina antequam sacerdotes primitias libassent.
9 III. Iugerum [1] vocabatur quod uno iugo boum in
die exarari posset, actus in quo boves agerentur cum
aratro uno impetu iusto; hic erat cxx pedum,
duplicatusque in longitudinem iugerum faciebat.
dona amplissima imperatorum ac fortium civium
quantum quis uno die plurimum circumaravisset,
item quartarii farris aut heminae, conferente populo.
10 cognomina etiam prima inde: Pilumni qui pilum
pistrinis invenerat, Pisonis a pisendo, iam Fabiorum,
Lentulorum, Ciceronum, ut quisque aliquod optime
genus sereret. Iuniorum e [2] familia Bubulcum
nominarunt quia bubus optime utebatur. quin et in
sacris nihil religiosius confarreationis vinculo erat,
11 novaeque nuptae farreum praeferebant. agrum male
colere censorium probrum iudicabatur, atque, ut
refert Cato, cum virum [3] laudantes bonum agricolam
bonumque colonum dixissent, amplissime laudasse

[1] Iugum *e Varronis R.R.* 1. 10 *Ursinus.*
[2] e (*aut* in ?) *add. Mayhoff.*
[3] virum ⟨bonum⟩ *e Catone Mayhoff.*

---

[a] It is not clear whether this means Segesta, including in the list the Termini as well as Seia, or whether a third guardian deity, Tutelina, is hinted at.

[b] The term 'plough-gate' might suggest the association of terms indicated.

[c] *Actus,* lit. a 'drive'; our furlong is $5\frac{1}{2}$ times as long. The *iugerum* described was 40 × 80 yards or 3200 square yards, our acre being 4840 square yards.

[d] *I.e.* the *cognomen* of the family, which was preceded by the *nomen* of the *gens,* and that by the *praenomen* of the individual.

Circus—the third[a] of these divinities it is irreverent even to mention by name indoors—and people used not even to taste the produce of a new harvest or vintage before the priests had offered a libation of the first-fruits.

Early customs recalled in nomenclature and vocabulary.

III. An area of land that one yoke of oxen could plough in a day used to be called an acre,[b] and a distance which oxen could be driven with a plough in a single spell of reasonable length was called a furlong[c]; this was 40 yards, and doubled longways this made an acre. The most lavish gifts bestowed on generals and valorous citizens were the largest area of land that a person could plough round in one day, and also a contribution from the whole people of one or two quarterns of emmer wheat a head. Moreover the earliest surnames[d] were derived from agriculture: the name 'Pilumnus' belonged to the inventor of the 'pestle' for corn-mills, 'Piso' came from 'pounding' corn, and again families were named Fabius or Lentulus or Cicero[e] according as someone was the best grower of some particular crop. One of the Junius family received the name of Bubulcus because he was very good at managing oxen. Moreover among religious rites none was invested with more sanctity than that of Communion in Wheat, and newly married brides used to carry in their hands an offering of wheat. Bad husbandry was judged an offence within the jurisdiction of the censors, and, as Cato[f] tells us, to praise a man by saying he was a good farmer and a good husbandman was thought to

[e] *Faba* 'bean', *lens* 'lentil', *cicer* 'chick-pea'. The personal names if actually derived from these vegetables were more probably nick-names than trade-names.

[f] Praef. 2, 3.

existimabantur. hinc et locupletes dicebant loci, hoc est agri, plenos. pecunia ipsa a pecore appellabatur et etiam nunc in tabulis censoris pascua dicuntur, omnia ex quibus populus reditus habet, quia diu hoc solum vectigal fuerat. multatio quoque non nisi ovium boumque inpendio dicebatur; nec omittenda priscarum legum benivolentia: cautum quippe est ne bovem prius quam ovem nominaret qui indiceret
12 multam. ludos boum causa celebrantes Bubetios vocabant. Servius rex ovium boumque effigie primum aes signavit. frugem quidem aratro quaesitam furtim noctu pavisse ac secuisse puberi XII tabulis capital erat, suspensumque Cereri necari iubebant gravius quam in homicidio convictum, inpubem praetoris arbitratu verberari noxiamve duplionemve[1]
13 decerni. iam distinctio honosque civitatis ipsius non aliunde erat. rusticae tribus laudatissimae eorum qui rura haberent, urbanae vero in quas transferri ignominia esset, desidiae probro. itaque quattuor solae erant a partibus urbis in quibus habitabant, Suburana, Palatina, Collina, Esquilina. nundinis urbem revisitabant et ideo comitia nundinis habere

[1] noxiamque duplione *Hardouin*: noxaeve duplionem *Lipsius*: noxiamve duplione decidi *Schoell.*

---

[a] Perhaps the text should be altered to give 'and'.
[b] 'Ninth-day', or by our form of expression, 'eighth-day', holidays.

be the highest form of commendation. That is the source of the word *locuples*, meaning 'wealthy', 'full of room', *i.e.* of land. Our word for money itself was derived from *pecus*, 'cattle', and even now in the censor's accounts all the sources of national revenue are termed 'pastures', because rent of pasture-land was for a long time the only source of public income. Moreover fines were only specified in terms of payment of sheep and oxen; nor must we omit the benevolent spirit of the law of early times, in that a judge imposing a fine was prohibited from specifying an ox before he had previously fined the offender a sheep. There were public games in honour of oxen, those conducting them being called the Bubetii. King Servius stamped first the bronze coinage with the likeness of sheep and oxen. Indeed the Twelve Tables made pasturing animals by stealth at night on crops grown under the plough, or cutting it, a capital offence for an adult, and enacted that a person found guilty of it should be executed by hanging, in reparation to Ceres, a heavier punishment than in a conviction for homicide; while a minor was to be flogged at the discretion of the praetor or[a] sentenced to pay the amount of the damage or twice that amount. In fact the system of class and office in the state itself was derived from no other source. The rural tribes were the most esteemed, consisting of those who owned farms, whereas the city tribes were tribes into which it was a disgrace to be transferred, this stigmatizing lack of activity. Consequently the city tribes were only four, named from the parts of the city in which their members resided, the Suburan, Palatine, Colline and Esquiline. They used to resort to the city on market-days,[b] and

14 non licebat, ne plebes rustica avocaretur. quies somnusque in stramentis erat. gloriam denique ipsam a farris honore adoriam appellabant. equidem ipsa etiam verba priscae significationis admiror: ita enim est in commentariis pontificum: 'Augurio canario agendo dies constituatur priusquam[1] frumenta vaginis exeant et antequam[2] in vaginas perveniant.'

15 IV. Ergo his moribus non modo sufficiebant fruges nulla provinciarum pascente Italiam, verum etiam annonae vilitas incredibilis erat. Manius Marcius aedilis plebis primum frumentum populo in modios assibus datavit. L. Minucius Augurinus, qui Spurium Maelium coarguerat, farris pretium in trinis nundinis ad assem redegit undecumus plebei tribunus, qua de causa statua ei extra portam trigeminam a populo
16 stipe conlata statuta est. T. Seius in aedilitate assibus populo frumentum praestitit, quam ob causam et ei statuae in Capitolio ac Palatio dicatae sunt, ipse supremo die populi umeris portatus in rogum est. quo verum anno Mater deum advecta Romam est, maiorem ea aestate messem quam antecedentibus
17 annis decem factam esse tradunt. M. Varro auctor

[1] postquam? *Rackham.* [2] nec antequam *Urlichs.*

---

[a] *Adoria,* or as other copies here and elsewhere give the word, *adorea,* was supposed to be derived from *ador,* grain of emmer wheat (*semen adoreum* Cato, Varro), particularly its flour; and to be a by-form of *gloria.*

[b] Perhaps the Latin should be altered to give 'after the corn comes out of the husk and not before', etc.

[c] He was co-opted as an additional tribune and appointed *praefectus annonae* in a time of famine, 439 B.C.

[d] In 204 B.C., during the Second Punic War, the statue of Cybele was brought from Pessinus in Galatia.

consequently elections were not allowed to be held on market-days, so that the common people of the country might not be called away from their homes. Beds of straw were used for a siesta and for sleeping on. Finally the actual word 'glory' used to be 'adory',[a] owing to the honour in which emmer was held. For my own part I admire even actual words used in their old signification; for the following sentence occurs in the *Memoranda of the Priesthood*: 'Let a day be fixed for taking augury by the sacrifice of a dog before the corn comes out of the sheath and before it penetrates through into the sheath.'[b]

IV. Accordingly these being the customs not only were the harvests sufficient for them without any of the provinces providing food for Italy, but even the market price of corn was unbelievably low. Manius Marcius when aedile of the plebs for the first time provided the people with corn at the price of an *as* a peck. Lucius Minucius Augurinus, who had procured the conviction of Spurius Maelius, when he was eleventh[c] tribune of the people reduced the price of emmer to an *as* for a fortnight, and consequently had his statue erected outside the Triplets' Gate, the cost being met by public subscription. Titus Seius during his aedileship supplied the public with corn at an *as* a peck, on account of which he too had statues erected to him on the Capitol and the Palatine, and he himself at the end of his life was carried to his cremation on the shoulders of the populace. Then it is recorded that in the summer of the year in which the Mother of the Gods was carried to Rome[d] there was a larger harvest than in the preceding ten years. Marcus Varro states that

Low prices in early days.

456 B.C.

345 B.C.

est, cum L. Metellus in triumpho plurimos duxit elephantos, assibus singulis farris modios fuisse, item vini congios ficique siccae pondo xxx, olei pondo x, carnis pondo xii. nec e latifundiis singulorum contingebat arcentium vicinos, quippe etiam lege Stolonis Licinii incluso modo quingentorum iugerum, et ipso sua lege damnato cum substituta filii persona amplius possideret. luxuriantis iam rei p. fuit ista
18 mensura. Manii quidem Curii post triumphos inmensumque terrarum adiectum imperio nota dictio est perniciosum intellegi civem cui septem iugera non essent satis; haec enim [1] mensura plebei post exactos
19 reges adsignata est. quaenam ergo tantae ubertatis causa erat? ipsorum tunc manibus imperatorum colebantur agri, ut fas est credere, gaudente terra vomere laureato et triumphali aratore, sive illi eadem cura semina tractabant qua bella eademque diligentia arva disponebant qua castra, sive honestis manibus omnia laetius proveniunt quoniam et curiosius fiunt.
20 serentem invenerunt dati honores Serranum, unde ei et cognomen. aranti quattuor sua iugera in Vaticano, quae Prata Quintia appellantur, Cincinnato viator

[1] *Rackham*: autem.

at the date when Lucius Metellus gave a procession of a very large number of elephants in his triumph, the price of a peck of emmer wheat was one *as*, as also was that of a gallon of wine, 30 pounds of dried figs, 10 pounds of oil and 12 pounds of meat. Nor was this the result of the large estates of individuals who ousted their neighbours, inasmuch as by the law of Licinius Stolo the limit was restricted to 500 acres, and Stolo himself was convicted under his own law because he owned a larger amount of land, held under his son's name instead of his own. Such was the scale of prices when the state had already some luxury. At any rate there is a famous utterance of Manius Curius, who after celebrating triumphs and making a vast addition of territory to the empire, said that a man not satisfied with seven acres must be deemed a dangerous citizen; for that was the acreage assigned for commoners after the expulsion of the kings. What therefore was the cause of such great fertility? The fields were tilled in those days by the hands of generals themselves, and we may well believe that the earth rejoiced in a laurel-decked ploughshare and a ploughman who had celebrated a triumph, whether it was that those farmers treated the seed with the same care as they managed their wars and marked out their fields with the same diligence as they arranged a camp, or whether everything prospers better under honourable hands because the work is done with greater attention. The honours bestowed on Serranus found him sowing seed, which was actually the origin of his surname. An apparitor brought to Cincinnatus his commission as dictator when he was ploughing his four-acre property on the Vatican, the land now

150 B.C.

368–7 B.C.

290 B.C.

Agriculture honoured.

257 B.C.

458 B.C.

attulit dictaturam et quidem, ut traditur, nudo, plenoque[1] nuntius morarum,[2] ‘Vela corpus’, inquit, ‘ut perferam senatus populique Romani mandata’.
21 tales tum etiam viatores erant, quod ipsum nomen inditum est subinde ex agris senatum ducesque arcessentibus. at nunc eadem illa vincti pedes, damnatae manus inscriptique vultus exercent, non tam surda tellure quae parens appellatur colique dicitur ut ipso opere[3] ab his adsumpto non invita ea et indignante credatur id fieri. et[4] nos miramur ergastulorum non eadem emolumenta esse quae fuerint imperatorum!

22 V. Igitur de cultura agri praecipere principale fuit etiam apud exteros, siquidem et reges fecere, Hiero, Philometor Attalus, Archelaus, et duces, Xenophon et Poenus etiam Mago, cui quidem tantum honorem senatus noster habuit Carthagine capta ut, cum regulis Africae bibliothecas donaret, unius eius duodetriginta volumina censeret in Latinam linguam transferenda,
23 cum iam M. Cato praecepta condidisset, peritisque Punicae dandum negotium, in quo praecessit omnes

[1] *Edd.*: plenosque *aut* plenusque.

[2] nuntius morarum *cd. Leid. n.* VII, *m.* 2: nunti ac morum *rell. Varia docti.*

[3] ipso *Mayhoff*, opere *Sillig*: ut onere (*aut* et ipsa honere *aut alia*).

[4] *C. F. W. Mueller*: sed.

---

[a] *Viator*, ‘setter on the way’; but the word commonly meant ‘wayfarer’.

[b] A play on two meanings of the word *colere*.

[c] *Ergastula*, ‘work-houses’, were private prisons kept on large estates in which refractory slaves were made to work in chains.

called the Quintian Meadows, and indeed it is said that he had stripped for the work, and the messenger as he continued to linger said, 'Put on your clothes, so that I may deliver the mandates of the Senate and People of Rome'. That was what apparitors were like even at that time, and their name itself[a] was given to them as summoning the senate and the leaders to put in an immediate appearance from their farms. But nowadays those agricultural operations are performed by slaves with fettered ankles and by the hands of malefactors with branded faces! although the Earth who is addressed as our mother and whose cultivation is spoken of[b] as worship is not so dull that when we obtain even our farm-work from these persons one can believe that this is not done against her will and to her indignation. And we forsooth are surprised that we do not get the same profits from the labour of slave-gangs[c] as used to be obtained from that of generals!

Early treatises on agriculture.

V. Consequently to give instructions for agriculture was an occupation of the highest dignity even with foreign nations, inasmuch as it was actually performed by kings such as Hiero, Attalus Philometor and Archelaus, and by generals such as Xenophon and also the Carthaginian Mago, on whom indeed our senate bestowed such great honour, after the taking of Carthage, that when it gave away the city's libraries to the petty kings of Africa it passed a resolution that in his case alone his twenty-eight volumes should be translated into Latin, in spite of the fact that Marcus Cato had already compiled his book of precepts, and that the task should be given to persons acquainted with the Carthaginian language, an accomplishment in

vir clarissimae familiae D. Silanus. sapientiae vero auctores et carminibus excellentes quique alii illustres viri conposuissent quos sequemur praetexuimus hoc in volumine, non in grege nominando M. Varrone qui LXXXI vitae annum agens de ea re prodendum putavit.

24 Apud Romanos multo serius [1] vitium cultura esse coepit, primoque, ut necesse erat, arva tantum coluere, quorum a nobis nunc ratio tractabitur non volgari modo verum, ut adhuc fecimus, et vetustis et postea inventis omni cura perquisitis causaque rerum et ratione simul eruta. dicemus et sidera, siderumque ipsorum terrestria signa dabimus indubitata, quandoquidem qui adhuc diligentius ea tractavere quibusvis potius quam agricolis scripsisse possunt videri.

25 VI. Ac primum omnium oraculis maiore e parte agemus, quae non in alio vitae genere plura certiorave sunt: cur enim non videantur oracula a certissimo die maximeque veridico usu profecta?

26 Principium autem a Catone sumemus: 'Fortissimi viri et milites strenuissimi ex agricolis gignuntur minimeque male cogitantes.' 'Praedium ne cupide emas.' in re rustica 'operae ne parcas, in agro emendo' minime; quod male emptum est semper

[1] *Rackham*: serior.

---

[a] *Praef.* 4; and I. 1; 3.

which Decimus Silanus, a man of most distinguished family, surpassed everybody. But we have given at the beginning a list of the philosophers of originality and the eminent poets and other distinguished authors whom we shall follow in this volume, although special mention must be made of Marcus Varro, who felt moved to publish a treatise on this subject in the eighty-first year of his life.

Vol. I. p. 87.

Method followed in the present essay.

Vine-growing began among the Romans much later, and at the beginning, as of necessity, they only practised agriculture, the theory of which we will now deal with, not in the common method but, as we have done hitherto, by making an exhaustive research into both ancient practices and subsequent discoveries, and at the same time delving into causes and principles. We shall also treat of astronomy, and shall give the indubitable signs which the stars themselves afford as regards the earth, inasmuch as authors who have hitherto handled these subjects with some degree of thoroughness may be thought to have been writing for any class of people rather than farmers.

207 ff.

VI. And first of all we will proceed for the most part by the guidance of oracular precepts, which in no other department of life are more numerous or more trustworthy—for why not assign oracular value to precepts originating from the infallible test of time and the supremely truthful verdict of experience?

Cato's advice and other wise rules as to buying a farm.

We will borrow a commencement from Cato:[a] 'The agricultural class produces the bravest men, the most gallant soldiers and the citizens least given to evil designs.' 'In buying a farm do not be too eager.' In rural affairs 'do not be sparing of trouble, least of all in buying land'; a bad purchase is always

paenitet[b]. agrum paraturos ante omnia intueri oportet 'aquam, viam, vicinum'. Singula magnas interpreta-
27 tiones habent nec dubias. Cato in conterminis hoc amplius aestimari iubet, quo pacto niteant[1]; 'in bona enim', inquit, 'regione bene nitent'. Atilius Regulus ille Punico bello[a] bis consul aiebat neque fecundissimis locis insalubrem agrum parandum, neque effetis saluberrimum. salubritas loci non semper incolarum colore detegitur, quoniam adsueti etiam in pestilentibus durant. praeterea sunt quaedam partibus anni salubria, nihil autem salutare est nisi quod toto anno
28 salubre est. 'Malus est ager cum quo dominus luctatur.' Cato inter prima spectari iubet ut solum sua virtute valeat qua dictum est positione, ut operariorum copia prope sit oppidumque validum, ut navigiorum evectus vel itinerum, ut bene aedificatus et cultus, in quo falli plerosque video, segnitiem enim prioris domini pro emptore esse arbitrantur: nihil est damnosius deserto agro. itaque Cato de bono domino melius emi, nec temere contemnendam alienam disciplinam, agroque ut homini, quamvis

[1] *Caesarius e Catone*: vivant *edd. vett.*: iubeant.

---

[a] The First, 264–241 B.C.
[b] Columella I. iii.

repented. Those about to buy land should before
all things give an eye to 'the water supply, the road,
and the neighbour'. Each of these rules admits
of an important and unquestionable interpretation.
Cato advises that in regard to the neighbouring I. 2.
farmers further consideration should be given to the
question how prosperous they look; 'for in a good
district', he says, 'the people look in good condition'.
Atilius Regulus who was twice consul during the
Punic war[a] used to say that it is a mistake to buy
unhealthy land in the most fertile districts or the
most healthy land in districts that have been worked
out. The healthy quality of the district is not always
disclosed by the complexion of the inhabitants,
because people can carry on even in very unhealthy
localities when they are used to them. Moreover
some districts are healthy during portions of the
year, but no place is really salubrious unless it is
healthy all the year round. 'Land with which the
owner has a continual struggle is bad land.'[b] Cato
bids us as one of the first points to see that the land I. ff.
in the position stated above has a good quality of XVII. 36.
its own, that there is a supply of labour near, and a
thriving town, routes for carrying produce away by
water or by road, and that the farm is furnished
with good buildings and has been well farmed—it
is in this that I notice most people make a mistake,
as they think that the purchaser scores from slack
farming on the part of the previous landlord, whereas
nothing is a greater source of loss than a farm that
has been neglected. For this reason Cato says that
it is better to purchase from a good landlord, and that
the lessons to be learnt from others should not be
despised, and that it is the same with land as with a

quaestuosus sit, si tamen et sumptuosus, non multum
29 superesse. ille in agro quaestuosissimam iudicat vitem—non frustra, quoniam ante omnia de inpensae ratione cavit—proxime hortos irriguos. nec id falso, si sub oppido sint—et prata antiqui parata dixere. idemque Cato interrogatus qui[1] esset certissimus quaestus, respondit 'Si bene pascas', qui proximus?
30 'Si sat bene': summa omnium in hoc spectando fuit ut fructus is maxime probaretur qui quam minimo inpendio constaturus esset. hoc ex locorum occasione aliter alibi decernitur; eodemque pertinet quod
31 agricolam Cato vendacem esse oportere dixit, fundum in adulescentia conserendum sine cunctatione, aedificandum non nisi consito agro, tunc quoque cunctanter (optimumque est, ut volgo dixere, aliena insania frui, sed ita ut villarum tutela non sit oneri), eum tamen qui bene habitet saepius ventitare in agrum—frontemque domini plus prodesse quam occipitium non mentiuntur.

32 VII. Modus hic probatur ut neque fundus villam quaerat neque villa fundum, non, ut fecere[2] iuxta diversis in[3] eadem aetate exemplis L. Lucullus et Q. Scaevola, cum villa Scaevolae fructus non caperet,

[1] qui? *Mayhoff*: quis.
[2] *Mayhoff*: fecerit.
[3] *Mayhoff* (diversis *Erasmus ed. Bas.*): diversum.

---

[a] *I.e.* to buy houses built by others.

human being—it may make large profits, yet if it also involves large expenses, not much balance is left over. In Cato's opinion the most profitable I. 7.
part of a farm is a vineyard—and not without reason, since above everything he has been cautious as to the matter of outlay of money—and next he puts kitchen-gardens well supplied with water; and this is true, if they are near a town—and the old word for 'meadows' means 'land ready to hand'. Cato moreover when asked what was the most reliable source of profit said, 'Good pasture', and when asked what was the next best, said, 'Fairly good pasture': the most important point in considering profit being that the crop that was going to cost the smallest outlay in expenses was the crop most to be recommended. This is a question decided differently in different places, in accordance with the suitability of the various localities; and the same applies to Cato's dictum that a farmer ought to be a good seller; and that he should begin to plant his farm without delay, in his youth, but only build when the land is fully under cultivation, and even then go slowly (and the best course is, as the common saying was, to profit by the folly of other people,[a] provided however that keeping up houses is not allowed to be a burden on your estate); but that the owner who is well housed should nevertheless keep visiting his farm rather frequently—and it is a true saying that 'the master's face does more good than the back of his head'.

The farm-house: size and situation.

VII. The satisfactory plan is that the house shall not be inadequate to the farm nor the farm to the house, not as was done on adjacent estates by Lucius Lucullus and Quintus Scaevola, acting on opposite principles though at the same period, when

villam Luculli ager, quo in genere censoria castigatio erat minus arare quam verrere. nec hoc sine arte quadam est. novissimus villam in Misenensi posuit C. Marius VII cos. sed peritia castra metandi, sic ut conparatos ei ceteros etiam Sulla Felix caecos fuisse
33 diceret. convenit neque iuxta paludes ponendam esse neque adverso amne, quamquam Homerus omnino e[1] flumine semper antelucanas auras insalubres verissime tradidit. spectare in aestuosis locis septentriones debet, meridiem in frigidis, in temperatis exortum aequinoctialem.

34 Agri ipsius bonitas quibus argumentis iudicanda sit, quamquam de terrae genere optimo disserentes abunde dixisse possumus videri, etiamnum tamen traditas notas subsignabimus Catonis[2] maxime verbis: 'Ebulum vel prunus silvestris vel rubus, bulbus minutus, trifolium, herba pratensis, quercus, silvestris pirus malusque frumentarii soli notae, item nigra terra et cinerei coloris. omnis creta coquet nisi permacra, sabulumque nisi id etiam pertenue est; et multo campestribus magis quam clivosis respondent eadem.'

[1] e *add. edd.*
[2] Columellae *Pintianus*: Magonis *Klotz.*

---

[a] Marius's great enemy.
[b] *I.e.* whether the river is in front of the house or behind it. *Od.* V. 469. Αὔρη δ' ἐκ ποταμοῦ ψυχρὴ πνέει ἠῶθι πρό.
The passage quoted does not occur in the extant writings of Cato.

Scaevola's farmhouse would not hold the produce of his farm and Lucullus's farm was not big enough for his house—a sort of extravagance that occasioned the censor's rebuke that there was less ground to plough than floor-space to sweep. The proper arrangement requires a certain amount of technical skill. Quite recently Gaius Marius, who was seven times consul, built a country house in the district of Miseno, but he relied on the skill he had acquired in planning the lay-out of a camp, so that even Sulla [a] the Fortunate declared that all the others had been blind men in comparison with Marius. It is agreed that a country house ought not to be put near a marsh nor with a river in front of it—although Homer has stated with the greatest truth that in any case [b] there are always unhealthy currents of air rising from a river before dawn. In hot localities the house should look north, in cold ones south and in temperate situations due east.

As to proofs by which the quality of the land itself can be judged, we may possibly be thought to have spoken of these with sufficient fullness when discussing the best kind of soil, but nevertheless we will still supplement the indications we have given by some words of Cato [c] more particularly: 'The danewort or the wild plum or the bramble, the small-bulb, trefoil, meadow grass, oak, wild pears and wild apple are indications of a soil fit for corn, as also is black or ash-coloured earth. All chalk land will scorch the crop unless it is an extremely thin soil, and so will sand unless it also is extremely fine; and the same soils answer much better for plantations on level ground than for those on a slope.'

Quality of land.

XVII. 25 ff.

35 Modum agri in primis servandum antiqui putavere, quippe ita censebant, satius esse minus serere et melius arare, qua in sententia et Vergilium fuisse video. verumque confitentibus latifundia perdidere Italiam, iam vero et provincias—sex domini semissem Africae possidebant, cum interfecit eos Nero princeps —non fraudando magnitudine hac quoque sua Cn. Pompeio qui numquam agrum mercatus est conterminum. agro empto domum vendendam inclementer atque non ex utilitate publici status Mago censuit hoc exordio praecepta pandere ingressus, ut tamen appareat adsiduitatem desideratam ab eo.

36 Dehinc peritia vilicorum in cura habenda est, multaque de his Cato praecepit. nobis satis sit dixisse quam proximum domino corde esse debere et tamen sibimet ipsi non videri. coli rura ab ergastulis pessumum est, ut quidquid agitur a desperantibus. temerarium videatur unam vocem antiquorum posuisse, et fortassis incredibile ni [1] penitus aestimetur: 'nihil minus expedire quam agrum optime colere.'

37 L. Tarius Rufus infima natalium humilitate consulatum militari industria meritus, antiquae alias parsi-

[1] ni *om. v.l.*

---

[a] *Georgics* II. 412, Laudato ingentia rura, Exiguum colito.
[b] *R.R.* V.
[c] 17 B.C.

In old times it was thought that to observe moderation in the size of a farm was of primary importance, inasmuch as the view was held that it was more satisfactory to sow less land and plough it better; and I observe that Virgil[a] was of this opinion. And if the truth be confessed, large estates have been the ruin of Italy, and are now proving the ruin of the provinces too—half of Africa was owned by six landlords, when the Emperor Nero put them to death; though Gnaeus Pompeius must not be cheated out of this mark of his greatness also: he never bought land belonging to a neighbouring estate. Mago's opinion that a landlord after buying a farm ought to sell his town house—that being the opening with which he begins the exposition of his instructions—was too rigorous, and not to the advantage of public affairs, though nevertheless it has the effect of showing that he laid stress on the need for constant oversight. *Size of farm.*

The next point requiring attention is the efficiency of bailiffs, and Cato has given[b] many instructions with regard to these. Let it be enough for us to say that the bailiff ought to be as near as possible to his master in intelligence, and nevertheless not think so himself. Farming done by slave-gangs hired from houses of correction is utterly bad, as is everything else done by desperate men. It may appear rash to quote one dictum of the old writers, and perhaps it may be judged impossible to credit unless its value is closely examined—it is that nothing pays less than really good farming. Lucius Tarius Rufus, who, though of extremely humble birth, by his soldierly efficiency won[c] a consulship, though in other respects a man of old-fashioned economy, spent the whole *Qualifications of farm bailiff.* *Economic farming.*

moniae, circiter |M| HS. liberalitate divi Augusti congestorum[1] usque ad detrectationem heredis exhausit agros in Piceno coemendo colendoque in gloriam.[2] internicionem ergo famemque censemus? immo, Hercules, modum iudicem rerum omnium
38 utilissimum. bene colere necessarium est, optime damnosum, praeterquam subole sua[3] colono aut pascendis alioqui colente. domino aliquas[4] messes colligere non expedit si conputetur inpendium operae, nec temere olivam, nec quasdam terras diligenter colere, sicut in Sicilia tradunt, itaque decipi advenas.

39 VIII. Quonam igitur modo utilissime colentur agri? ex oraculo scilicet: 'malis bonis.' sed defendi aequum est abavos qui praeceptis suis prospexere vitae; namque cum dicerent 'malis', intellegere voluere vilissimos, summumque providentiae illorum fuit ut quam minimum esset inpendii. praecipiebant enim ista qui triumphales denas argenti libras in supellectile crimini dabant, qui mortuo vilico relinquere victorias et reverti in rura sua postulabant, quorum heredia colenda suscipiebat res p., exercitusque ducebant

[1] congestorum? *Mayhoff*: congestum.
[2] in gloria (*ad sequ. relatum*) *Hermolaus*.
[3] *Edd.*: suo.
[4] amplas? *Mayhoff*.

---

[a] The term *heredium* was used to denote a small estate of 2 *iugera*, about 1¼ acres.

of the money he had accumulated through the generosity of his late Majesty Augustus, about 100 million sesterces, in buying up farms in Picenum and farming them with the purpose of making a name for himself, so that his heir refused to take over the estate. Is it our opinion then that this policy means ruin and starvation? Nay rather, I vow, it is that moderation is the most valuable criterion of all things. Good farming is essential, but superlatively good farming spells ruin, except when the farmer runs the farm with his own family or with persons whom he is in any case bound to maintain. There are some crops which it does not pay the landlord to harvest if the cost of the labour is reckoned, and olives are not easily made to pay; and some lands do not repay very careful farming—this is said to be the case in Sicily, and consequently newcomers there find themselves deceived.

General principles of farming.

VIII. What then will be the most profitable way of farming land? Presumably to follow the oracular dictum: *By making good from bad.* But it is only fair to justify our forefathers who laid down rules for conduct by their teachings; for the term 'bad lands' they meant to be understood to mean the cheapest lands, and the chief point in their economy was to keep down expenses to the minimum. For the sort of instructions in question were given by men who though they had headed triumphal processions deemed ten pounds of silver as part of one's furniture a criminal extravagance, who when their bailiff died insisted on leaving their victories and returning to their farms, and the cultivation of whose estates [a] was taken over by the government and who commanded

40 senatu illis vilicante. inde illa reliqua oracula:
'nequam agricolam esse quisquis emeret quod
praestare ei fundus posset, malum patrem familias
quisquis interdiu faceret quod noctu posset, nisi in
tempestate caeli, peiorem qui profestis diebus ageret
quod feriatis deberet, pessimum qui sereno die sub
41 tecto potius operaretur quam in agro.' nequeo mihi
temperare quominus unum exemplum antiquitatis
adferam ex quo intellegi possit apud populum etiam
de culturis agendi morem fuisse, qualiterque defendi
soliti sint illi viri. C. Furius Chresimus e servitute
liberatus, cum in parvo admodum agello largiores
multo fructus perciperet quam ex amplissimis
vicinitas, in invidia erat magna, ceu fruges alienas
42 perliceret veneficiis. quamobrem ab Spurio Albino
curuli aedile [1] die dicta metuens damnationem, cum
in suffragium tribus oporteret ire, instrumentum
rusticum omne in forum attulit et adduxit familiam
suam validam atque, ut ait Piso, bene curatam ac
vestitam, ferramenta egregie facta, graves ligones,
43 vomeres ponderosos, boves saturos. postea dixit:
'Veneficia mea, Quirites, haec sunt, nec possum vobis
ostendere aut in forum adducere lucubrationes meas
vigiliasque et sudores.' omnium sententiis absolutus
itaque est. profecto opera inpensa cultura constat

[1] aedile *add. Sillig.*

armies while the senate acted as their bailiff. Then come all those other oracular utterances: 'Whoever buys what his farm could supply him with is a worthless farmer; whoever does by day work that he could do by night, except during bad weather, is a bad head of a family, and he who does on working days things that he ought to do on holidays is a worse; and one who works indoors on a fine day rather than in the field is the worst farmer of all.' I cannot refrain from adducing one instance from old times which will show that it was customary to bring before the Commons even questions of agriculture, and will exhibit the kind of plea that men of those days used to rely on to defend their conduct. Gaius Furius Chresimus, a liberated slave, was extremely unpopular because he got much larger returns from a rather small farm than the neighbourhood obtained from very large estates, and he was supposed to be using magic spells to entice away other people's crops. He was consequently indicted by the curule aedile Spurius Albinus; and as he was afraid he would be found guilty, when the time came for the tribes to vote their verdict, he brought all his agricultural implements into court and produced his farm servants, sturdy people and also according to Piso's description well looked after and well clad, his iron tools of excellent make, heavy mattocks, ponderous ploughshares, and well-fed oxen. Then he said: 'These are my magic spells, citizens, and I am not able to exhibit to you or to produce in court my midnight labours and early risings and my sweat and toil.' This procured his acquittal by a unanimous verdict. The fact is that husbandry depends on expenditure of labour, and this is the reason for the saying of our

et ideo maiores fertilissimum in agro oculum domini esse dixerunt.

44 Reliqua praecepta reddentur suis locis, quae propria generum singulorum erunt. interim communia quae succurrunt non omittemus, et in primis Catonis humanissimum utilissimumque, id agendum ut diligant te[1] vicini; causas reddit ille, nos existimamus nulli esse dubias. inter prima idem cavet ne familiae male sit. nihil sero faciendum in agricultura omnes censent, iterumque suo quaeque tempore facienda, et tertio praecepto praetermissa frustra revocari. de terra cariosa execratio Catonis abunde indicata est, quamquam praedicere non cessantis: quidquid per asellum fieri potest vilissime
45 constare. filix biennio moritur si frondem agere non patiaris; id efficacissime contingit germinantibus ramis baculo decussis, sucus enim ex ipsa defluens necat radices. aiunt et circa solstitium avolsas non renasci nec harundine sectas aut exaratas vomeri harundine inposita. similiter et harundinem exarari
46 filice vomeri inposita praecipiunt. iuncosus ager
47 verti pala debet, ante infractus bidentibus. frutecta igni optime tolluntur. umidiorem agrum fossis

[1] te *Urlichs*: se *aut om.*

[a] *R.R.* IV. Vicinis bonus esto . . . si te libenter vicinitas videbit, facilius tua vendes.

[b] *R.R.* V. 2.

forefathers that on a farm the best fertilizer is the master's eye.

The remaining rules will be given in their proper places, according as they belong to the various kinds of agriculture. In the meantime we will not omit the principles of general application which occur to us, and particularly that most humane and most profitable advice of Cato,[a] to do your best to win the esteem of your neighbours. Cato gives reasons for this advice, but for our part we imagine that nobody can doubt what the reasons are. Also one of Cato's first pieces of advice[b] is a warning to keep your farm hands in good condition. That in agriculture nothing must be done too late is a rule universally held, as is a second rule that each thing must be done at its own time, and a third that it is no use calling back lost opportunities. The malediction uttered by Cato against rotten land has been pointed out at sufficient length; though he is never tired of declaring that whatever can be done by means of an ass costs the least money. Bracken dies in two years if you do not let it make leaf, the best way to kill it is to knock off the stalk with a stick when it is budding, as the juice trickling down out of the fern itself kills the roots. It is also said that ferns plucked up about midsummer do not spring up again, nor do those cut with a reed or ploughed up with a reed placed on the ploughshare. Similarly they also advise ploughing up reed with bracken placed on the ploughshare. A field grown over with rushes should be turned up with the spade after having been first broken with two-pronged forks. Brushwood is best removed by setting fire to it. When land is too damp it is very useful to cut ditches

Neighbourliness. Treatment of farm hands.

Keep the land clean. XVII. 3.

Drainag of land.

concidi atque siccari utilissimum est, fossas autem cretosis locis apertas relinqui, in solutiore terra saepibus firmari vel[1] proclivibus ac[2] supinis lateribus procumbere; quasdam obcaecari et in alias dirigi maiores patentioresque et, si sit occasio, silice vel glarea sterni, ora autem earum binis utrimque lapidibus statuminari et alio superintegi.—Silvae extirpandae rationem Democritus prodidit, lupini flore in suco cicutae uno die macerato sparsoque radicibus.

48 IX. Et quoniam praeparatus est ager, nunc indicabitur natura frugum. sunt autem duo prima earum genera: frumenta, ut triticum, hordeum, et legumina, ut faba, cicer. differentia notior quam ut indicari deceat.

49 X. Frumenti ipsius totidem genera per tempora satu divisa: hiberna, quae circa vergiliarum occasum sata terra per hiemem nutriuntur, ut triticum, hordeum; aestiva, quae aestate ante vergiliarum exortum seruntur, ut milium, panicum, sesama, horminum, irio, Italiae dumtaxat ritu: alioquin in Graecia et in Asia omnia a vergiliarum occasu seruntur, quaedam autem utroque tempore in Italia,
50 ex his quaedam et tertio veris. aliqui verna milium, panicum, lentem, cicer, alicam appellant, sementiva autem triticum, hordeum, fabam, rapam. et in

[1] *Mayhoff*: ne *aut* in *aut* ine. [2] *Edd.*: aut.

---

[a] *alica* was properly groats made from *far* or emmer wheat; by *triticum* Pliny here means common or bread-wheats.

through it and drain it; and in clayey places to leave the ditches open, but in looser soil to strengthen them with hedges or let them have their sides sloping and on a slant; and to block up some and make them run into other larger and wider ones, and, if opportunity offers, to pave them with flint or gravel; and to stay their mouths with two stones, one on each side, and roof them over with another stone on top.—Democritus has put forward a method of clearing away forest by soaking lupin-flower for one day in hemlock juice and sprinkling it on the roots of the trees.

Classes of cereals.

IX. And now that the ground has been prepared, we shall proceed to describe the nature of the various kinds of grain. There are two primary varieties, the cereals, such as wheat and barley, and the legumina, such as the bean and chick-pea. The difference between them is too well known to need description.

Grain, its varieties and seasons.

X. There are also two varieties of corn itself distinguished by the different seasons at which they are sown: winter grains, which are sown about the setting of the Pleiads and get their nourishment through the winter from the earth, for instance wheat and barley, and summer grains, which are sown in summer before the rising of the Pleiads, for instance common and Italian millet, sesame, clary and hedge mustard: at all events this is the method of Italy. In Greece and Asia however all grains are sown after the setting of the Pleiads, while in Italy some are sown at both dates, and some of these have a third sowing, in spring. Some persons give the name of spring grain to common millet, Italian millet, lentils, chick-pea and groats-wheat, but term bread-wheat,[a] barley, beans and

tritici genere pars aliqua pabuli est quadripedum causa sati, ut farrago, et in leguminibus, ut vicia; ad communem quadripedum hominumque usum lupinum.

51 Legumina omnia singulas habent radices praeter fabam, easque surculosas, quia non in multas[1] dividuntur, altissimas autem cicer. frumenta multis radicantur fibris sine ramis. erumpit a primo satu hordeum die septimo, legumen quarto vel, cum tardissime, septimo, faba a xv ad xx, legumina in Aegypto tertio die. ex hordeo alterum caput grani in radicem exit, alterum in herbam, quae et prior floret; radicem crassior pars grani fundit, tenuior florem, ceteris seminibus eadem pars et radicem et florem.

52 Frumenta hieme in herba sunt, verno tempore fastigantur in stipulam quae sunt hiberni generis, at milium et panicum in culmum geniculatum et
53 concavum, sesama vero in ferulaceum. omnium sativorum[2] fructus aut spicis continetur, ut tritici, hordei, muniturque vallo aristarum contra aves et parvas quadripedes, aut includitur siliquis, ut leguminum, aut vasculis, ut sesamae ac papaveris. milium et panicum tantum pro indiviso et parvis avibus expositum est; indefensum[3] quippe membranis continetur.[4] panicum a paniculis dictum, cacumine languide nutante, paulatim extenuato

[1] multas? *Mayhoff*: multa.
[2] *V.ll.* sativorum, saturorum.
[3] *Mayhoff*: indefensa. [4] *V.l.* continentur.

[a] Perhaps all these numbers should be reduced by 1 in English, as the Roman idiom would describe *e.g.* Saturday as the seventh day after Sunday, not the sixth.

turnip autumn-sowing grains. In the class of wheat one division consists of fodder sown for animals, such as mixed feed, and the same also in the leguminous plants, such as vetch; but lupine is grown for the use of animals and men in common.

All the leguminous plants except the bean have a single root, which has a woody substance because it is not divided into many branches; the chick-pea has the deepest root. Corn has a number of fibrous roots without ramifications. Barley bursts out of the ground seven days[a] after it is first sown, leguminous plants on the fourth day, or at latest the seventh, beans from fifteen to twenty days; in Egypt leguminous plants emerge on the third day. In barley one end of the grain sends out a root and the other a blade, which flowers before the other corn; and the root shoots out from the thicker end of the grain and the flower from the thinner, whereas with all other seeds both root and flower come from the same end.

Corn is in the blade during winter; in the spring time corn of the winter variety shoots up into a stalk, but common and Italian millets into a knotted hollow straw, and sesame into a stalk like fennel. The fruit of all kinds of sown grain is either contained in ears, as in the case of wheat and barley, and is protected against birds and small animals by a fence of beard, or is enclosed in pods, as with leguminous plants, or in capsules, as with sesame and poppy. Both millets are accessible also to small birds, in what can only be called joint ownership with the grower, inasmuch as they are contained in thin skins, leaving them unprotected. Panic, named from its panicles *Italian millet.* or tufts, has a head that droops languidly and a

culmo paene in surculum, praedensis acervatur granis cum longissima pedali phoba.[1] milio comae granum
54 complexae fimbriato capillo curvantur. sunt et panico genera: mammosa, e pano parvis racemata paniculis, et cacumine gemino; quin et colore distinguntur candido, nigro, rufo, etiam purpureo. panis multifariam et a milio fit, e panico rarus; sed nullum ponderosius frumentum est aut quod coquendo magis crescat: LX pondo panis e modio reducunt[2]
55 modiumque pultis ex tribus sextariis madidis. milium intra hos X annos ex India in Italiam invectum est nigrum colore, amplum grano, harundineum culmo. adolescit ad pedes altitudine VII, praegrandibus comis—iubas[3] vocant—omnium frugum fertilissimum: ex uno grano sextarii terni gignuntur. seri debet in umidis.

56 Frumenta quaedam in tertio genu spicam incipiunt concipere, quaedam in quarto, sed etiamnum occultam. genicula autem sunt tritico quaterna, farri sena, hordeo octona; sed non ante supra dictum geniculorum numerum conceptus est spicae, qui ut spem sui fecit, quattuor aut quinque cum[4] tardissime diebus florere incipiunt totidemque aut paulo pluribus deflorescunt, hordea vero cum tardissime diebus septem. Varro quater novenis diebus fruges absolvi tradit et mense nono meti.

[1] *Turnebus*: loba *Hermolaus*: obba *Gelen.*: obfa *aut* offa.
[2] *V.l.* redicunt (redire dicunt *Sillig*).
[3] *V.l.* lobas (phobas *Scaliger*).
[4] cum *add.* ? *Mayhoff*.

---

[a] Mostly bare varieties of the older *far* or emmer, including also spelt and 'Rivet' and 'poulard' wheats.
[b] *R.R.* I. 32. 1.

stalk that tapers gradually almost into a twig; it is heaped with very closely packed grains, with a corymb that is at its longest a foot in length. In millet the hairs embracing the seed curve over with a fringed tuft. There are also varieties of panic, for instance the full-breasted kind, clustered with small tufts growing out of the ear, and with a double point; moreover these grasses are of various colours, white, black, red and even purple. Bread of several kinds is made even from millet, but very little from panic; but there is no grain heavier in weight or that swells more in baking: they get sixty pounds of bread out of a peck, and a peck of porridge out of three-sixteenths of a peck soaked in water. A millet has been introduced into Italy from India within the last ten years that is of a black colour, with a large grain and a stalk like that of a reed. It grows to seven feet in height, with very large hairs—they are called the mane—and is the most prolific of all kinds of corn, one grain producing three-sixteenths of a peck. It should be sown in damp ground.

Common millet.

Some kinds of grain begin to form the ear at the third joint of the stalk and some at the fourth, but it still remains concealed. Wheat [a] has four articulations in each stalk, emmer six and barley eight; but the ear does not begin to form before the above-mentioned number of articulations is complete; when this has given signs of occurring, in four or at latest five days they begin to blossom, and after the same number of days or a few more they finish flowering; but with barley this happens in seven days at latest. Varro states [b] that the grains are fully formed in thirty-six days and are ready for reaping after eight months.

Formation of ear.

57 Fabae in folia exeunt ac deinde caulem emittunt
nullis distinctum internodiis. reliqua legumina surcu-
losa sunt. ex his ramosa cicer, ervum, lens. quorundam caules sparguntur in terram si non habeant
adminiculum, at pisa scandunt si habuere, aut[1]
deteriora fiunt. leguminum unicaulis faba sola,
unus et lupino, sed ⟨non rectus,⟩[2] ceteris ramosis[3]
58 praetenui surculo, omnibus vero fistulosis. folium
quaedam ab radice emittunt,[4] quaedam a cacumine,
ut[5] frumentum et hordeum. utrumque[6] et quidquid
in stipula est in cacumine unum folium habet—sed
hordeo scabra sunt, ceteris levia—multifolia[7] contra
faba, cicer, pisum. frumentis folium harundina-
ceum, fabae rotunda et magnae leguminum parti,
longiora erviliae et piso, phasiolis venosa, sesamae et
59 irioni sanguinea. cadunt folia lupino tantum et
papaveri. legumina diutius florent, et ex his ervum
ac cicer, sed diutissime faba XL diebus, non autem
singuli scapi tamdiu, quoniam alio desinente alius
incipit, nec tota seges sicut frumenti pariter, siliquantur vero omnia diversis diebus et ab ima primum
parte paulatim flore subeunte.

60 Frumenta cum defloruere, crassescunt maturantur-
que cum plurimum diebus XL, item faba, paucissimis

[1] at . . . aut *Mayhoff*: ut piscandum nisi habuere aut *aut alia*: ut pisa scandunt aut nisi habuere *Urlichs*: ut pisa; scandunt si habuere aut *Warmington*.

[2] *Add. Mayhoff*.

[3] *Mayhoff*: ramosus.

[4] *Mayhoff*: mittunt.

[5] ut *add. Mayhoff*.

[6] *Gelen.*: utrimque *cdd. pler.*

[7] *Detlefsen*: multificia.

---

[a] A type of chick-pea or chickling vetch.

Leaves of leguminous plants and of corn.

Beans shoot out into leaves and then throw out a stalk which is divided by no joints. The rest of the leguminous plants are tough and woody. Some of them are branching—the chick-pea, the bitter vetch and the lentil. In some the stems spread along the ground if they are not propped up, but peas climb if given a prop, or else they deteriorate. The bean is the only one of the leguminous plants that has a single stem; the lupine also has only one but it does not stand up straight, all the others having branches with a very thin woody stalk, but all of them hollow. Some send out a leaf from the root, some from the top, for instance wheat and barley. Each of these and all the plants that make straw have one leaf at the top—though barley leaves are rough and those of the rest smooth—whereas the bean, the chick-pea and the pea are many-leaved. In corn the leaf is like that of a reed; those of the bean and a large part of the leguminous plants are round; those of the chickling [a] and pea rather long, that of calavance veined, that of sesame and hedge mustard the colour of blood. Only the lupin and the poppy shed their leaves. Leguminous plants remain longer in flower, and among them more particularly bitter vetch and chick-pea, but longest of all the bean, which flowers for forty days, though the single stalks do not keep their flowers so long, since when one goes off another begins, nor does the whole crop flower at the same time, as with corn, but all the pods form on different days, the blossom starting first at the bottom and rising gradually.

Time taken in ripening.

When cereals have finished flowering, they gradually swell and ripen in 40 days at most, and the same is the case with the bean, but the chick-pea ripens in the fewest days, as it is completely ready in 40 days

cicer; id enim a sementi diebus XL perficitur. milium et panicum et sesama et omnia aestiva XL diebus maturantur a flore, magna terrae caelique differentia; in Aegypto enim hordeum sexto a satu mense, frumenta septumo metuntur, in Hellade VII hordeum, in Peloponneso octavo, et frumenta etiamnum tardius. grana in stipula crinito textu spicantur; in faba leguminibusque alternis lateribus siliquantur. fortiora contra hiemes frumenta, legumina in cibo.

61 Tunicae frumento plures, hordeum maxime nudum et arinca, set praecipue avena. calamus altior frumento quam hordeo, arista mordacior hordeo. in area exteruntur triticum et siligo et hordeum; sic et seruntur pura qualiter moluntur, quia tosta non sunt. e diverso far, milium, panicum purgari nisi tosta non possunt; itaque haec cum suis folliculis seruntur cruda. et far in vaginulis suis servant ad satus atque non torrent.

62 XI. Levissimum ex his hordeum raro excedit XV libras et faba XXII. ponderosius far magisque etiamnum triticum. farina in Aegypto ex olyra conficitur: tertium genus spicae hoc ibi est. Galliae quoque suum genus farris dedere, quod illic bracem vocant, apud nos scandalam,[1] nitidissimi grani. est et alia differentia quod fere quaternis libris plus reddit

[1] *V.l.* sandalam.

[a] *Siligo* was chiefly soft bread-wheat (common wheat) but included club-wheat and spelt.

[b] Greek *ὄλυρα = ζειὰ δίκοκκος*. A two-grained wheat. The word was used especially for the hulled grains.

[c] Hence French *brasser*, 'to brew'.

from sowing. Millet (common and Italian) and sesame and all the summer grains ripen within 40 days of blossoming, although with considerable differences due to soil and weather; for in Egypt barley is reaped in the sixth month after sowing and wheat in the seventh, while in Greece barley is cut in the seventh month and in the Peloponnese in the eighth, and wheat even later. Grains growing on a stalk form ears with a texture like a tuft of hairs; in beans and leguminous plants the grains are in pods shooting on each side alternately. Cereals are stronger to withstand winter, but the leguminous plants provide a more substantial article of food.

Husks.

In wheat the grain has several coats, but barley and good emmer wheat are largely naked, and the oat is especially so. Wheat has a taller stalk than barley, but barley has a more prickly ear. Hard wheat, common wheat[a] and barley are threshed on a threshing floor; thus they are also sown without the husk, just as they are milled, because they are not dried first. On the other hand emmer wheat, and common and Italian millet cannot be freed of husk until they have been dried, and consequently these grains are sown unthreshed, with their husks on. People also keep emmer in its little husks for sowing, and do not dry it by heat.

Weight of various grains.

XI. Of these grains the lightest is barley, which rarely exceeds fifteen pounds to the peck, and beans twenty-two pounds. Emmer is heavier and wheat heavier still. In Egypt they make flour out of olyra,[b] a third kind of corn that grows there. The Gallic provinces have also produced a special kind of emmer, the local name for which is bracê,[c] while with us it is called scandala; it has a very glossy grain. There is also another difference in that it gives about four

panis quam far aliud. populum Romanum farre tantum e frumento CCC annis usum Verrius tradit.

63 XII. Tritici genera plura quae fecere gentes. Italico nullum equidem comparaverim candore ac pondere, quo maxime discernitur.[1] montanis modo comparetur Italiae agris externum, in quo principatum tenuit Boeotia, dein Sicilia, mox Africa. tertium pondus erat Thracio, Syrio, deinde et Aegyptio, athletarum tum [2] decreto, quorum capacitas iumentis similis quem diximus ordinem fecerat. Graecia et Ponticum laudavit, quod in Italiam non
64 pervenit; ex omni autem genere grani praetulit dracontian et strangian [3] et Selinusium argumento crassissimi calami; itaque pingui solo haec genera adsignabat. levissimum et maxime inane speudian, tenuissinit calami, in umidis seri iubebat, quoniam
65 multo egeret alimento. hae fuere sententiae Alexandro Magno regnante, cum clarissima fuit Graecia atque in toto orbe terrarum potentissima, ita tamen ut ante mortem eius annis fere CXLV Sophocles poeta in fabula Triptolemo frumentum Italicum ante cuncta laudaverit ad verbum tralata sententia: 'Et fortunatam Italiam frumento canere [4] candido,' quae laus peculiaris hodieque Italico est; quo magis admiror

[1] *Rackham*: decernitur.
[2] *Detlefsen*: cum ([cum] *vel* olim *vel* quidem *Mayhoff*).
[3] *Caesarius*: stelepan *aut* istelepant.
[4] *V.l.* serere.

[a] See p. 224, note *a*.
[b] This and the following were apparently 'poulard' wheats.
[c] Sophocles *Fr.* 600 (Pearson II. p. 246).

pounds more bread per peck than other emmer wheats. According to Verrius emmer was the only corn used by the Roman nation for 300 years.

Wheat, its qualities and local varieties.

XII. There are several kinds of wheat[a] that have been produced by various races. For my own part I should not rank any of them with Italian wheat for whiteness and for weight, for which it is particularly distinguished. Foreign wheat can only be compared with that of the mountain regions of Italy; among foreign kinds Boeotia has obtained the first rank, then Sicily, and after that Africa. The third place for weight used to belong to Thracian and Syrian wheat and later also to Egyptian, by the vote of athletes in those days, whose capacity for cereals, resembling that of cattle, had established the order of merit that we have stated. Greece also gave praise to wheat from Pontus, which did not get through to Italy; but of all the varieties of grain Greece gave the preference to dracontias,[b] strangias and the wheat of Selinunte, recognized by the thickness of the straw, because of which it used to count these kinds as appropriate for a rich soil. For sowing in damp soils Greece prescribed speudias, a very light and extremely scanty-growing grain with a very thin stalk, because it required a great deal of nourishment. These were the opinions held in the reign of Alexander the Great, when Greece was most famous and the most powerful state in the whole world, although nevertheless about 145 years before his death the poet Sophocles in his play *Triptolemus* praised Italian corn before all other kinds, in the phrase[c] of which a literal translation is: 'And that happy Italy glows white with bright white wheat'; and also to-day the Italian wheat is especially dis-

posteros Graecorum nullam mentionem huius fecisse frumenti.

66 Nunc ex iis[1] generibus quae Romam[2] invehuntur
levissimum est Gallicum atque Chersoneso advectum,
quippe non excedunt modii vicenas libras, si quis
granum ipsum ponderet. Sardum adicit selibram,
Alexandrinum et trientem—hoc et Siculi pondus—,
Baeticum totam libram addit, Africum et dodrantem.
in transpadana Italia scio vicenas quinas libras farris
67 modios pendere, circa Clusium et senas. lex certa
naturae ut in quocumque genere pani militari[3] tertia
portio ad grani pondus accedat, sicut optumum
frumentum esse quod in subactum congium aquae
capiat. quibusdam generibus per se pondus, sicut
Baliarico modio tritici panis p. xxxv redit,[4] quibusdam
non nisi[5] mixtis, ut Cyprio et Alexandrino xx per se[6]
68 libras non excedentibus. Cyprium fuscum est
panemque nigrum facit, itaque miscetur Alexandrinum candidum, redeuntque xxv pondo. Thebaicum libram adicit. marina aqua subigi, quod plerique in maritimis locis faciunt occasione lucrandi salis, inutilissimum: non alia de causa opportuniora morbis corpora existunt. Galliae et Hispaniae

[1] *Rackham*: his.
[2] *Edd.*: Roma *aut* Romae.
[3] miliari *Detlefsen.*
[4] *Detlefsen*: reddit.
[5] non nisi *cd. Vat. Lat.* 3861, *m.* 2: in pinis *rell.*: in binis *Gelen.*: binis *Hardouin.*
[6] *Rackham*: xx prope.

---

[a] A conjectural emendation gives 'of bread made from millet'.

tinguished for whiteness, which makes it more surprising to me that the later Greeks have made no mention of this corn.

Imported wheats and their yield. At the present the lightest in weight among the kinds of wheat imported to Rome is the wheat of Gaul, and that brought from the Chersonese, as they do not exceed twenty pounds a peck, if one weighs the grain by itself. Sardinian grain adds half a pound to this figure, and Alexandrian a third of a pound more—this is also the weight of Sicilian wheat—while that of Southern Spain scores a whole pound more and that of Africa a pound and three-quarters. In Italy north of the Po the peck of emmer to my knowledge weighs 25 pounds, and in the Chiusi neighbourhood even 26 pounds. It is a fixed law of nature that in any kind of commissariat bread[a] a third part is added in the making to the weight of the grain, just as that the best wheat is that which absorbs three quarts of water into the peck of grain kneaded. Some kinds of grain used by themselves give their full weight, for instance a peck of Balearic wheat produces 35 pounds of bread, but some only do so when blended—for example, Cyprian wheat and Alexandrian, which used by themselves do not go beyond 20 pounds a peck. Cyprus wheat is of a dusky colour and makes black bread, and consequently the white Alexandrian is mixed with it, and that gives 25 pounds of bread to the peck. The wheat of the Thebaid in Egypt makes a pound more. To knead the flour with sea water, which they frequently do in seaside places for the sake of economizing salt, is extremely inexpedient, as there is nothing else that renders the body more liable to disease. When the corn of Gaul and Spain of the

frumento in potum resoluto quibus diximus generibus
spuma ita concreta pro fermento utuntur, qua de
69 causa levior illis quam ceteris panis est. est differentia et calami, crassior quippe melioris est generis.
plurimis tunicis Thracium triticum vestitur ob nimia
frigora illi plagae requisitum.[1] eadem causa et
trimenstre [2] invenit detinentibus terras nivibus quod
tertio fere a satu mense cum et in reliquo orbe metitur.
totis hoc Alpibus notum, et hiemalibus provinciis
nullum hoc frumento laetius; unicalamum praeterea
nec usquam capax, seriturque non nisi tenui terra.
70 est et bimestre circa Thraciae Aenum, quod XL die e[3]
quo satum est maturescit, mirumque nulli frumento
plus esse ponderis et furfuribus carere. utitur eo et
Sicilia et Achaia, montuosis utraque partibus, Euboea
quoque circa Carystum. in tantum fallitur Columella
qui ne trimestri quidem proprium genus existimaverit
esse, cum sit antiquissimum. Graeci setanion vocant.
tradunt in Bactris grana tantae magnitudinis fieri ut
singula spicas nostras aequent.
71 XIII. Primum ex omnibus frumentis seritur
hordeum. dabimus et dies serendo cuique generi
natura singulorum exposita. hordeum Indis sativum
et silvestre, ex quo panis apud eos praecipuus et alica.[4]

[1] *Rackham*: exquisitum. [2] *Dalec.*: trimestria.
[3] e *add. Mayhoff*. [4] *Hardouin*: praecipuus Italica.

---

[a] This of course is an absur d exaggeration, the quickest-growing wheat, used for example in Northern Canāda, taking five months.

[b] *Σιτανίας*. Here a common or a club-wheat; but the word was also used for a 'poulard' wheat.

[c] Theophrastus, *Hist. Plant.* 8. 4, 5, says as big as an olive stone.

[d] *Alica* was normally groats made from two-grained wheat.

kinds we have stated is steeped to make beer the §§ 62, 67.
foam that forms on the surface in the process is used for leaven, in consequence of which those races have a lighter kind of bread than others. There is also a difference in the stalk, that of the better sort of grain being thicker. Thracian wheat is clothed with a great many husks, which is necessary for that region because of the excessive frosts. The same reason has also led to the discovery of a three-month wheat, because the snow holds back the ground; it is reaped about three months[a] after sowing, at the same time as wheat is harvested in the rest of the world. This wheat is known all over the Alps, and in the provinces with cold climates no corn flourishes better than this; moreover it has a single stem and in no region holds much grain, and it is never sown except in a thin soil. There is actually a two-month variety in the neighbourhood of Aenus in Thrace, which begins to ripen six weeks after it is sown; and it is surprising that no corn weighs heavier, and that it produces no bran. It is also used in Sicily and Achaia, in both cases in mountain districts, and in Euboea in the neighbourhood of Carystus. So greatly is Columella mistaken in his II. 9. 8.
opinion that even three-month wheat is not a distinct variety, although it is of extreme antiquity. The Greeks call it setanion.[b] It is said that in Bactria the grains of wheat grow so large that a single grain is as big as our ears of corn.[c]

XIII. The one sown first of all the cereals is barley. *Barley.*
After explaining the nature of each variety we will also give the date for sowing. India has both cultivated and wild barley, and from it the natives make their best bread and also porridge.[d] Their favourite

maxume quidem oryza gaudent, ex qua tisanam conficiunt quam reliqui mortales ex hordeo. oryzae folia carnosa, porro similia sed latiora, altitudo cubitalis, flos purpureus, radix gemmeae[1] rotunditatis.

72 XIV. Antiquissimum in cibis hordeum, sicut Atheniensium ritu Menandro auctore apparet et gladiatorum cognomine qui hordearii vocabantur. polentam quoque Graeci non aliunde praeferunt. pluribus fit haec modis: Graeci perfusum aqua hordeum siccant nocte una ac postero die frigunt, dein
73 molis frangunt. sunt qui vehementius tostum rursus exigua aqua adspergant et siccent prius quam molant. alii vero virentibus spicis decussum hordeum recens purgant madidumque in pila tundunt atque in corbibus eluunt ac siccatum sole rursus tundunt et purgatum molunt. quocumque autem genere praeparato vicenis hordei libris ternas seminis lini et coriandri selibram salisque acetabulum, torrentes ante
74 omnia, miscent in mola. qui diutius volunt servare cum polline ac furfuribus suis condunt novis fictilibus. Italia sine perfusione tostum in subtilem farinam molit, isdem additis atque etiam milio.

XV. Panem ex hordeo antiquis usitatum vita damnavit, quadripedumque fere cibus est, cum tisanae inde usus validissimus saluberrimusque tanto opere
75 probetur: unum laudibus eius volumen dicavit

[1] *V.l.*: geminae.

---

[a] A prize of barley was given to victors in the Eleusinian games. The passage referred to in Menander is not extant.

grain is however rice, of which they make a drink like the barley-water made by the rest of mankind. Rice leaves are fleshy, resembling leek but broader; the plant is 18 inches high, with a purple blossom and a root of a round shape like a precious stone.

XIV. Barley is the oldest among human foods, as is proved by the Athenian ceremony[a] recorded by Menander, and by the name given to gladiators, who used to be called 'barley-men'. Also the Greeks prefer it to any other grain for porridge. There are several ways of making barley porridge: the Greeks soak some barley in water and then leave it for a night to dry, and next day dry it by the fire and then grind it in a mill. Some after roasting it more thoroughly sprinkle it again with a small amount of water and dry it before milling; others however shake the young barley out of the ears while green, clean it and while it is wet pound it in a mortar, and wash it of husk in baskets and then dry it in the sun and again pound it, clean it and grind it. But whatever kind of barley is used, when it has been got ready, in the mill they mix in three pounds of flax seed, half a pound of coriander seed, and an eighth of a pint of salt, previously roasting them all. Those who want to keep it for some time in store put it away in new earthenware jars with fine flour and its own bran. Italians bake it without steeping it in water and grind it into fine meal, with the addition of the same ingredients and millet as well.

Uses of barley.

XV. Barley bread was much used in earlier days, but has been condemned by experience, and barley is now mostly fed to animals, although the consumption of barley-water is proved so conclusively to be very conducive to strength and health: Hippocrates, one

Barley-water.

Hippocrates e clarissimis medicinae scientia. tisanae bonitas praecipua Uticensi. in Aegypto vero est quae fiat ex hordeo cui sunt bini anguli. in Baetica et Africa genus ex quo fiat hordei glabrum appellat Turranius. idem olyran et oryzan eandem esse existimat. tisanae conficiendae volgata ratio est.

76 XVI. Simili modo e tritici semine tragum fit, in Campania dumtaxat et Aegypto, XVII. amylum vero ex omni tritico ac siligine, sed optimum e trimestri. inventio eius Chio insulae debetur, et hodie laudatissimum inde. est appellatum ab eo quod sine mola fiat. proximum trimestri quod e minime ponderoso tritico. madescit dulci aqua in ligneis vasis, ita ut integatur quinquies in die mutata, melius si et noctu, ita ut integatur quinquies in die mutata,
77 melius si et noctu, ita ut misceatur pariter. emollitum, prius quam acescat, linteo aut sportis saccatum[1] tegulae infunditur inlitae fermento atque ita in sole densatur. post Chium maxime laudatur Creticum, mox Aegyptium. probatur autem levore et levitate atque ut recens sit. iam et Catoni dictum apud nos.

[1] saccatum *cd. Par. Lat.* 6797: siccatum *rell.*

---

[a] See p. 228, note *b*.
[b] See p. 224, note *a*; p. 228, note *a*.
[c] Ἄμυλον.
[d] *R.R.* LXXXVII.

of the most famous authorities on medical science, has devoted one whole book to its praises. Utica barley-water is of outstanding quality. There is a kind in Egypt made of the double-pointed grain. The kind of barley used for making this drink in Andalusia and Africa is called by Turranius smooth barley. The same authority is of opinion that *olyra*,[a] and *oryza* (rice) are the same plant. The recipe for making barley-water is universally known.

XVI. Hulled-wheat grain is used in a similar way for making pap, at all events in Campania and in Egypt; XVII. and starch is made from every kind of wheat and common wheat,[b] but the best from three-month wheat. For its discovery we are indebted to the island of Chios, and that is where the best kind comes from to-day. Its name[c] is Greek, and means 'made without milling'. Next to the starch made from three-month wheat is the kind made of the lightest sort of wheat. This is soaked with fresh water in wooden tubs, with the grain completely covered, the water being changed five times in the course of a day, and preferably in the night time as well, so as to get it mixed up evenly with the grain. When it is quite soft but before it goes sour it is strained through linen or wicker baskets and poured out on a tiled surface that has been smeared with leaven, and left to thicken in the sun. Next to the starch of Chios that from Crete is most highly spoken of; and then comes the Egyptian kind. The test of its quality is smooth consistency and light weight, and the condition of being fresh. It has moreover been mentioned already by Cato[d] among ourselves. *Starch.*

78 XVIII. Hordei farina et ad medendum utuntur, mirumque in usu iumentorum ignibus durato ac postea molito offisque humana manu demissis in alvum maiores eis vires torosque corporis fieri. spicae quaedam binos ordines habent, quaedam plures usque ad senos. grano ipsi aliquot differentiae: longius leviusque aut brevius ac[1] rotundius, candidius nigriusve, cui purpura est opimo[2] ad polentam; contra
79 tempestates candido maxima infirmitas. hordeum frugum omnium mollissimum est. seri non volt nisi in sicca et soluta terra ac nisi laeta. palea ex optimis, stramento vero nullum conparatur. hordeum ex omni frumento minime calamitosum, quia ante tollitur quam triticum occupet rubigo (itaque sapientes agricolae triticum cibariis tantum serunt, hordeum sacculo seri dicunt), propterea celerrime
80 redit; fertilissimumque est quod in Hispaniae Carthagine Aprili mense collectum est. hoc seritur eodem mense in Celtiberia, eodemque anno bis nascitur. rapitur omne a prima statim maturitate festinantius quam cetera; fragili enim stipula et tenuissima palea granum continetur. meliorem etiam polentam fieri tradunt si non excocta maturitate tollatur.[3]

81 XIX. Frumenti genera non eadem ubique, nec ubi eadem sunt isdem nominibus. volgatissima ex his

[1] *Mayhoff*: aut.
[2] optimo *cd. Vat. Lat.* 3861: ultimo *rell.*
[3] §§ 78–80 *fortasse ita transponenda sunt ut caput* XV (§ 74) *antecedant.*

XVIII. Barley meal is used as a medicine, and it is remarkable how in treating cattle pills made of it after it has been hardened by roasting at the fire and afterwards ground, sent down into the animal's stomach by the human hand, serve to increase the strength and enlarge the muscles of the body. Some ears of barley have two rows of grains and some more, up to as many as six. In the grain itself there are some varieties: it is longer and smoother or shorter and rounder, lighter or darker in colour, the kind with a purple shade being of a rich consistency for porridge; the light-coloured grain offers the weakest resistance to storms. Barley is the softest of all the grains. It likes to be sown only in a dry, loose soil, which must also be of rich quality. Its chaff is one of the best, indeed for straw there is none that compares with it. Barley is the least liable to damage of all corn, because it is harvested before the wheat is attacked by mildew (and so wise farmers only sow wheat for the larder, whereas barley is sown by the sack, as the saying is), and consequently it brings in a return very quickly; and the most prolific kind is the barley harvested at Carthage in Spain in the month of April. In Celtiberia this barley is sown in the same month, and there are two crops in the same year. All barley is cut sooner than any other grain, as soon as it first ripens, because the grain is carried on a brittle straw and contained in a very thin chaff. Moreover we are told that it makes better pearl-barley if it is lifted before its ripening has been completed.

More details about barley.

XIX. Varieties of wheat are not the same everywhere, and where they are the same they do not always bear the same names. The most widely

Varieties of wheat. Emmer.

atque pollentissima far (quod adoreum veteres appellavere), siligo, triticum: haec plurimis terris communia. arinca Galliarum propria copiosa et Italiae est; Aegypto autem ac Syriae Ciliciaeque et Asiae ac Graeciae peculiares zea, ⟨olyra,⟩ oryza ⟨sive⟩[1] tiphe.
82 Aegyptus similaginem conficit e tritico suo nequaquam Italicae parem. qui zea utuntur non habent far. est et haec Italiae in Campania maxime, semenque appellatur; hoc habet nomen res praeclara, ut mox docebimus, propter quam Homerus ζείδωρος ἄρουρα dixit, non ut aliqui arbitrantur quoniam vitam donaret. amylum quoque ex ea fit priore crassius:
83 haec sola differentia est. ex omni genere durissimum far et contra hiemes firmissimum. patitur frigidissimos locos et minus subactos vel aestuosos sitientesque. primus antiquo is[2] Latio cibus, magno argumento in adoriae donis, sicuti diximus. pulte autem, non pane, vixisse longo tempore Romanos manifestum, quoniam
84 et pulmentaria hodieque dicuntur, et Ennius antiquissimus vates obsidionis famem exprimens offam eripuisse plorantibus liberis patres commemorat. et hodie sacra prisca atque natalium pulte fitilla[3] conficiuntur; videturque tam puls ignota Graeciae fuisse quam Italiae polenta.

[1] ⟨olyra,⟩ oryza ⟨sive⟩ *coll.* §§ 62, 93, *Theophr. Warmington.*
[2] *C. F. W. Mueller*: antiquis (antiquis Latii *Mayhoff*).
[3] *V.l.* fritilla.

---

[a] Emmer.
[b] Ζειὰ (δίκοκκος) and ὄλυρα were both varieties of two-grained or 'emmer' wheat, while τίφη = ζειὰ ἁπλῆ was one-grained or 'einkorn' wheat (*Triticum monococcum*). The

known of them and the most prevalent are emmer (the old name for which was adoreum), common wheat and hard wheat—these are common to most countries. *Arinca*[a] wheat which is indigenous in the Gallic provinces is also frequent in Italy; while *zea*, *olyra*, and 'rice' or *tiphe*[b] are only found in Egypt, Syria, Cilicia and Asia and Greece. Egypt makes a prime flour out of its own wheat, but it by no means matches that of Italy. The places that use zea have not got our emmer. Zea also is found in Italy, particularly in Campania, and is called 'seed'; it has that name as being a remarkable thing, as we shall soon explain, §§ 112, 198.
which is the reason for Homer's expression *zeidoros* *Il.* II. 534
aroura, 'the tilth that gives us zea'—it is not on account of its 'bestowing life', as some people think. Starch of a coarser quality than the kind mentioned before but otherwise identical is made from it. Emmer is the most hardy of every kind and the one that resists winter best. It stands the coldest localities and those that are under-cultivated or extremely hot and dry. It was the first food of the Latium of old times, a strong proof of this being found in the offerings of adoria, as we have said. It is clear § 14.
however that for a long time the Romans lived on pottage, not on bread, since even to-day foodstuffs are also called 'pulmentaria', and Ennius, the oldest of our bards, describing a famine during a siege, recalls how fathers snatched away a morsel from their crying children. Even nowadays primitive rituals and birthday sacrifices are performed with gruel-pottage; and it appears that pottage was as much unknown to Greece as pearl-barley was to Rome.

Latin *far* was properly ζειὰ δίκοκκος, but Pliny misses this point.

85 XX. Tritici semine avidius nullum est nec quod plus alimenti trahat. siliginem proprie dixerim tritici delicias sive[1] candore esse sive virtute sive pondere.[2] conveniens umidis tractibus, quales Italiae sunt et Galliae Comatae, sed trans Alpes in Allobrogum tantum Remorumque agro pertinax, in ceteris ibi partibus biennio in triticum transit. remedium ut gravissima quaeque grana eius ser-
86 antur. e siligine lautissimus panis pistrinarumque opera laudatissima. praecellit in Italia si Campana Pisis natae misceatur: rufior illa, at Pisana candidior ponderosiorque cretacea. iustum est e grano Campanae quam vocant castratam e modio redire sextarios quattuor siliginis vel e gregali sine
87 castratura sextarios quinque, praeterea floris semodium et cibarii, quod secundarium vocant, sextarios quattuor, furfuris sextarios totidem, e Pisana autem siliginis sextarios quinque, cetera paria sunt. Clusina Arretinaque etiamnum sextarios siliginis adiciunt, in reliquis pares. si vero pollinem facere libeat, XVI pondo panis redeunt et cibarii III furfurumque semodius. molae discrimine hoc constat; nam quae sicca moluntur plus farinae reddunt, quae salsa aqua sparsa candidiorem medullam, verum plus retinent in
88 furfure. farinam a farre dictam nomine ipso apparet. siligineae farinae modius Gallicae XX libras panis

[1] sive *add. Rackham.*

[2] candore virtute pondere *cd. Vat. Lat.* 3861, *m.* 2: candor (candore *cd. Leid. n.* VII, *m.* 1) est et sine virtute sine pondere *rell.*: esse *pro* est et *Warmington*: candore sive virtute sive pondere *Mayhoff.*

XX. No grain is greedier than wheat or draws more nourishment out of the soil. Common wheat I may properly designate the choicest variety, whether in whiteness or goodness or weight. It is suitable for moist districts like those in Italy and Gallia Comata, but across the Alps it only keeps its character in the territory of Savoy and Reims, while in the other parts of that country it changes in two years into ordinary wheat. The cure for this is to select its heaviest grains for sowing. Common wheat flour makes bread of the highest quality and the most famous pastry. The top place in Italy is taken by a mixture of Campanian common wheat flour with that grown at Pisa, the former being reddish but the chalk-like Pisa variety whiter and heavier. A fair yield from the Campanian grain called 'bolted' is to give four sixteenths of fine flour to the peck, or from what is called common grain, not bolted, five sixteenths, as well as half a peck of fine flour and four sixteenths of the coarse meal called 'seconds', and the same amount of bran; whereas Pisa wheat should give four sixteenths of prime flour, while of the other kinds the yield is the same. The wheats of Chiusi and Arezzo give an additional sixteenth of prime flour, but in the remaining qualities they are on a level. If however it is wished to make special flour, the return is sixteen pounds of bread and three pecks of seconds and half a peck of bran. This depends on different methods of milling; for grain ground when dry gives more flour, but if sprinkled with salt water it makes a whiter meal, but keeps more back in the bran. The name for flour, *farina*, is obviously derived from *far*, emmer. A peck of flour made of Gallic common wheat gives 20

Local varieties of wheat.

Flour yield of wheat.

reddit, Italicae duabus tribusve amplius in artopticio pane: nam furnaceis binas adiciunt libras in quocumque genere.

89 Similago e tritico fit, laudatissima ex Africa. iustum est e modiis redire semodios et pollinis sextarios quinque—ita appellant in tritico quod florem in siligine; hoc aerariae officinae chartariaeque utuntur —praeterea secundarii sextarios quattuor furfurumque tantundem, panis vero e modio similaginis p.
90 XXII, e floris modio p. XVI. pretium huic annona media in modios farinae XL asses, similagini octonis assibus amplius, siligini castratae duplum. est et alia distinctio semel[1] pollinatam XVII p. panis reddere, bis XVIII, ter XIX cum triente et secundarii panis quinas selibras, totidem cibarii, et furfurum sextarios VI.

91 Siligo numquam maturescit pariter, nec ulla segetum minus dilationem patitur propter teneritatem spicis[2] quae maturuere protinus granum dimittentibus. sed minus quam cetera frumenta in stipula periclitatur, quoniam semper rectam habet spicam nec
92 rorem continet qui robiginem faciat. ex arinca dulcissimus panis; ipsa spissior quam far, et maior spica, eadem et ponderosior: raro modius grani non XVI libras implet. exteritur in Graecia difficulter, ob id iumentis dari ab Homero dicta: haec enim est quam

[1] semel ⟨tenuiore cribro⟩ ? *Mayhoff.*
[2] *Rackham*: iis.

[a] Especially the flour from hard bare wheats or 'macaroni' wheats. *Cf.* p. 224, note a; p. 228, note a.
[b] *Iliad* V. 195.

pounds of bread, that of the Italian kind two or three pounds more, in the case of bread baked in a tin—for loaves baked in the oven they add two pounds in either kind of wheat.

'Hard' flour[a] is made from hard wheat, the most highly esteemed coming from Africa. A fair return is half a peck from a peck with five sixteenths of special flour—that is the name given in the case of hard wheat to what in common wheat is called the 'flower'; this is used in copper works and paper mills—and in addition four sixteenths of second quality flour and the same amount of bran, but from a peck of 'hard' flour 22 pounds of bread and from a peck of flower of wheat 16 pounds. The price for this when the market rate is moderate is 40 *asses* a peck for flour, 8 *asses* more for 'hard' flour and twice as much for bolted common wheat. There is also another distinction, that when bolted a single time it gives 17 pounds of bread, when twice 18, when three times $19\frac{1}{3}$, and $2\frac{1}{2}$ pounds of second quality bread, the same amount of shorts and six sixteenths of bran.

Common wheat, etc

Common wheat never ripens evenly, and yet no corn crop is less able to stand delay as, owing to its delicacy of structure, the ears that have ripened shed their grain at once. But it is less exposed to danger in the straw than other cereals, because it always has the ear on a straight stalk and it does not hold dew to cause rust. Best emmer makes the sweetest bread; the grain itself is of closer fibre than ordinary emmer and the ear is at once larger and heavier: a peck of the grain seldom fails to make 16 pounds. In Greece it is difficult to thresh and consequently Homer[b] speaks of it as being fed to cattle—for his word *olyra* means this grain;

olyram vocat; eadem in Aegypto facilis fertilisque.
93 far sine arista est, item siligo, excepta quae Laconica appellatur. adiciuntur his genera bromos et tragos, externa omnia, ab oriente invectae oryzae similia. tiphe et ipsa eiusdem est generis, ex qua fit in nostro orbe oryza. apud Graecos est et zea, traduntque eam ac tiphen, cum sint degeneres, redire ad frumentum, si pistae serantur, nec protinus, sed tertio anno.
94 XXI. Tritico nihil est fertilius—hoc ei Natura tribuit quoniam eo maxime alebat hominem—utpote cum e modio, si sit aptum solum quale in Byzacio Africae campo, centeni quinquageni modii reddantur. misit ex eo loco divo Augusto procurator eius ex uno grano—vix credibile dictu—cccc paucis minus ger-
95 mina, exstantque de ea re epistulae. misit et Neroni similiter CCCLX stipulas ex uno grano. cum centesimo quidem et Leontini Siciliae campi fundunt aliique et tota Baetica et in primis Aegyptus. fertilissima tritici genera ramosum ac quod centigranium vocant. inventus est iam et scapus unus centum fabis onustus.
96 XXII. Aestiva frumenta diximus sesimam, milium, panicum. sesima ab Indis venit; ex ea et oleum faciunt; colos eius candidus. huic simile est in

---

[a] Perhaps *bromos* is a variety of oats; tragos, τράγος = ὄλυρα, the grain a d groats of emmer wheats.

[b] For *tiphe* etc. see pp. 242–3.

[c] Examples given here may include exaggerated records of 'tillering' or production of numbers of side-shoots by one plant.

[d] A branch-eared kind of 'poulard' wheat.

but on the other hand in Egypt it is easy to thresh and gives a good yield. Emmer has no beard, nor has common wheat, excepting the kind called Laconian. With these are also to be classed bromos and tragos,[a] entirely foreign grains, resembling rice imported from the east. *Tiphe* itself also belongs to the same class—the grain from which a rice is produced in our part of the world. With the Greeks there is also *zea*, and according to their account that grain and *tiphe* degenerate and go back to wheat, if they are sown after being ground, though not at once, but two years later.[b]

Fertility of wheat.

XXI. Nothing is more prolific than wheat—Nature having given it this attribute because it used to be her principal means of nourishing man—inasmuch as a peck of wheat, given suitable soil like that of the Byzacium plain in Africa, produces a yield of 150 pecks. The deputy governor of that region sent to his late Majesty Augustus—almost incredible[c] as it seems—a parcel of very nearly 400 shoots obtained from a single grain as seed, and there are still in existence despatches relating to the matter. He likewise sent to Nero also 360 stalks obtained from one grain. At all events the plains of Lentini and other districts in Sicily, and the whole of Andalusia, and particularly Egypt reproduce at the rate of a hundredfold. The most prolific kinds of wheat are branched wheat[d] and what they call hundred-grain wheat. Also a single beanstalk has before now been found laden with a hundred beans.

Summer grains. § 49.

XXII. We have specified sesame and common and Italian millets as summer grains. Sesame comes from India, where it is also used for making oil; the colour of the grain is white. A grain that resembles

Asia Graeciaque erysimum, idemque erat nisi pinguius esset quod apud nos vocant irionem, medicaminibus adnumerandum potius quam frugibus. eiusdem naturae et horminum Graecis dictum, sed cumino simile, seritur cum sesama; hac et irione nullum animal vescitur virentibus.

97 XXIII. Pistura non omnium facilis, quippe Etruria
spicam farris tosti pisente pilo praeferrato, fistula
serrata et stella intus denticulata, ut, si intenti pisant,
concidantur grana ferrumque frangatur. maior pars
Italiae nudo utitur pilo, rotis etiam quas aqua verset
obiter et mola.[1] de ipsa ratione pisendi Magonis
98 proponemus sententiam: triticum ante perfundi aqua
multa iubet, postea evalli, dein sole siccatum in [2] pila
repeti, simili modo hordeum; huius sextarios xx
spargi duobus sextariis aquae. lentem torreri prius,
dein cum furfuribus leviter pisi aut addito in sextarios
xx lateris crudi frusto et harenae semodio. erviliam
iisdem modis quibus lentem. sesimam in calida
maceratam exporrigi, dein confricari et frigida mergi
ut paleae fluctuentur, iterumque exporrigi in sole
super lintea, quod nisi festinato peragatur, lurido
99 colore mucescere. et ipsa autem quae evalluntur

[1] *Ian*: molat.
[2] in *coll.* XXXIII 87 *add. Mueller.*

---

[a] Winter cress.
[b] Clary.

it in Asia and Greece is erysimum, and the grain called with us irio[a] would be identical with it were it not that that is more filled out, and is to be reckoned as a drug rather than a cereal. Of the same nature is also the grain[b] called in Greece horminum, though it resembles cummin; it is sown with gingelly. No animal will eat either this or irio while green.

XXIII. Not all grains are easy to crush, in fact Etruria pounds the ears of emmer, after it has been roasted, with a pestle shod with iron at the end, in a handmill that is serrated and denticulated inside with grooves radiating from a centre, so that if people put their weight into it while pounding the grains are only splintered up and the iron is broken. The greater part of Italy uses a bare pestle, and also wheels turned by moving water, and a millstone. As to the actual method of pounding corn we will put forward the opinion of Mago: he says that wheat should be steeped in a quantity of water beforehand, and afterwards shelled of husk and then dried in the sun and well pounded in a mortar; and barley should be treated in a similar way; of the latter, he says, 20 sixteenths should be wetted with two sixteenths of water. Lentils must be roasted first and then mixed with bran and lightly pounded, or with a fragment of unbaked brick and half a peck of sand added to each 20 sixteenths. Chickling to be treated in the same ways as lentils. Sesame to be steeped in warm water and spread out, and then rubbed well and dipped in cold water so that the chaff may float to the top, and again spread out in the sun on a linen sheet; and if this is not done very quickly it turns musty with a livid colour. Also there are various methods of pounding the

Methods of milling.

variam pistrinarum rationem habent. acus vocatur cum per se pisitur spica tantum, aurificum ad usus, si vero in area teritur cum stipula, palea, in maiore terrarum parte ad pabula iumentorum. milii et panici et sesimae purgamenta apludam vocant et alibi aliis nominibus.

100 XXIV. Milio Campania praecipue gaudet pultemque candidam ex eo facit; fit et panis praedulcis. Sarmatarum quoque gentes hac maxime pulte aluntur et cruda etiam farina, equino lacte vel sanguine e cruris venis admixto. Aethiopes non aliam frugem quam milii hordeique novere.

101 XXV. Panico et Galliae quidem, praecipue Aquitania utitur, sed et circumpadana Italia addita faba sine aqua.[1] Ponticae gentes nullum panico praeferunt cibum. cetera aestiva frumenta riguis magis etiam quam imbribus gaudent, milium et panicum aquis minime, cum in folia exeant.[2] vetant ea inter vites arboresve frugiferas seri, terram emaciari [3] hoc satu existimantes.

102 XXVI. Milii praecipuus ad fermenta usus e musto subacti in annuum tempus. simile fit e tritici ipsius furfuribus minutis et optimis e musto albo triduo maceratis, subactis ac sole siccatis. inde pastillos in pane faciendo dilutos cum similagine seminis ferve-

[1] *Detlefsen*: sine qua (*lacunam vel* solida *Mayhoff*).
[2] exeant *Rackham*: exeunt (quoniam folia exuunt? *coll. Theophr.* φυλλοβολοῦσι *Mayhoff*).
[3] *Hardouin*: emactari *aut* emacerari.

---

[a] It made a very hot small fire.
[b] Italian millet.
[c] Probably the tribes at the eastern and south-eastern end of the Black Sea are meant.

grains themselves which are cleaned of husk. When only the ear is pounded by itself, to be used by goldsmiths,[a] it is called flakes, but if it is beaten out on a threshing-floor together with the straw it is called chaff; this in the larger part of the world is used as fodder for cattle. The refuse from millet, panic[b] and sesame is called apluda, and by other names in other places.

Common (Russian) millet.

XXIV. Millet flourishes particularly well in Campania, where it is used for making a white porridge; it also makes extremely sweet bread. Moreover the Sarmatian tribes live chiefly on millet porridge, and even on the raw meal, mixed with mare's milk or with blood taken from the veins in a horse's leg. Millet and barley are the only grains known to the Ethiopians.

Italian millet.

XXV. The provinces of Gaul, and particularly Aquitaine, also use panic,[b] and so also do the parts of Italy on the banks of the Po, though adding to it beans without water. The races of the Black Sea[c] prefer panic to any other food. All the other kinds of summer corn flourish even better in land watered by streams than in rainy districts, but millet and panic are not at all fond of water, as it makes them run to leaves. People advise not growing them among vines or fruit trees, as they believe that this crop impoverishes the soil.

Leaven.

XXVI. Millet is specially used for making leaven; if dipped in unfermented wine and kneaded it will keep for a whole year. A similar leaven is obtained by kneading and drying in the sun the best fine bran of the wheat itself, after it has been steeped for three days in unfermented white wine. In making bread cakes made of this are soaked in water and

faciunt atque ita farinae miscent, sic optimum panem
103 fieri arbitrantes. Graeci in binos semodios farinae satis esse bessem fermenti constituere. et haec quidem genera vindemiis tantum fiunt, quo libeat vero tempore ex aqua hordeoque bilibres offae ferventi foco vel fictili patina torrentur cinere et carbone usque dum rubeant; postea operiuntur in vasis donec acescant; hinc fermentum diluitur. cum fieret autem panis hordeacius, ervi aut cicerculae farina ipse fermentabatur; iustum erat duas libras[1]
104 in quinos[2] semodios. nunc fermentum fit ex ipsa farina quae subigitur prius quam addatur sal, ad pultis modum decocta et relicta donec acescat. vulgo vero nec suffervefaciunt, sed tantum pridie adservata materia utuntur; palamque est naturam[3] acore fermentari, sicut invalidiora[4] esse corpora quae fermentato pane alantur, quippe cum apud veteres ponderosissimo cuique tritico praecipua salubritas perhibita sit.

105 XXVII. Panis ipsius varia genera persequi supervacuum videtur, alias ab opsoniis appellati, ut ostrearii, alias a deliciis, ut artolagani, alias a festinatione, ut speustici,[5] nec non a coquendi ratione, ut furnacei vel artopticii aut in clibanis cocti, non pridem etiam e

[1] *Rackham*: duae librae (II libras ? *Mayhoff*).
[2] *Rackham* (V *Mayhoff*): quinque.
[3] ⟨materiae⟩ naturam ? *Rackham*.
[4] invalidiora ? *Mayhoff*: evalidiora.
[5] speustici *Gelen.*: sceptrice (sceptrici *cd. Leid. n.* VII, *m.* 2) *cdd.*: a fastigatione, ut streptici ? *coll. Athen.* III 113a *Mayhoff*.

[a] An alteration of the text, based on Athenaeus's στρεπτίκιος ἄρτος, gives 'from its pointed shape, like twisted bread'.

boiled with prime flour of emmer and then mixed with the flour, this process being thought to produce the best bread. The Greeks have decided that two-thirds of an ounce of leaven is enough for every two half-pecks of flour. Moreover though these kinds of leaven can only be made in the vintage season, it is possible at any time one chooses to make leaven from water and barley, making two-pound cakes and baking them in ashes and charcoal on a hot hearth or an earthenware dish till they turn brown, and afterwards keeping them shut up in vessels till they go sour; then soaked in water they produce leaven. But when barley bread used to be made, the actual barley was leavened with flour of bitter vetch or chickling; the proper amount was two pounds of leaven to every two and a half pecks of barley. At the present time leaven is made out of the flour itself, which is kneaded before salt is added to it and is then boiled down into a kind of porridge and left till it begins to go sour. Generally however they do not heat it up at all, but only use the dough kept over from the day before; manifestly it is natural for sourness to make the dough ferment, and likewise that people who live on fermented bread have weaker bodies, inasmuch as in old days outstanding wholesomeness was ascribed to wheat the heavier it was.

XXVII. As for bread itself it appears superfluous to give an account of its various kinds—in some places bread called after the dishes eaten with it, such as oyster-bread, in others from its special delicacy, as cake-bread, in others from the short time spent in making it, as hasty-bread,[a] and also from the method of baking, as oven bread or tin loaf or baking-pan bread; while not long ago there was

Ways of making bread.

Parthis invecto quem aquaticum vocant quoniam aqua trahitur ad tenuem et spongiosam inanitatem, alii Parthicum. summa laus siliginis bonitate et cribri tenuitate constat. quidam ex ovis aut lacte subigunt, butyro vero gentes etiam pacatae, ad operis pistorii
106 genera transeunte cura. durat sua Piceno in panis inventione gratia ex alicae materia; eum novem diebus maceratum decumo ad speciem tractae subigunt uvae passae suco, postea in furnis ollis inditum, quae rumpantur ibi, torrent. neque est ex eo cibus nisi madefacto, quod fit lacte maxime vel mulso.

107 XXVIII. Pistores Romae non fuere ad Persicum usque bellum annis ab urbe condita super DLXXX. ipsi panem faciebant Quirites, mulierumque id opus maxime erat, sicut etiam nunc in plurimis gentium. artoptas iam Plautus appellat in fabula quam Aululariam inscripsit, magna ob id concertatione erudi
108 torum an is versus poetae sit illius, certumque fit Ateii Capitonis sententia cocos tum panem lautioribus coquere solitos, pistoresque tantum eos qui far pisebant nominatos; nec cocos vero habebant in servitiis, eosque ex macello conducebant. cribrorum genera Galliae ex saetis equorum invenere, Hispania e lino

---

[a] The Third Macedonian War, 171–168 B.C.

[b] Plautus uses this word for millers, but later it meant bakers.

even bread imported from Parthia, called water bread because by means of water it is drawn out into a thin spongy consistency full of holes; others call it just Parthian bread. The highest merit depends on the goodness of the wheat and the fineness of the bolter. Some use eggs or milk in kneading the dough, while even butter has been used by races enjoying peace, when attention can be devoted to the varieties of pastry-making. The Ancona country still retains the popularity it won in the invention of bread from using groats as the material; this bread is steeped for nine days and on the tenth day they knead it up with raisin juice into the shape of a long roll and afterwards put it in earthenware pots and bake it in ovens, the pots breaking in the process. It is not used for food unless it has been soaked, for which chiefly milk or honey-water is employed.

Bakers at Rome comparatively modern.

XXVIII. There were no bakers at Rome down to the war with King Perseus,[a] over 580 years after the foundation of the city. The citizens used to make bread themselves, and this was especially the task of the women, as it is even now in most nations. Plautus already speaks of bakers, using the Greek word, in his play named *Aulularia*, which has caused great debate among the learned as to the authenticity of the line, and it is proved by the expression occurring in Ateius Capito that it was in his day usual for bread to be baked for more luxurious people by cooks, and only those who ground spelt were called 'grinders'[b]; nor used people to have cooks on their regular staff of servants, but they hired them from the provision market. The Gallic provinces invented the kind of bolter made of horse-hair, while Spain

Aul. 400.

excussoria et pollinaria, Aegyptus e papyro atque iunco.

109 XXIX. Sed inter prima dicatur et alicae ratio praestantissimae saluberrimaeque, qua[1] palma frugum indubitata Italiae contigit. fit sine dubio et in Aegypto, sed admodum spernenda, in Italia vero pluribus locis, sicut Veronensi Pisanoque agro, in Campania tamen laudatissima. campus est subiacens montibus nim-
110 bosis, totus quidem $\overline{\text{XL}}$ p. planitie. terra eius, ut protinus soli natura dicatur, pulverea summa, inferiore[2] bibula et pumicis vice fistulosa quoque, montium culpa in bonum cedit; crebros enim imbres percolat atque transmittit, nec dilui aut madere voluit propter facilitatem[3] culturae, eadem acceptum umorem nullis fontibus reddit sed temperate concoquens intra se
111 vice suci[4] continet. seritur toto anno, panico semel, bis farre; et tamen vere segetes quae interquievere fundunt rosam odoratiorem sativa, adeo terra non cessat parere; unde volgo dictum plus apud Campanos unguenti quam apud ceteros olei fieri. quantum autem universas terras campus Campanus antecedit, tantum ipsum pars eius quae Leboriae vocantur, quem Phlegraeum Graeci appellant. finiuntur Leboriae via ab utroque latere consulari quae a Puteolis et quae

[1] *Rackham*: saluberrimam quae *aut sim.*
[2] *Rackham*: inferior.
[3] felicitatem *cdd. pler.*
[4] suci *cd. Par. Lat.* 6797: fusi *rell.*

---

[a] The cereal mentioned at § 50 and elsewhere, groats made from *far* = emmer wheat.

made sieves and meal-sifters of flax, and Egypt of papyrus and rush.

XXIX. But among the first things let us give a recipe for alica,[a] a very excellent and healthy food, by means of which Italy has undoubtedly won the palm for cereals. It is no doubt also made in Egypt, but of a rather contemptible quality, whereas in Italy it occurs in a number of places, for instance in the districts of Verona and Pisa, but the most highly recommended variety in Campania. There beneath cloud-capped mountains lies a plain extending in all for about 40 miles on the level. The ground of this plain, to begin by stating the nature of the soil, being dusty on the surface but spongy underneath and also porous like pumice, what is a fault in mountain country turns into an advantage, as the earth allows the frequent rainfall to percolate and passes it through, and so as to facilitate cultivation has refused to become soaked or swampy, while at the same time it does not give back the moisture it receives by any springs, but warms it up inside itself to a moderate temperature and retains it as a kind of juice. The land is in crop all the year round, being sown once with Italian millet and twice with emmer wheat; and yet in spring the fields having had an interval of rest produce a rose with a sweeter scent than the garden rose, so far is the earth never tired of giving birth; hence there is a common saying that the Campanians produce more scent than other people do oil. But as the Campanian plain surpasses all the lands of the world, so in the same degree is Campania itself surpassed by the part of it called Leboriae, and by the Greeks the Phlegraean Plain. This district is bounded on either side by consular roads that run from Pozzuoli and

Campanian alica.

112 a Cumis Capuam ducit.—Alica fit e zea quam semen appellavimus. tunditur granum eius in pila lignea ne lapidis duritia conterat, mobili, ut notum est, pilo vinctorum poenali opera; primori inest pyxis ferrea. excussis inde tunicis iterum isdem armamentis nudata conciditur medulla. ita fiunt alicae tria genera: minimum ac secundarium, grandissimum vero aphae-
113 rema appellant. nondum habent candorem suum quo praecellunt, iam tamen Alexandrinae praeferuntur. postea—mirum dictu—admiscetur creta quae transit in corpus coloremque et teneritatem adfert.
114 invenitur haec inter Puteolos et Neapolim in colle Leucogeo appellato, extatque divi Augusti decretum quo annua ducena milia Neapolitanis pro eo numerari iussit e fisco suo, coloniam deducens Capuam, adiecitque causam adferendi,[1] quoniam negassent Campani alicam confici sine eo metallo posse. (In eodem reperitur et sulpur, emicantque fontes Araxi oculorum claritati et volnerum medicinae dentiumque firmitati.)

115 Alica adulterina fit maxime quidem e zea quae in Africa degenerat; latiores eius spicae nigrioresque et

[1] adserendi *Strack.*

---

[a] That is, *far* or emmer wheat.

from Cumae to Capua.—Alica is made from 'zea' which we have already called by the name of 'seed'.[a] § 82. Its grain is pounded in a wooden mortar so as *Recipe for alica.* to avoid the hardness of stone grating it up, the motive power for the pestle, as is well known, being supplied by the labour of convicts in chains; on the end of the pestle there is a cap of iron. After the grain has been stripped of its coats, the bared kernel is again broken up with the same implements. The process produces three grades of alica—very small, seconds, and the largest kind which is called in Greek 'select grade'. Still these products have not yet got their whiteness for which they are distinguished, though even at this stage they are preferable to the Alexandrian alica. In a subsequent process, marvellous to relate, an admixture of chalk is added, which passes into the substance of the grain and contributes colour and fineness. The chalk is found at a place called White Earth Hill, between Pozzuoli and Naples, and there is extant a decree of his late Majesty Augustus ordering a yearly payment of 200,000 sesterces from his privy purse to the people of Naples as rent for this hill—the occasion was when he was establishing a colony at Capua; and he added that his reason for importing this material was that the Campanians had stated that alica could not be made without that mineral. (In the same hill sulphur is also found, and the springs of the Araxus which issue from it are efficacious for improving the sight, healing wounds and strengthening the teeth.)

A spurious alica is manufactured chiefly from *Adulterated alica.* an inferior kind of zea growing in Africa, the ears of which are larger and blacker and on a short

brevi stipula. pisunt cum harena et sic quoque difficulter deterunt utriculos, fitque dimidia nudi mensura, posteaque gypsi pars quarta inspargitur atque, ut cohaesit, farinario cribro subcernunt. quae in eo remansit excepticia appellatur et grandissima est. rursus quae transiit[1] artiore cribro[2] cernitur et secundaria vocatur, item cribraria quae simili modo in tertio remansit cribro angustissimo et tantum harenas
116 transmittente. alia ratio ubique adulterandi: ex tritico candidissima et grandissima eligunt grana ac semicocta in ollis postea arefaciunt sole ad dimidium[3] rursusque leviter adspersa aqua[4] molis frangunt. ex zea pulchrius quam e tritico fit tragum,[5] quamvis id alicae vitium sit; candorem autem ei pro creta lactis incocti mixtura confert.

117 XXX. Sequitur leguminum natura, inter quae maximus honos fabae, quippe ex qua temptatus sit etiam panis. lomentum appellatur farina ex ea,[6] adgravaturque pondus illa et omni legumine, iam vero et pabulo, in pane venali. fabae multiplex usus omni[7] quadripedum generi, praecipue homini. frumento etiam miscetur apud plerasque gentes, et
118 maxime panico solida aut[8] delicatius fracta. quin et

[1] *Rackham*: transit.
[2] cribro *add. Rackham.*
[3] *Mayhoff*: ad initum *cdd. pler.*: ad initium *cd. Par. Lat.* 6797: admittunt *cd. Vat. Lat.* 3861, *m.* 2.
[4] aqua *add. Rackham.*
[5] tragum *Turnebus*: granaeum? *Hardouin*: gracum *cdd.* (grana cum *cd. Par. Lat.* 6795).
[6] ex *add. Mayhoff*: eius *cd. Leid. n.* VII, *m.* 2.
[7] *Rackham*: omnium.
[8] *Dalec.*: ac.

[a] Τράγος = ὄλυρα = shelled grains of emmer wheat.

stalk. These are mixed with sand and pounded, and even so there is a difficulty in rubbing off the husks, and only half the quantity of naked grain is produced; and afterwards a quarter the amount of white lime is sprinkled into the grain, and when this has stuck together with it they bolt it through a flour-sieve. The grain that stays behind in the sieve is called residuary and is the largest in size. That which goes through is sifted again in a finer sieve, and is called seconds, and likewise the name of sieve-flour is given to that which in a similar manner stays behind in a third extremely fine sieve that only lets grains like sand through. There is another method of adulteration which is everywhere used: they pick out from wheat the whitest and largest grains, half boil them in pots and afterwards dry them in the sun to half their former size and then again lightly sprinkle them with water and crush them in a mill. A more attractive kind of groats called *tragum*[a] is made from zea than from other wheat, although it is in fact merely a spurious alica; but it is given whiteness by an admixture of milk boiled in it instead of chalk.

XXX. The next subject is the nature of the leguminous plants, among which the highest place of honour belongs to the bean, inasmuch as the experiment has been made of using it for making bread. Bean meal is called lomentum, and it is used in bread made for sale to increase the weight, as is meal made from all the leguminous plants, and nowadays even cattle fodder. Beans are used in a variety of ways for all kinds of beasts and especially for man. With most nations it is also mixed with corn, and most of all with panic, for this purpose it is either used whole or broken up rather fine. Moreover in ancient ritual

Leguminous plants. Beans.

prisco ritu puls fabata[1] suae religionis diis in sacro est. praevalens pulmentarii cibo set[2] hebetare sensus existimata, insomnia quoque facere, ob haec Pythagoricae sententiae damnata, aut[3] ut alii tradidere, quoniam mortuorum animae sint in ea, qua de causa
119 parentando utique adsumitur. Varro et ob haec flaminem ea non vesci tradit et quoniam in flore eius litterae lugubres reperiantur. in eadem peculiaris religio, namque fabam utique ex frugibus referre mos est auspicii causa, quae ideo referiva appellatur. et auctionibus adhibere eam lucrosum putant. sola certe frugum etiam exesa repletur crescente luna. aqua marina aliave salsa non percoquitur.

120 Seritur ante vergiliarum occasum leguminum prima, ut antecedat hiemem. Vergilius eam per ver seri iubet circumpadanae Italiae ritu, sed maior pars malunt fabalia maturae sationis quam trimestrem fructum; eius namque siliquae caulesque gratissimo sunt pabulo pecori. aquas in flore maxime concupiscit, cum vero defloruit, exiguas desiderat. solum in quo

[1] *Mayhoff*: pulsa fabata.
[2] *Mayhoff*: et *aut* sed.
[3] aut *add. Rackham.*

bean pottage has a sanctity of its own in sacrifice to the gods. It occupies a high place as a delicacy for the table, but it was thought to have a dulling effect on the senses, and also to cause sleeplessness, and it was under a ban with the Pythagorean system on that account—or, as others have reported, because the souls of the dead are contained in a bean, and at all events it is for that reason that beans are employed in memorial sacrifices to dead relatives. Moreover according to Varro's account it is partly for these reasons that a priest abstains from eating beans, though also because certain letters of gloomy omen are to be found inscribed on a bean-flower. There is also a special religious sanctity attached to the bean; at all events it is the custom to bring home from the harvest a bean by way of an auspice, this being consequently called the harvest-home bean. Also it is supposed to bring luck at auctions if a bean is included in a lot for sale. It is undoubtedly the case that the bean is the only grain that even when it has been grazed down by cattle fills out again when the moon is waxing. It cannot be thoroughly boiled in sea water or other water with salt in it.

The bean is sown first of the leguminous plants, before the setting of the Pleiads, so that it may get ahead of winter. Virgil advises sowing it all through *Georg.* I. 215. the spring, as is the custom of Italy near the river Po, but the majority of people prefer bean crops of early sowing to the produce of three months' growth, for the pods and stalks of beans sown early make the most acceptable fodder for cattle. When the bean is in flower it particularly wants water, but when it has shed its blossom it only needs little. It serves

sata est laetificat stercoris vice; ideo circa Macedoniam Thessaliamque, cum florere coepit, vertunt
121 arva. nascitur et sua sponte plerisque in locis, sicut septentrionalis oceani insulis, quas ob id nostri Fabarias appellant, item in Mauretania silvestris passim, sed praedura et quae percoqui non possit. nascitur et in Aegypto spinoso caule, qua de causa
122 crocodili oculis timentes refugiunt. longitudo scapo quattuor cubitorum est amplissima, crassitudo ut digito; ni[1] genicula abessent, molli calamo similis, caput papaveri, colore roseo, in eo fabae non supra tricenas, folia ampla, fructus ipse amarus et odore, sed radix perquam grata incolarum cibis, cruda et omnimodo cocta, harundinum radicibus similis. nascitur et in Syria Ciliciaque et in Toronaeo[2] Chalcidices lacu.

123 XXXI. Ex leguminibus autumno vereve seruntur lens et in Graecia pisum. Lens amat solum tenue magis quam pingue, caelum utique siccum. duo genera eius Aegypto, alterum rotundius nigriusque, alterum sua figura, unde vario usu tralatum est in lenticulas nomen. invenio apud auctores aequanimitatem fieri vescentibus ea. pisum in apricis seri debet frigorum inpatientissimum; ideo in Italia et in austeriore caelo non nisi verno tempore terra facili, soluta.

[1] ut digito ni? *Mayhoff*: *alii alia*: intoni.
[2] *Rackham*: Toronae *Ian*: Torone.

instead of stable manure to fertilize the ground it is grown in; consequently in the districts of Macedon and Thessaly when it begins to blossom the farmers plough up the fields. It also grows wild in most places, for example the islands of the North Sea, for which our name is consequently the Bean Islands,[a] and it also grows wild all over Mauretania, though this bean is very hard and incapable of being cooked. It[b] also grows in Egypt, where it has a thorny stalk which makes the crocodiles keep away from it for fear of injuring their eyes. The stalk is two yards long at most and the thickness of a finger: if it had knots in it, it would be like a soft reed; it has a head like a poppy, is rose-coloured, and bears not more than thirty beans on each stalk; the leaves are large; the actual fruit is bitter even in smell, but the root is a very popular article of diet with the natives, and is eaten raw and cooked in every sort of way; it resembles the roots of reeds. The Egyptian bean also grows in Syria and Cilicia, and at the Lake of Torone in Chalcidice. *Egyptian bean.*

XXXI. Vegetables sown in autumn or spring are the lentil and in Greece the pea. The lentil likes a thin soil better than a rich one, and in any case a dry climate. Egypt has two kinds of lentil, one rounder and blacker, the other the normal shape, which has given the name of lenticle applied to small flasks. I find it stated in writers that a lentil diet conduces to an equable temper. Peas must be sown in sunny places, as they stand cold very badly; consequently in Italy and in severer climates they are only sown in spring, in yielding soil that has been well loosened. *Lentils and peas.*

[a] Borkum in the North Sea.

[b] *Nelumbo nucifera.*

124 XXXII. Ciceris natura est gigni cum salsilagine, ideo solum urit nec nisi madefactum pridie seri debet. differentiae plures, magnitudine, colore, figura, sapore. est enim arietino capiti simile, unde ita appellatur, album nigrumque, est et columbinum quod alii Venerium appellant, candidum, rotundum, leve, arietino minus, quod religio pervigiliis adhibet. est et cicercula minuti ciceris, inaequalis, angulosi veluti pisum, dulcissimum autem id quod ervo simillimum; firmiusque quod nigrum et rufum quam quod album.

125 XXXIII. Siliquae rotundae ciceri, ceteris leguminum longae et ad figuram seminis latae, piso cylindratae. passiolorum cum ipsis manduntur granis; serere eos qua velis terra licet ab idibus Octobribus[1] in kal. Novembres. legumina cum maturescere coeperint rapienda sunt, quoniam cito exiliunt latentque cum decidere, sicut et lupinum. quamquam prius de rapis
126 dixisse conveniat, XXXIV. (in transcursu ea attigere nostri, paulo diligentius Graeci, et ipsi tamen inter hortensia) si iustus ordo fiat, a frumento protinus aut

[1] *Rackham* (Octobr. *Mayhoff*): Octobris.

XXXII. It is the nature of the chick-pea to contain an element of saltness, and consequently it scorches the soil, and ought not to be sown without having been soaked the day before. There are several varieties differing in size, colour, shape and flavour. One resembles a ram's head and so is called 'ram's chick-pea'; of this there is a black variety and a white one. There is also the dove-pea, another name for which is Venus's pea, bright white, round, smooth and smaller than the ram's chick-pea; it is used by religious ritual in watch-night services. There is also the chickling vetch, belonging to a diminutive variety of chick-pea, uneven in shape and with corners like a pea. But the chick-pea with the sweetest taste is one that closely resembles the bitter vetch; the black and red varieties of this are firmer than the white. *Chick-peas and other varieties.*

XXXIII. The chick-pea has round pods, whereas those of other leguminous plants are long, and broad to fit the shape of the seed; the pod of the pea is cylindrical. The pods of calavance are eaten with the seeds themselves. They may be sown in any ground you like from the middle of October to the beginning of November. Leguminous plants ought to be plucked as soon as they begin to ripen, because the seeds quickly jump out and when they have fallen on the ground cannot be found; and the same as regards lupine. Nevertheless it would be proper to speak first about the turnip, XXXIV. (authors of our nation have only touched on it in passing, but the Greeks have dealt with it rather more carefully, although even they have placed it among kitchen-garden plants), if we are to follow the proper order, as the turnip should be mentioned di- *Calavance.* *Turnip.*

certe faba dicendis, quando alius usus praestantior his non est. ante omnia namque cunctis animalibus nascuntur, nec in novissimis satiant ruris alitum quoque genera, magisque si decoquantur aqua.
127 quadripedes et fronde eorum gaudent, et homini non minore rapiciorum suis horis gratia quam cymarum, flavidorum quoque et in horreis enecatorum vel maiore quam virentium. ipsa vero durant et in sua terra servata et postea passa paene ad alium proventum, famemque sentiri prohibent. a vino atque
128 messe tertius hic transpadanis fructus. terram non morose eligit, paene ubi nihil aliud seri possit. nebulis et pruinis ac frigore ultro aluntur, amplitudine mirabili: vidi XL libras excedentia. in cibis quidem nostris pluribus modis commendantur, durantque [1] acetaria [2] sinapis acrimonia domita, etiam coloribus picta praeter suum sex aliis, purpureo quoque: neque
129 aliud in cibis tingui decet. genera eorum Graeci duo prima fecere, masculinum femininumque, et ea serendi modum [3] ex eodem semine docuere,[4] densiore enim satu masculescere, item in terra difficili. semen praestantius quo subtilius; species vero omnium tres;
130 aut enim in latitudinem fundi, aut in rotunditatem globari; tertiam speciem silvestrem appellavere, in longitudinem radice procurrente raphani similitudine

[1] aduruntque ? *Warmington.*
[2] acetaria ? *Mayhoff*: ad alia.
[3] *Urlichs*: modi.
[4] docuere *add. Rackham.*

rectly after corn or at all events after the bean, since its utility surpasses that of any other plant. For to begin with it grows as fodder for all animals, nor is it the lowest in rank among herbs to satisfy the needs of the various kinds of birds as well, and the more so if it is well boiled in water. Cattle also are fond of its leaves, even man esteeming turnip tops when in season no less than cabbage sprouts, also liking them when they are yellow and have been left to die in barns even more than when green. But turnip itself keeps if left in the earth where it grows, and also afterwards if left spread out, almost till the next crop comes, and it serves as a precaution against scarcity of food. It ranks third after wine and corn among the products of the country north of the Po. It is not particular in its choice of soil, growing where almost nothing else can be grown. It actually thrives on mist and frost and cold, growing to a marvellous size: I have seen turnips weighing over 40 pounds. Among our own articles of diet it is popularized by several modes of dressing, and it holds the field for salads when subdued by the pungency of mustard, and is actually stained six different colours beside its own, even purple: indeed that is the only suitable colour served at table. The Greeks have produced two primary classes of turnip, the male and the female, and have shown a way of growing both from the same seed, as they turn male when sown more thickly, and also in difficult ground. The smaller the seed is the better its quality. The Greeks distinguish in all three kinds of turnip, as it either spreads out into breadth or makes a round ball, while a third kind they have named wild turnip, with a root running out to a great length like a

et folio anguloso scabroque, suco acri qui circa messem exceptus oculos purget medeaturque caligini admixto lacte mulierum. frigore dulciora fieri existimantur et grandiora; tepore in folia exeunt. palma in Nursino agro nascentibus—taxatio in libras sestertii singuli et in penuria bini—proxima in Algido natis, XXXV.
131 napis[1] vero Amiterni. quorum eadem fere natura:[2] gaudent aeque frigidis. seruntur et ante kalendas Martias, in iugero sextarii IV. diligentiores quinto sulco napum seri iubent, rapa quarto, utrumque stercorato; rapa laetiora fieri si cum palea semen inaretur.[3] serere nudum volunt precantem sibi et
132 vicinis serere se. satus utrique generi iustus inter duorum numinum dies festos, Neptuni atque Volcani, feruntque subtili observatione, quota luna praecedente hieme nix prima ceciderit, si totidem luminum die intra praedictum temporis spatium serantur, mire provenire. seruntur et vere in calidis atque umidis.
133 XXXVI. Lupini usus proximus, cum sit et homini et quadripedum generi ungulas habenti communis. remedium eius, ne metentes fugiat exiliendo, ut ab

[1] napis *Mayhoff*: napi.
[2] *V.l.* natura est.
[3] *Mayhoff*: seminaretur.

---

[a] July 23 and August 23.

radish, and an angular leaf with a rough surface and an acid juice which if extracted at harvest time and mixed with a woman's milk makes an eye-wash and a cure for dim sight. They are believed to grow sweeter and bigger in cold weather; warm weather makes them run to leaves. The prize goes to turnip grown in the Norcia district—it is priced at a sesterce per pound, and at two sesterces in a time of scarcity—and the next to those grown on Monte Compatri; XXXV. but the prize for navews goes to those grown at San Vettorino. Navews have almost the same nature as turnips: they are equally fond of cold places. They are sown even before the first of March, 4 sixteenths of a peck in an acre. The more careful growers recommend ploughing five times before sowing navew and four times for turnip, and manuring the ground in both cases; and they say that turnip grows a finer crop if the seed is ploughed in with some chaff. They advise that the sower should strip for the work, and should offer a prayer in the words, 'I sow for myself and my neighbours.' For both these kinds sowing is properly done between the holidays [a] of two deities, Neptune and Vulcan, and as a result of careful observation it is said that these seeds give a wonderfully fine crop if they are sown on a day that is as many days after the beginning of the period specified as the moon was old when the first snow fell in the preceding winter. In warm and damp localities turnip and navew are also sown in spring.

Navew and turnip.

XXXVI. The next most extensively used plant is the lupine, as it is shared by men and hoofed quadrupeds in common. To prevent its escaping the reapers by jumping out of the pod the best remedy is

Lupine, its fertility, manure value and soil preferences.

imbre tollatur. nec ullius quaequae[1] seruntur natura ad sensum siderum terraeque[2] mirabilior est. primum omnium cotidie cum sole circumagitur horasque agricolis etiam nubilo demonstrat. ter praeterea floret, ter germinat; atqui[3] terra operiri
134 non vult, et unum hoc seritur non arata.[4] quaerit maxime sabulosam et siccam atque etiam harenosam,[5] coli utique non vult. tellurem adeo amat ut quamvis frutectoso solo coiectum inter folia vepresque ad terram tamen radice perveniat. pinguescere hoc satu arva vineasque diximus; itaque adeo non eget fimo ut optimi vicem repraesentet, nihilque aliud nullo inpendio constat, ut quod ne serendi quidem gratia
135 opus sit adferre: protinus seritur ex arvo,[6] ac ne spargi quidem postulat decidens sponte. primumque omnium seritur, novissimum tollitur, utrumque Septembri fere mense, quia si non antecessit hiemem frigoribus obnoxium est. inpune praeterea iacet vel derelictum etiam, si non protinus secuti obruant imbres, ab omnibus animalibus amaritudine sua tutum; plerumque tamen levi sulco integunt. ex densiore terra rubricam maxime amat; ad hanc alendam post tertium florem verti debet, in sabulo

[1] quaequae? *Mayhoff*: quae.
[2] *Sic*? *Mayhoff*: adsensu terraeque.
[3] *Detlefsen*: floret terram amat atque.
[4] *Rackham*: arato.
[5] *Rackham*: sabulosa . . . sicca . . . harenosa.
[6] ex area *Pintianus*.

---

[a] *I.e.* while being reaped.

to gather it immediately after rain. And of all crops sown none has a more remarkable quality of sensitiveness to the heavenly bodies and the soil. In the first place it turns round every day with the sun, and tells the time to the husbandman even in cloudy weather. Moreover it blossoms three times and buds three times; all the same, it does not like to be covered with earth, and it is the only seed that is sown without the ground being ploughed. It requires most of all a gravelly and dry and even sandy soil, and in any case needs no cultivation. It has such a love for the earth that when it falls on soil however much overgrown with briars it penetrates among leaves and brambles and gets through with its root to the ground. We have stated that fields and vineyards are enriched XVII. 54.
by a crop of lupines; and thus it has so little need for manure that it serves instead of manure of the best quality, and there is no other crop that costs no expenditure at all—seeing that it does not require carrying to the spot even for the purpose of sowing: it sows itself directly from the crop,[a] and does not even need to be scattered, falling on the ground of its own accord. And it is the earliest of all crops to be sown and the latest to be carried, both operations generally taking place in September, because if it does not grow ahead of winter it is liable to suffer from frost. Moreover it can be left just lying on the ground with impunity, as it is protected from all animals by its bitter flavour if a fall of rain does not occur immediately so as to cover it up; although nevertheless growers usually cover it up in a light furrow. Among thicker soils it likes red earth best; to enrich this it must be turned up after the plant has blossomed three times, but when planted in gravel the

post secundum. cretosam tantum limosamque odit
136 et in his non provenit. maceratum calida aqua homini quoque in cibo est; nam bovem unum modii singuli satiant validumque praestant, quando etiam inpositum puerorum ventribus pro remedio est. condi in fumo maxime convenit, quoniam in umido vermiculi umbilicum eius in sterilitatem castrant. si depastum sit in fronde, inarari protinus solum opus est.

137 XXXVII. Et vicia pinguescunt arva, nec ipsa agricolis operosa: uno sulco sata non saritur, non stercoratur, nec aliud quam deoccatur. sationis eius tria tempora: circa occasum Arcturi, ut Decembri mense pascat—tum optime seritur in semen, aeque namque fert depasta; secunda satio mense Ianuario est, novissima Martio, tum ad frondem utilissima.
138 siccitatem ex omnibus quae seruntur maxime amat; non aspernatur etiam umbrosa. ex semine eius, si lecta matura est, palea ceteris praefertur. vitibus praeripit sucum languescuntque, si in arbusto seratur.

139 XXXVIII. Nec ervi operosa cura est. hoc amplius quam vicia runcatur, et ipsum medicaminis vim optinens, quippe quo[1] divom Augustum curatum epistulis ipsius memoria exstet. sufficiunt singulis

[1] *Urlichs*: cum.

soil must be turned after every second blossoming. The only kinds of soil it positively dislikes are chalky and muddy soils, and in these it comes to nothing. It is used as a food for mankind as well after being steeped in hot water; as for cattle, a peck per head of stock makes ample and strength-giving feed, while it is also used medicinally for children as a poultice on the stomach. It suits the seed best to be stored in a smoky place, as in a damp place maggots attack the germ and reduce it to sterility. If lupine is grazed off by cattle while in leaf, the only thing to be done is to plough it in at once.

Vetch.

XXXVII. Vetch also enriches the soil, and it too entails no labour for the farmer, as it is sown after only one furrowing, and it is not hoed or manured, but only harrowed in. There are three seasons for sowing it—about the time of the setting of Arcturus, so that it may provide pasture in December—at that date it is best sown for seed, for it bears seed just as well when grazed down; the second sowing is in January, and the last in March, which is the best crop for providing green fodder. Of all crops sown vetch is the one that is fondest of a dry soil; it does not dislike even shady localities. If it is picked when ripe, its grain supplies chaff that is preferred to all others. If sown in a vineyard planted with trees it takes away the juice from the vines and makes them droop.

Bitter-Vetch.

XXXVIII. Bitter vetch also is not difficult to cultivate. This needs weeding more than the vetch; and it too has medicinal properties, indeed the fact that his late Majesty Augustus was cured by it stands on record in his own letters. Five pecks of seed are enough for one yoke of oxen in a day.

boum iugis modi quini. Martio mense satum noxium esse bobus aiunt, item autumno gravedinosum, innoxium autem fieri primo vere satum.

140 XXXIX. Et silicia, hoc est fenum Graecum, scariphatione seritur, non altiore quattuor digitorum sulco, quantoque peius tractatur tanto provenit melius—rarum dictu esse aliquid cui prosit neglegentia; id autem quod secale ac farrago appellatur occari tantum desiderat.

141 XL. Secale Taurini sub Alpibus asiam vocant, deterrimum et[1] tantum ad arcendam famem, fecunda sed gracili stipula, nigritia triste, pondere praecipuum. admiscetur huic far ut mitiget amaritudinem eius, et tamen sic quoque ingratissimum ventri est. nascitur qualicumque solo cum centesimo grano, ipsumque pro laetamine est.

142 XLI. Farrago ex recrementis farris praedensa seritur, admixta aliquando et vicia. eadem in Africa fit ex hordeo. omnia haec pabularia, degeneransque ex leguminibus quae vocatur cracca, in tantum columbis grata ut pastas ea negent fugitivas illius loci fieri.

143 XLII. Apud antiquos erat pabuli genus quod Cato ocinum vocat, quo sistebant alvom bubus. id erat e pabuli segete viride desectum antequam generaret.[2] Sura Mamilius aliter id interpretatur et tradit fabae modios x, viciae ii, tantundem erviliae in iugero

[1] *Mayhoff*: sed.
[2] *Strack*: gelaret (genicularet *vel* siliquaret *Ursinus*).

It is said to be injurious to oxen if sown in March and to cause cold in the head if sown in autumn, but sowing it in early spring makes it harmless.

XXXIX. Silicia or fenugreek also is sown after a mere scratching of the ground, in a furrow not more than four inches deep, and the worse it is treated the better it comes on—a singular proposition that there is something that is benefited by neglect; however the kinds called black spelt and cattle mash need harrowing, but no more. *Fenugreek.*

XL. The name for secale in the subalpine district of Turin is asia; it is a very poor food and only serves to avert starvation; its stalk carries a large head but is a thin straw; it is of a dark sombre colour, and exceptionally heavy. Wheat is mixed in with this to mitigate its bitter taste, and all the same it is very unacceptable to the stomach even so. It grows in any sort of soil with a hundred-fold yield, and serves of itself to enrich the land. *Secale.*

XLI. Cattle-mash obtained from the refuse of wheat is sown very thick, occasionally with an admixture of vetch as well. In Africa the same mash is obtained from barley. All of these plants serve as fodder, and so does the throw-back of the leguminous class of plant called wild vetch, which pigeons are so fond of that they are said never to leave a place where they have been fed on it. *Grains for fodder.*

XLII. In old times there was a kind of fodder which Cato calls ocinum, used to stop scouring in oxen. This was got from a crop of fodder cut green before it seeded. Mamilius Sura gives another meaning to the name, and records that the old practice was to mix ten pecks of bean, two of vetch and the *R.R.* XXVII. sqq. *Ocinum.*

autumno misceri et seri solitos, melius et avena Graeca, cui non cadat[1] semen, admixta; hoc vocitatum ocinum boumque causa seri solitum. Varro appellatum a celeritate proveniendi e Graeco quod ὠκέως dicunt.

144 XLIII. Medica externa etiam Graeciae est, ut a Medis advecta per bella Persarum quae Darius intulit, sed vel in primis dicenda tanta dos est,[2] cum ex uno satu amplius quam tricenis annis duret. similis est trifolio caule foliisque, geniculata; quidquid in caule adsurgit folia contrahuntur. unum de ea et
145 cytiso volumen Amphilochus conposuit. solum in quo seratur elapidatum purgatumque subigitur autumno, mox aratum et occatum integitur creta[3] iterum ac tertium, quinis diebus interpositis et fimo addito—poscit autem siccum sucosumque vel riguum —et ita praeparato seritur mense Maio, alias pruinis
146 obnoxia. opus est densitate seminis omnia occupari internascentesque herbas excludi—id praestant in iugera modi iii[4]—et cavendum[5] ne adurat sol, terraque protinus integi debet. si sit umidum solum herbosumve, vincitur et desciscit in pratum; ideo protinus altitudine unciali herbis omnibus liberanda est, manu potius quam sarculo. secatur incipiens

[1] *Rackham*: cadit.
[2] *Mayhoff*: *alii alia*: et.
[3] *Detlefsen*: crate (inducitur crate? *Mayhoff*).
[4] *Mayhoff*: vi.
[5] et cavendum *Mayhoff*: *varia cdd.* (cavendam, cinavendam, vindem).

same of chickling for each acre of land and sow this mixture in autumn, preferably with some Greek oats mixed in as well, as this does not drop its seed; he says that the usual name for this mixture was ocinum, and that it used to be grown for cattle. Varro explains the name as due to its rapid growth, deriving it from the Greek word for 'quickly'. *R.R.* I. 31. 4.

XLIII. Lucerne is foreign even to Greece, having been imported from Media during the Persian invasions under Darius; but so great a bounty deserves mention even among the first of the grains, since from a single sowing it will last more than thirty years. In stalk and leaf it resembles trefoil, being jointed, and as the stalk rises higher the leaves become narrower. Amphilochus devoted one volume to lucerne and tree-medick. The land for it to be sown in is broken in autumn after being cleared of stones and weeded, and is afterwards ploughed over and harrowed and then covered with chalk, the process being repeated a second and a third time at intervals of five days, and after the addition of manure —it requires a dry and rich soil or else a well-watered one—and after the land has been thus prepared the seed is sown in May, as otherwise it is liable to damage from frost. It is necessary for the whole plot to be occupied with closely sown seed, and for weeds shooting up in between to be debarred—this is secured by sowing three modii to the acre—, and care must be taken that the sun may not scorch the seed up, and it ought to be covered over with earth immediately. If the soil be damp or weedy, the lucerne is overpowered and goes off into meadow; consequently as soon as it is an inch high it must be freed from all weeds, by hand in preference to hoeing.

Lucerne. 492–490 B.C.

florere et quotiens refloruit: id sexies evenit per annos,
147 cum minimum, quater. in semen maturescere prohibenda est, quia pabulum utilius est usque ad trimatum. verno sariri debet liberarique ceteris herbis, ad trimatum marris ad solum radi: ita reliquae herbae intereunt sine ipsius damno propter altitudinem radicum. si evicerint herbae, remedium unicum in aratro, saepius vertendo donec omnes aliae
148 radices intereant. dari non ad satietatem debet, ne deplere sanguinem necesse sit. et viridis utilior est; arescit surculose ac postremo in pulverem inutilem extenuatur.

De cytiso, cui et ipsi principatus datur in pabulis, adfatim diximus inter frutices. et nunc frugum omnium natura peragenda est, cuius in parte de morbis quoque dicatur.

149 XLIV. Primum omnium frumenti vitium avena est. et hordeum in eam degenerat, sic ut ipsa frumenti sit instar, quippe cum Germaniae populi serant eam neque alia pulte vivant. soli maxime caelique umore hoc evenit vitium; sequentem causam habet inbecillitas seminis, si diutius retentum est terra prius
150 quam erumpat. eadem ratio est et si cariosum fuit cum sereretur. prima autem statim eruptione agnoscitur, ex quo apparet in radice esse causam. est et aliud ex vicino avenae vitium, cum ampli-

[a] Long-stalked, useless grasses, rather than oats, which are not a 'disease' and need a cooler climate than the Italian.

[b] This is real oats.

It is cut when it is beginning to flower and every time it flowers again: this happens six times, or at the least four times, in a year. It must be prevented from running to seed, because till it is three years old it is more useful as fodder. It must be hoed in springtime and rid of all other plants, and till the third year shaved down to the earth with weeding-hoes: this makes the rest of the plants die without damaging the lucerne itself, because of the depth of its roots. If weeds get the upper hand, the sole remedy is in the plough, by repeatedly turning the soil till all the other roots die. It must not be fed to cattle to the point of repletion, lest it should be necessary to let blood. Also it is more useful when green, as it dries into a woody state and finally thins out into a useless dust.

About tree-medick, which itself also is given a very high rank among fodder, we have spoken sufficiently among the shrubs. And now we have to complete XIII. 130. our account of the nature of all the cereals, in one part of which we must also speak about diseases.

Diseases affecting cereals; oats.

XLIV. The first of all forms of disease in wheat is the oat.[a] Barley also degenerates into oats, in such a way that the oat[b] itself counts as a kind of corn, inasmuch as the races of Germany grow crops of it and live entirely on oatmeal porridge. The degeneration in question is principally due to dampness of soil and climate, but a subsidiary cause is contained in weakness of the seed, if it is held back too long in the ground before it shoots out. There is also the same explanation if it was rotten when it was sown. But it is recognizable the moment it breaks out of the ground, which shows that the cause is contained in the root. There is also another disease arising in close connection with oats, when

tudine inchoata granum sed nondum matura, prius quam roboret corpus, adflatu noxio cassum et inane in spica evanescit quodam abortu.

151 Venti autem tribus temporibus nocent frumento et hordeo: in flore aut protinus cum defloruere vel maturescere incipientibus; tum enim exinaniunt grana, prioribus causis nasci prohibent. nocet et sol creber ex nube. nascuntur et vermiculi in radice cum sementem imbribus secutis inclusit repentinus
152 calor umorem. gignuntur et in grano cum spica e pluviis calore infervescit. est et cantharis dictus scarabaeus parvus, frumenta erodens. omnia ea animalia cum cibo deficiunt. oleum, pix, adips contraria seminibus, cavendumque ne contacta his serantur. imber in herba utilis a partu,[1] florentibus autem frumento et hordeo nocet, leguminibus innocuus praeterquam ciceri. maturescentia fru-
153 menta imbre laeduntur et hordeum magis. nascitur et herba alba panico similis occupans arva, pecori quoque mortifera. nam lolium et tribulos et carduos lappasque non magis quam rubos inter frugum morbos potius quam inter ipsius terrae pestes
154 numeraverim. caeleste frugum vinearumque malum nullo minus noxium est robigo. frequentissima haec in roscido tractu convallibusque ac perflatum non

[1] utilis ac parturientibus? *Mayhoff.*

after the grain has begun to fill out but its growth is not yet mature, before it makes a strong body it becomes hollow and empty owing to some noxious blast and fades away in the ear by a sort of abortion.

Other cause of damage: wind, weeds, small creatures.

Wind is injurious to wheat and barley at three seasons—when they are in flower or directly after they have shed their flower or when they are beginning to ripen; at the last stage it shrivels up the grain, while in the preceding cases its influence is to prohibit the seed from forming. Successive gleams of sun appearing out of cloud are also injurious. Also maggots breed in the root when after rains following seed-time a sudden spell of heat has enclosed the moisture in the ground. They also grow in the grain when heat following rain causes the ear to ferment. There is also a small beetle called the cantharis which gnaws away corn crops. When food fails, all these creatures disappear. Olive oil, pitch and grease are detrimental to seeds, and care must be taken not to let seed come in contact with them before it is sown. Rain is beneficial to crops while in the stalk from the time of germination, but it damages wheat and barley when in blossom; although it does no harm to leguminous plants, excepting chick-pea. Corn crops when beginning to ripen are damaged by rain, and particularly barley. Also there is a white grass like Italian millet that springs up all over the fields, and is also fatal to cattle. As for darnel, caltrops, thistle and bur, I should not count these any more than brambles among diseases of cereals, but rather among pestilences of the soil itself. One of the most harmful climatic maladies of corn crops and vines is rust. This is most frequent in a district exposed to dew

habentibus; e diverso carent ea ventosa et excelsa. inter vitia segetum et luxuria est, cum oneratae fertilitate procumbunt. commune autem omnium satorum vitium uricae, etiam ciceris cum salsilaginem eius abluendo imber dulcius id facit.

155 Est herba quae cicer enecat et ervum circumligando se, vocatur orobanche; tritico simili modo aera, hordeo festuca quae vocatur aegilops, lenti herba securiclata quam Graeci a similitudine pelecinum vocant; et hae conplexu necant. circa Philippos ateramum nominant in pingui solo herbam qua faba necatur, teramum qua in macro, cum udam
156 quidam ventus adflavit. aerae granum minimum est in cortice aculeato. cum est in pane, celerrime vertigines facit, aiuntque in Asia et Graecia balneatores, cum velint turbam pellere, carbonibus id semen inicere. nascitur et phalangion in ervo, bestiola aranei generis, si hiems aquosa sit. limaces nascuntur in vicia, et aliquando e terra cocleae minutae mirum in modum erodentes eam.—Et morbi quidem fere hi sunt.

157 XLV. Remedia eorum quaecumque pertinent ad herbas in sarculo et, cum semen iactatur, cinere; qui[1] vero in semine et circa radicem consistunt prae-

[1] *Rackham*: quae.

[a] 'Vetch-strangler.' Not the modern botanists' *orobanche* or broom-rape but plants such as dodder and bindweed.

[b] 'Aegilops' is *Aegilops ovata*; axle-grass is axe-weed (*Securigera coronilla*), or perhaps climbing persicaria or a bindweed; but axe-leaved is vague.

[c] This comes from Theophrastus *De causis* IV. 14 who only says that at Philippi a cold wind makes the bean ἀτεράμων, hard and difficult to cook. From this adjective Pliny coins two proper names.

and in shut-in valleys that have no current of air through them, whereas windy places and high ground on the contrary are free from it. Among the vices of corn is also over-abundance, when the stalks fall down under the burden of fertility. But a vice common to all cultivated crops is caterpillars, which even attack chick-pea when rain makes it taste sweeter by washing away its saltness.

There is a weed that kills off chick-pea and bitter vetch by binding itself round them, called orobanche[a]; and in a similar way wheat is attacked by darnel, barley by a long-stalked plant called aegilops and lentils by an axe-leaved plant[b] which the Greeks call axe-grass from its resemblance; these also kill the plants by twining round them. In the neighbourhood of Philippi[c] they give the name of ateramum to a weed growing in rich soil that kills the bean plant, and the name teramum to one that has the same effect in thin soil, when a particular wind has been blowing on the beans when damp. Darnel has a very small seed enclosed in a prickly husk. When used in bread it very quickly causes fits of giddiness, and it is said that in Asia and Greece when the managers of baths want to get rid of a crowd they throw darnel seed on to hot coals. Also the phalangium, a little creature of the spider class, breeds in bitter vetch, if there is a wet winter. Slugs breed amongst vetch, and sometimes small snails which are produced from the ground and eat away the vetch in a surprising manner. —These broadly speaking are the diseases of grain.

XLV. Such cures of these diseases as pertain to grain in the blade are to be found in the hoe, and when the seed is being sown, in ashes; but the diseases that occur in the seed and round the root can

Protections for seeds against diseases, worms, birds, mice.

cedente cura caventur. vino ante semina perfusa minus aegrotare existimant. Vergilius nitro et amurca perfundi iubet fabam; sic etiam grandescere
158 promittit. quidam vero si triduo ante satum urina et aqua maceretur praecipue adolescere putant; ter quidem saritam modium fractae e modio solidae reddere; reliqua semina cupressi foliis tusis si misceantur non esse vermiculis obnoxia, nec si interlunio serantur. multi ad milii remedia rubetam noctu arvo circumferri iubent prius quam sariatur, defodique in medio inclusam fictili: ita nec passerem nec vermes nocere, sed eruendam prius quam seratur,[1] alioquin amarum fieri. quin et armo talpae contacta semina
159 uberiora esse. Democritus suco herbae quae appellatur aizoum, in tegulis nascens, et ab aliis hypogaesum,[2] Latine vero sedum aut digitillum, medicata seri iubet omnia semina. vulgo vero, si uredo [3] noceat et vermes radicibus inhaereant, remedium est amurca pura ac sine sale spargere, dein sarire, et[4] si in articulum seges exire[5] coeperit, runcare, ne herbae
160 vincant. pestem a milio atque panico, sturnorum passerumve agmina, scio abigi herba cuius nomen

[1] seratur? *coll. Geopon. Mayhoff*: sariatur.
[2] *Urlichs* (hypogaeson): aesum.
[3] *V.ll.* dulcedo, ulcedo.
[4] et *add. Rackham.*
[5] exire? *Mayhoff*: ire.

---

[a] *Semper vivum*, 'ever alive', our house-leak.

be guarded against by taking precautions. It is believed that seed steeped in wine before sowing is less liable to disease. Virgil recommends steeping bean in native soda and dregs from oil-presses, and also guarantees this as a method of increasing its size. Others however hold the view that it grows specially well if it is kneaded in a mixture of urine and water three days before sowing; and at all events that if the crop is hoed three times it will yield a peck of crushed beans from a peck of whole beans; and that the other kinds of seeds are not liable to maggots if mixed with crushed cypress leaves, and also if sown just before a new moon. As a cure for diseases of millet many recommend carrying a toad round the field at night before it is hoed and then burying it in the middle of the field, with a pot for a coffin; it is then prevented from being damaged by a sparrow or by worms; but it must be dug up before the field is sown, otherwise the land turns sour. They also say that seed is made more fertile if it is touched by the forequarters of a mole. Democritus advises soaking all seeds before they are sown in the juice of the plant that grows on roof-tiles, called in Greek *aeizoon* [a] and by other people 'under-the-eaves', and in our language 'squat' or 'little finger'. But if damage is being done by blight and by worms adhering to the roots, a common remedy is to sprinkle the plant with pure olive oil lees, not salted, and then to hoe, and if the crop is beginning to shoot out into knots to weed it, so that weeds may not get the upper hand. I know for a fact that flights of starlings or sparrows, the plague of common and Italian millets, can be driven away from them by burying a plant, the name of which is unknown to me,

Georg. I. 193.

ignotum est, in quattuor angulis segetis defossa, mirum dictu, ut omnino nulla avis intret. mures abiguntur cinere mustelae vel felis diluto et semine sparso vel decoctarum aqua, sed redolet virus animalium eorum etiam in pane: ob id felle bubulo semina
161 attingi utilius putant. rubigo quidem, maxima segetum pestis, lauri ramis in arvo defixis transit in ea folia ex arvis. luxuria segetum castigatur dente pecoris in herba dumtaxat, et depastae quidem vel saepius nullam in spica iniuriam sentiunt. retonsarum etiam semel omnino certum est granum longius fieri et inane cassumque ac satum non nasci. Babylone tamen bis secant, tertium depascunt, alioquin
162 folia tantum fierent. sic quoque cum quinquagesimo[1] fenore messes reddit eximia fertilitas soli, diligentioribus vel[2] cum centesimo. neque est cura difficilis quam diutissime aqua rigandi, ut praepinguis et densa ubertas diluatur. limum autem non invehunt Euphrates Tigrisque sic ut in Aegypto Nilus, nec terra ipsa herbas gignit; ubertas tamen tanta est ut sequente anno sponte restibilis fiat seges inpressis vestigio seminibus. quae tanta soli differentia admonet terrae genera in fruges discribere.

[1] *E Theophrasto Hermolaus*: quinto decimo.
[2] *Mayhoff*: venum *et alia*.

[a] This hides a fact: the living leaves of some barberries are the springtime host of wheat black-rust.

at the four corners of the field, with the remarkable result that no bird whatever will enter it. Mice are driven away by sprinkling the seed with the ashes of a weasel or a cat dissolved in water or with water in which those animals have been boiled; but their poison makes an odour even in bread, and consequently it is thought more satisfactory to steep the seed in ox-gall. As for the greatest curse of corn, mildew, fixing branches of laurel in the ground makes it pass out of the fields into their foliage.[a] Excessive luxuriance in corn-crops is corrected by grazing cattle on them, provided the corn is still in the blade, and although it is eaten down even several times it suffers no injury in the ear. It is absolutely certain that if the ears are lopped off even once the grain becomes longer in shape and hollow inside and worthless, and if sown does not grow. Nevertheless at Babylon they cut the corn twice and the third time pasture it off with cattle, as otherwise it would make only leaves. Even so the exceptional fertility of the soil returns crops with a fifty-fold increase, and to more industrious farmers even with a hundredfold. Nor is there any difficulty in the method of letting the ground be under water as long as possible, in order that its extremely rich and substantial fertility may be diluted. But the Euphrates and the Tigris do not carry mud on to the land in the same way as the Nile does in Egypt, nor does the soil itself produce vegetation; but nevertheless its fertility is so great that a second crop grows of its own accord in the following year from the seeds trodden in by the reapers. This extreme difference of soil prompts me to distribute my description of the various kinds of land among the different crops.

163 XLVI. Igitur Catonis haec sententia est: 'in agro crasso et laeto frumentum seri, si vero nebulosus sit idem, rapa[1], raphanos, milium, panicum. in frigido vel aquoso prius serendum, postea in calido; in solo autem rubricoso vel pullo vel harenoso, si non sit aquosum, lupinum, in creta et rubrica et aquosiore agro adoreum, in sicco et non herboso nec umbroso
164 triticum, in solo valido fabam, viciam vero quam minime in aquoso herbidoque, siliginem et triticum in loco aperto, edito, qui sole quam diutissime torreatur, lentem in rudecto et rubricoso qui non sit herbidus, hordeum in novali et in arvo quod restibile possit fieri, trimestre ubi sementem maturam facere non possis[2] et cuius crassitudo sit restibilis.'

165 Subtilis et illa sententia: 'Serenda ea in tenuiore terra quae non multo indigent suco, ut cytisus et, cicere excepto, e leguminibus[3] quae velluntur e terra, non subsecantur—unde et legumina appellata, quia ita leguntur—, in pingui autem quae cibi sunt maioris, ut olus, triticum, siligo, linum. sic ergo tenue solum hordeo dabitur—minus enim alimenti radix poscit—,
166 lenior[4] terra densiorque tritico. in loco umidiore[5] far adoreum potius quam triticum seretur, temperato et triticum et hordeum. colles robustius sed minus reddunt triticum. far, siligo et cretosum et uliginosum solum patiuntur.'

[1] rapa e *Catone add. Pintianus.*
[2] *E Catone Hardouin*: possit.
[3] *Sic? Mayhoff*: cicer exceptis leguminibus.
[4] laetior *Pintianus.*
[5] *E Varrone Sillig*: humili.

---

[a] *R.R.* VI. 1, XXXIV. 1, 2.
[b] Varro *R.R.* I. 23.

XLVI. This then is the opinion of Cato[a]: 'In thick and fertile land wheat should be sown; but if the same land is liable to fog, turnip, radishes, common and Italian millets. In cold or damp land sowing should be done earlier, but in warm land later. In a ruddle-soil or in dark or sandy soil, if it is not damp, sow lupine; in chalk and red earth and rather damp land, emmer wheat; in dry land that is free from grass and not overshaded, wheat; beans in strong soil, but vetch in the least damp and weedy soil; common and other bare wheats in an open and elevated locality that gets the warmth of the sun as long as possible; lentils in poor and ruddle-soil that is free from grass; barley in fallow land and also in land that can produce a second crop; three-month wheat where the land could not ripen an ordinary crop and which is rich enough to produce a second crop.'

Cato's advice for various crops.

The following also is acute advice:[b] 'In a rather thin soil crops should be sown that do not need much moisture, for instance tree-medick, and such of the leguminous plants, except chick-pea, as are gathered by being pulled up out of the ground and not by being cut—which is the reason why they are called "crops", because that is how they are "cropped"—, but in rich land the plants that need greater nutriment, such as greens, wheat, common wheat, flax. Under this method consequently thin soil will be assigned to barley, as its root demands less nourishment, while more easily worked and denser earth will be allotted to wheat. In a rather damp place emmer will be sown in preference to other wheat, but in soil of medium quality this and also barley. Hillsides produce a stronger wheat but a smaller crop of it. Emmer and common wheat can do with both chalky and marshy soil.'

Varro's advice.

Ex[1] frugibus ostentum semel, quod equidem invenerim, accidit P. Aelio Cn. Cornelio cos., quo anno superatus est Hannibal: in arboribus enim tum nata produntur frumenta.

167 XLVII. Et quoniam de frugum terraeque generibus abunde diximus, nunc de arandi ratione dicemus, ante omnia Aegypti facilitate commemorata. Nilus ibi coloni vice fungens evagari incipit, ut diximus, solstitio a nova luna, primo lente, dein vehementius, quamdiu in leone sol est. mox pigrescit in virginem
168 transgresso atque in libra residit. si XII cubita non excessit, fames certa est, nec minus si XVI exsuperavit; tanto enim tardius decedit quanto abundantius crevit, et sementem arcet. vulgo credebatur a decessu eius serere solitos mox sues inpellere vestigiis semina deprimentes in madido solo, et credo antiquitus
169 factitatum, nunc quoque non multo graviore opera; sed tamen inarari certum est abiecta prius semina in limo degressi amnis. hoc fit Novembri mense incipiente, postea pauci runcant—botanismon vocant—, reliqua pars non nisi cum falce arva visit paulo ante

[1] *Detlefsen*: et.

[a] At the battle of Zama, 202 B.C.
[b] Varro *R.R.* I. 9, 4.

The only portent arising from grain crops that I for my part have come across occurred in the consulship of Publius Aelius and Gnaeus Cornelius, the year in which Hannibal was overcome [a]: it is stated [b] that on that occasion corn grew on trees.

A portentous growth.

XLVII. And now that we have spoken fully about the kinds of grain and of soil, we will now speak about the method of ploughing, beginning with an account of the easy conditions prevailing in Egypt. In that country the Nile plays the part of farmer, beginning to overflow its banks at the new moon in midsummer, as we have said, at first gently and then more violently, as long as the sun is in the constellation of the Lion. Then when the sun has passed over into the Virgin it slows down, and when the sun is in the Scales it subsides. If it has not risen more than 18 feet, there is certain to be a famine, and likewise if it has exceeded 24 feet; for it retires more slowly in proportion as it has risen in greater flood, and prevents the sowing of seed. It used to be commonly believed that the custom was to begin sowing after the subsidence of the Nile and then to drive swine over the ground, pressing down the seed in the damp soil with their footprints, and I believe that in former days this was the common practice, and that at the present day also the sowing is done without much heavier labour; but nevertheless it is certain that the seed is first scattered in the mud of the river after it has subsided and then ploughed in. This is done at the beginning of November, and afterwards a few men stub up the weeds—their name for this process is botanismus—, but the rest of the labourers only visit the fields a little before the first of April, taking a sickle with

Cultivation. Effects of flooding by the Nile and other rivers.

V. 57.

kal. Apriles. peragitur autem messis mense Maio, stipula numquam cubitali, quippe sabulum subest
170 granumque limo tantum continetur. excellentius Thebaidis regioni frumentum, quoniam palustris Aegyptus. similis ratio sed felicitas maior Babyloniae Seleuciae, Euphrate atque Tigri restagnantibus, quoniam rigandi modus ibi manu temperatur. Syria quoque tenui sulco arat, cum multifariam in Italia octoni boves ad singulos vomeres anhelent. in omni quidem parte culturae, sed in hac maxime valet oraculum illud: 'quid quaeque regio patiatur.'

171 XLVIII. Vomerum plura genera: culter vocatur infixus prae dentali[1] priusquam proscindatur terram secans futurisque sulcis vestigia praescribens incisuris quas resupinus in arando mordeat vomer. alterum genus est volgare rostrati[2] vectis. tertium in solo facili non toto porrectum dentali sed exigua cuspide
172 in rostro. latior haec quarto generi et acutior in mucronem fastigata eodemque gladio scindens solum et acie laterum radices herbarum secans. non pridem inventum in Raetia Galliae ut duas adderent tali rotulas, quod genus vocant plaumorati; cuspis
173 effigiem palae habet. serunt ita non nisi culta terra[3] et fere nova[4]; latitudo vomeris caespites versat,

[1] infixus prae dentali? *Mayhoff*: infelix (inflexus *Sillig*) praedensam.
[2] *Gelenius*: rostratum uti *aut* rostra uti.
[3] cultrata *vel* cultro arata t. *Strack*: inculta t. *Frobeen*: cultatra *aut* cultratatra.
[4] novali? *Mayhoff*.

them. However the harvest is completed in May, and the straw is never more than an ell long, as the subsoil is sand and the corn only gets its support from the mud. The district of the Thebaid has corn of better quality, because Egypt is marshy. Seleucia in Babylon has a similar method but greater fertility, owing to the overflow of the Euphrates and the Tigris, as there the amount of flooding is controlled by the hand of man. Syria also ploughs with a narrow furrow, whereas in Italy in many parts eight oxen strain panting at one ploughshare. In every department of agriculture but most of all in this one the greatest value attaches to the oracular precept: 'what the particular district will stand.'

Ploughs of various patterns.

XLVIII. Ploughshares are of several kinds. The coulter is the name for the part fixed in front of the share-beam, cutting the earth before it is broken up and marking out the tracks for the future furrows with incisions which the share sloping backward is to bite out in the process of ploughing. Another kind is the ordinary share consisting of a lever with a pointed beak, and a third kind used in easy soil does not present an edge along the whole of the share-beam but only has a small spike at the extremity. In a fourth kind of plough this spike is broader and sharper, ending off in a point, and using the same blade both to cleave the soil and with the sharp edge of the sides to cut the roots of the weeds. An invention was made not long ago in the Grisons fitting a plough of this sort with two small wheels—the name in the vernacular for this kind of plough is *plaumorati*; the share has the shape of a spade. This method is only used for sowing in cultivated land and land that is nearly fallow; the breadth of

semen protinus iniciunt cratesque dentatas supertrahunt. nec sarienda sunt hoc modo sata, sed protelis binis ternisque sic arant. uno boum iugo censeri anno facilis soli quadragena iugera, difficilis tricena iustum est.

174 XLIX. In arando magnopere servandum est Catonis oraculum: 'Quid est bene agrum colere? bene arare. quid secundum? arare.[1] quid tertium? stercorare.' 'sulco varo[2] ne ares. tempestive ares.' Tepidioribus locis a bruma proscindi arva oportet, frigidioribus ab aequinoctio verno, et maturius sicca regione quam umida, maturius densa terra quam
175 soluta, pingui quam macra. ubi siccae et graves aestates, terra cretosa aut gracilis, utilius inter solstitium et autumni aequinoctium aratur, ubi leves aestus, frequentes imbres, pingue herbosumque solum, ibi mediis caloribus. altum et grave solum etiam hieme moveri placet, tenue valde et aridum paulo ante sationem.

176 Sunt et huic[3] suae leges: lutosam terram ne tangito. vi omni arato. prius quam ares proscindito. hoc utilitatem habet quod inverso caespite herbarum radices necantur. quidam utique ab aequinoctio verno proscindi volunt. quod vere semel aratum est a temporis argumento vervactum vocatur;

[1] arare *add. Sillig.*
[2] varo *coll.* § 179 *Rackham*: vario (*sic et Cato*).
[3] *Mayhoff*: hic.

the share turns the turves over; men at once scatter the seed on it and draw toothed harrows over the furrows. Fields that have been sown in this way do not need hoeing, but this method of ploughing requires teams of two or three pairs of oxen. It is a fair estimate for forty acres of easy soil and thirty of difficult to be rated as a year's work for one team of oxen.

XLIX. In ploughing it is extremely important to obey the oracular utterance of Cato: 'What is good farming? Good ploughing. What is second best? Ploughing. What third? Manuring.' 'Do not plough a crooked furrow. Plough in good time.' In comparatively mild places breaking the ground should begin at midwinter, but in colder districts at the spring equinox; and it should begin earlier in a dry region than in a damp one, and earlier in a dense soil than a loose one and in a rich soil than in a poor one. Where the summers are dry and oppressive and the land chalky or thin, it pays better to plough between midsummer and the autumnal equinox, but in the middle of the hot weather in places where summer heat is moderate, rainfalls frequent and the soil rich and grassy. It is the rule to stir a deep heavy soil even in the winter, but a very thin and dry one a little before sowing.

Season for ploughing. R.R. LXI.

Ploughing also has rules of its own: Do not touch a muddy soil. Plough with all your might. Break the ground before you plough. The value of the last process is that turning the turf kills the roots of the weeds. Some people recommend beginning to break the ground at all events at the spring equinox. Land ploughed once in spring is called 'spring-worked land', from the fact of the date; spring-

Rules for ploughing.

hoc in novali aeque necessarium est: novale est quod
177 alternis annis seritur. araturos boves quam artissime iungi oportet, ut capitibus sublatis arent—sic minime colla contundunt; si inter arbores vitesque aretur, fiscellis capistrari ne germinum tenerrima[1] praecerpant; securiculam in stiva pendere qua intercidantur radices—hoc melius quam convelli aratro bovesque luctari; in arando versum peragi nec strigare in actu
178 spiritus. iustum est proscindi sulco dodrantali iugerum uno die, iterari sesquiiugerum, si sit facilitas soli, si minus, proscindi semissem, iterari assem, quando et animalium labori natura leges statuit. omne arvum rectis sulcis, mox et obliquis subigi debet. in collibus traverso tantum monte aratur, sed modo in superiora modo in inferiora rostrante vomere; tantumque est laboris homini ut etiam boum vice fungatur: certe sine hoc animali montanae gentes
179 sarculis arant. arator nisi incurvus praevaricatur—inde tralatum hoc crimen in forum: ibi utique caveatur ubi inventum est. purget vomerem subinde stimulus cuspidatus rallo. scamna inter duos sulcos cruda ne relinquantur, glaebae ne exultent. male

[1] *Rackham*: tenera.

---

[a] *I.e.* the furrows do not run straight up hill and the cross-furrows horizontally, but both are diagonal to the slope of the hill, so that the plough runs alternately up the slope and down it diagonally.

working is equally necessary in the case of fallow land—fallow is land sown every other year. Oxen when going to plough should be harnessed to the yoke as tightly as possible, to make them hold their heads up when ploughing—that makes them least liable to gall their necks; if the ploughing is in between trees and vines, they must wear basket-work muzzles to prevent their nibbling off the tenderest of the buds; a small billhook should be hung on the plough-tail to cut through roots with—this is better than letting the plough tear them up, which is a strain on the oxen; when ploughing finish the row and do not halt in the middle while taking breath. It is a fair day's work to break an acre with a nine-inch furrow and to plough over again an acre and a half, given an easy soil, but otherwise, to break half an acre and plough over one acre, since Nature has appointed laws even for the labour of animals. Every field must be worked with straight furrows and then with slanting furrows as well. Hilly ground is ploughed only across the slope of the hill, but with the share pointing now up hill and now down;[a] and man has such capacity for labour that he can actually perform the function of oxen—at all events mountain races dispense with this animal and do their ploughing with hoes. Unless a ploughman bends his back to his work he goes crooked—the charge of 'prevarication' is a metaphorical term transferred to public life from ploughing: anyhow it must be avoided in the department of its origin. The share should be cleaned now and then with a stick tipped with a scraper. The ridges between two furrows should not be left untidy, so that clods of earth may not fall off them. A field that needs harrowing after the

aratur arvum quod satis frugibus occandum est: id demum recte subactum erit ubi non intellegetur utro vomer ierit. in usu est et collicias interponere, si ita locus poscat, ampliore sulco, quae in fossas aquam educant.

180 Aratione per traversum iterata occatio sequitur, ubi res poscit, crate vel rastro, et sato semine iteratur[1] haec quoque, ubi consuetudo patitur, crate contenta[2] vel tabula aratro adnexa—quod vocant lirare—operiente[3] semina; ni operiantur, quae[4] primum appellata
181 deliratio est. quarto seri sulco Vergilius existimatur voluisse, cum dixit optimam esse segetem quae bis soles, bis frigora sensisset. spissius solum, sicut plerumque in Italia, quinto sulco seri melius est, in Tuscis vero nono. at fabam et viciam non proscisso serere sine damno conpendium operae est.

182 Non omittemus unam etiamnum arandi rationem in transpadana Italia bellorum iniuria excogitatam. Salassi cum subiectos Alpibus depopularentur agros, panicum miliumque iam excrescens temptavere; postquam respuebat natura, inararunt; at illae messes multiplicatae docuere quod nunc vocant artrare, id est aratrare, ut credo tunc dictum. hoc fit

[1] *Schneider*: iteratio.
[2] dentata *edd.*
[3] *Dalec.*: operientes.
[4] ni . . . quae *Mayhoff*: operianturque.

---

[a] *I.e. deliratio*, delirium, 'going off the ridge', was originally an agricultural term meaning bad ploughing in of seed.

[b] This Alpine tribe in the Val d'Aosta caused much frontier trouble from 143 B.C. onward; they were finally exterminated 25 B.C.

crop has been sown is badly ploughed: the ground will only have been worked properly where it is impossible to tell in which of two opposite directions the share went. It is also usual to make intermediate runnels by means of a larger furrow, if the place requires this, for these to draw off the water into the ditches.

Harrowing and raking. After the cross-ploughing has been done there follows the harrowing of clods with a framework or a rake where circumstances require it, and, where local custom allows, this second breaking is also repeated after the seed has been sown, by means of a harrow-framework or with a board attached to the plough covering up the seeds—this process is called ridging; if they are not covered, this is 'unridging'—the original use of the word that means 'raving'.[a] Virgil when he said that the best crop is one that 'twice hath felt the sun and twice the cold', is understood to have desired a fourth ploughing before sowing. *Georg.* I. 47. Where the soil is rather dense, as it usually is in Italy, it is better to plough five times before sowing, but in Tuscany nine times. With beans and vetch however it is a labour-saving plan involving no loss to dispense with preliminary breaking before sowing.

Ploughing in. We will not omit one additional method of ploughing that has been devised in Italy north of the Po owing to damage caused by war. When the Salassi[b] were devastating the farms lying below the Alps they made an attempt to destroy the crops of panic and millet that were just appearing above the ground: but after Nature proved contemptuous of their efforts, they ploughed in the crops; these however came up in multiplied abundance, and thus taught us the practice of ploughing in—*artrare* as it is now

vel incipiente culmo vel[1] cum iam se[2] ad bina
183 ternave emiserit folia. nec recens subtrahemus exemplum in Treverico agro tertio ante hunc anno[3] conpertum: nam cum hieme praegelida captae segetes essent, reseverunt etiam campos mense Martio uberrimasque messes habuerunt.

Nunc reliqua cultura tradetur per genera frugum.

184 L. Siliginem, far, triticum, semen, hordeum occato, sarito, runcato quibus dictum erit diebus; singulae operae cuique generi in iugero sufficient. sarculatio induratam hiberno rigore soli tristitiam laxat temporibus vernis novosque soles admittit. qui sariet caveat ne frumenti radices subfodiat. triticum,
185 semen, hordeum, fabam bis sarire melius. runcatio, cum seges in articulum exiit, evolsis[4] inutilibus herbis frugum radices vindicat segetemque discernit a caespite. leguminum cicer eadem quae far desiderat; faba runcari non gestit, quoniam evincit herbas; lupinum occatur tantum; milium et panicum occatur et saritur, non iteratur, non runcatur; silicia
186 et phasioli occantur tantum. sunt genera terrae quorum ubertas pectinari segetem in herba cogat—cratis et hoc genus dentatae stilis ferreis—eademque

[1] vel *add. edd.*
[2] *Mayhoff*: si.
[3] *Rackham*: annum.
[4] *Mayhoff*: *alii alia*: in articulo esse in molsis.

called, that as I believe being the form at that time in use of the word *aratrare*. This is done either when the stem is beginning to grow or when it has already shot up as far as the second or third set of leaves. Nor will we withhold a recent instance that was ascertained two years ago in the Trier country: the crops having been nipped by an extremely cold winter, in March they actually sowed the fields again, and had a very bounteous harvest.

We will now give the remaining methods of cultivation corresponding to the various kinds of corn.

Ways of growing and weeding various kinds of corn, etc.

L. Common, emmer, hard naked and other emmer wheats and barley should be harrowed, hoed and stubbed on the days that will be stated; a single hand per acre will be enough for each of these kinds of grain. Hoeing loosens in the spring season the harshness of the soil that has been hardened by the rigour of winter, and lets in the fresh sunshine. One who is going to hoe must beware of digging underneath the roots of the corn. Naked and emmer wheats, barley and beans are better for two hoeings. Stubbing, when the crop has begun to make a joint, liberates the roots of the corn by pulling up useless weeds and disengages the crop from clods of turf. Of the leguminous plants chick-pea needs the same treatment as emmer; beans do not want much stubbing, as they overpower weeds; lupine is only harrowed; common and Italian millets are harrowed and hoed, but not hoed a second time and not stubbed; fenugreek and calavances are harrowed only. There are some kinds of ground the fertility of which necessitates combing the crop while in the blade—the comb is another kind of harrow fitted with pointed iron teeth—and even then they also

nihilominus et depascuntur; quae depasta sunt sarculo iterum excitari necessarium. at in Bactris, Africa, Cyrenis omnia haec supervacua facit[1] indulgentia caeli, et a semente non nisi messibus in arva redeunt, quia siccitas coercet herbas, fruges nocturno
187 tantum rore nutriente. Vergilius alternis cessare arva suadet, et[2] si patiantur ruris spatia, utilissimum procul dubio est; quod si neget condicio, far serendum unde lupinum aut vicia aut faba sublata sint et quae terram faciunt laetiorem. in primisque et hoc notandum, quaedam propter alia seri obiter si parum provenere, ut priore diximus[3] volumine, ne eadem saepius dicantur; plurimum enim refert soli cuiusque ratio.

188 LI. Civitas Africae in mediis harenis petentibus Syrtes Leptimque Magnam vocatur Tacape, felix[4] super omne miraculum riguo solo. ternis fere milibus passuum in omnem partem fons abundat, largus quidem, sed certis horarum spatiis dispensatur inter incolas. palmae ibi praegrandi subditur olea, huic ficus, fico punica, illi vitis; sub vite seritur frumentum, mox legumen, deinde olus, omnia eodem anno, omniaque aliena umbra aluntur.

[1] *Rackham*: fecit.
[2] et *add. edd.*
[3] *Mayhoff*: si parum provenire diximus.
[4] *Rackham*: felici.

---

[a] *Georg.* I. 71:

Alternis idem tonsas cessare novales
Et segnum patiere situ durescere campum.

afford pasture for cattle; and the crops that have been eaten down as pasture have to be resuscitated with the hoe. But in Bactria and Africa and at Cyrene all these operations are rendered superfluous by the indulgence of the climate, and after sowing they only go back into the fields at harvest, because the dry atmosphere prevents weeds, the crops depending for nourishment on the dew-fall at night. Virgil advises letting the fields 'lie fallow turn and turn about',[a] and if the extent of the farm allows it, this is undoubtedly extremely useful; but if conditions forbid it, emmer wheat should be sown in ground which has borne a crop of lupines or vetch or beans, and plants that enrich the land. And another point to be noticed as of first importance is this, that some interim crops are sown for the sake of other crops if these have made an unsatisfactory return, as we have said in the preceding volume—not to repeat the same things too often; for the quality of each particular soil is of the greatest importance. XVII. 56.

Land of exceptional fertility.

LI. There is a city-state of Africa called Tacape, in the middle of the desert on the route to the Syrtes and Great Leptis, which has the exceptionally marvellous blessing of a well-watered soil. There is a spring that distributes water over a space of about three miles in every direction, giving a generous supply, but nevertheless it is distributed among the population only at special fixed periods of the day. Here underneath palms of exceptional size there are olives, under the olives figs, under the figs pomegranates, and under those vines; and underneath the vines is sown corn, and later leguminous plants, and then garden vegetables, all in the same year, and all nourished in the shade of something else.

189 quaterna cubita eius soli in quadratum, nec ut a porrectis metiantur digitis sed in pugnum contractis, quaternis denariis venundantur. super omnia est bifera vite bis anno vindemiare; et nisi multiplici partu exinaniatur ubertas, pereant luxuria singuli fructus: nunc vero toto anno metitur aliquid, constatque fertilitati non occurrere[1] homines.

190 Aquarum quoque differentia magna riguis. est in Narbonensi provincia nobilis fons Orgae nomine; in eo herbae nascuntur in tantum expetitae bubus ut mersis capitibus totis eas quaerant; sed illas in aqua nascentis certum est non nisi imbribus ali. ergo suam quisque terram aquamque noverit.

191 LII. Si fuerit illa terra quam appellavimus teneram, poterit sublato hordeo seri milium, eo condito rapa, his sublatis hordeum rursus vel triticum, sicut in Campania; satisque talis terra aratur cum saritur.[2] alius ordo ut, ubi adoreum fuerit, cesset quattuor mensibus hibernis et vernam fabam recipiat; ante[3] hiemalem ne cesset.[4] nimis pinguis alternari potest, ita ut[5] frumento sublato legumen tertio seratur;

[1] succurrere? *Mayhoff.*
[2] *Strack*: seritur.
[3] *Mayhoff*: recipi ut aut ante *aut sim.*
[4] *Edd.*: nec exiet.
[5] *Mayhoff*: fit *aut* fit ut.

A plot of soil there measuring four cubits either way, a cubit being measured not from the elbow to the finger-tips but to the closed fist, is sold for four denarii. But the unique point is that there are two vintages a year, the vines bearing twice over; and if fertility were not exhausted by multiplied production, each crop would be killed by its own exuberance, but as it is, something is being gathered all the year round, and yet it is an absolute fact that this fertility receives no assistance from human beings.

There is also a great difference of quality in the water supplied to watered places. In the province of Narbonne there is a celebrated spring with the name of Orga, in which plants grow that are so much sought after by oxen that they put their whole heads under water in trying to get them; but it is a well-known fact that those plants though growing in water only get their nutriment from showers of rain. Consequently it is necessary for everybody to know the nature of the soil and of the water in his own district. *Varieties of water.*

LII. If the land is of the kind which we designated 'tender', after harvesting the barley it will be possible to sow millet, and when that has been got in turnip-seed, and when the millet and turnip have been harvested barley again, or else wheat, as is done in Campania; and land of that nature is sufficiently ploughed by being hoed. Another order of rotation is for ground where there has been a crop of emmer wheat to lie fallow during the four winter months and to be given spring beans; but it should not lie fallow before being sown with winter-beans. With a soil that is too rich it is possible to employ rotation, sowing a leguminous crop at a third sowing after the wheat has been carried; but a thin soil had better be XVII. 36. *Succession of crops.*

gracilior et in annum tertium cesset. frumentum seri quidam vetant nisi in ea quae proximo anno quieverit.

192 LIII. Maximam huius loci partem stercorationis optinet ratio, de qua et priore diximus volumine. hoc tantum nemini incompertum [1] est, nisi stercorato seri non oportere, quamquam et huic leges sunt propriae. milium, panicum, rapa, napos nisi in stercorato ne serito; [2] non stercorato frumentum potius quam hordeum serito. item in novalibus, tametsi in illis fabam seri volunt, eandem ubicumque quam recen-
193 tissime stercorato solo. autumno aliquid saturus Septembri mense fimum in agro acervet,[3] post imbrem utique; sin [4] verno erit saturus, per hiemem fimum disponat—iustum est vehes XVIII iugero tribui; dispergere caveto [5] priusquam ares. at iacto semine, si haec omissa sit stercoratio, sequens est, priusquam sarias, ut fimi ex aviariis seminis vice spargas [6] ante
194 pulverem. quod ut hanc quoque curam determinemus, iustum mense [7] singulas vehes fimi redire [8] in singulas pecudes minores, in maiores denas.[9] nisi contingat hoc, male substravisse pecori colonum appareat. sunt qui optime stercorari putent sub diu retibus inclusa pecorum mansione. ager si non

[1] *Mayhoff* (*vel* inconfessum ?) : tantum enim inconpessum.

[2] serito *Detlefsen*: seritor *Mayhoff*: serantur *edd. vett.*: *seritur*.

[3] *Mayhoff*: fimum inarguet.

[4] sin ? *Mayhoff*: si.

[5] caveto *Mayhoff*: autem.

[6] ut . . . spargas *add Mayhoff coll.* XVII 50, 53 *et Colum.* II. 15. 2.

[7] *Mayhoff*: iustum est.

[8] redire *Mayhoff*: definire *Detlefsen*: terdenis redire *Urlichs*: denario ire.

[9] denas <tricenis diebus> *L. Poinsinet de Sivry ex Columella.*

left fallow till the year after next. Some people forbid sowing wheat except in land that has lain fallow the year before.

Rules for manuring with dung. XVII. 50.

LIII. A very important part of this topic is occupied by the proper way of using dung, about which we have also spoken in the preceding volume. The one thing known to everybody is that the land must not be sown unless it has been manured, although even this matter has special rules applying to it. You must not sow millet, panic, turnip or navew except in ground that has been manured, but if the ground has not been manured, you should sow wheat in it rather than barley. Similarly also in the case of fallows, although it is held that in these beans should be sowed, in every case you must sow that crop after the soil has been manured as recently as possible. A person intending to sow something in the autumn should pile dung on the land in September, at all events after rain has fallen; but if intending to sow in the spring-time, he should spread dung during the winter—eighteen loads of dung is the proper amount to be given to an acre; but be careful not to spread it before ploughing. But after the seed has been sown, if this manuring has been neglected, the following stage is, before you weed, first to scatter like seed some dust of droppings obtained from hen-coops. But to fix a precise limit for this treatment also, the right amount is to get one load of manure per head of smaller animals and ten loads per head of oxen. If that be not forthcoming, it would look as if the farmer had been slack in providing litter for his stock. Some people think that manuring is best done by keeping the flocks and herds permanently out of doors penned up with netting.

stercoratur alget, si nimium stercoratus est aduritur; satiusque est id saepe quam supra modum facere. quo calidius solum est, eo minus addi stercoris ratio est.

195 LIV. Semen optimum anniculum, bimum deterius, trimum pessimum, ultra sterile; etenim[1] omnium definita generatio est. quod in ima area subsedit ad semen reservandum est, id enim optimum quoniam gravissimum, neque alio modo utilius discernitur. quae spica intervallata[2] semina habebit abicietur. optimum granum quod rubet et dentibus fractum eundem habet colorem, deterius cui plus intus albi est.
196 certum terras alias plus seminis recipere, alias minus, religiosumque inde et[3] primum colonis augurium: cum avidius accipiat, esurire creditur et comesse semen. sationem locis umidis celerius fieri ratio est, ne semen imbre putrescat, siccis serius, ut pluviae sequantur ne diu iacens atque non concipiens evanescat; itemque festinata satione densum spargi semen, quia tarde concipiat, serotina rarum, quia densitate
197 nimia necetur. artis quoque cuiusdam est aequaliter spargere; manus utique congruere debet cum gradu semperque cum dextro pede. fit[4] quoque quorundam

[1] *Mayhoff*: et in imo *aut* et in uno.
[2] *Ian*: intervalla.
[3] et *add. Mayhoff.*
[4] *Edd.*: sit.

If the land is not manured it gets chilled, and if it is given too much manure it becomes burnt up; and it pays better to do the manuring frequently than to manure to excess. It stands to reason that the warmer the soil is the less manure it should be given.

LIV. The best seed is last year's; two-year old seed is inferior, three-year old very poor, and beyond that it is barren; in fact all things have a limited period of fertility. The seed that falls to the bottom on the threshing-floor should be kept for sowing, as it is the best because the heaviest, and there is no other more efficient way of distinguishing it. An ear having its seeds separated by gaps will be discarded. The best grain is that which is reddish in colour and which when crushed by the teeth shows the same colour inside, and one that has more white inside is inferior. It is a well-known fact that some lands take more seed and others less, and this supplies farmers with a binding and primary augury: when the earth receives the seed more greedily, it is believed to be hungry and to devour the seed. The plan is for sowing to be done more quickly in damp places, to prevent the seed from being rotted by moisture, but later in dry places, so that the rainfalls may come afterwards to prevent the seed from lying for a long time without germinating and so withering away; and similarly when sowing is hurried on it pays to scatter the seed thickly, because it conceives slowly, but when sowing is late, to scatter it thin, because excessive closeness kills it. Also there is a certain science in scattering the seed evenly; at all events the hand must keep in time with the pace of walking, and always go with the right foot. Also it comes about by some not obvious

Qualities of seed and times for sowing.

occulta ratione quod sors[1] genialis atque fecunda est. non transferendum est ex frigidis locis semen in calida, neque ex praecocibus in serotina[2] nihilque[3] in contrarium ut[4] praecepere quidam falsa diligentia.

198 LV. Serere in iugera temperato solo iustum est tritici aut siliginis modios v, farris aut seminis, quod frumenti genus ita appellamus, x, hordei vi, fabae quinta amplius quam tritici, viciae xii, ciceris et cicerculae et pisi iii, lupini x, lentis iii (sed hanc cum fimo arido seri volunt), ervi vi, siliciae vi, passiolorum iv, pabuli xx, milii, panici sextarios iv,
199 pingui solo plus, gracili minus. est et alia distinctio: in denso aut cretoso aut uliginoso tritici aut siliginis modios vi, in soluta terra et sicca et laeta iv; macrum[5] enim solum, nisi rarum culmum habeat, spicam minutam facit et inanem, pinguia arva ex uno semine fruticem numerosum fundunt densamque segetem
200 ex raro semine emittunt. ergo inter quattuor et sex modios, pro natura soli quinto minus seri plusve praecipiunt, item in consito aut clivoso ut in macro. huc[6] pertinet oraculum illud magno opere custodiendum: 'Segetem ne defruges.'[7] adiecit his Attius in Praxidica,[8] ut sereretur cum luna esset in ariete, geminis, leone, libra, aquario, Zoroastres sole

[1] *Edd.*: fors.
[2] in serotina *coll.* xvii 79 *add. edd.*
[3] nihilque *v.l. om.*
[4] ut *add. Mayhoff.*
[5] *V.l.* macies (macie *Mayhoff*).
[6] *Rackham*: hoc.
[7] defrudes *Sillig ex Catone.*
[8] *Ribbeck*: Praxidico.

---

[a] That is, zea, § 82. See pp. 198–9, 242–3, 248–9.

method used by certain people that luck is kind to them and brings a good return. Seed should not be transferred from cold places to warm ones nor from early ripening districts to late ones, and nothing should be transferred in the contrary directions either, as some people out of mistaken ingenuity have advised.

LV. The right amounts of seed per acre to sow in soil of medium quality are: bare or common wheat 5 pecks, emmer or seed (the kind of grain[a] to which we give that name) 10; barley 6, beans a fifth more than in the case of wheat, vetch 12, chick-pea, chickling vetch and peas 3, lupine 10, lentil 3 (but people like to sow lentils mixed with dry dung), bitter vetch 6, fenugreek 6, calavances 4, hay-grass 20, common and Italian millets a quarter of a peck, or more in a rich soil and less in a thin one. There is also another distinction to make: in thick or chalky or moist soil 6 pecks of bare or common wheat, but in loose and dry and fertile soil 4; for a meagre soil makes a small and empty ear unless it has the corn stalks far apart, whereas fields with a rich soil produce a number of stalks from a single seed and yield a thick crop from thinly scattered seed. Consequently the rule given is to sow between four and six pecks, adding or subtracting a fifth in accordance with the nature of the soil, and the same in a densely planted place or on sloping land as in thin soil. To this applies that oracular utterance, which it is so important to observe: 'Do not grudge the cornfield its seed.' To this Attius in his *Praxidike* added the advice to sow when the moon is in the constellations of the Ram, the Twins, the Lion, the Scales and Aquarius, but Zoroaster advised

Amount of seed needed.

Time of sowing.

scorpionis duodecim partes transgresso cum luna esset in tauro.

201 LVI. Sequitur huc dilata et maxima indigens cura de tempore fruges serendi quaestio, magnaque ex parte rationi[1] siderum conexa, quamobrem sententias omnium in primis ad id pertinentes exponemus. Hesiodus, qui princeps hominum de agricultura praecepit, unum tempus serendi tradidit a vergiliarum occasu; scribebat enim in Boeotia Helladis,
202 ubi ita seri diximus. inter diligentissimos convenit, ut in alitum quadripedumque genitura, esse quosdam ad conceptum impetus et terrae; hoc Graeci ita definiunt, cum sit calida et umida. Vergilius triticum et far a vergiliarum occasu seri iubet, hordeum inter aequinoctium autumni et brumam, viciam vero et passiolos et lentem boote occidente; quo fit ut horum siderum aliorumque exortus et occasus digerendi sint
203 in suos dies. sunt qui et ante vergiliarum occasum seri iubeant, dumtaxat in arida terra calidisque provinciis, custodiri enim semen non[2] corrumpente umore, et a proximo imbre uno die erumpere; alii statim ab occasu vergiliarum, sequi enim[3] imbres a septimo fere die; aliqui in frigidis ab aequinoctio autumni, in calidis serius, ne ante hiemem luxurient.

[1] *Mayhoff*: ratione.
[2] non *add. Hardouin* (a *add.* ? *Mayhoff*).
[3] enim *add. Rackham.*

sowing when the sun has crossed 12 degrees of the Scorpion and the moon is in the Bull.

LVI. There follows the question postponed to this place, a question that needs very careful consideration—that of the proper date for sowing the crops; it is in a large degree connected with astronomy, and consequently we will begin by setting out the views of all authors in regard to it. Hesiod, the leader of mankind in imparting agricultural instruction, gave only one date for sowing, to begin at the setting of the Pleiads; for he wrote in the Greek country of Boeotia where, as we have said, that is the custom for sowing. It is agreed among the most careful observers that, as in the propagation of birds and animals, so with the earth, there exist certain impulses leading to conception; and the Greeks define this as the period when the earth is warm and moist. Virgil prescribes sowing bare and emmer wheats after the setting of the Pleiads, barley between the autumnal equinox and mid-winter, but vetch and calavances and lentils at the setting of Boötes; with the consequence that it is important to ascertain the exact dates of the rising and setting of these and other stars. There are some who advise sowing before the setting of the Pleiads, at all events in dry land and in the provinces with a warm climate, because the seed keeps safely, there being no damp to make them rot, and within a day after the next fall of rain they break out; while others recommend sowing immediately after the setting of the Pleiads, because about a week later rains follow; and some advise beginning to sow at the autumnal equinox in cold places, but later in warm districts, so that the crops may not be too far forward before winter.

Works and Days, 384.

§ 49.

Cf. Georg. I 219, 208–210, 227–229.

204 inter omnes autem convenit circa brumam serendum non esse, magno argumento, quoniam hiberna semina, cum ante brumam sata sint, septimo die erumpant, si post brumam, vix quadragesimo. sunt qui properent atque ita pronuntient, festinatam sementem saepe decipere, serotinam semper. e contrario alii vel vere potius serendum quam malo autumno, atque ubi fuerit necesse, inter favonium et vernum
205 aequinoctium. quidam omissa caelesti subtilitate temporibus definiunt: vere linum et avenam et papaver atque, uti nunc etiam transpadani servant, usque in quinquatrus, fabam, siliginem Novembre mense, far Septembri extremo usque in idus Octobres, alii post hunc diem in kal. Novembris. ita his nulla naturae cura est, illis nimia, et ideo caeca subtilitas, cum res geratur inter rusticos litterarumque expertes,
206 non modo siderum. et confitendum est caelo maxime constare ea, quippe Vergilio iubente praedisci ventos ante omnia ac siderum mores, neque aliter quam navigantibus servari. spes ardua et inmensa misceri posse caelestem divinitatem inperitiae rusticae, sed temptanda tam[1] grandi vitae emolumento. prius tamen sideralis difficultas, quam sensere etiam periti,

[1] iam *Mayhoff*.

---

[a] See page 341.
[b] The festival of Minerva beginning March 19.
[c] *Georg.* I. 50 ff.:

Ac prius ignotum ferro quam scindimus aequor,
ventos ac varium caeli praediscere morem
cura sit ac patrios cultusque habitusque locorum
et quid quaeque ferat regio, quid quaeque recuset.

But it is universally agreed that sowing must not be done in the period of mid-winter, for the convincing reason that winter seeds when sown before mid-winter break out in a week, but if sown after it scarcely begin to appear in four weeks. There are some who hasten matters on and put forward the dictum that, while sowing in haste often proves deceptive, sowing late always does. Others on the opposite side think that sowing even in spring is preferable to sowing in a bad autumn, and that if this is necessary it should be done between the arrival of the west wind [a] and the spring equinox. Some people ignore nice points of meteorology and fix limits by the calendar: flax, oats and poppy in spring and up to the Feast of the Five Days,[b] a practice even now observed in the districts north of the Po, beans and common wheat in November, emmer wheat at the end of September on to October 15, and others after that date on to November 1. Thus these latter writers pay no attention to Nature, while the previous set pay too much, and consequently their elaborate theorizing is all in the dark, as the issue lies between countrymen and literary, not merely astronomical, pundits! And it must be confessed that these matters do chiefly depend on the weather—as in fact Virgil[c] enjoins first before all else to learn the winds and the habits of the stars, and to observe them just in the same way as they are observed for navigation. It is an arduous and a vast aspiration—to succeed in introducing the divine science of the heavens to the ignorance of the rustic, but it must be attempted, owing to the vast benefit it confers on life. Nevertheless we must first submit to contemplation the difficulties of astronomy, which

subicienda contemplationi est, quo deinde laetior mens discedat a caelo et facta sentiat quae futura praenosci non possint.

207 LVII. Primum omnium dierum ipsorum anni solisque motus prope inexplicabilis ratio est, ad CCCLXV adiciente anno[1] intercalario diei noctisque quadrantes; ita fit ut tradi non possint certa siderum tempora. accedit confessa rerum obscuritas, nunc praecurrente nec paucis diebus tempestatum significatu, quod προχειμάζειν Graeci vocant, nunc postveniente, quod ἐπιχειμάζειν, et plerumque alias celerius[2] alias tardius caelesti effectu ad terram deciduo; inde[3] vulgo serenitate reddita confectum
208 sidus audimus. praeterea cum omnia haec statis sideribus caeloque adfixis constent, interveniunt motus[4] stellarum, grandines, imbres et ipsi non levi effectu, ut docuimus, turbantque conceptae spei ordinem. idque ne nobis tantum putemus accidere, et reliqua fallit animalia, sagaciora circa hoc ut quo vita eorum constet; aestivasque alites praeposteri aut
209 praepróperi rigores necant, hibernas aestus. ideo Vergilius errantium quoque siderum rationem edis-

[1] *Detlefsen*: adicient eam non.
[2] *Mayhoff*: serius.
[3] inde? *Mayhoff*: unde *aut om. plerique codd.*
[4] motus *quidam apud Dalec*: motu.

---

[a] Aristotle uses προχειμάζειν in the sense of 'to be stormy before', and ἐπιχειμάζειν 'to be stormy at' a certain date. In Thucydides ἐπιχ. means 'to pass the winter at' a place.

even experts have been conscious of, in order that subsequently our minds may more happily pass on from the study of the heavens and discern the actual events of the past whose future occurrence cannot be known in advance.

LVII. First of all it is almost impossible to explain the system of the actual days of the year and that of the movement of the sun, because to the 365 days an intercalary year adds a quarter of a day and of a night, and consequently definite periods of the stars cannot be stated. In addition to this there is the admitted obscurity of the facts, as sometimes the specification of the seasons runs in advance, and by a considerable number of days (the Greek term [a] for this is προχειμάζειν), whereas at other times it comes behind (in Greek ἐπιχειμάζειν), and in general the influence of the heavens falls down to the earth in one place more quickly and in another place more slowly; this is the cause of the remark we commonly hear on the return of fine weather, that a constellation has been completed. Moreover although all these things depend on stars that are stationary and fixed in the sky, there intervene movements of stars and hailstorms and rain, these also having no inconsiderable effect, as we have shown, and they disturb the regularity of the expectation that has been conceived. And we must not think that this occurs only to ourselves—it also deceives the rest of the animals, which have greater sagacity about this matter, inasmuch as it is a thing on which their life depends; and the birds of summer are killed by exceptionally late or exceptionally early frosts, and those of winter by untimely spells of heat. This is why Virgil teaches the

Principles of astronomy.

§ 152.

Georg. I. 335.

cendam praecipit, admonens observandum frigidae Saturni stellae transitum. sunt qui certissimum veris indicium arbitrentur, ob infirmitatem animalis, papiliones; sed[1] eo ipso anno cum commentaremur haec notatum est proventum eorum ter repetito frigore extinctum, advenasque volucres a. d. VI kal. Febr. spem veris adtulisse mox saevissima hieme

210 conflictatam.[2] res anceps: primum omnium a caelo peti legem, deinde eam argumentis esse quaerendam. super omnia est mundi convexitatis terrarumque globi differentia, eodem sidere alio tempore aliis aperiente se gentibus, quo fit ut causa eius non isdem diebus ubique valeat. addidere difficultatem et auctores diversis in locis observando, mox etiam in isdem diversa prodendo. tres autem fuere sectae,

211 Chaldaea, Aegyptia, Graeca; his addidit quartam apud nos Caesar dictator annos ad solis cursum redigens singulos Sosigene perito scientiae eius adhibito—et ea ipsa ratio postea conperto errore correcta est ita ut[3] duodecim annis continuis non intercalaretur, quia

[1] *Mayhoff*: id.
[2] *Rackham*: conflictatas.
[3] ut *add. edd.*

[a] A misinterpretation of Caesar's instructions.

necessity of acquiring a thorough knowledge of the system of the planets also, warning us to watch the transit of the cold star Saturn. Some people think that butterflies are the most reliable sign of spring, on account of the extremely delicate structure of that insect; but in the very year in which I am writing this treatise it has been noticed that their supply has been three times annihilated by a return of cold weather, and that migratory birds arriving on January 27 brought a hope of spring that was soon dashed to the ground by a spell of very severe winter. The procedure is two-fold: first of all it consists in trying to obtain a general principle from celestial phenomena, and then this principle has to be investigated by special signs. Above all there is the variation due to the convexity of the world and the terrestrial globe, the same star revealing itself to different nations at a different time, with the consequence that its influence is not operative everywhere on the same days. Additional difficulty has also been caused by authors through their observations having been taken in different regions, and because in the next place they actually publish different results of observations made in the same regions. But there were three main schools, the Chaldaean, the Egyptian and the Greek; and to these a fourth system was added in our own country 46 B.C.
by Caesar during his dictatorship, who with the assistance of the learned astronomer Sosigenes brought the separate years back into conformity with the course of the sun—and this theory itself was afterwards corrected (when an error [a] had been found), so as to dispense with an intercalary day for a period of twelve successive years, for the reason that the

coeperat ad[1] sidera annus morari qui prius ante-
212 cedebat. et Sosigenes ipse trinis commentationibus
—quamquam diligentior ceteris, non cessavit tamen
addubitare ipse semet corrigendo—et alii[2] auctores
prodidere ea quos praetexuimus volumini huic, raro
ullius sententia cum alio congruente. minus hoc in
reliquis mirum, quos diversi excusaverint tractus;
eorum qui in eadem regione dissedere, unam discor-
diam ponemus exempli gratia: occasum matutinum
213 vergiliarum Hesiodus—nam huius quoque nomine
exstat astrologia—tradidit fieri cum aequinoctium
autumni conficeretur, Thales xxv die ab aequinoctio,
Anaximander xxx, Euctemon xliv, Eudoxus[3] xlviii.
214 nos sequimur observationem Caesaris maxime: haec
erit Italiae ratio; dicemus autem et aliorum placita,
quoniam non unius terrae sed totius naturae inter-
pretes sumus, non auctoribus positis—id enim verbo-
sum est—sed regionibus. legentes tantum memin-
erint brevitatis gratia, cum Attica nominata fuerit,
215 simul intellegere Cycladas insulas; cum Macedonia,
Magnesiam, Threciam; cum Aegyptus, Phoenicen,
Cyprum, Ciliciam; cum Boeotia, Locridem, Phocidem
et finitimos semper tractus; cum Hellespontus,
Chersonesum et continentia usque Atho montem;

[1] ad *add. Mayhoff.*
[2] et alii *add. Mayhoff.*
[3] xliv Eudoxus *add. Boeckh.*

---

[a] Presumably the reference is to the list of astronomers included among the authorities used for Book XVIII that is given in Book I.

[b] Fragments are extant of an Ἀστρικὴ Βίβλος ascribed to Hesiod.

year which had previously been getting in advance of the constellations had begun to lag behind in relation to them. Both Sosigenes himself in his three treatises—though more careful in research than the other writers he nevertheless did not hesitate to introduce an element of doubt by correcting his own statements—and also other authors whose names we prefixed to this volume [a] have published these theories, although it is seldom that the opinions of any two of them agree. This is less surprising in the case of the rest, as they had the excuse of difference of localities; but as for those who have differed in their views in the same country, we will give one case of disagreement as an example: the morning setting of the Pleiads is given by Hesiod [b] —for there is extant an astronomical work that bears his name also—as taking place at the close of the autumnal equinox, whereas Thales puts it on the 25th day after the equinox, Anaximander on the 30th, Euctemon on the 44th, and Eudoxus on the 48th. We follow the observation of Caesar specially: this will be the formula for Italy; but we will also state the views of others, since we are not treating of a single country but of the whole of nature, though we shall not arrange them under the head of their authors, for that would be a lengthy matter, but of the regions concerned. Only readers should remember that, for the sake of brevity, when Attica is mentioned they must understand the Cyclades islands to be included; when Macedonia, Magnesia and Thrace; when Egypt, Phoenicia, Cyprus and Cilicia; when Boeotia, Locris and Phocis and the adjoining regions always as well; when the Dardanelles, the Gallipoli peninsula as far as Monte Santo; when

cum Ionia, Asiam et insulas Asiae, cum Peloponnesus,
216 Achaiam et ad vesperam adiacentes[1] terras; Chaldaei Assyriam et Babyloniam demonstrabunt. Africam, Hispanias, Gallias sileri non erit mirum; nemo enim eas[2] observavit ex iis qui proderent siderum exortus. non tamen difficili ratione dinoscentur in illis quoque
217 terris digestione circulorum quam in sexto volumine fecimus, qua cognatio caeli non gentium modo verum urbium quoque singularum intellegitur. ergo ex iis terris quas nominavimus sumpta convexitate circuli pertinentis ad quas quisque quaeret terras idem erunt siderum exortus per omnium circulorum pares umbras. indicandum et illud, tempestates ipsas cardines[3] suos habere quadrinis annis, et easdem non magna differentia reverti ratione solis, octonis vero augeri easdem centesima revolvente se luna.

218 LVIII. Omnis autem ratio observata est tribus modis, exortu siderum occasuque et ipsorum temporum cardinibus: exortus occasusque binis modis intelleguntur, aut enim adventu solis occultantur stellae et conspici desinunt, aut eiusdem abscessu proferunt se (ut[4] emersum hoc melius quam exortum consuetudo

[1] *Rackham*: iacentes.
[2] *Rackham*: ea *cd. Leid. n.* VII, *m.* 2: *om. rell.*
[3] *Pintianus*: ardores *edd. vett.*: arbores.
[4] ut *Mayhoff*: in.

Ionia, Asia and the islands belonging to it; when the Morea, Achaia and the lands lying to the west of it; and the term 'Chaldaeans' will indicate Assyria and Babylonia. That the names of Africa and the provinces of Spain and Gaul are not mentioned will cause no surprise, because none of those who have published accounts of the risings of the constellations have made observations in respect of those countries. Still it will not involve a difficult calculation to ascertain them in those countries as well, by means of the explanation of parallels which we have set out in Book Six, which indicates the astronomical relationship not only of nations but of individual cities as well. Therefore by taking the circular parallel belonging to the countries we have specified and applying it to those that the particular student is seeking, the risings of the constellations will be the same throughout the parts of all the parallels where shadows are of equal length. It is also necessary to point out that the seasons themselves have their own periods every four years, and that they too return without great variation under the system of the sun, but that they are also lengthened every eight years at the hundredth revolution of the moon.

VI. 212 ff.

Rising and setting of constellations.

LVIII. The whole system however is based on three lines of observation—the rising and the setting of the constellations and the periods of the seasons themselves: there are two modes of observing the risings and settings, as the stars are either hidden by the arrival of the sun and cease to be visible, or they present themselves to the view on the sun's departure (so that custom would have done better to designate the latter as the stars' 'emergence' rather than

dixisset et illud occultationem potius quam occasum);
219 aut illo[1] modo, quo die incipiunt apparere vel desinunt oriente sole aut occidente, matutini vespertinive cognominati, prout alteruter eorum mane vel crepusculo contingit. dodrantes horarum cum minimum intervalla ea desiderant ante solis ortum vel post occasum ut aspici possint. praeterea bis quaedam exoriuntur et occidunt; omnisque sermo de iis est stellis quas adhaerere caelo diximus.

220 LIX. Cardines temporum quadripertita anni distinctione constant per incrementa ac decrementa[2] lucis. augetur haec a bruma, et aequatur nocti[3] verno aequinoctio diebus XC horis tribus. dein superat noctem ad solstitium diebus XCIV horis XII,**[4] usque ad aequinoctium autumni, et tum aequata diei procedit nox[5]
221 ex eo ad brumam diebus LXXXVIII horis tribus—horae nunc in omni accessione ac decessione[6] aequinoctiales, non cuiuscumque diei, significantur—omnesque eae differentiae fiunt in octavis partibus signorum, bruma capricorni a. d. VIII kal. Ian. fere, aequinoctiam vernum arietis, solstitium cancri, alterumque aequinoctium librae, qui et ipsi dies raro non aliquos tem-
222 pestatum significatus habent. rursus hi cardines

[1] *Rackham*: occasum ullo (alio *Hermolaus*).
[2] ac decrementa *add. Rackham.*
[3] *Rackham*: noctibus.
[4] *Lacunam Petavius.*
[5] *Mayhoff*: die procedit ex.
[6] ac decessione *add. Warmington.*

---

[a] *E.g.* Aquila; see § 288.
[b] The Romans, telling the time by the sundial, normally divided each of the two daily periods from sunrise to sunset and from sunset to sunrise into twelve hours all the year round, so that an hour was one twenty-fourth part of the day.

'rising', and the former as their 'occultation' rather than 'setting'); or by means of the following mode —by the day on which the risings and settings of the stars begin or cease to be visible at the rising or setting of the sun, these being designated their morning or evening risings and settings according as each of them occurs at dawn or at dusk. They require intervals of at least three-quarters of an hour before sunrise or after sunset in order to be visible. Moreover there are some stars that rise and set twice[a]; and all that is said here refers to the stars which we have stated to be fixed stars. II. 7 ff.

Solar seasons.

LIX. The divisions of the seasons are fixed by the fourfold distribution of the year corresponding with the increases and decreases of daylight. From midwinter onward this increases in length, and in 90 days 3 hours at the spring equinox the day becomes equal to the night. From then to the summer solstice, a period of 94 days 12 hours, the day is longer than the night . . . until the autumn equinox, and then the night having become equal to the day goes on increasing from that point until midwinter, a period of 88 days 3 hours (in the present passage the term 'hours' in each addition and subtraction denotes equinoctial hours and not the hours of any day in particular[b]) and all these changes occur at the eighth degree of the signs of the zodiac, midwinter at the eighth degree of Capricorn, about December 26, the equinox at the eighth of the Ram, the summer solstice at the eighth of the Crab and the other equinox at the eighth of the Scales—which days themselves also usually give some indications of changes of weather. Again these

and night together only at the equinoxes, and at other periods was longer by day and shorter by night, or *vice versa.*

singulis etiamnum articulis temporum dividuntur, per media omnes dierum spatia, quoniam inter solstitium et aequinoctium autumni fidiculae occasus autumnum inchoat die XLVI, ab aequinoctio eo ad brumam vergiliarum matutinus occasus hiemem die XLIV,[1] inter brumam et aequinctium die XLV flatus favoni vernum tempus, ab aequinoctio verno initium aestatis die
223 XLVII [2] vergiliarum exortus matutinus. nos incipiemus a sementibus frumenti, hoc est vergiliarum occasu matutino: nec deinde parvorum siderum mentione concidenda ratio est et difficultas rerum augenda, cum sidus vehemens Orionis isdem diebus longo decidat spatio.

224 LX. Sementibus tempora plerique praesumunt et ab XI die autumnalis aequinoctii fruges serunt, novem a [3] coronae exortu continuis diebus certo prope imbrium promisso; Xenophon non antequam deus signum dederit—hoc Cicero noster imbre fieri interpretatus est, cum sit vera ratio non prius serendi
225 quam folia coeperint decidere. hoc ipso vergiliarum occasu fieri putant aliqui a. d. III idus Novembris, ut diximus, servantque id sidus etiam vestis institores, et est in caelo notatu facillimum: ergo ex occasu eius de hieme augurantur quibus est cura insidiandi, negotiatores avari: ita[4] nubilo occasu pluviosam hiemem denuntiat, statimque augent lacernarum

[1] *Pintianus*: XLIII.
[2] *Detlefsen*: XLVIII.
[3] *Mayhoff*: fruges servitio venta *aut alia codd.*
[4] *Mayhoff*: negotiatoris avaritia.

---

[a] In his now lost translation of Xenophon's *Oeconomicus*, referred to in *De Off.* II. 87.
[b] The text here has been suspected.

periods are also divided by particular moments of time, all of them at midday—since between the solstice and the autumnal equinox the setting of the Lyre on the 46th day marks the beginning of autumn, and from that equinox to midwinter the morning setting of the Pleiads on the 44th day marks that of winter, and between midwinter and the equinox the prevalence of a west wind on the 45th day marks the period of spring, and the morning rising of the Pleiads on the 47th day from the spring equinox marks the beginning of summer. We will start from sowing-time of wheat, that is from the morning setting of the Pleiads; and we need not interrupt our explanation and increase the difficulty of the subject by mentioning the minor stars, inasmuch as it is at the same date that the stormy constellation of Orion sets after its extensive course.

LX. Most people anticipate the times for sowing, *Signs of the weather for sowing.*
and begin to sow corn at the eleventh day of the autumnal equinox, as for nine days after the rising of the Crown there is an almost certain expectation of rain. But Xenophon tells us not to begin before *Oec.* 17. 2.
the Deity has given the signal—this our Roman author Cicero [a] understood as being done by a fall of rain; although the true method is not to sow before the leaves have begun to fall. Some think that this occurs exactly at the setting of the Pleiads on November 10, as we have said, and even clothes- II. 125.
dealers go by that constellation,[b] and it is very easy to identify in the sky; consequently dealers out to make money, who are careful to watch for chances, make forecasts as to the winter from its setting: thus by a cloudy setting it foretells a wet winter, and they at once raise their prices for cloaks, whereas by a

pretia, sereno asperam, et reliquarum vestium
226 accendunt. sed ille indocilis caeli agricola hoc signum habeat inter suos vepres humumque suam aspiciens, cum folia decidere viderit: sic iudicetur anni temperies, alibi tardius, alibi maturius; ita enim sentitur ut caeli locique adficit natura, idque in hac ratione praecellit quod eadem et in mundo publica est
227 et unicuique loco peculiaris. miretur hoc qui non meminerit ipso brumali die puleium in carnariis florere: adeo nihil occultum esse natura voluit; et serendi igitur hoc dedit signum. haec est vera interpretatio argumenta naturae secum adferens, quippe sic terram peti suadet promittitque quandam stercoris vicem et contra rigores terram satusque operiri a se nuntiat ac monet festinare.

228 LXI. Varro in fabae utique satu hanc observationem custodiri praecepit. alii plena luna serendam, lentim vero a vicesima quinta ad tricesimam, viciam quoque iisdem lunae diebus: ita demum sine limacibus fore. quidam pabuli causa sic iubent seri, seminis autem vere.

Est et alia manifestior ratio mirabiliore naturae

---

[a] *I.e.* the rule to be guided by the weather at the setting of the Pleiads, § 225.

fine weather setting it foretells a hard winter, and they screw up the prices of all other clothes. But our friend the farmer, not learned in astronomy, may find this sign of the weather among his hedgerows and merely by looking at his own land, when he has seen the leaves fall: in that way the year's weather can be estimated, as they fall later in some cases and earlier in others, for the weather is perceived as it is affected by the nature of the climate and the locality, and this method contains the advantage that while it is universal and world-wide it is also at the same time peculiar to each particular locality. This may surprise anyone who does not remember that the pennyroyal hung up in our larders blossoms exactly on midwinter day: so fully has Nature willed that nothing shall be hidden; consequently she has also given us this signal for sowing. This is the true account of the situation, bringing with it Nature's own proofs, inasmuch as she actually advises this mode of approaching the land and promises it will serve as a substitute for manure, and tells us that the land and the crops are shielded by herself against the rigours of frost, and warns us to make haste.

LXI. Varro has advised keeping this rule[a] at all events in sowing beans. Others say that beans should be sown at a full moon, but lentils between the 25th and 30th day of the lunar month, and also vetch on the same days, that being the only way to keep them free from slugs. Some people advise that date for sowing for fodder, but recommend sowing in the spring to obtain seed. *R.R.* I. 34, 2.

Other rules for sowing. There is also another more obvious method due to still more remarkable foresight on the part of

providentia, in qua Ciceronis sententiam ipsius verbis subsignabimus:

Iam vero semper viridis semperque gravata
Lentiscus triplici solita est grandescere fetu;
Ter fruges fundens tria tempora monstrat arandi.

229 Ex his unum hoc erit idem et lino ac papaveri serendo. Cato de papavere ita tradit: 'Virgas et sarmenta quae tibi usioni[1] supererunt in segete comburito. ubi eas combusseris, ibi papaver serito.' silvestre in miro usu est melle decoctum ad faucium remedia, visque somnifera etiam sativo.—Et hactenus de hiberna semente.

230 LXII. Verum ut pariter omnis culturae quoddam breviarium peragatur, eodem tempore conveniet arbores stercorare, adcumulare item vineas—sufficit in iugerum una[2] opera—et ubi patietur loci ratio arbusta ac vineas putare, solum seminariis bipalio praeparare, incilia aperire, aquam de agro pellere,
231 torcular lavare et recondere. a kal. Novemb. gallinis ova supponere nolito donec bruma conficiatur; in eum diem ternadena subicito aestate tota, hieme pauciora, non tamen infra novena. Democritus talem futuram hiemem arbitratur qualis fuerit brumae dies et circa eum terni, item solstitio aestatem. circa brumam plerisque bis septeni[3] halcyonum feturae[4]

[1] *Hardouin e Catone*: osioni *aut* cisioni *aut* usui.
[2] una *add. Sillig.*
[3] *Mayhoff*: septem.
[4] *Mayhoff*: fetura.

---

[a] *De Div.* I. 9, 15, from Aratus *Diosem.* 1050 sqq.

Nature, under the head of which we will register the opinion of Cicero[a] in his own words:

> The mastich, ever green and ever teeming,
> Is wont to swell with thrice-repeated produce:
> Thrice bearing fruit, she marks three ploughing seasons.

One of these seasons, this last one, is the same also for sowing flax and poppy. For poppy Cato gives the following rule: 'On land used for corn burn any twigs and brushwood left over from your utilization of them. Sow poppy in the place where you have burnt them'. Wild poppy boiled in honey is wonderfully serviceable for making throat-cures, and also cultivated poppy is a powerful soporific. So far as to winter sowing. *R.R.* XXVIII. 4.

Management of vineyards.

LXII. But correspondingly to complete a sort of summary of the whole subject of cultivation, it will be suitable at the same time to manure the trees, also to bank up the vines—one hand is enough to do an acre—and where the nature of the locality will allow, to prune the trees and the vines, to prepare the ground with a double mattock for seed-plots, to open up the ditches, to drain water off the land, and to wash out and put away the wine-press. Do not put eggs under the hens to hatch after November 1 until mid-winter is past; all through the summer till that date give thirteen eggs to each hen, but fewer in winter, though not less than nine. Democritus thinks that the weather through the winter will be the same as it was on the shortest day and the three days round it, and he thinks so too in regard to the summer and the weather at the summer solstice. In most cases the fourteen days round mid-winter

Poultry-keeping, etc.

ventorum quiete molliunt caelum. sed et in his et in aliis omnibus ex eventu significationum intellegi sidera debebunt, non ad dies utique praefinitos expectari tempestatum vadimonia.

232 LXIII. Per brumam vitem ne colito. vina tum defaecari vel etiam diffundi Hyginus suadet a confecta ea septimo die, utique si septima luna conpetat; cerasa circa brumam seri. bubus glandem tum adspergi convenit in iuga singula modios: largior valetudinem infestat; et quocumque tempore detur, si minus XXX diebus continuis data sit, narrant verna scabie poenitere.[1] materiae caedendae tempus hoc dedimus; reliqua opera nocturna maxime vigilia
233 constent, cum sint noctes tanto ampliores, qualos, crates, fiscinas texere, faces incidere, ridicas praeparare interdiu XXX, palos LX et in lucubratione vespertina ridicas V, palos X, totidem antelucana[2].

234 LXIV. A bruma in favonium Caesari nobilia sidera significant, III kal. Ian. mututino canis occidens, quo die Atticae et finitimis regionibus aquila vesperi occidere traditur; pridie nonas Ian. Caesari delphinus matutino exoritur et postero die fidicula, quo

[1] *Mendosum? Mayhoff.*
[2] *Caesarius*: antelucano *aut* -anum.

[a] Hence the phrase 'halcyon days'. This bird was believed to lay its eggs and hatch them floating on the surface of the sea.

bring mild weather with calm winds for the sitting of the kingfishers.[a] But in these and all other matters we shall have to conjecture the influence of the stars from the outcome of their indications, and at all events not expect changes of weather to answer to bail on dates fixed in advance.

Winter farm operations.

LXIII. Avoid attending to the vine at mid-winter. Hyginus recommends straining the wine then, or even racking it off a week after the shortest day has passed, provided a week-old moon coincides with it; and planting cherries about mid-winter. It is proper at that date to put acorns in soak as fodder for oxen, a peck *per* yoke—a larger quantity is injurious to their health; and it is said that whenever they are given this feed, if it is not fed to them for at least 30 days in succession, an outbreak of mange in the spring will cause you to repent. We have given XVI. 188. this as the time for cutting timber; and the other kinds of work may be arranged chiefly in the night time, as the nights are so much longer—weaving wicker baskets, hampers and rush baskets, cutting torches, preparing squared vine-props at the rate of thirty and rounded poles at the rate of sixty a day in day-time, and by artificial light five props and ten poles in an evening and the same number in the early morning.

Winter dates told by the stars. Suitable farm work.

LXIV. From midwinter till the west wind blows the important stars that mark the dates, according to Caesar's observations, are—the Dogstar setting at dawn on December 30, the day on which the Eagle is reported to set in the evening for Attica and the neighbouring regions; on January 4 according to Caesar's observations the Dolphin rises at dawn and the next day the Lyre, the Arrow setting in the evening on

235 Aegypto sagitta vesperi occidit; item ad VI idus Ian. eiusdem delphini vespertino occasu continui dies hiemant Italiae, et cum sol in aquarium sentiatur transire, quod fere XVI kal. Feb. evenit. VIII kal. stella regia appellata Tuberoni in pectore leonis occidit matutino[1] et pridie nonas Feb. fidicula vespere[2]
236 occidit. huius temporis novissimis diebus, ubicumque patietur caeli ratio, terram ad rosarum[3] et vineae satum vertere bipalio oportet—iugero operae LXX sufficiunt—fossas purgare aut novas facere, antelucanis ferramenta acuere, manubria aptare, dolia quassa sarcire, ovium tegimenta concinnare ipsarumque lanas scabendo purgare.

237 LXV. A favonio in aequinoctium vernum Caesari significat XIV kal. Mart. triduum varie, et VIII kal. hirundinis visu et postero die arcturi exortu vespertino, item III non. Mart.—Caesar cancri exortu id fieri observavit, maior pars auctorum vindemitoris inmersu—VIII idus aquilonii piscis exortu et postero die Orionis; in Attica milvum apparere servatur. Caesar et idus Mart. ferales sibi notavit scorpionis occasu, XV kal. vero April. Italiae milvum ostendi, XII kal. equum occidere matutino.

[1] *Edd.*: matutina.
[2] *V.l.* vespera.
[3] *V.l.* rosaria *aut* rosariam.

the same day for Egypt; likewise on January 8 the Dolphin before mentioned sets in the evening and there are some days of continuous wintry weather for Italy; and so also when the sun is seen to pass into Aquarius, which happens about January 17. On January 25 the star in the breast of the Lion called according to Tubero the Royal Star sets in the morning and the Lyre sets in the evening of February 4. In the concluding days of this period, whenever the weather conditions allow, the ground should be turned up with a double mattock for planting roses and vines —seventy hands are enough for an acre—and ditches should be cleaned or new ones made, and the time before daybreak should be used for sharpening iron tools, fitting handles, repairing broken vats, doing up the shelters used for sheep and cleaning the sheeps' fleeces by scraping them.

Late winter weather and suitable farm work.

LXV. Between the period of west wind and the spring equinox, February 16 for Caesar marks three days of changeable weather, as also does February 22 by the appearance of the swallow and on the next day the rising of Arcturus in the evening, and the same on March 5—Caesar noticed that this bad weather took place at the rising of the Crab, but the majority of the authorities put it at the setting of the Vintager—on March 8 at the rising of the northern part of the Fish, and on the next day at the rising of Orion; in Attica it is noticed that the constellation Kite appears. Caesar also noted March 15—the day that was fatal to him—as marked by the setting of the Scorpion, but stated that on March 18 the Kite becomes visible in Italy and on March 21 the Horse sets in the morning.

238 Hoc intervallum temporis vegetissimum agricolis maximeque operosum est, in quo praecipue falluntur; neque enim eo die vocantur ad munia quo favonius flare debeat sed quo coeperit. hoc acri intentione servandum est, hoc illo mense signum dies[1] habet observatione minime fallaci aut dubia, si quis adtendat.
239 unde autem spiret is ventus quaque parte veniat, diximus secundo volumine et dicemus mox paulo operosius. interim ab eo die, quisquis ille fuerit, quo flare coeperit—non utique VI id. Feb., sed sive ante, quando[2] praevernat,[3] sive postea, quando hiemat post diem hunc,[4] innumera rusticos cura distringat et prima quaeque peragantur quae differri nequeunt.
240 trimestria serantur, vites putentur qua diximus ratione, oleae curentur, poma serantur inseranturque, vineae pastinentur, seminaria[5] digerantur, instaurentur alia, harundines, salices, genistae serantur caedanturque, serantur vero ulmi, populi, fraxini uti
241 dictum est. tum et segetes convenit purgare, sarire hibernas fruges maximeque far; lex certa in eo, cum quattuor fibrarum esse coeperit, in[6] faba vero non antequam trium foliorum, tunc quoque levi sarculo purgare verius quam fodere, florentem utique

[1] *Mayhoff*: deus.
[2] *cd. Par. Lat.* 6797: quo 6795: $\overline{\mathrm{qm}}$. *rell.*
[3] *Gelen.*: praevenerat (praeverat *cd. Tolet.*).
[4] hunc *Mayhoff*: tunc *cd. Leid. n.* VII, *m.* 2: diemat *rell.*; quando posthiemat tunc *Detlefsen*).
[5] *C. F. W. Mueller*: semina.
[6] in *add. Rackham*: coeperit, fabam? *Warmington*.

This space of time is an extremely busy period
for farmers and specially toilsome, and it is one as
to which they are particularly liable to go wrong—
the fact being that they are not summoned to their
tasks on the day on which the west wind ought to
blow but on which it actually does begin to blow.
This must be watched for with sharp attention, and
is a signal possessed by a day in that month that is
observable without any deception or doubt whatever, if one gives close attention. We have stated
in Volume Two the quarter in which that wind blows II. 122.
and the exact point from which it comes, and we
shall speak about it rather more fully a little later. § 317.
In the meantime, starting from the day, whichever
it is, on which it begins to blow—not however necessarily February 8, but whether before that date,
when the spring is early, or afterwards, when winter
goes on after that day, countrymen should find
themselves torn between innumerable anxieties and
should finish off all the primary tasks which cannot
be postponed. Three-month wheat must be sown,
vines pruned by the method we have stated, olives XVII. 176.
attended to, fruit-trees planted and grafted, vineyards dug over, seed-plots arranged and others restored, reeds, willows and brooms planted and cut, and
elms, poplars and ash trees planted in the manner
stated above. Then it is also suitable to weed the XVII. 78.
cornfields and hoe the winter crops, and especially
emmer wheat; for the latter there is a definite
rule, to hoe when it has begun to have four blades
showing, but in the case of beans not before they
have three leaves out, and even then they should
be cleaned with a light hoe rather than dug over,
and anyway when they flower they must not be

xv primis diebus non attingere. hordeum nisi sicco ne sarito. putationem aequinoctio peractam habeto. vineae iugerum quaternae operae putant, alligant
242 in arbusto singulae operae arbores xv. eodem hoc tempore hortorum rosariorumque cura est, quae separatim proximis voluminibus dicetur, eodem et topiarii; tum optime scrobes fiunt. terra in futurum proscinditur Vergilio maxime auctore, ut glaebas sol excoquat. utilior sententia quae non nisi temperatum solum medio vere arari iubet, quoniam in pingui statim sulcos occupant herbae, gracili insecuti aestus exsiccant omnemque sucum venturis seminibus auferunt; talia autumno melius arari certum est.

243 Cato verna opera sic definit: 'scrobes fieri seminariis, ⟨vitiaria⟩[1] propagari, in locis crassis et umidis ulmos, ficos, poma, oleas seri, prata stercorari luna sitiente quae rigua non erunt, a flatu favonii defendi, purgari, herbas malas radicitus erui, ficos interputari, seminaria fieri et vetera sarciri, haec antequam vineam fodere incipias.' idemque, 'piro florente arare incipito[2] macra harenosaque; postea uti quaeque gravissima et aquosissima ita postremo
244 arato.' ergo haec aratio duas[3] habebit notas,

[1] *Ian*: seminaria (seminaria *et lac. Pontedera*: seminariis, vitiariis locum verti, vites propagari *Cato* XL).
[2] *Mayhoff*: incipiat.
[3] duas? *Mayhoff*: has.

---

[a] Presumably this sentence refers to one day's work.
[b] What follows in § 243 is loosely quoted or paraphrased from Cato *R.R.* cc. XL, L, CXXXI.

touched during the first fortnight. You should only hoe barley in dry weather. You should have your pruning finished by the equinox. An acre of vineyard takes four hands to prune, and tying up the vines on a tree takes one hand for each fifteen trees.[a] This is the time moreover for kitchen-gardens and rose-beds to be attended to, a subject which will be dealt with separately in the following Books, and it is also the time for landscape gardening; and then is the best occasion for making ditches. The ground is now opened for future operations, as Virgil in particular advises, to allow the sun thoroughly to dry the clods. The more useful opinion recommends ploughing only ground of medium quality in the middle of spring, because in a rich soil the furrows are at once seized on by weeds and in a thin soil the spells of heat that follow dry them up and take away all moisture from the seeds that are to come; there is no question that it is best to plough land of these sorts in the autumn.

XIX. 49 ff., XXI. 14 ff.

Georg. I. 6.

Spring operations.

The following are the rules given by Cato[b] for operations in spring: 'to make ditches for the seed-plots, layer vine-nurseries, plant elms, figs, fruit-trees and olives in thick and damp soils, under a dry moon to manure meadows that are not going to be irrigated, and to protect them from westerly winds, and to clean them and root up noxious weeds; to prune fig-trees lightly, make new seed-beds and repair old ones—these operations to be done before you begin to dig over the vineyard.' Cato also says: 'You should begin to plough thin and sandy soils when the pear-tree blossoms, and afterwards plough the successively heaviest and wettest lands last of all.' Consequently there will be two signs for this

lentisci primum fructum ostendentis ac piri florentis.
erit et tertia in bulborum satu scillae, item in corona-
mentorum narcissi; namque et haec ter florent
primoque flore primam arationem ostendunt, medio
secundam, tertio novissimam, quando inter sese alia
245 aliis notas praebent. ac non in novissimis caveatur[1]
ne fabis florentibus attingatur hedera; id enim
noxium et exitiale ei[2] est tempus. quaedam vero
et suas habent notas, sicuti ficus: cum folia pauca in
cacumine acetabuli modo germinent, tunc maxime
serendas ficus.

246 LXVI. Aequinoctium vernum a. d. viii kal. April.
peragi videtur. ab eo ad vergiliarum exortum
matutinum Caesari significant kal. April. iii non.
April. in Attica vergiliae vesperi occultantur, eaedem
postridie in Boeotia, Caesari autem et Chaldaeis
nonis, Aegypto Orion et gladius eius incipiunt
247 abscondi. Caesari vi idus significatur imber librae
occasu. xiv kal. Mai. Aegypto suculae occidunt
vesperi, sidus vehemens et terra marique turbidum;
xvi Atticae, xv Caesari continuo quatriduo significat,
Assyriae autem xii kal. hoc est vulgo appellatum
sidus Parilicium, quoniam xi kal. Mai. urbis Romae
natalis, quo fere serenitas redditur, claritatem
observationi dedit, nimborum argumento hyadas

[1] *Rackham*: cavetur.
[2] eis? *Rackham*.

[a] A variant reading gives *terra* 'with the ground.'

ploughing, the sign of the mastich showing its first fruit and that of the pear blossoming. There will also be a third sign, that of the squill in the growing bulbs and that of the narcissus among the plants used for wreaths; for these also flower three times, marking the first ploughing by their first flowering, the second by the middle one and the last by the third—inasmuch as things afford hints for other things different from them. And one of the first precautions to be taken is to prevent beans when in flower from coming in contact with ivy;[a] for that season is a baneful and deadly one with ivy. Some plants however also have special signs of their own, for instance the fig: when a few leaves are sprouting from the top, like a vinegar-cup, that indicates that it is the best time for planting fig-trees.

Constellations of late spring.

LXVI. The vernal equinox appears to end on March 25. Between that day and the morning rising of the Pleiads the first of April according to Caesar indicates bad weather. The Pleiads set on the evening of April 3 in Attica and on the day after in Boeotia, but for Caesar and the Chaldaeans on April 5, when for Egypt Orion and his sword begin to set. The setting of the Scales on April 8 according to Caesar announces rain. In the evening The Little Pigs, a stormy constellation bringing boisterous weather on land and sea, sets for Egypt on April 18; it sets on April 16 for Attica and April 17 for Caesar, indicating four successive days of bad weather, but on the 20th for Assyria. This constellation is commonly called Parilicium, because April 21, the birthday of the city of Rome, on which fine weather usually returns, has given a clear sky for observing the heavens, although because of the clouds that it brings with

appellantibus Graecis[1] quod nostri a similitudine cognominis Graeci propter sues inpositum arbitrantes
248 inperitia appellavere suculas. Caesari et VIII kal. notatur dies. VII kal. Aegypto haedi exoriuntur, VI Boeotiae et Atticae canis vesperi occultatur, fidicula mane oritur. V kal. Assyriae Orion totus absconditur, IV autem canis. VI non. Mai. Caesari suculae matutino exoriuntur et VIII id. capella pluvialis, Aegypto autem eodem die canis vesperi occultatur. sic fere in VI id. Mai., qui est vergiliarum exortus, decurrunt sidera.

249 In hoc temporis intervallo XV diebus primis agricolae rapienda sunt quibus peragendis ante aequinoctium non suffecerit, dum[2] sciat inde natam exprobrationem foedam putantium vites per imitationem cantus alitis temporariae quam cuculum vocant; dedecus enim habetur obprobriumque meritum falcem ab illa volucre in vite deprehendi, et ob id petulantiae sales etiam, cum primo vere ludantur,[3] auspicio tamen detestabiles videntur. adeo minima quaeque in agro naturalibus trahuntur argumentis.

250 Extremo autem hoc tempore panici miliique satio est: iustum haec seri maturato hordeo. atque etiam in eodem arvo signum illius maturitatis et horum sationis commune lucentes vespere per arva cicindelae

[1] *Mayhoff*: Graecis eas stellas *aut alia.*
[2] tum? *Mayhoff.*
[3] *Edd.*: laudantur (ludant *cd. Vat. Lat.* 3861, *m.* 2).

---

[a] From ὕειν, 'to rain', not from ὗς, 'pig'.

it the Greek name for the constellation is Hyades [a], which our countrymen, owing to the similarity of the Greek name supposed in their ignorance to have been given it with reference to the word for 'pigs', and so have called the stars the Little Pigs. In Caesar's calendar April 24 is also a marked day. On April 25 the Kids rise for Egypt, and on April 26 the Dog sets in the evening and the Lyre rises in the morning for Boeotia and Attica. On April 27 Orion entirely disappears for Assyria, and on the 28th the Dog. On May 2 the Little Pigs rise in the morning for Caesar, and on May 8 the She-goat, portending rain, while the Dog sets for Egypt in the evening of the same day. That is a fairly precise account of the movements of the constellations down to May 10, which is the date of the rising of the Pleiads.

Farm work in spring.

In this space of time the farmer must hurry on during the first fortnight with work which he has not had time to finish before the equinox, while realising that this is the origin of the rude habit of jeering at people pruning their vines by imitating the note of the visiting bird called the cuckoo, as it is considered disgraceful and deserving of reproach for that bird to find the pruning-hook being used on the vine; and consequently wanton jokes, though men are merely being made sport of in early spring, are thought to be objectionable as bringing bad luck. To such an extent on the land is every trifle set down as a hint given by Nature.

End of cold weather marked by appearance of glow-worms.

In the latter part of this period Italian and common millets are sown, the proper time for sowing them being when the barley has ripened. And the sign alike of the barley being ripe and for sowing these crops consists in the fields in the evening shining with glow-

(ita appellant rustici stellantes volatus, Graeci vero
251 lampyridas) incredibili benignitate naturae. LXVII. Iam vergilias in caelo notabiles caterva fecerat; non tamen his contenta terrestres fecit alias, veluti vociferans: 'Cur caelum intuearis, agricola? cur sidera quaeras, rustice? iam te breviore somno fessum premunt noctes. ecce tibi inter herbas tuas spargo peculiares stellas easque vespera et ab opere disiungenti ostendo ac ne possis praeterire miraculo sollicito:
252 videsne ut fulgor igni similis alarum conpressu obtegatur secumque lucem habeant[1] et nocte?[2] dedi tibi herbas horarum indices et, ut ne sole quidem oculos tuos terra avoces, heliotropium ac lupinum circumaguntur cum illo. cur etiamnum altius spectes
253 ipsumque caelum scrutere? habes ante pedes tuos ecce vergilias.' incertis hae diebus proveniunt durantque, sed esse sideris huiusce partum eas certum est. proinde quisquis aestivos fructus ante illas severit 'ipse frustrabitur sese.' hoc intervallo et apicula procedens fabam florere indicat, fabaque florescens eam evocat. dabitur et aliud finiti frigoris indicium: cum germinare videris morum, iniuriam postea frigoris timere nolito.

[1] habeant? *Mayhoff*: habeat.
[2] noctem? *Mayhoff*.

---

[a] *Sese frustrabitur ipse* might be a half-line from a poem, as Sillig suggests.

worms (that is what the country-people call those starlike flights of insects, the Greek name for which is *lampyrides*) thanks to Nature's unbelievable kindness. LXVII. She had already formed the remarkable group of the Pleiads in the sky; yet not content with these she has made other stars on the earth, as though crying aloud: 'Why gaze at the heavens, husbandman? Why, rustic, search for the stars? Already the slumber laid on you by the nights in your fatigue is shorter. Lo and behold, I scatter special stars for you among your plants, and I display them to you in the evening and as you unyoke to leave off work, and I stimulate your attention by a marvel so that you may not be able to pass them by: do you see how their fire-like brilliance is screened by their folded wings, and how they carry daylight with them even in the night? I have given you plants that mark the hours, and in order that you may not even have to avert your eyes from the earth to look at the sun, the heliotrope and the lupine revolve keeping time with him. Why then do you still look higher and scan the heavens themselves? Lo! you have Pleiads at your very feet.' Glow-worms do not make their appearance on fixed days or last a definite period, but certain it is that they are the offspring of this particular constellation. Consequently anybody who does his summer sowing before they appear 'will have himself to thank for labour wasted'.[a] In this interval also the little bee comes forth and announces that the bean is flowering, and the bean begins to flower to tempt her out. We will also give another sign of cold weather being ended: when you see the mulberry budding, after that you need not fear damage from cold.

254 Ergo opera: taleas olivarum ponere ipsasque oleas interradere, rigare prata aequinoctii diebus primis, cum herba creverit in festucam arcere aquas, vineam pampinare (et huic lex sua, cum pampini quattuor digitos longitudine expleverint—pampinat una opera iugerum), segetes iterare (saritur diebus xx). ab aequinoctio sartura nocere et vineae et segeti existimatur. et oves lavandi hoc idem tempus est.

255 A vergiliarum exortu significant Caesari postridie
arcturi occasus matutinus, iii id. Mai. fidiculae
exortus, xii kal. Iun. capella vesperi occidens et in
Attica canis. xi kal. Caesari Orionis gladius occidere
incipit, iv non. Iun. Caesari et Assyriae aquila vesperi
oritur, vii id. arcturus matutino occidit Italiae, iv
256 delphinus vesperi exoritur. xvii kal. Iul. gladius
Orionis exoritur, quod in Aegypto post quadriduum.
xi kal. eiusdem Orionis gladius Caesari occidere
incipit; viii kal. vero Iul. longissimus dies totius anni
257 et nox brevissima solstitium conficiunt. in hoc
temporis intervallo vineae pampinantur, curatur ut
vinea vetus semel fossa sit, bis novella; oves
tondentur, lupinum stercorandi causa vertitur, terra
proscinditur, vicia in pabulum secatur, faba metitur,
dein cuditur.

258 Prata circa kal. Iun. caeduntur, quorum facillima agricolis cura ac minimi inpendii haec de se postulat

Well then, a list of things to be done: to plant olive-cuttings and rake over between the olive trees themselves; in the first days of the equinox to irrigate the meadows; when the grass has grown to a stalk, to shut off the water; to trim the vine (the vine too has a rule of its own: it must be trimmed when the shoots have made four inches in length—one hand can trim an acre); to stir over the corn crops again (hoeing takes 20 days). It is thought that to start hoeing at the equinox injures both vines and corn. This is also the time for washing sheep. *Appropriate operations.*

After the rise of the Pleiads the weather is indicated for Caesar by the morning setting of Arcturus on the following day, the rise of the Lyre on May 13, the setting of the She-goat, and in Attica of the Dog, in the evening of May 21. On May 22, as observed by Caesar, Orion's Sword begins to set; in the evening of June 2, according to Caesar, and for Assyria also, the Eagle rises; on the morning of June 7 Arcturus sets for Italy, and on the evening of June 10 the Dolphin rises. On June 15 Orion's Sword rises, but in Egypt this takes place four days later. Moreover on June 21 Orion's Sword, as observed by Caesar, begins to set; while on June 24 the longest day and shortest night of the whole year make the summer solstice. In this interval of time the vines are pruned, and care is taken to give an old vine one digging round and a new one two; sheep are sheared, lupins are ploughed in to manure the land, the ground is dug over, vetches are cut for fodder, beans are gathered and then threshed. *Constellations of early summer.* *Appropriate work.*

Meadows are mown about June 1. The cultivation of these is extremely easy for the farmer and *Meadows. Hay.*

dici. relinqui debent in laeto solo vel umido vel riguo, eaque aqua pluvia rigari aut [1] publica. utilissimum, si malae herbae, arare, dein cratire, sarire,[2] florem ex fenilibus atque e praesepibus feno dilapsum spargere priusquam cratiantur, nec primo anno rigari, nec pasci ante secunda fenisecia, ne herbae

259 vellantur obtrituque hebetentur. senescunt prata restituique debent faba in iis sata vel rapis vel milio, mox insequente anno frumento, rursusque inarata [3] tertio relinqui, praeterea quotiens secta sint siciliri, hoc est quae feniseces praeterierunt secari; est enim in primis inutile enasci herbas sementaturas. herba optima in prato trifolii, proxima graminis, pessima nummuli siliquam etiam diram ferentis; invisa et

260 equisaeti est, a similitudine equinae saetae.[4] secandi tempus cum spica deflorescere coepit atque roborari; secandum antequam inarescat. Cato 'Fenum,' inquit, 'ne sero seces; prius quam semen maturum sit secato.'[5] quidam pridie rigant; ubi non sunt rigua, noctibus roscidis secari melius. quaedam partes

261 Italiae post messem secant. fuit hoc quoque maioris

[1] *Detlefsen*: uta *aut* via *aut* e via.
[2] *Mayhoff*: sirare *aut* serere.
[3] *Mayhoff*: in prata.
[4] [a . . . saetae] ? *gloss. Rackham.*
[5] secato *e Cat. add. Erasmus ed. Bas.*

[a] The plant now called 'horse-tail.'

involves very little outlay; it requires the following remarks to be made about it. Land should be left in grass where the soil is rich or damp or watered by streams, and the meadows should be watered by the rainfall or by a public aqueduct. If there are weeds, the best plan is to plough up the land and then harrow and hoe it, and sprinkle it with seed fallen out of the hay from haylofts and from mangers before the weeds are harrowed; and it is best not to irrigate the land in the first year, nor to use it for grazing before the second cutting of the hay, so that the grass may not be torn up by the roots or trodden down and weakened. Meadows go off with age, and need to be revived by sowing in them a crop of beans or turnip or millet, and afterwards in the following year corn, and in the third year they should again be left fallow; and moreover every time they are cut they should be gone over with the sickle, for the purpose of cutting all the growth that the mowers have passed over; for it is very detrimental indeed for any weeds to spring up that will scatter seeds. The best crop in meadow land is trefoil, the next best grass; money-wort is the worst, and it also bears a terrible pod; horse-hair,[a] named from its resemblance to horses' hair, is also a hateful weed. The time for mowing is when the stalk has begun to shed its blossom and to grow strong; the grass must be cut before it begins to dry up. 'Do not mow your hay too late,' says Cato; 'cut it before the seed is ripe.' *R.R.* LIII.
Some farmers irrigate the fields the day before mowing, but where there is no means of doing this it is better to mow when there are heavy falls of dew at night. Some parts of Italy mow after harvest. Mowing was also a more expensive operation in

inpendii apud priores, Creticis tantum transmarinisque cotibus notis nec nisi oleo aciem falcis excitantibus; igitur cornu propter oleum ad crus ligato fenisex incedebat. Italia aquarias cotes dedit limae vice imperantes ferro, set aqua protinus virentes.[1] falcium ipsarum duo genera: Italicum brevius ac vel inter vepres quoque tractabile, Galliarum latifundiis maiores,[2] conpendio quippe medias caedunt herbas brevioresque praetereunt. Italus fenisex dextra una
262 manu secat. iustum est una opera in die iugerum desecari, alligarique manipulos CC[3] quaterna pondo. sectum verti ad solem nec nisi siccum construi oportet; ni fuerit observatum hoc diligenter, exhalare matutino nebulam quandam metas, mox sole accendi et
263 conflagrare certum est. rursus rigari desecta oportet, ut secetur autumnale fenum quod vocant cordum. Interamnae in Umbria quater anno secantur etiam non rigua, rigua vero ter plerisque in locis, et postea in ipso pabulo non minus emolumenti est quam e feno. armentorum ideo[4] cura iumentorumque progeneratio suum cuique consilium dabit, opimo[5] maxime quadrigarum quaestu.

[1] aqua . . . virentes? *Mayhoff*: aquaria . . . virent.
[2] *Sic*? *Mayhoff*: latifundia a maioribus.
[3] *Rackham*: MCC.
[4] *Urlichs*: id.
[5] *Mayhoff*: optimo.

former days, when only Cretan and other imported whetstones were known, and these would only liven up the blade of a scythe with the help of olive oil; and consequently a man mowing hay used to walk along with a horn to hold the oil tied to his leg. Italy gave us whetstones used with water, which keep the iron in order instead of a file, though the water very soon makes them go green with rust. Of scythes themselves there are two kinds: the Italian kind is shorter, and handy to use even among brambles, whereas the scythe used on the large farms of the Gallic provinces are bigger, in fact they economize labour by cutting through the stalks of the grass in the middle and missing the shorter ones. An Italian mower holds the sickle with only his right hand. It is a fair day's work for one labourer to cut an acre of grass, or to bind 200[a] sheaves weighing four pounds each. After the grass is cut it must be turned towards the sun, and it must not be piled in shocks till it is dry; unless this rule is carefully kept, the shocks are certain to give off a sort of vapour in the morning and then to be set alight by the sun and to burn up. A hayfield should be irrigated again after it has been mown, so as to provide a crop of autumn hay called the aftermath. At Terni in Umbria even hayfields not irrigated are mown four times a year, but those with irrigation are in most places mown three times, and afterwards as much profit is made out of the pasture as from the hay. Accordingly keeping herds and breeding draft-animals will supply each farmer with his own policy, a most lucrative trade being breeding horses for chariot-racing.

[a] The MSS. give 1200.

264 LXVIII. Solstitium peragi in octava parte cancri et VIII kal. Iul. diximus. magnus hic anni cardo, magna res mundi. in hoc usque a bruma crescunt dies [creverunt][1]. sex mensibus[2] sol ipse ad aquilonem scandens ac per ardua enisus[3] ab ea meta incipit flecti ac degredi ad austrum, aucturus noctes aliis
265 sex mensibus ablaturusque diei mensuram. ex hoc deinde rapiendi convehendique fructus alios atque alios tempus et praeparandi se contra saevam feramque hiemem, decebatque hoc discrimen indubitatis notis signasse naturam; quam ob rem eas manibus ipsis agricolarum ingessit, vertique iussit ea[4] ipsa die[5] folia et esse confecti sideris signum, nec silvestrium arborum remotarumque, ut in saltus devios montesque eundum esset quaerentibus signa, non rursus urbanarum quaeque topiario tantum coluntur,
266 quamquam his et in villa visendis; vertit oleae ante pedes satae, vertit tiliae ad mille usus petendae, vertit populi albae etiam vitibus nuptae. adhuc parum est. 'Ulmum,' inquit, 'vite dotatam habes; et huius vertam. pabulo folia eius stringis aut deputas: aspice et tenes sidus, alia parte caelum

[1] *V.ll.* creverat, creverunt sata: *secl. Mayhoff.*
[2] *cd. Par. Lat.* 6795?: *om. rell., Mayhoff.*
[3] *Gelenius*: emissus *aut sim.*
[4] ea *add. Rackham.*
[5] inde *vel* die⟨eo⟩ *coni. Mayhoff.*

Farm work after mid-summer. §§ 221, 256.

LXVIII. We have said that the summer solstice comes round on June 24, in the eighth degree of the Crab. This is an important turning-point of the year, an important matter in the world. From mid-winter to this point the days continually grow longer. The sun itself climbing northward for six months and having scaled the heights of heaven, from that goal begins to slope and to descend towards the south, proceeding for another six months to increase the length of the nights and to subtract from the measurement of the day. From this point onward is the time for plucking and collecting the various successive crops and for preparing against the fierce cruelty of winter, and to have this change marked with unmistakable signs was only Nature's duty; consequently she has placed such signs in the very hands of the farmers, and has bidden the foliage to turn round on that very day and to indicate that the heavenly body has completed its course—and not the leaves of the forests and of trees distant from human habitation, so compelling those seeking the signs to have to go into remote valleys and mountains, nor yet again the foliage of the trees of the city and those that are only grown by the ornamental gardener, albeit these may be seen at a country house as well; but Nature turns round the foliage of the olive that confronts us at every step, of the lime-tree which we employ for a thousand practical purposes, and even of the white poplar that is married to the vines. Nor is that yet sufficient. 'You have the elm,' she says, 'that is enriched with the vine; I will turn the foliage of this tree also. You strip its leaves for fodder, or prune them off: look at these, and you have a sign of the heavens,

267 respiciunt quam qua spectavere pridie. salice omnia alligas, humillima [1] arborum ipse toto capite altior; et huius circumagam. quid te rusticum quereris? non stat per me quo minus caelum intellegas et caelestia scias. dabo et auribus signum: palumbium utique exaudi gemitus; transisse solstitium caveto putes nisi cum incubantem videris palumbem.'

268 Ab solstitio ad fidiculae occasum VI kal. Iul. Caesari Orion exoritur, zona autem eius IV non. Assyriae; Aegypto vero procyon matutino aestuosus, quod sidus apud Romanos non habet nomen nisi caniculam hanc volumus intellegi [hoc est minorem canem] [2] [sane ut in astris pingitur] [3] ad aestum magno opere pertinens, sicut paulo mox docebimus.

269 IV non. Chaldaeis corona occidit matutino, Atticae Orion totus eo die exoritur. prid. id. Iul. Aegyptiis Orion desinit exoriri, XVI kal. Aug. Assyriae procyon exoritur, dein post triduum [4] fere ubique confessum inter omnes sidus ingens quod canis ortum vocamus, sole partem primam leonis ingresso: hoc fit post

270 solstitium XXIII die. sentiunt id maria et terrae, multae vero et ferae, ut suis locis diximus; neque est minor ei veneratio quam discriptis [5] in deos stellis, accenditque solem et magnam aestus obtinet causam.

[1] *Edd.*: humilia.
[2] *Secl. Rackham.*
[3] *Secl. Detlefsen.*
[4] *Schol. Germ.*: postridie.
[5] *Mayhoff*: descriptis.

---

[a] Really Canicula or the Dog-Star belongs to the constellation Canis Major, but Procyon, 'the fore-runner of the dog', is in the constellation Canis Minor which precedes it.

for they look towards another quarter of the sky than that towards which they faced yesterday. You use the willow to make withes for binding all things—the lowliest of trees, you yourself are a whole head taller: its leaves also I will turn round. Why complain that you are a mere peasant? It is not owing to me that you do not understand the heavens and know the things thereof. I will bestow a sign upon your ears also: only listen to the cooing of the ring-doves, and beware of thinking that midsummer is past until you have seen the dove sitting on her nest.'

Between the solstice and the setting of the Lyre, on June 26 by Caesar's reckoning, Orion rises, and Orion's Belt on July 4, in the region of Assyria, while in that of Egypt in the morning rises the scorching constellation of Procyon, which has no name with the Romans, unless we take it to be the same as the Little Dog[a]; it has a great effect in producing hot weather as we shall show a little later. On July 4 the Crown sets in the morning for the people of Chaldaea and for Attica the whole of Orion rises on that day. On July 14 Orion ceases rising for the Egyptians, on July 17 Procyon rises for Assyria, and then three days later the great constellation recognized almost everywhere among all people, which we call the rising of the Dogstar, when the sun has entered the first quarter of the Lion: this occurs on the 23rd day after midsummer. Its rising influences both the seas and the lands, and indeed many wild animals, as we have said in the proper places; nor is this constellation less reverenced than the stars that are assigned to various gods; and it kindles the fire of the sun, and constitutes

Constellations of late summer. *Cf.* § 214.

§ 272.

II. 107 IX. 58.

XIII kal. Aug.[1] Aegypto aquila occidit matutino etesiarumque prodromi flatus incipiunt, quod Caesar x kal.
271 sentire Italiam existimavit. aquila Atticae matutino occidit, III kal. regia in pectore leonis stella matutino Caesari emergit. VIII id. Aug. arcturus medius occidit, III id. fidicula occasu suo autumnum inchoat,[2] ut is adnotavit, sed vera ratio id fieri invenit VI id. easdem.

272 In hoc temporis intervallo res summa vitium agitur decretorio uvis sidere illo quod caniculam appellavimus, unde carbunculare dicuntur ut quodam uredinis carbone exustae. non conparantur huic malo grandines, procellae, quaeque umquam annonae intulere caritatem; agrorum quippe mala sunt illa, carbunculus autem regionum late patentium, non difficili remedio, nisi calumniari naturam rerum homines
273 quam sibi prodesse mallent. ferunt Democritum, qui primus intellexit ostenditque caeli cum terris societatem, spernentibus hanc curam eius opulentissimis civium, praevisa olei caritate futura ex[3] vergiliarum ortu qua diximus ratione ostendemusque iam planius, magna tum vilitate propter spem olivae, coemisse in toto tractu omne oleum, mirantibus qui

[1] Aug. *add. Warmington.*
[2] *V.l.* indicat.
[3] *Pintianus* : ex futuro.

an important cause of the summer heat. On July 20 the Eagle sets in the morning for Egypt, and the breezes that herald the seasonal winds begin to blow, which in Caesar's opinion is perceived in Italy on July 23. The Eagle sets for Attica on the morning of that day, and the Royal Star in the breast of the Lion rises, according to Caesar, on the morning of July 30. On August 6 one-half of Arcturus disappears; and on August 11 the setting of the Lyre brings the beginning of autumn, according to Caesar's note, but a true calculation has discovered that the date of this is really August 8.

Late summer coal-blight in vineyards.

In this interval of time the crisis for the vines occurs, the constellation which we have called the Little Dog deciding the fate of the grapes, as it is the date at which they begin to be 'charred', as it is called, as though they had been scorched up by a blighting red-hot coal. Hail and stormy weather do not compare with this disaster, nor any of the disasters which have ever caused high market prices, inasmuch as these are misfortunes affecting single farms, whereas charring affects a wide expanse of country—although the remedy would not be difficult if mankind did not prefer slandering Nature to benefiting themselves. The story goes that Democritus, who was the first person to realise and point out the alliance that unites the heavens with the earth, when the wealthiest of his fellow-citizens despised his devotion to these studies, foresaw, on the principle which we have stated and shall now explain more fully, that the rising XVII. 11. of the Pleiads would be followed by an increase in the price of oil, which at the time was very cheap because of the crop of olives expected; and he bought up all the oil in the whole of the country, to

paupertatem quietemque doctrinarum ei sciebant in
274 primis cordi esse, atque ut apparuit causa et ingens
divitiarum concursus,[1] restituisse mercedem anxiae
et avidae dominorum poenitentiae, contentum ita
probavisse opes sibi in facili, cum vellet, fore. hoc
postea Sextius e Romanis sapientiae adsectatoribus
Athenis fecit eadem ratione. tanta litterarum
occasio est, quas equidem miscebo agrestibus negotiis
quam potero dilucide atque perspicue.

275 Plerique dixere rorem inustum sole acri frugibus
robiginis causam esse et carbunculi vitibus, quod ex
parte falsum arbitror, omnemque uredinem frigore
tantum constare sole innoxio. id manifestum fiet
adtendentibus; nam primum omnium non hoc evenire
nisi noctibus et ante solis ardorem deprehenditur,
totumque lunari ratione constat, quoniam talis iniuria
non fit nisi interlunio plenave luna, hoc est praevalente
—utroque enim habitu plena est, ut saepius diximus,
sed interlunio omne lumen quod a sole accepit caelo
regerens. differentia utriusque habitus magna, sed[2]
276 manifesta: namque interlunio aestate calidissima
est, hieme gelida,[3] e diverso in plenilunio aestate
frigidas facit noctes, hieme tepidas. causa evidens,
sed alia quam redditur a Fabiano Graecisque auctori-
277 bus. aestate enim interlunio necesse est cum sole

[1] concursus? *Mayhoff*: cursus.
[2] magna est et manifesta *Mayhoff*.
[3] *fortasse* gelidissima.

the surprise of those who knew that the things he most valued were poverty and learned repose; and when his motive had been made manifest and they had seen vast wealth accrue to him, he gave back the money paid him for the olives to the anxious and covetous landlords, now repentant, being content to have given this proof that riches would be easily within his reach when he chose. A similar demonstration was later given by Sextius, a Roman student of philosophy at Athens. Such is the opportunity afforded by learning, which it is my intention to introduce, in treating of the operations of agriculture, as clearly and convincingly as I am able.

Blights due to frost and the moon. Cf. 278, 293.

Most people have stated that rust in corn and glowing-coal blight in vines are caused by dew burnt into them by very hot sunshine, but I think this is partly erroneous, and that all blight is caused by frost only, the sun being guiltless. Close attention to the facts will make this clear; for first of all blight is never found to occur except at night and before the sun gives any heat, and it depends entirely on the phases of the moon, since damage of this sort only takes place at the moon's conjunction or at full moon, that is, when the moon's influence is powerful —for the moon is at the full at both phases, as we have often said, but at the point of its conjunction (II. 46.) it reflects back to the sky all the light it has received from the sun. The difference between the two phases is great, but it is obvious: the moon is hottest in summer and cold in winter at the conjunction, whereas on the contrary when full it makes the nights cold in summer and warm in winter. The reason is clear, but it is not the one given by Fabianus and the Greek authors. During the moon's conjunction in

proximo nobis circulo currat igne eius comminus recepto candens, eadem interlunio absit hieme, quoniam abscedit et sol, item in plenilunio aestivo procul abeat adversa soli, hieme autem ad nos per aestivum circulum accedat. ergo per se roscida quotiens alget, infinitum quantum illo tempore cadentes pruinas congelat.

278 LXIX. Ante omnia autem duo genera esse caelestis iniuriae meminisse debemus: unum quod tempestates vocamus, in quibus grandines, procellae ceteraque similia intelleguntur, quae cum acciderint, vis maior appellatur; haec ab horridis sideribus exeunt, ut saepius diximus, veluti arcturo, Orione, haedis.

279 alia sunt illa quae silente caelo serenisque noctibus fiunt nullo sentiente nisi cum facta sunt; publica haec et magnae differentiae a prioribus, aliis robiginem, aliis uredinem, aliis carbunculum appellantibus, omnibus vero sterilitatem. de his nunc dicemus a nullo ante nos prodita, priusque causas reddemus.

280 Duae sunt praeter lunarem, paucisque caeli locis constant. namque vergiliae privatim attinent ad

summer she must necessarily run with the sun in an orbit very near to our earth, glowing with the heat that she receives from his fire close at hand, whereas in winter she must be further away at her conjunction, because the sun also withdraws, and likewise when at the full in summer she must retire a long way from the earth, being in opposition to the sun, whereas in winter the full moon comes towards us following the same orbit as in summer. Consequently, being herself naturally humid, whenever she is cold she freezes up the hoar-frosts falling at that season to an unlimited extent.

LXIX. But before all things we ought to remember that there are two kinds of damage done by the heavens. One we entitle tempests, a term understood to include hail-storms, hurricanes and the other things of a similar nature, the occurrence of which is termed exceptionally violent weather; these take their origin from certain noxious constellations, as we have said more than once, for instance Arcturus, Orion, the Kids. The other are those that occur when the sky is quiet and the nights fine, nobody perceiving them except after they have taken place; these are universal, and widely different from the former ones, being termed by some people rust, by others burning and by others coal-blight, though sterility is a term universally applied to them. Of these last we will now speak, as they have never been treated by any writer before us; and we will begin by stating their causes.

Damage by storm, etc., different.

II. 106, XVIII. 223.

These are two in number, in addition to that depending on the moon, and they are situated in only a few quarters of the heavens. For the Pleiads specially concern farm produce, inasmuch as their

Blight due to influence of stars.

fructus, ut quarum exortu aestas incipiat, occasu hiems, semenstri spatio intra se messes vindemiasque et omnium maturitatem conplexis.[1] est praeterea in caelo qui vocatur lacteus circulus, etiam visu facilis
281 [huius defluvio velut ex ubere aliquo sata cuncta lactescunt] [2] duorum siderum observatione, aquilae in septentrionali parte et in austrina caniculae, cuius mentionem suo loco fecimus. ipse circulus fertur per sagittarium atque geminos, solis centro bis aequinoctialem circulum secans, commissuras eorum optinente
282 hinc aquila illinc canicula. ideo effectus utriusque ad omnes frugiferas pertinent terras, quoniam in his tantum locis solis terraeque centra congruunt. igitur horum siderum diebus si purus atque mitis aer genitalem illum lacteumque sucum transmisit in terras, laeta adulescunt sata; si luna qua dictum est ratione roscidum frigus aspersit, admixta amaritudo
283 ut in lacte puerperium necat. modus in terris huius iniuriae quem fecit in quacumque convexitate comitatus utriusque causae, et ideo non pariter in toto orbe sentitur, ut nec dies. aquilam diximus in Italia exoriri a. d. XIII kal. Ian. nec patitur ratio naturae quicquam in satis ante eum diem spei esse certae; si vero interlunium incidat, omnis hibernos fructus et praecoces laedi necesse est.

[1] *Rackham*: complexit *aut sim. aut* complexas.
[2] *Mayhoff*.

---

[a] The MSS. insert here: 'By the emanation of this all the crops derive milk as from an udder.'
[b] *I.e.* the days of their rising and setting.
[c] At XVI. 99 and 103 it was merely indicated that the Eagle rises in winter.

rising marks the beginning of summer and their setting that of winter, embracing in the six months' space between them the harvest and vintage and ripening of all vegetation. And the sky also contains the constellation called the Milky Way, which is also easily recognized[a] by observing two others, the Eagle in the northern region and in the southern the Little Dog, which we have mentioned in its proper place. The Milky Way itself passes through § 268.
the Archer and the Twins, cutting the equinoctial orbit twice at the sun's centre-point, the intersections being marked by the Eagle on one side and the Little Dog on the other. Consequently the influences of each of these constellations reach to all cultivated lands, inasmuch as these are the only points at which the centres of the sun and earth correspond. Consequently if on the dates[b] of these constellations the atmosphere is clear and mild and transmits this genial milky juice to the lands of the earth, the crops grow luxuriantly; but if the moon scatters a dewy cold after the manner previously described, § 277.
the admixture of bitterness, like sourness in milk, kills off the infant offspring. The measure of this injury in various countries is that occasioned in each part of earth's convex surface by the combination of each of these two causes, and so it is not perceived simultaneously in the whole of the world, as daybreak is not either. We have said[c] that the Eagle rises in Italy on December 20, and Nature's system does not permit any of the crops sown to be of certain promise before that day; but if the moon happens then to be in conjunction, all the winter and early spring produce is bound to suffer damage.

284 Rudis fuit priscorum vita atque sine litteris; non minus tamen ingeniosam fuisse in illis observationem apparebit quam nunc esse rationem. tria namque tempora fructibus metuebant, propter quod instituerunt ferias diesque festos, Robigalia, Floralia, Vinalia.
285 Robigalia Numa constituit anno regni sui xi, quae nunc aguntur a. d. vii kal. Mai., quoniam tunc fere segetes robigo occupat. hoc tempus Varro determinavit sole tauri partem x obtinente, sicut tunc ferebat ratio; sed vera causa est quod post dies undetriginta[1] ab aequinoctio verno per id quatriduum varia gentium observatione in iv kal. Mai. canis occidit, sidus et per se vehemens et cui praeoccidere
286 caniculam necesse sit. itaque iidem Floralia iv kal. easdem instituerunt urbis anno dxvi ex oraculis Sibyllae, ut omnia bene deflorescerent. hunc diem Varro determinat sole tauri partem xiv obtinente: ergo si in hoc quadriduum inciderit plenilunium, fruges et omnia quae florebunt laedi necesse erit.
287 Vinalia priora, quae ante hos dies sunt ix kal. Mai. degustandis vinis instituta, nihil ad fructus attinent, nec quae adhuc diximus ad vites oleasque, quoniam earum conceptus exortu vergiliarum incipit a. d. vi id. Mai., ut docuimus. aliud hoc quatriduum est quo

[1] *Pintianus*: undeviginti.

---

[a] The MSS. give 'nineteenth'. The idioms of Roman arithmetic and chronology and the liability of Roman numerals to miscopying render the transmission of a passage of this kind extremely uncertain.

[b] As a matter of fact Canicula sets after Canis, although it rises before it, as its Greek name Procyon implies. It is possible however that the Latin means 'before whose setting it is essential to sacrifice a puppy'.

The life of men in early times was rude and illiterate; but nevertheless it will be found that mere observation was not less ingenious among them than theory is now. There were three seasons which they had to fear for their crops, and on this account they instituted the holidays and festivals of Robigalia, Floralia and Vinalia. Numa in the eleventh year of his reign established the Feast of Robigalia, which is now kept on April 25, because that is about the time when the crops are liable to be attacked by mildew. Varro has given this date as fixed by the sun occupying the tenth degree of the Bull, as theory then stated; but the true explanation is that on one or other (according to the latitude of the various observers) of the four days from the twenty-ninth[a] day after the spring equinox to April 28 the Dog sets, a constellation of violent influence in itself and the setting of which is also of necessity preceded[b] by the setting of the Little Dog. So the same people in 238 B.C. in obedience to the Sibyl's oracles, instituted the Floralia on April 23, in order that all vegetation might shed its blossom favourably. This day is dated by Varro at the sun's entering the 14th degree of the Bull; consequently if full moon falls within these four days, the crops and all the vegetation then in flower will inevitably suffer injury. The First Vinalia,[c] established in former days on April 23 for tasting the wines, has no reference to the fruits of the earth, nor yet have the festivals so far mentioned to the vines and olives, because their sprouting begins at the rise of the Pleiads, on May 10, as we have explained. This is another four-day period in

Danger periods.

trad. dates 715–672 B.C.

XVI. 104, XVII. 11, XVIII. 248.

[c] This corresponds to the Greek *Pythoigia*, the feast of broaching the casks of the new vintage.

neque rura rore[1] sordida esse[2] velim—exurit enim frigidum sidus arcturi postridie occidens—et multo
288 minus plenilunium incidere. IV non. Iun. iterum aquila exoritur vesperi, decretorio die florentibus oleis vitibusque si plenilunium in eum incidat. equidem et solstitium VIII kal. Iul. in simili causa duxerim et canis ortum post dies a solstitio XXIII, sed interlunio accidente, quoniam vapore constat culpa acinique praecocuntur in callum. rursus plenilunium nocet a. d. IV non. Iul., cum Aegypto canicula exoritur, vel certe XVI kal. Aug. cum Italiae; item XIII kal. Aug., cum aquila occidit, usque in X kal. easdem.
289 extra has causas sunt Vinalia altera, quae aguntur a. d. XIV kal. Sept. Varro ea fidicula incipiente occidere mane determinat, quod vult initium autumni esse et hunc diem festum tempestatibus leniendis institutum: nunc fidiculam occidere a. d. VI id. Aug. servatur.

290 Intra haec constat caelestis sterilitas, neque negaverim posse eam permutari algentium[3] locorum et[4] aestuantium natura. set[5] a nobis rationem demonstratam esse satis est, reliqua observatione cuiusque constabunt: alterutrum quidem fore in causa, hoc est aut[6] plenilunium aut interlunium, non
291 erit dubium. et in hoc mirari benignitatem naturae

[1] rore *cdd.* (rorare *cd. Vat. Lat.* 3861, *m.* 2).
[2] *Detlefsen* : *alii alia* : sordidae.
[3] *Pintianus* : legentium.
[4] et *add. Ian.*
[5] *Mayhoff* : naturas et.
[6] aut *add. Rackham.*

which it is desirable that the fields may not be fouled by dew—for the cold constellation of Arcturus, setting the next day, nips them—and much more is it desirable that a full moon may not come at this period. On June 2 the Eagle for a second time rises in the evening, and this is a critical day for olives and vines in blossom if a full moon coincides with it. For my own part I am also inclined to consider that June 24, the solstice, is in a similar case, and also the rising of the Dog 23 days after the solstice, though only if the moon's conjunction falls then, as harm is done by the extreme heat and the young grapes are ripened prematurely into a hard knob. Again, harm is done by a full moon on July 4, when the Little Dog rises for Egypt, or at all events on July 17 when it rises for Italy, and similarly between July 20, when the Eagle sets, and July 23. The festival of the Second Vinalia, kept on August 19, has no connexion with these influences. Varro fixes it at the time when the Lyre is beginning to set in the morning, which he holds to be the beginning of autumn and a holiday established for propitiating the weather; but at the present day observation shows that the Lyre sets on August 8.

Within these periods falls the sterilizing influence of the heavens, though I would not deny the possibility that it is liable to alteration by local climatic conditions, whether cold or hot. But it is enough for us to have demonstrated the principle, leaving the details to be ascertained by individual observation; at all events it will not be doubted that one or other of two things, full moon or the moon's conjunction, is responsible. And in this matter admiration for Nature's benevolence suggests itself, as to the

Danger can be forecast by observation.

succurrit: iam primum hanc iniuriam omnibus annis accidere non posse propter statos siderum cursus, nec nisi paucis noctibus anni, idque quando sit futurum facile nosci ac, ne per omnes menses timeretur, eorum [1] quoque lege provisum [2]; aestate interlunia praeterquam biduo secura esse, hieme plenilunia, nec nisi aestivis brevissimisque noctibus
292 metui, diebus non idem valere; praeterea tam facile intellegi ut formica minimum animal interlunio quiescat, plenilunio operetur etiam noctibus; avem parram oriente sirio ipso die non apparere et donec occidat, e diverso chlorionem prodire ipso die solstitii; neutrum vero lunae statum noxium esse ne noctibus quidem nisi serenis et omni aura quiescente, quoniam neque in nube neque in flatu cadunt rores, sic quoque
293 non sine remedio. LXX. Sarmenta aut palearum acervos et evulsas herbas fruticesque per vineas camposque, cum timebis, incendito, fumus medebitur his [3]; e paleis et contra nebulas auxiliatur ubi nebulae nocent. quidam tres cancros vivos cremari iubent in
294 arbustis ut carbunculus non [4] noceat, alii siluri carnem leniter uri a vento, ut per totam vineam fumus dispergatur. Varro auctor est, si fidiculae occasu,

[1] eorum? *Mayhoff*: stellarum? *Warmington*: earum.
[2] provisum? *Mayhoff*: divisum.
[3] his? *Mayhoff*: hic.
[4] ne *Mayhoff*.

[a] Probably the lapwing.

fact that, in the first place, because of the fixed courses of the stars this disaster cannot possibly happen every year, and only on a few nights in the year, and that its occurrence is easy to forecast, and that, in order to prevent its being apprehended through all the months, it has also been foreseen by the law that governs the stars; that the moon's conjunctions are safe in summer except for a period of two days, and a full moon safe in winter and only formidable in summer and when the nights are shortest, but they have not the same potency by day; moreover that this is so easily understood that that tiny creature the ant, at the moon's conjunction keeps quite quiet, but at full moon works busily even in the nights; that the bird called the parra[a] disappears on the very day when Sirius rises, and remains concealed till it sets, while the oriole, on the contrary, comes out exactly on midsummer day; but that neither phase of the moon is harmful even at night except in fine weather and when there is not a breath of wind, because dews do not fall when it is cloudy or a wind is blowing, and even so there are remedies available. LXX. When you have occasion for alarm, make bonfires about the vineyards and fields of trimmings or heaps of chaff and weeds and bushes that have been rooted up, and the smoke will act as a cure for them; smoke from chaff is also helpful against fogs, in places where fogs do damage. Some people advise burning three crabs alive among the trees to prevent the vines being injured by coal-blight, others roasting the flesh of a sheat-fish in a slow fire to windward, so that the smoke may spread all through the vineyard. Varro gives the information that a vineyard suffers less damage from storms

Precautions to be taken.

quod est initium autumni, uva picta consecretur inter vites, minus nocere tempestates. Archibius ad Antiochum Syriae regem scripsit, si fictili novo obruatur rubeta rana in media segete, non esse noxias tempestates.

295 LXXI. Opera rustica huius intervalli: terram iterare, arbores circumfodere aut, ubi aestuosa regio poscat, adcumulare—germinantia nisi in solo luxurioso fodienda non sunt—, seminaria purgare sarculo, messem hordeaciam facere, aream messi praeparare, Catonis sententia amurca temperatam, Vergilii operosius creta.[1] maiore ex parte aequant tantum et fimo bubulo dilutiore inlinunt; id satis ad pulveris remedium videtur.

296 LXXII. Messis ipsius ratio varia. Galliarum latifundiis valli praegrandes dentibus in margine insertis duabus rotis per segetem inpelluntur iumento in contrarium iuncto; ita dereptae in vallum cadunt spicae. stipulae alibi mediae falce praeciduntur atque inter duas mergites spica destringitur. alibi ab radice caeduntur, alibi cum radice evelluntur; quique id faciunt proscindi ab se obiter agrum interpretantur,
297 cum extrahant sucum. differentia et[2] haec: ubi stipula domos contegunt quam longissimam servant, ubi feni

[1] creta *hic Urlichs*: *ante* Vergilii *cd. Par. Lat.* 6797: *om. rell.* [2] et *add. Rackham.*

if, at the setting of the Lyre, which marks the beginning of autumn, a picture of a bunch of grapes is placed among the vines as a votive offering. Archibius in his letter to Antiochus, king of Syria, says that if a toad is buried in a new earthenware jar in the middle of a corn-field, the crop will not be damaged by storms.

Operations of late summer.

LXXI. The following are the rural operations belonging to this interval: to turn up the ground again, to dig round the trees, or to bank them up where a hot locality calls for it—except in a very rich soil crops just budding must not be dug—, to clean seed-plots with the hoe, to harvest barley, to prepare the threshing-floor for the harvest, in Cato's opinion by dressing it with olive-lees, and in Virgil's with chalk, a more laborious method. But for the most part people only level it and smear it with a rather weak solution of cow-dung; this appears to be enough to prevent dust.

R.R. CXXIX.

Georg. I. 178.

Methods of harvesting.

LXXII. There are various methods of actually getting in the harvest. On the vast estates in the provinces of Gaul very large frames fitted with teeth at the edge and carried on two wheels are driven through the corn by a team of oxen pushing from behind; the ears thus torn off fall into the frame. Elsewhere the stalks are cut through with a sickle and the ear is stripped off between two pitchforks. In some places the stalks are cut off at the root, in others they are plucked up with the root; and those who use the latter method explain that in the course of it they get the land broken, although really they are drawing the goodness out of it. There are also these differences: where they thatch the houses with straw, they keep it as long as possible, but where

inopia est,[1] stramento paleam quaerunt. panici
culmo non tegunt, milii culmum fere inurunt, hordei
stipulam bubus gratissimam servant. panicum et
milium singillatim pectine manuali legunt Galliae.
298 Messa spica[2] ipsa alibi tribulis in area, alibi
equarum gressibus exteritur, alibi perticis flagellatur.
triticum quo serius metitur hoc copiosius invenitur,
quo celerius vero hoc speciosius ac robustius. lex
apertissima, 'antequam granum indurescat et cum
iam traxerit colorem,' oraculum vero 'biduo celerius
messem facere potius quam biduo serius.' siliginis et
tritici eadem[3] ratio in area horreoque. far, quia
difficulter excutitur, convenit cum palea sua condi, et
299 stipula tantum et aristis liberatur. palea plures
gentium pro feno utuntur; melior ea quo tenuior
minutiorque et pulveri propior, ideo optima e milio,
proxima ex hordeo, pessima ex tritico, praeterquam
iumentis opere laborantibus. culmum saxosis locis
cum inaruit baculo frangunt, substraturi[4] animali-
300 bus; si palea defecit, et culmus teritur. ratio haec:
maturius desectus, muria dura sparsus, dein siccatus
in manipulos convolvitur atque ita pro feno bubus
datur. sunt qui accendant in arvo et stipulas, magno
Vergilii praeconio; summa autem eius ratio ut her-

[1] inopia est *edd.*: inopiae *aut* inopia.
[2] Messa spica? *Mayhoff*: Messis.
[3] *Pintianus*: etiam.
[4] *Mayhoff*: substracta *aut* subtracta.

[a] Moved by oxen.

there is a shortage of hay, they require chaff for litter. Straw of Italian millet is not used for thatch; common millet stalks are usually burnt on the ground; barley stalks are kept as extremely acceptable to oxen. The Gallic provinces gather both millets ear by ear, with a comb held in the hand.

Threshing and subsequent treatment.

The ear itself when reaped in some places is beaten out with threshing-sledges[a] on a threshing-floor, in others by being trodden on by mares, and in other places it is thrashed out with flails. Wheat is found to give a larger yield the later it is reaped, but to be of finer quality and stronger the earlier it is reaped. The most obvious rule is to reap it 'before the grain hardens and when it has begun to gain colour', but there is an oracular utterance, 'Better to do your reaping two days too soon than two days too late.' Common and bare wheats require the same method on the threshing-floor and in the granary. Emmer being difficult to thresh is best stored with its chaff, and only has the straw and the beard removed. The majority of countries use chaff for hay; the thinner and finer it is and the nearer to dust, the better, and consequently the best chaff is obtained from millet, the next best from barley, and the worst from wheat, except for beasts that are being worked hard. In rocky places they leave straw to dry and then break it up with a flail, to use it as litter for cattle, but if there is a shortage of chaff the straw also is ground for fodder. The method is as follows: it is cut rather early, and sprinkled with strong brine and then dried and rolled up into trusses, and so fed to oxen instead of hay. Some people also set fire to the stubble in the field, a process advertised by the high authority of Virgil; their chief reason however for *Georg.* I. 85.

barum semen exurant. ritus diversos magnitudo facit messium et raritas operariorum.

301 LXXIII. Conexa est ratio frumenti servandi. horrea operose tripedali crassitudine parietis latericii exaedificari iubent aliqui, praeterea superne impleri nec adflatus admittere aut fenestras habere ullas, alii ab exortu tantum aestivo aut septentrione, eaque sine calce construi, quoniam sit frumento inimicissima; nam quae de amurca praeciperentur indicavimus.
302 alibi contra suspendunt granaria lignea columnis et perflari undique malunt, atque etiam a[1] fundo. alii omnino pendente tabulato extenuari granum arbitrantur et si tegulis subiaceat confervescere. multi ventilare quoque vetant; curculionem enim non descendere infra quattuor digitos, nec amplius
303 periclitari. Columella et favonium ventum conlecto[2] frumento praedicit, quod miror equidem, siccissimum alioqui. sunt qui rubeta rana in limine horrei pede e longioribus suspensa invehere iubeant. nobis referre plurimum tempestivitas condendi videbitur; nam si parum tostum atque robustum collectum sit aut calidum conditum, vitia innasci necesse est.

304 Diuturnitatis causae plures: aut in ipsius grani corio cum est numerosius, ut milio, aut suci pingue-

[1] a *add. edd.*
[2] conlecto *vel* contecto *Mayhoff*: confecto.

this plan is to burn up the seed of weeds. The size of the crops and scarcity of labour cause various procedures to be adopted.

LXXIII. A connected subject is the method of storing corn. Some people recommend building elaborate granaries with brick walls a yard thick, and moreover filling them from above and not letting them admit draughts of air or have any windows; others say they should only have windows facing north-east or north, and that they should be built without lime, as lime is very injurious to corn: the recommendations made with regard to the dregs of olive-oil have been pointed out above. In other places, on the contrary, they build their granaries of wood and supported on pillars, preferring to let the air blow through them from all sides, and even from below. Others think the grain shrinks in bulk if laid on a floor entirely off the ground, and that if it lies under a tile roof it gets hot. Many moreover forbid turning over the grain to air it, as the weevil does not penetrate more than four inches down, and beyond that the grain is in no danger. Columella also advises a west wind when corn is harvested, at which I for my part am surprised, as generally it is a very dry wind. Some people tell us to hang up a toad by one of its longer legs at the threshold of the barn before carrying the corn into it. To us storing the corn at the proper time will seem most important, as if it is got in when insufficiently ripened and firm, or stored while hot, pests are certain to breed in it.

Storage of grain.

XV. 33.

II. 20, 5.

There are several causes that make grain keep: they are found either in the husk of the grain when this forms several coats, as with millet, or in the

Methods of protecting stored grain.

dine, qui pro umore sufficiat tantum, ut sesimae, aut amaritudine, ut lupino et cicerculis. in tritico maxime nascuntur animalia, quoniam spissitate sua concalescit et furfure crasso vestitur. tenuior hordeo palea, exilis et legumini, ideo non generant. faba crassioribus tunicis operitur, ob hoc effervescit.
305 quidam ipsum triticum diuturnitatis gratia adspergunt amurca, mille modios quadrantali, alii Chalcidica aut Carica creta aut etiam absinthio. est et Olynthi ac Cerinthi Euboeae terra quae corrumpi non sinat; nec
306 fere condita in spica laeduntur. utilissime tamen servantur in scrobibus, quos siros vocant, ut in Cappadocia ac Threcia et Hispania, Africa; et[1] ante omnia ut sicco solo fiant curatur, mox ut palea substernantur; praeterea cum spica sua conduntur ita frumenta. si nullus spiritus penetret, certum est nihil maleficum
307 innasci.[2] Varro auctor est sic conditum triticum durare annis L, milium vero C, fabam et legumina in oleariis cadis oblita cinere longo tempore servari. idem refert fabam a Pyrrhi regis aetate in quodam specu Ambraciae usque ad piraticum Pompeii Magni
308 bellum durasse annis circiter CCXX. ciceri tantum nullae bestiolae in horreis innascuntur. sunt qui urceis cinere substratis et pice[3] inlitis acetum habentibus leguminum acervos superingerant, ita non innasci[4]

[1] *Mayhoff*: Africae.
[2] *Rackham*: nasci.
[3] pice *add. quidam ap. Dalec.*
[4] *Rackham*: nasci.

---

[a] *I.e.* to repel insects. [b] In 67 B.C.

richness of the juice, which may be enough to supply moisture, as with sesame, or in bitter flavour,[a] as with lupine and chickling vetch. It is specially in wheat that grubs breed, because its density makes it get hot and the grain becomes covered with thick bran. Barley chaff is thinner, and also that of the leguminous plants is scanty, and consequently these do not breed grubs. A bean is covered with thicker coats, and this makes it ferment. Some people sprinkle the wheat itself with dregs of olive oil to make it keep better, eight gallons to a thousand pecks; others use chalk from Chalcis or Caria for this purpose, or even wormwood. There is also an earth found at Olynthus and at Cerinthus in Euboea which prevents grain from rotting; also if stored in the ear corn hardly ever suffers injury. The most paying method however of keeping grain is in holes, called *siri*, as is done in Cappadocia and Thrace, and in Spain and Africa; and before all things care is taken to make them in dry soil and then to floor them with chaff; moreover the corn is stored in this way in the ear. If no air is allowed to penetrate, it is certain that no pests will breed in the grain. Varro states I. 58.
that wheat so stored lasts fifty years, but millet a hundred, and that beans and leguminous grain, if put away in oil jars with a covering of ashes, keep a long time. He also records that beans stored in a cavern in Ambracia lasted from the period of King Pyrrhus to Pompey the Great's war with the pirates,[b] a period of about 220 years. Chick-pea is the only grain which does not breed any grubs when kept in barns. Some people pile leguminous seed in heaps on to jars containing vinegar, placed on a bed of ashes and coated with pitch, believing that this prevents

malificia credentes, aut [1] in salsamentariis cadis gypso inlinant; alii qui lentem aceto laserpiciato respergant siccatamque oleo unguant. sed brevissima observatio quod vitiis carere velis interlunio legere. quare plurimum refert condere quis malit an vendere; crescente enim luna frumenta grandescunt.

309 LXXIV. Sequitur ex divisione temporum autumnus a fidiculae occasu ad aequinoctium ac deinde vergiliarum occasum initiumque hiemis. in his intervallis significant prid. id. Aug. Atticae equus oriens vespera, Aegypto et Caesari delphinus occidens. XI kal. Sept. Caesari et Assyriae stella quae vindemitor appellatur exoriri mane incipit vindemiae maturitatem promittens; eius argumentum erunt acini colore mutati. Assyriae V kal, et sagitta
310 occidit et etesiae desinunt. vindemitor Aegypto nonis exoritur, Atticae arcturus matutino, et sagitta occidit mane. V id. Sept. Caesari capella oritur vesperi, arcturus vero medius prid. id. vehementissi-
311 mo significatu terra marique per dies quinque. ratio eius haec traditur: si delphino occidente imbres fuerint, non futuros [2] per arcturum. signum orientis eius sideris servetur hirundinum abitus, namque

[1] aut? *Mayhoff*: alii qui *edd. vett.*: alii.
[2] defuturos *Sillig*.

---

[a] Or, with Sillig's conjecture, 'it is sure to rain'.

pests from breeding in them, or else they put them in casks that have held salted fish and coat them over with plaster; and there are others who sprinkle lentils with vinegar mixed with silphium, and when they are dry give them a dressing of oil. But the speediest precaution is to gather anything you want to save from pests at the moon's conjunction. So it makes a very great difference who wants to store the crop or who to put it on the market, because grain increases in bulk when the moon is waxing.

LXXIV. Next in accordance with the division of the seasons comes autumn, from the setting of the Lyre to the equinox and then the setting of the Pleiads and the beginning of winter. In these periods important stages are marked by the Horse rising in the region of Attica and the Dolphin setting for Egypt and by Caesar's reckoning on the evening of August 12. On August 22 the constellation called the Vintager begins to rise at dawn for Caesar and for Assyria, announcing the proper time for the vintage; an indication of this will be the change of colour in the grapes. On August 28 the Arrow sets for Assyria and also the seasonal winds cease to blow. On September 5 the Vintager rises for Egypt, and in the morning Arcturus for Attica, and the Arrow sets at dawn. On September 9, according to Caesar, the She-goat rises in the evening, while half of Arcturus becomes visible on September 12, indicating very unsettled weather on land and at sea for five days. The account given of this is that if there has been rain while the Dolphin was setting it will not rain[a] while Arcturus is visible. The departure of the swallows may be noted as the sign of the rise of that constellation, since if they are over-

Astronomical signs of autumn.

deprehensae intereunt. xvi kal. Oct. Aegypto spica quam tenet virgo exoritur matutino etesiaeque desinunt; hoc idem Caesari xiv kal., xiii Assyriae significat,[1] et xi kal. Caesari commissura piscium
312 occidens ipsumque aequinoctii sidus viii kal., Oct. dein consentiunt, quod est rarum, Philippus, Callippus. Dositheus, Parmeniscus, Conon, Criton, Democritus, Eudoxus iv kal. Oct. capellam matutino exoriri et iii kal. haedos. vi non. Oct. Atticae corona exoritur mane, Asiae et Caesari v heniochus occidit matutino. iv Caesari corona exoriri incipit, et postridie occidunt
313 haedi vespere. viii id. Oct. Caesari fulgens in corona stella exoritur, et vi id. vergiliae vesperi, idibus corona tota. xvii kal. Nov. suculae vesperi exoriuntur. prid. kal. Caesari arcturus occidit et suculae exoriuntur cum sole. iv non. arcturus occidit vesperi. v id. Nov. gladius Orionis occidere incipit; dein iii id. vergiliae occidunt.

314 In his temporum intervallis opera rustica: rapa, napos serere quibus diximus diebus. vulgus agreste rapa post ciconiae discessum male seri putat, nos omnino post Vulcanalia, et praecocia cum panico, a fidiculae autem occasu viciam, passiolos, pabulum;

[1] *Rackham*: significant.

taken by it they are killed off. On September 16 the Ear of Corn held by the Virgin rises for Egypt in the morning and the seasonal winds cease; this also appears for Caesar on September 18 and for Assyria on September 19; and on September 21 for Caesar the knot in the Fishes setting and the Equinoctial Constellation itself on September 24. Then there is general agreement, which is a rare occurrence, between Philippus, Callippus, Dositheus, Parmeniscus, Conon, Crito, Democritus and Eudoxus, that the She-goat rises in the morning of September 28 and the Kids on September 29. On October 2 the Crown rises for Attica at dawn, and the Charioteer sets for Asia and for Caesar in the morning of October 3. On October 4 the Crown begins to rise for Caesar, and in the evening of the next day the Kids set. On October 8 for Caesar the bright star in the Crown rises, and in the evening of October 10 the Pleiads; and on October 15 the whole of the Crown. In the evening of October 16 the Little Pigs rise. At day-break on October 31 for Caesar Arcturus sets and the Little Pigs rise. In the evening of November 2 Arcturus sets. On November 9 Orion's Sword begins to set; and then on November 11 the Pleiads set.

Autumn farm operations. § 131.

The agricultural operations that come in these periods of time include sowing turnip and navew, on the days that we have stated. It is commonly thought by country people that it is a mistake to sow turnip after the departure of the stork; our own view however is that it should be sown in any case after the Feast of Vulcan, and the early kind when Italian millet is sown, but that the time for vetch and calavance and plants for fodder is after the setting of the Lyre; it is recommended that this should take place

hoc silente luna seri iubent. et frondis praeparandae tempus hoc est; unus frondator quattuor frondarias fiscinas complere in die iustum habet. si decrescente luna praeparetur, non putrescit; aridam colligi non oportet.

315 Vindemiam antiqui numquam existimavere maturam ante aequinoctium, iam passim rapi cerno; quamobrem et huius tempora notis argumentisque signentur. leges ita se habent: 'Uvam caldam ne legito,' hoc est continua[1] siccitate ac nisi imber intervenerit. 'Uvam rorulentam ne legito,' hoc est si ros nocturnus fuerit, nec prius quam sole discutiatur.
316 'Vindemiare incipito cum ad palmitem pampinus procumbere coeperit aut cum exempto acino ex densitate intervallum non conpleri apparuerit ac iam non augeri acinos.' plurimum refert si contingat
317 crescente luna vindemiare. pressura una culleos xx implere debet: hic est pes iustus. ad totidem culleos et lacus xx iugeribus unum sufficit torculum. premunt aliqui singulis, utilius binis, licet magna sit vastitas singulis. longitudo in his refert, non crassitudo; spatiosa melius premunt. antiqui funibus vittisque loreis

[1] continua? *coll.* XXI 82 *Mayhoff*: in nimia *cd. Leid. n.* VII, *m.* 2: in ea *rell.*: in eius *edd. vett.*

---

[a] *Silente luna* = § 322 *interlunio:* the phrase comes from Cato.

[b] For fodder.

[c] Columella, XI. 2, 67.

[d] *Pressura* presumably means the amount that the vat would hold at one time.

[e] *Culleus,* supposed to be the same measure as a *dolium,* cask, held 20 *amphorae,* pitchers, each holding nearly 7 gallons.

when the moon is silent.[a] This is also the time for getting ready a store of leaves;[b] to collect four leaf-baskets full is a fair day's work for one woodman. If they are stored when the moon is on the wane they do not decay; but they ought not to be dry when collected.

Dates of vintage and use of wine-press. In old days the vines were never thought to be ripe for the vintage before the equinox, but nowadays I notice they are commonly pulled at any time; consequently we must also specify the times for this by their signs and indications. The rules[c] are as follows: 'Do not pick a bunch of grapes when they are warm'—that is during unbroken dry weather, with no rain in between; 'Do not pick a bunch of grapes if wet with dew', that is if there has been dew in the night, and not before it has been dispelled by the sun. 'Begin the vintage when the grape-shoot begins to droop down to the stem, or when after a grape has been removed from a cluster it has been clearly noticed that the gap does not fill up and that the grapes are no longer getting bigger.' It is a very great advantage for the vintage to coincide with a crescent moon. One pressing[d] ought to fill twenty wine-skins[e]: that is a fair basis. A single wine press is enough for twenty wine-skins and vats to serve twenty acres of vineyard. Some press the grapes with a single press-beam, but it pays better to use a pair, however large the single beams may be. It is length that matters in the case of the beams, not thickness;[f] but those of ample width press better. In old days people used to drag down the press-beams with ropes and leather straps,

[f] *I.e.* the work is done by leverage, not by the mere weight of the beam.

ea detrahebant et vectibus; intra c annos inventa Graecanica, mali rugis per cocleam[1] ambulantibus, ab aliis adfixa arbori stella, aliis[2] arcas lapidum adtollente secum arbore, quod maxime probatur. intra XXII hos annos inventum parvis prelis et minore torculario aedificio, breviore malo in media derecto, tympana inposita vinaceis superne toto pondere
318 urguere et super prela construere congeriem. hoc et poma colligendi tempus; observato[3] cum aliquod maturitate, non tempestate, deciderit. hoc et faeces exprimendi, hoc et defrutum coquendi silente luna noctu aut, si interdiu, plena, ceteris diebus aut ante exortum lunae aut post occasum, nec de novella vite aut palustri, nec nisi e matura uva.[4] si ligno contingatur vas, adustum et fumosum fieri putant.
319 iustum vindemiae tempus ab aequinoctio ad vergiliarum occasum dies XLIV; ab eo die oraculum occurrit frigidum picari pro nihilo ducentium. sed iam et kal. Ian. defectu vasorum vindemiantes vidi piscinisque musta condi aut vina effundi priora ut dubia recipe-
320 rentur. hoc non tam saepe proventu nimio evenit

[1] *Mayhoff*: cocleas.
[2] *Mayhoff*: ab alis.
[3] *Mayhoff*: observatio (observatur *cd. Leid. n.* VII, *m.* 2).
[4] *V.ll.* quasi, uva si, uva quia si.

and by means of levers: but within the last hundred years the Greek pattern of press has been invented, with the grooves of the upright beam running spirally, some makers fitting the tree with a star, but with others the tree raises with it boxes of stones, an arrangement which is very highly approved. Within the last twenty years a plan has been invented to use small presses and a smaller pressing-shed, with a shorter upright beam running straight down into the middle, and to press down the drums placed on top of the grape-skins with the whole weight and to pile a heap of stones above the presses. This is also the time for gathering fruit; one should watch when any falls off owing to ripeness and not because of windy weather. This is also the season for pressing out the lees of wine and for boiling down grape-juice, on a night when there is no moon, or, if done in the day time, it should be at full moon, or on any other days either before the moon rises or after it sets; and the grapes should not be obtained from a young vine nor from one growing on marshy ground; and only a ripe bunch should be used. It is thought that if wood is brought in contact with the vessel, the liquor gets a burnt and smoky flavour. The proper time for the vintage is the period of 44 days from the equinox to the setting of the Pleiads; we meet with a wise saying of growers who hold that from that day onward it is no good at all to tar a cold wine-butt. Still, before now I have seen vintagers at work even on the first of January owing to shortage of vats, and must being stored in tanks, or last year's wine being poured out of the casks to make room for new wine of doubtful quality. This is not so often due to an over-abundant crop as to slackness, or else to

quam segnitia aut avaritia insidiantium caritati. civilis aequi patrisfamilias modus est annona cuiusque anni uti; id peraeque etiam lucrosissimum. reliqua de vinis adfatim dicta sunt, item vindemia facta olivam esse rapiendam, et quae ad oleum pertinent quaeque a vergiliarum occasu agi debent.

321 LXXV. His quae sunt necessaria adicientur de luna ventisque et praesagiis, ut sit tota sideralis ratio perfecta. namque Vergilius etiam in numeros lunae digerenda quaedam putavit Democriti secutus ostentationem; nos legum utilitas, quae in toto opere, in hac quoque movet parte.

Omnia quae caeduntur, carpuntur, tondentur innocentius decrescente luna quam crescente fiunt.
322 stercus nisi decrescente luna ne tangito, maxime autem intermenstrua dimidiaque stercorato. verres, iuvencos, arietes, haedos decrescente luna castrato. ova luna nova supponito. scrobes luna plena noctu facito. arborum radices luna plena operito. umidis locis interlunio serito et circa interlunium quatriduo. ventilari quoque frumenta ac legumina et condi circa extremam lunam iubent, seminaria cum luna supra terram sit fieri, calcari musta cum luna sub terra, item

avarice lying in wait for a rise in prices. The public-spirited method of an honest head of a household is to use the output of each year as it comes; and this is also quite equally the most profitable plan. As for the other matters relating to wines enough has been said already, and also it has been stated that as soon as the vintage is done the olives must at once be picked; and we have given the facts concerning olive-growing and the operations that must be done after the setting of the Pleiads. XIV. 59 ff., XV. 5ff. 49.

Times for various minor farm operations.

LXXV. To these statements we will add what is necessary about the moon and winds and about weather forecasts, so as to complete our account of astronomic considerations. Virgil following the statement paraded by Democritus has even thought proper to assign particular operations to numbered days of the moon, but our own motive, in this section also of our work as in the whole of it, is the practical value of general rules. *Georg.* I. 276.

All cutting, gathering and trimming is done with less injury to the trees and plants when the moon is waning than when it is waxing. Manure must not be touched except when the moon is waning, but manuring should chiefly be done at new moon or at half moon. Geld hogs, steers, rams and kids when the moon is waning. Put eggs under the hen at the new moon. Make ditches at full moon, in the night-time. Bank up the roots of trees at full moon. In damp land sow seed at the new moon and in the four days round that time. They also recommend giving corn and leguminous grains an airing and storing them away towards the end of the moon, making seed-plots when the moon is above the horizon, and treading out grapes when it is below

323 materias caedi quaeque alia suis locis diximus. neque est facilior observatio ac iam dicta nobis secundo volumine; sed quod intellegere vel rustici possint: quotiens ab occidente sole cernetur prioribusque horis noctis lucebit, crescens erit et oculis dimidiata iudicabitur, cum vero ab occidente sole orietur ex adverso ita ut pariter aspiciantur, tum erit plenilunium. quotiens ab ortu solis orietur prioribusque noctis horis detrahet lumen et in diurnas extendet, decrescens erit iterumque dimidia, in coitu vero, quod interlunium vocant,
324 cum apparere desierit. supra terras autem erit quamdiu et sol interlunio et prima tota die, secunda horae noctis unius dextante sicilico, ac deinde tertia et usque xv multiplicatis horarum isdem portionibus. xv tota supra terras nocte [1] erit eademque sub terris
325 tota die. xvi ad primae horae nocturnae dextantem sicilicum sub terra aget, easdemque portiones horarum per singulos dies adiciet [2] usque ad interlunium, et quantum primis partibus noctis detraxerit quoad [3] sub terris aget,[4] tantundem novissimis ex die adiciet supra terram. alternis autem mensibus xxx implebit numeros, alternis vero detrahet singulos. haec erit ratio lunaris; ventorum paulo scrupulosior.

[1] *Mayhoff*: noctu.
[2] *Caesarius*: adicit.
[3] quoad? *Mayhoff*: quod.
[4] *Mayhoff*: agat.

[a] *I.e.* for 51¼ minutes after sunset.

it, as well as felling timber and the other operations which we have specified in their proper places. Nor is the observation of the moon specially easy, and we have already spoken of it in Volume II; but to give what even countrymen may be able to understand: whenever the moon is seen at sunset and in the earlier hours of the night, she will be waxing and will appear to be cut in half, but when she rises at sunset opposite the sun, so that sun and moon are visible at the same time, then it will be full moon. When she rises with the sunrise and withholds her light in the earlier hours of the night and prolongs it into daytime, she will be waning and will again show only half; but when she has ceased to be visible she is in conjunction, the period designated 'between moons'. During the conjunction she will be above the horizon as long as the sun is and during the whole of the first day, on the second day ten and a quarter twelfths of an hour of the night,[a] and then on the third day and on to the 15th with the same fractions of an hour added in progression. On the 15th day she will be above the horizon all night and also below it all day. On the 16th she will remain below the horizon ten and a quarter twelfths of the first hour of the night, and she will go on adding the same fraction of an hour every day in succession until the period of conjunction, and will add from the day-time to the last parts of the night above the horizon as much as she subtracts from its first parts when below the earth. She will complete thirty revolutions in alternate months but subtract one from that number every alternate month. This will be the theory of the course of the moon; that of the winds is somewhat more intricate.

II. 41 sqq.

Phases, etc., of the moon.

326 LXXVI. Observato solis ortu quocumque die libeat stantibus hora diei sexta sic ut ortum eum a sinistro umero habeant, contra mediam faciem meridies et a vertice septentrio erit; qui ita limes per agrum curret[1] cardo appellabitur. circumagi deinde melius est ut umbram suam quisque cernat, alioquin post
327 hominem erit. ergo permutatis lateribus, ut ortus illius diei ab dextro umero fiat, occasus a sinistro, tunc erit hora sexta cum minima umbra contra medium fiet hominem. per huius mediam longitudinem duci sarculo sulcum vel cinere[2] liniam verbi gratia pedum xx conveniet, mediamque mensuram, hoc est in decumo pede, circumscribi circulo parvo,
328 qui vocetur umbilicus. quae pars fuerit a vertice umbrae, haec erit venti septentrionis: illo tibi, putator, arborum plagae ne spectent, neve arbusta vineaeve nisi in Africa, Cyrenis, Aegypto; illinc flante vento ne arato, quaeque alia praecipiemus. quae pars liniae fuerit a pedibus umbrae meridiem
329 spectans, haec ventum austrum dabit quem a Graecis notum diximus vocari; illinc flatu veniente materiam vinumque, agricola, ne tractes. umidus aut aestuosus Italiae est, Africae quidem incendia cum serenitate adfert. in hunc Italiae palmites spectent, sed non

[1] *Mayhoff*: currit.
[2] cultro (*vel* vomere) *Mayhoff*.

Observation of the winds to regulate work to be done to trees

LXXVI. After observing the position of sunrise on any given day, let people stand at midday so as to have the point of sunrise at their left shoulder: then they will have the south directly in front of them and the north directly behind them; a path running through a field in this way will be called a cardinal line. It is better then to turn round, so as to be able to see your own shadow, which will otherwise be behind you. So, having interchanged your flanks, so as to have the sunrise of that day at your right shoulder and the sunset at your left, it will be midday when your shadow directly in front of you becomes smallest. Through the middle of the length of this shadow you will have to draw a furrow with a hoe or make a line with ashes let us say 20 ft. long, and at the centre of this line, that is 10 ft. from each end, to draw a small circle, which may be called the *umbilicus* or navel. The part of the line towards the head of the shadow will be in the direction of the north wind. You who prune trees, do not let the cut ends of them face in that direction, nor should trees carrying vines or vines themselves do so except in the province of Africa, in the Cyrenaica and in Egypt; when the wind is in that quarter, do not plough or perform any of the other operations we § 334. shall mention. The part of the line towards the feet of the shadow, facing south, will indicate the south wind, the Greek name of which is as we said II. 119. Notus: when the wind comes from that quarter, husbandman, do not deal with timber or the vine. For Italy this is a damp wind or else extremely hot, —indeed for Africa it brings fiery heat together with fine weather. In Italy bearing branches should face in this direction, but not the pruned branches of

plagae arborum vitiumve; hic oleae timeatur vergiliarum quatriduo, hunc caveat insitor calamis
330 gemmisque inoculator. de ipsa regionis eius hora praemonuisse conveniat. frondem medio die, arborator, ne caedito. cum meridiem adesse senties, pastor, [aestate][1] contrahente se umbra, pecudes a sole in opaca cogito. cum aestate pasces, in occidentem spectent ante meridiem, post meridiem in orientem; aliter noxium, sicut hieme et vere in rorulentum educere [nec contra septentrionem paveris supra dictum][2]: clodunt[3] ita lippiuntque ab adflatu et alvo cita pereunt. qui feminas concipi voles, in hunc ventum spectantes iniri cogito.

331 LXXVII. Diximus ut in media linia designaretur umbilicus. per hunc medium transversa currat alia: haec erit ab exortu aequinoctiali ad occasum aequinoctialem, et limes qui ita secabit agrum decumanus vocabitur. ducantur deinde aliae duae liniae in decussem[4] obliquae, ita ut ab septentrionis dextra laevaque ad austri laevam dextramque[5] descendant.
332 omnes per eundem currant umbilicum, omnes inter se pares sint, omnium intervalla paria. quae ratio semel in quoque agro ineunda erit vel, si saepius libeat uti, e ligno facienda, regulis paribus in tympanum exiguum sed circinatum adactis. ratione

[1] *Secl. Mayhoff.*
[2] *Gloss. secl. Mayhoff.*
[3] *Edd.* (cluduntur *Mayhoff*): cludantur *aut* clodantur.
[4] decussem *Warmington*: decussis *aut sim.*
[5] *Rackham*: dextram ac laevam.

[a] This is not the case.

trees or vines; and this wind in the four days of the Pleiads is to be dreaded for the olive, and avoided for their slips by the grafter or for their buds by those engaged in budding. It may be suitable to give some warnings as to the times of day in this region. Woodman, do not prune foliage at midday. Shepherd, when you perceive noon to be approaching as the shadow contracts, drive your flocks out of the sun into a shady place. When you are pasturing your flocks in summer, let them face west in the forenoon and east in the afternoon; otherwise it is harmful, as it is in winter and spring to lead them out into pasture wet with dew [and it has been said[a] above that you must not let them feed facing north], as they go lame, and get blear-eyed from the wind, and die of looseness of the bowels. You must make the ewes face this wind when they are being covered, if you want them to have ewe lambs.

Directions for making a compass.

LXXVII. We have said that the umbilicus must be drawn at the middle of the line. Let another line run transversely through the middle of the umbilicus; this line will run due east and west, and a path that cuts across the land on this line will be called the 'decuman'. Then two other lines must be drawn obliquely to form an X, so as to run down from the right and left of the northern point to the left and right of the southern point. All these lines must run through the same umbilicus, and they must all be equal and the spaces between all of them must be equal. This system will have to be worked out once in each plot of land, or, if you mean to employ it frequently, a wooden model of it may be made consisting of rods of equal length fitted into a small but circular drum. Under the method I am explaining

§ 327.

quam[1] doceo occurrendum ingeniis quoque inperi-
333 torum est:[2] meridiem excuti[3] placet, quoniam semper idem est, sol autem cotidie ex alio caeli momento quam pridie oritur, ne quis forte ad exortum capiendam putet liniam.[4]

Ita caeli exacta parte quod fuerit liniae caput septentrioni proximum a parte exortiva solstitialem habebit exortum, hoc est longissimi diei, ventumque
334 aquilonem borean Graecis dictum. in hunc ponito arbores vitesque; sed hoc flante ne arato, frugem ne serito, semen ne iacito; praestringit enim atque praegelat hic radices arborum quas positurus adferes. praedoctus[5] esto: alia robustis prosunt, alia infanti-
335 bus. (Nec sum oblitus in hac parte ventum Graecis poni quem *καικίαν* vocant; sed idem Aristoteles, vir inmensae subtilitatis, qui id ipsum fecit, rationem convexitatis mundi reddit qua contrarius aquilo Africo flet.[6]) nec tamen eum toto anno in praedictis timeto agricola; mollitur sidere aestate media mutatque nomen[7]—etesias vocatur. ergo cum frigidum senties, caveto, atque cum aquilo praedicetur[8]: tanto perni-
336 ciosior septentrione[9] est. in hunc Asiae, Graeciae, Hispaniae, maritimae Italiae, Campaniae, Apuliae arbusta vineaeque spectent. qui mares concipi voles,

[1] *Rackham*: qua.
[2] esse *Mayhoff*.
[3] exigi? *Mayhoff*.
[4] ratione (§ 322) . . . liniam *transponenda ad* § 326? *Warmington*.
[5] *Gelen.*: praedictus (-um *Detlefsen*).
[6] *Rackham*: flat.
[7] nomen et? *Warmington*.
[8] *Mayhoff*: praedicitur.
[9] *Mayhoff*: septentrio.

[a] Properly north-north-east.

help must be afforded to the understanding even of persons unacquainted with the subject: the rule is to examine the position of the sun at noon, as that is always the same, whereas the sunrise is at a different point in the sky every day from where it was yesterday, so nobody must suppose that the right plan is to take a line on sunrise.

Having thus worked out a part of the heavens, the end of the line next to north on the east side of it will give the point of sunrise at the summer solstice, that is on the longest day, and the position of the north-east [a] wind, the Greek name for which is Boreas. *North-east wind.* You should plant trees and vines facing this point; but beware of ploughing or sowing corn or scattering seed when this wind is blowing, for it nips and chills the roots of trees that you will bring to plant. Be taught in advance: some conditions are good for strong full-grown trees and others for saplings. (Nor have I forgotten that the Greeks place in this quarter the wind they call Caecias; but Aristotle, a man of immense acuteness, who took that very view, also gives the earth's convexity as the reason why the north-east wind blows in the opposite direction to the African wind.) And nevertheless the farmer need not fear a north-east wind all the year round in the operations mentioned above; at midsummer it is softened by the sun, and changes its name—it is called Etesias. Consequently be on your guard when you feel the wind cold, and when a north-easter is forecast, as it does so much more damage than a wind due north. North-east is the direction in which the trees and vines should face in Asia, Greece, Spain, the coastal parts of Italy, Campania and Apulia. Breeders who desire to get male stock

in hunc pascito, ut sic ineuntem ineat. ex adverso aquilonis ab occasu brumali Africus flabit, quem Graeci liba vocant; in hunc a coitu cum se pecus circumegerit, feminas conceptas esse scito.

337 Tertia a septentrione linia, quam per latitudinem umbrae duximus et decumanam vocavimus, exortum habebit aequinoctialem ventumque subsolanum, Graecis aphelioten dictum. in hunc salubribus locis villae vineaeque spectent. ipse leniter pluvius; lenior[1] tamen est[2] siccior favonius, ex adverso eius ab aequinoctiali occasu, zephyrus Graecis nominatus. in hunc spectare oliveta Cato iussit; hic ver inchoat aperitque terras tenui frigore saluber, hic vites putandi frugesque curandi, arbores serendi, poma inserendi, oleas tractandi ius dabit adflatuque
338 nutricium exercebit. quarta a septentrione linia, eadem austro ab exortiva parte proxima, brumalem habebit exortum ventumque volturnum, eurum Graecis dictum, sicciorem et ipsum tepidioremque; in hunc apiaria et vineae Italiae Galliarumque spectare debent. ex adverso volturni flabit corus, ab occasu solstitiali et occasuro latere[3] septentrionis, Graecis dictus argestes, ex frigidissimis et ipse, sicut
339 omnes qui a septentrionis parte spirant; hic et grandines infert, cavendus et ipse non secus ac

[1] lenior *add.* ? *Mayhoff.*
[2] et ? *Warmington.*
[3] occasuro latere *Mayhoff coll.* II 92: occidentali l. *edd. vett.*: occasu lateri *aut* o. lateris.

[a] We should say the *second*, i.e. running due east; cp. § 331.

should pasture their flocks exposed to this wind, so that it may thus fecundate the sire when coupling. The African wind, the Greek name for which is Libs, will blow from the south-west, directly opposite to Aquilo; when animals after coupling turn towards this quarter, you may be sure that they have got females.

The third[a] line from the north, which we have drawn transversely to the shadow and have called the decuman, will have the sunrise at the equinoxes and the Subsolanus wind, called by the Greeks Apheliotes. This is the proper aspect for farm-houses and vineyards in healthy localities. This wind itself brings gentle rains; still Favonius, the wind in the opposite quarter, blowing from the equinoctial sunset, the Greek name for which is Zephyrus, is gentler and drier. This is the direction in which Cato recommended that olive-yards should face; this wind inaugurates the spring, and opens up the land, having a healthy touch of cold, and it will give the right time for pruning vines, tending crops, planting trees, grafting fruit-trees and treating olives; and its breeze will have a nutritive effect. The fourth line from the north, lying nearest the south on the eastern side, will have the sunrise at midwinter and the wind Volturnus, the Greek name for which is Eurus, which itself also is rather dry and warm; this is the proper aspect for beehives and for vineyards in Italy, and the provinces of Gaul. Directly opposite to Volturnus will blow Corus, from the point of sunset at midsummer, on the sunset side of north, its Greek name being Argestes; it also is one of the coldest winds, as are all those blowing from the north; it also brings hailstorms, and is quite as much to be avoided as the

Other winds.

R.R. VI. 2.

septentrio. volturnus si a serena caeli parte coeperit flare, non durabit in noctem, at subsolanus in maiorem partem noctis extenditur. quisquis erit ventus, si fervidus sentietur, pluribus diebus permanebit. aquilonem praenuntiat terra siccescens repente, austrum umescens rore occulto.[1]

340 LXXVIII. Etenim praedicta ventorum ratione, ne saepius eadem dicantur, transire convenit ad reliqua tempestatum praesagia, quoniam et hoc placuisse Vergilio magno opere video, siquidem in ipsa messe saepe concurrere proelia ventorum damnosa imperitis
341 refert. tradunt eundem Democritum metente fratre eius Damaso ardentissimo aestu orasse ut reliquae segeti parceret raperetque desecta sub tectum, paucis mox horis saevo imbre vaticinatione adprobata. quin immo et harundinem non nisi inpendente pluvia seri iubent et fruges insecuturo imbre. quamobrem et haec breviter attingimus, scrutati maxime pertinentia,[2] primumque a sole capiemus praesagia.

342 Purus oriens atque non fervens serenum diem nuntiat, at hibernum[3] pallidus grandine.[4] si et occidit pridie serenus [et oritur],[5] tanto certior fides serenitatis. concavus oriens pluvias praedicit, idem ventos cum ante exorientem eum nubes rubescunt; quod si et nigrae rubentibus intervenerint,

[1] rore nocturno? *Mayhoff.*

[2] ⟨ad usum vitae⟩ pertinentia? *coll.* XIX 2, XXIX 2 *Mayhoff.*

[3] *V.l.* hibernam.

[4] grandine? *Mayhoff*: grandinem.

[5] *Mayhoff.*

---

[a] *Cf.* Virgil, *Georg.* I. 441: Ille ubi nascentem maculis variaverit ortum Concavus in nubem medioque refugerit orbe, Suspecti tibi sint imbres.

north wind. If Volturnus begins to blow from a clear part of the sky, it will not last till night, whereas Subsolanus goes on for the greater part of the night. Whatever the wind is, if it is felt to be hot it will last for several days. The earth suddenly drying up foretells a north-east wind, and if it becomes damp from no visible fall of moisture, a south wind.

LXXVIII. The theory of the winds having now in fact been set out, in order to avoid repetition it is the best plan to pass on to the remaining means of forecasting the weather, since I see that this subject also appealed greatly to Virgil, inasmuch as he records that even in harvest time the winds often engage in battles that are ruinous to inexpert farmers. It is recorded that Democritus above mentioned when his brother Damasus was reaping his harvest, in extremely hot weather besought him to leave the rest of the crop and make haste to get what he had already cut under cover, his prophecy being confirmed a few hours later by a fierce storm of rain. Moreover it is also recommended only to plant reeds when rain is impending and to sow corn when a shower is about to follow. We therefore briefly touch on these subjects also, examining the most relevant facts, and we will take first weather forecasts derived from the sun.

Weather forecasts from the sun, moon and stars.

Georg. I. 318.

A clear sunrise without burning heat announces a fine day, but a pale sunrise promises a wintry day with hail. If there was also a fine sunset the day before, the promise of fine weather is all the more reliable. If the sun rises in a vault of clouds[a] it foretells rain, and likewise when the clouds are red before it rises it foretells wind, or if black clouds also mingle with the red, rain as well; when the rays of the rising

Forecasts from the sun.

et pluvias; cum occidentis aut orientis radii videntur
343 coire, pluvias. si circa occidentem rubescunt nubes, serenitatem futuri diei spondent; si in exortu spargentur partim ad austrum partim ad aquilonem, pura circa eum serenitas sit licet, pluviam tamen ventosque significabunt, si in ortu aut in occasu contracti cernentur radii, imbrem. si in occasu eius pluet aut radii nubem in se trahent, asperam in
344 proximum diem tempestatem significabunt. cum oriente radii non inlustres eminebunt, quamvis circumdatae nubes non sint, pluviam portendent. si ante exortum nubes globabuntur, hiemem asperam denuntiabunt, si ab ortu repellentur et ad occasum abibunt, serenitatem. si nubes solem circumcludent, quanto minus luminis relinquent tanto turbidior tempestas erit, si vero etiam duplex orbis fuerit, eo
345 atrocior; quod si in exortu aut in occasu fiet, ita ut rebescant nubes, maxima ostendetur tempestas. si non ambibunt sed incumbent, a quocumque vento fuerint eum portendent, si a meridie, et imbrem. si oriens cingetur orbe, ex qua parte is se ruperit expectetur ventus; si totus defluxerit aequaliter,
346 serenitatem dabit. si in exortu longe radios per nubes porriget et medius erit inanis, pluviam significabit, si ante ortum radii se ostendent, aquam et ventum, si circa occidentem candidus circulus erit,

or setting sun seem to coalesce, that means rain. If the setting sun is surrounded by red clouds, these guarantee fine weather the next day; but if at sunrise the clouds are scattered some to the south and some to the north, although the sky round the sun may be fine and clear, they will nevertheless indicate rain and winds, while if when the sun is rising or setting its rays appear shortened, that will be a sign of rain. If at sunset it rains or the sun's rays attract cloud towards them, they will denote stormy weather for the following day. When at sunrise the rays do not shoot out with great brilliance, although the sun is not surrounded by clouds, they will portend rain. If before sunrise clouds form in masses, they will foretell rough stormy weather, but if they are driven away from the east and go away westward, fine weather. If clouds form a ring round the sun, the less light they leave the more stormy will be the weather, but if even a double ring of cloud is formed, the storm will be all the more violent; and if this occurs at sunrise or sunset, so that the clouds turn red, that will be a sign of a very bad storm indeed. If the clouds do not surround the sun but hang over it they will presage wind in the quarter they come from, and if they are from the south, rain as well. If the rising sun is surrounded with a ring, wind is to be expected in any quarter in which the ring breaks; but if the whole of it slips away equally, it will give fine weather. If the sun when rising stretches out its rays a long way through the clouds and the middle of its disk is free of cloud, it will be a sign of rain; if the sun's rays become visible before it rises this will mean rain and wind; if the setting sun has a white ring round it, it means a slight storm in the

noctis levem tempestatem, si nebula, vehementiorem, si candentem solem,[1] ventum, si ater circulus fuerit, ex qua regione is ruperit se, ventum magnum.

347 LXXIX. Proxima sint iure lunae praesagia. quartam eam maxime observat Aegyptus. si splendens exorta puro nitore fulsit, serenitatem, si rubicunda, ventos, si nigra, pluvias portendere creditur in xv. cornua eius obtusa pluviam, erecta et infesta ventos semper significant, quarta tamen maxime; cornu superius[2] acuminatum septentrionalem[3] atque rigidum illum praesagit ventum, inferius austrum, utraque erecta[4] noctem ventosam. si quartam orbis
348 rutilus cinget, et ventos et imbres praemonebit. apud Varronem ita est: 'Si quarto die luna erit directa, magnam tempestatem in mari praesagiet, nisi si coronam circa se habebit et eam sinceram, quoniam illo modo non ante plenam lunam hiematurum ostendit. si plenilunio per dimidium pura erit, dies serenos significabit; si rutila, ventos; nigrescens
349 imbres; si caligo orbisve[5] nubium[6] incluserit, ventos qua se ruperit; si gemini orbes cinxerint, maiorem tempestatem, et magis, si tres erunt aut nigri, interrupti atque distracti. nascens luna si cornu superiore obatrato surget, pluvias decrescens dabit, si inferiore, ante plenilunium, si in media nigritia illa fuerit,

[1] *Rackham*: candente sole.
[2] *Mayhoff coll.* 349, II 58: eius.
[3] *Mayhoff*: septentrionale acuminatum.
[4] *Mayhoff*: recta *aut* rectam.
[5] *Mayhoff*: orbis.
[6] *Mayhoff*: nubem.

night; if mist, a more violent storm; if the sun when so surrounded is bright, wind; if the ring is very dark, there will be a strong wind in the quarter in which the ring breaks.

Forecasts from the moon.

LXXIX. The prognostics of the moon must rightfully come next. Egypt pays most attention to the moon's fourth day. It is believed that if she rises bright and shines with clear brilliance, she portends fine weather, if red, wind, if dark, rain, for the next fortnight. The moon's horns being blunted are always a sign of rain, and when they shoot up threateningly, of wind, but particularly on the fourth day of the moon. If the upper horn points stiffly north it presages a north wind, if the lower horn a south wind; if both horns are upright, a windy night. If the moon on her fourth night is surrounded by a bright ring, this will be a warning of both wind and rain. Varro writes as follows: 'If on the fourth day of the moon her horns are upright, this will presage a great storm at sea, unless she has a circlet round her, and that circlet unblemished, since that is the way in which she shows that there will not be stormy weather before full moon. If the moon at full has half of her disk clear, this will be a sign of fine weather, but if it is red, that will mean wind, and if darkish, rain. If the moon is enclosed in mist or in a circle of clouds, it will signify wind in the quarter in which the circle breaks; if she is surrounded by two rings, it will mean stormier weather, and the more so if there are three rings or if the rings are dark, broken and torn apart. If the new moon at her birth rises with her upper horn blacked out, she will bring rain when she wanes, but if it is the lower horn, before she is full, and if the blackness is at her centre,

imbrem in plenilunio. si plena circa se habebit orbem, ex qua parte is maxime splendebit ex ea ventum ostendet, si in ortu cornua crassiora fuerint, horridam tempestatem. si ante quartam non apparuerit vento favonio flante, hiemalis toto mense erit. si XVI vehementius flammea apparuerit, asperas tempestates praesagiet.'

350 Sunt et ipsius lunae VIII articuli, quotiens in angulos solis incidat, plerisque inter eos tantum observantibus praesagia eius, hoc est III, VII, XI, XV, XIX, XXIII, XXVII et interlunium.

351 LXXX. Tertio loco stellarum observationem esse oportet. discurrere hae videntur interdum, ventique protinus secuntur in quorum parte ita praesagiere. caelum cum aequaliter totum erit splendidum articulis temporum quos proposuimus, autumnum serenum praestabit et frigidum. si ver et aestas non sine refrigerio aliquo transierint, autumnum serenum ac

352 densum [1] minusque ventosum facient. autumni serenitas ventosam hiemem facit. cum repente stellarum fulgor obscuratur et id neque nubilo nec caligine, pluvia aut [2] graves denuntiantur tempestates. si volitare plures stellae videbuntur, quo ferentur albescentes ventos ex is partibus nuntiabunt, si coruscabunt,[3] certos, si id in pluribus partibus fiet, inconstantes ventos et undique. si stellarum erran-

[1] tersum *Hoffius*.
[2] *Gelen.*: fluviant.
[3] *Mayhoff*: aut si cura stabunt.

---

[a] *Cf.* II. 100.
[b] Not those of § 350 just above, but those given in § 222.

she will bring rain at full moon. If when full she has a circle round her, it will denote wind in the quarter where the circle shines brightest, and if at her rising the horns are thicker, it will denote a terrible storm. If when there is a west wind blowing the moon does not make an appearance before her fourth day, she will be accompanied by wintry weather for the whole month. If on her sixteenth day she has a more violently flaming appearance, this will presage violent storms.'

There are also eight periodic points of the moon herself, corresponding to her angles of incidence with the sun, and most observers only notice the moon's prognostics between those points; they are the 3rd, 7th, 11th, 15th, 19th, 23rd and 27th days of the moon, and the day of her conjunction.

Forecasts from the stars.

LXXX. In the third place must come the observation of the stars. These are sometimes seen to move to and fro [a], and this is immediately followed by wind in the quarter in which they have given this presage. When at the periodic points [b] that we have set out the whole sky is equally brilliant, it will afford a fine and cold autumn. If spring and summer do not pass without a chilly period, they will cause a fine and misty autumn, with less wind. Fine weather in autumn makes a windy winter. When the brightness of the stars becomes suddenly obscured, and that not by cloud or mist, rain or heavy storms are threatened. If several shooting stars are seen, they will announce winds from the quarters in the direction of which they travel, making a white track, steady winds if the stars twinkle, but if this occurs in several parts of the sky, shifting winds and blowing from all quarters. If one of the planets is enclosed by a

353 tium aliquam orbis incluserit,[1] imbrem. sunt in signo cancri duae stellae parvae aselli appellatae, exiguum inter illas spatium obtinente nubecula quam praesepia appellant; haec cum caelo sereno apparere desiit, atrox hiems sequitur; si vero[2] alteram earum aquiloniam caligo abstulit, auster saevit, si austrinam, aquilo. arcus cum sunt duplices, pluvias nuntiant, a pluviis serenitatem non perinde certam, circulus nubis circa sidera aliqua pluviam.

354 LXXXI. Cum aestate vehementius tonuit quam fulsit, ventos ex ea parte denuntiat, contra si minus tonuit, imbrem. cum sereno caelo fulgetrae erunt et tonitrua, hiemabit, atrocissime autem cum ex omnibus quattuor partibus caeli fulgurabit; cum ab aquilone tantum, in posterum diem aquam portendet, cum a septentrione, ventum eum. cum ab austro vel coro aut favonio nocte serena fulgurabit, ventum et imbrem ex isdem regionibus demonstrabit. tonitrua matutina ventum significant, imbrem meridiana.

355 LXXXII. Nubes cum sereno in caelum ferentur, ex quacumque parte id fiet venti expectentur. si eodem loco globabuntur adpropinquanteque sole discutientur et hoc ab aquilone fiet, ventos, si ab austro, imbres portendent. sole occidente si ex utraque parte eius caelum petent, tempestatem significabunt; vehementius atrae ab oriente in noctem aquam minantur, ab occidente in posterum

[1] *V.l.* incluserint.
[2] *Mayhoff*: si in *aut sim.*

circle, it means rain. In the constellation of the Crab there are two small stars called the Little Asses, with a small gap between them containing a little nebula called the Manger; when this nebula ceases to be visible in fine weather, a fierce storm follows; but if the northern one of the two stars is obscured by mist, there is a southerly gale, and if the southern one, a gale from the north. A double rainbow foretells rain, or coming after rain, fine weather, but this is not so certain; a ring of clouds round certain stars is a sign of rain.

Weather forecasts from thunder and lightning, clouds and mist.

LXXXI. A thunderstorm in summer with more violent thunder than lightning foretells wind in that quarter, but one with less thunder than lightning is a sign of rain. If there are flickers of lightning and claps of thunder in a clear sky, there will be stormy weather, but this will be extremely severe when it lightens from all four quarters of the sky; lightning in the north-east only will portend rain for the next day, and lightning in the north a north wind. Lightning on a fine night in the south, west or north-west will indicate wind and rain from the same quarters. Thunder in the morning signifies wind, and thunder at midday rain.

LXXXII. When clouds sweep over the sky in fine weather, wind is to be expected in whichever quarter the clouds come from. If they mass together in the same place and when the sun approaches are scattered, and if this takes place from a northern direction, they will portend winds, but if from a southern, rain. If when the sun is setting clouds rise into the sky on either side of the sun, they will signify stormy weather; if they are more lowering in the east they threaten rain for the night, but if in the west, rain the next day.

diem. si nubes ut vellera lanae spargentur multae
356 ab oriente, aquam in triduum praesagient. cum in cacuminibus montium nubes consident, hiemabit; si cacumina pura fient, disserenabit. nube gravida candicante, quod vocant tempestatem albam, grando imminebit. caelo sereno[1] nubecula quamvis parva flatum procellosum dabit.

357 LXXXIII. Nebulae montibus descendentes aut caelo cadentes vel in vallibus sidentes serenitatem promittent.

LXXXIV. Ab his terreni ignes proxime significant. pallidi namque murmurantesque tempestatum nuntii sentiuntur, pluviae etiam si in lucernis fungi, si flexuose volitet flamma. ventum nuntiant[2] lumina cum ex
358 sese flammas elidunt aut vix accenduntur; item cum in aeno pendente scintillae coacervantur, vel cum tollentibus ollas carbo adhaerescit, aut cum contectus ignis e se favillam discutit scintillamve emittit, vel cum cinis in foco concrescit et cum carbo vehementer perlucet.

359 LXXXV. Est et aquarum significatio. mare si tranquillum in portu cursitabit murmurabitve intra se, ventum praedicit, si idem hieme, et imbrem, litora ripaeque si resonabunt tranquillo, asperam tempestatem, item maris ipsius tranquillo sonitus spumaeve dispersae aut aquae bullantes. pulmones marini in pelago plurium dierum hiemem portendunt. saepe et silentio intumescit inflatumque?[3] altius solito iam intra se esse ventos fatetur.

[1] *Rackham*: caelo quamvis sereno.
[2] *Mayhoff*: et.
[3] *Excerpta astrom.*: flatumque *aut* flatuque *aut* inflatumque.

If a number of clouds spread like fleeces of wool in the east, they will presage rain lasting three days. When clouds settle down on the tops of the mountains, the weather will be stormy; but if the tops become clear, it will turn fine. When there is heavy white cloud, a hailstorm, a 'white storm' as it is called, will be imminent. A patch of cloud however small seen in a fine sky will give a storm of wind.

LXXXIII. Mists coming down from the mountains or falling from the sky or settling in the valleys will promise fine weather.

Weather signs in the fire.

LXXXIV. Next after these, signs are given by fires on the earth. When they are pallid and crackling they are perceived as messengers of storms; also it is a sign of rain if fungus forms in lamps, and if the flame is spiral and flickering. When the lights go out of themselves or are hard to light, they announce wind; and so do sparks piling up on the top of a copper pot hanging over the fire, or live coal sticking to saucepans when you take them off the fire, or if when the fire is banked up it sends out a scattering of ashes or emits a spark, or if cinders on the hearth cake together and if a coal fire glows with extreme brilliance.

Weather signs given by the sea.

LXXXV. Water also gives signs. If when the sea is calm the water in a harbour sways about or makes a splashing noise of its own, it foretells wind, and if it does so in winter, rain as well; if the coasts and shores re-echo during a calm, they foretell a severe storm, as also do noises from the sea itself in a calm, or scattered flakes of foam, or bubbles on the water. Jelly-fish on the surface of the sea portend several days' storm. Often also the sea swells in silence, and blown up in unusually high waves confesses that the winds are now inside it. IX. 154.

360 LXXXVI. Et quidam et montium sonitus nemorumque mugitus praedicunt et sine aura quae sentiatur folia ludentia, lanugo populi aut spinae volitans aquisque plumae innatantes, atque etiam in campanis[1] venturam tempestatem praecedens suus fragor. caeli quidem murmur non dubiam significationem habet.

361 LXXXVII. Praesagiunt et animalia: delphini tranquillo mari lascivientes flatum ex qua veniant[2] parte, item spargentes aquam iidem turbato tranquillitatem. lolligo volitans, conchae adhaerescentes, echini adfigentes sese aut harena saburrantes tempestatis signa sunt; ranae quoque ultra solitum vocales
362 et fulicae matutino clangore, item mergi anatesque pinnas rostro purgantes ventum, ceteraeque aquaticae aves concursantes, grues in mediterranea festinantes, mergi, gaviae maria aut stagna fugientes. grues silentio per sublime volantes serenitatem, sic et noctua in imbre garrula, at sereno tempestatem, corvique singultu quodam latrantes seque concutientes, si continuabunt, si vero carptim vocem
363 resorbebunt, ventosum imbrem. graculi sero a pabulo recedentes hiemem, et albae aves cum congregabuntur et cum terrestres volucres contra aquam clangores dabunt perfundentque[3] sese, sed maxime cornix; hirundo tam iuxta aquam volitans ut pinna saepe percutiat; quaeque in arboribus

[1] campis *edd.*: compactis (*sc.* lignis) ? *Mayhoff.*
[2] *V.ll.* veniunt, venient.
[3] *Mayhoff*: perfundentesque.

---

[a] The reading is questioned, the word only occurring elsewhere in very late Latin, and passing into Italian. A conjecture substitutes 'timber frames'.
[b] Perhaps egrets.

LXXXVI. And predictions are also given by certain sounds occurring in the mountains and by moanings of the forests and leaves rustling without any breeze being perceptible; and by the down off poplars and thorns fluttering, and feathers floating on the surface of water, and also in bells [a] a peculiar ringing sound foretelling a storm about to come.

Minor weather signs.

LXXXVII. Presages are also given by animals: for instance dolphins sporting in a calm sea prophesy wind from the quarter from which they come, and likewise when splashing the water in a billowy sea they also presage calm weather. A cuttle-fish fluttering out of the water, shell-fish adhering to objects, and sea-urchins making themselves fast or ballasting themselves with sand are signs of a storm; so also frogs croaking more than usual, and coots making a chattering in the morning, and likewise divers and ducks cleaning their feathers with their beak are a sign of wind, and the other water-birds flocking together, cranes hastening inland, and divers and seagulls forsaking the sea or the marshes. Cranes flying high aloft in silence foretell fine weather, and so also does the night-owl when it screeches during a shower, but it prophesies a storm if it screeches in fine weather, and so do crows croaking with a sort of gurgle and shaking themselves, if the sound is continuous, but if they swallow it down in gulps, this foretells gusty rain. Jays returning late from feeding foretell stormy weather, and so do the white birds [b] when they collect in flocks, and land birds when they clamour while facing a piece of water and sprinkle themselves, but especially a rook; a swallow skimming along so close to the water that she repeatedly strikes it with her wing; and birds

Weather signs given by animals, fish, birds.

habitant fugitantes in nidos suos; et anséres continuo clangore intempestivi, ardea in mediis harenis tristis.

364 LXXXVIII. Nec mirum aquaticas aut in totum volucres praesagia aeris sentire; pecora exultantia et indecora lascivia ludentia easdem significationes habent, et boves caelum olfactantes seque lambentes contra pilum, turpesque porci alienos sibi manipulos feni lacerantes, segniterque et contra industriam suam apes conditae, vel formicae concursantes aut ova progerentes, item vermes terreni erumpentes.

365 LXXXIX. Trifolium quoque inhorrescere et folia contra tempestatem subrigere certum et. XC. nec non et in cibis mensisque nostris vasa quibus esculentum additur sudorem repositoriis relinquentia diras tempestates praenuntiant.

that live in trees going to cover in their nests; and geese when they make a continuous clamouring at an unusual time; and a heron moping in the middle of the sands.

LXXXVIII. Nor is it surprising that aquatic birds or birds in general perceive signs of coming changes of atmosphere; sheep skipping and sporting with unseemly gambols have the same prognostications, and oxen sniffing the sky and licking themselves against the way of the hair, and nasty swine tearing up bundles of hay that are not meant for them, and bees keeping in hiding idly and against their usual habit of industry, or ants hurrying to and fro or carrying forward their eggs, and likewise earth-worms emerging from their holes.

Other weather signs.

LXXXIX. It is also a well-ascertained fact that trefoil bristles and raises its leaves against an approaching storm. XC. Moreover when we are at table during our meals vessels into which food is put foretell dreadful storms by leaving a smudge on the sideboard.

BOOK XIX

LIBER XIX

I. Siderum quidem[1] tempestatumque ratio vel imperitis facilis[2] atque indubitata[3] modo demonstrata est; vereque intellegentibus non minus conferunt rura deprehendendo caelo quam sideralis scientia agro colendo. proximam multi hortorum curam fecere;
2 nobis non protinus transire ad ista tempestivum videtur, miramurque aliquos scientiae gratiam eruditionisve gloriam ex his petentes tam multa praeterisse nulla mentione habita tot rerum sponte curave provenientium, praesertim cum plerisque earum pretio usuque vitae maior etiam quam frugibus perhibeatur auctoritas. atque, ut a confessis ordiamur utilitatibus quaeque non solum terras omnes verum etiam maria replevere, seritur ac dici neque inter fruges neque
3 inter hortensia potest linum; sed in qua non occurret vitae parte, quodve miraculum maius, herbam esse quae admoveat Aegyptum Italiae in tantum ut Galerius a freto Siciliae Alexandriam septimo die pervenerit, Balbillus sexto, ambo praefecti, aestate

[1] *Pintianus*: quoque.
[2] facilis ? *Mayhoff*: facili.
[3] ? *Mayhoff*: indubitato.

---

[a] This refers to kitchen-gardens, not to flower-gardens.
[b] *I.e.* sails are made from it.

BOOK XIX

I. An account of the constellations, seasons and weather has now been given that is easy even for non-experts to understand does not leave any room for doubt; and for those who really understand the matter the countryside contributes to our knowledge of the heavens no less than astronomy contributes to agriculture. Many writers have made horticulture [a] the next subject; we however do not think the time has come to pass straight to those topics, and we are surprised that some persons seeking from these subjects the satisfaction of knowledge, or a reputation for learning, have passed over so many matters without making any mention of all the plants that grow of their own accord or from cultivation, especially in view of the fact that even greater importance attaches to very many of these, in point of price and of practical utility, than to the cereals. And to begin with admitted utilities and with commodities distributed not only throughout all lands but also over the seas: flax is a plant that is grown from seed and that cannot be included either among cereals or among garden plants; but in what department of life shall we not meet with it, or what is more marvellous than the fact that there is a plant which brings [b] Egypt so close to Italy that of two governors of Egypt Galerius reached Alexandria from the Straits of Messina in seven days and Balbillus in six, and that in the summer

Between agriculture and horticulture comes flax-growing.

Importance of flax for navigation, as linking the empire.

A.D. 55.

vero post xv annos Valerius Marianus ex praetoriis senatoribus a Puteolis nono die lenissumo flatu?
4 herbam esse quae Gades ab Herculis columnis septimo die Ostiam adferat et citeriorem Hispaniam quarto, provinciam Narbonensem tertio, Africam altero, quod etiam mollissumo flatu contigit C. Flavio legato Vibii Crispi procos.? audax vita, scelerum plena, aliquid
5 seri ut ventos procellasque capiat, et parum esse fluctibus solis vehi, iam vero nec vela satis esse maiora navigiis, sed, quamvis vix[1] amplitudini velorum antemnarum singulae arbores sufficiant, super eas tamen addi alia vela praeterque alia[2] in proris et alia in puppibus pandi, ac tot modis provocari mortem, denique e[3] tam parvo semine nasci quod orbem terrarum ultro citro portet, tam gracili avena, tam non alte a tellure tolli, neque id viribus suis nexum, sed fractum tunsumque et in mollitiem lanae coactum iniuria ad[4]
6 summa audaciae pervenire.[5] nulla exsecratio sufficit contra inventorem dictum suo loco a nobis, cui satis non fuit hominem in terra mori nisi periret et insepultus. at nos priore libro imbres et flatus

[1] vix *add. Ian* (quom vix *Detlefsen*).
[2] alia *add. Brotier.*
[3] e *add.* ? *Mayhoff.*
[4] *Urlichs* : ac.
[5] pervehi mare *Mayhoff.*

---

[a] Daedalus. See VII. 206.

15 years later the praetorian senator Valerius Marianus made Alexandria from Pozzuoli in nine days with a very gentle breeze? or that there is a plant that brings Cadiz within seven days' sail from the Straits of Gibraltar to Ostia, and Hither Spain within four days, and the Province of Narbonne within three, and Africa within two? The last record was made by Gaius Flavius, deputy of the proconsul Vibius Crispus, even with a very gentle wind blowing. How audacious is life and how full of wickedness, for a plant to be grown for the purpose of catching the winds and the storms, and for us not to be satisfied with being borne on by the waves alone, nay that by this time we are not even satisfied with sails that are larger than ships, but, although single trees are scarcely enough for the size of the yard-arms that carry the sails, nevertheless other sails are added above the yards and others besides are spread at the bows and others at the sterns, and so many methods are employed of challenging death, and finally that out of so small a seed springs a means of carrying the whole world to and fro, a plant with so slender a stalk and rising to such a small height from the ground, and that this, not after being woven into a tissue by means of its natural strength but when broken and crushed and reduced by force to the softness of wool, afterwards by this ill-treatment attains to the highest pitch of daring! No execration is adequate for an inventor [a] in navigation (whom we mentioned above in the proper place), who was not content that mankind should die upon land unless he also perished where no burial awaits him. Why, in the preceding Book we were giving a warning to beware of storms of rain and wind for the

Growing of flax a sign of human temerity.

XVIII. 326 ff.

cavendos frugum causa victusque praemonebamus: ecce seritur hominis manu, nectitur[1] eiusdem hominis ingenio quod ventos in mari optet! praeterea, ut sciamus favisse Poenas, nihil gignitur facilius, ut sentiamus nolente seri[2] natura, urit agrum deterioremque etiam terram facit.

7 II. Seritur sabulosis maxime unoque sulco. nec magis festinat aliud: vere satum aestate evellitur, et hanc quoque terrae iniuriam facit. ignoscat tamen aliquis Aegypto serenti ut Arabiae Indiaeque merces inportet: itane et Galliae censentur hoc reditu? montesque mari oppositos esse non est satis et a latere oceani obstare ipsum quod vocant inane?
8 Cadurci, Caleti, Ruteni, Bituriges ultumique hominum existimati Morini, immo vero Galliae universae vela texunt, iam quidem et transrhenani hostes, nec pulchriorem aliam vestem eorum feminae novere. qua admonitione succurrit quod M. Varro tradit, in Serranorum familia gentilicium esse feminas lintea
9 veste non uti. in Germania autem defossae atque sub terra id opus agunt; similiter etiam in Italiae regione Aliana inter Padum Ticinumque amnes, ubi a Saetabi tertio in Europa lino palma, secundam enim

[1] nectitur? *Mayhoff*: netur? *Warmington*: metitur.
[2] *Mayhoff*: fieri *aut* id fieri.

---

[a] *I.e.* the Atlantic ocean is mere emptiness, τὸ κενόν of the philosophers.

[b] The humidity was supposed to be favourable to the manufacture of the tissue.

sake of the crops and of our food: and behold man's hand is engaged in growing and likewise his wits in weaving an object which when at sea is only eager for the winds to blow! And besides, to let us know how the Spirits of Retribution have favoured us, there is no plant that is grown more easily; and to show us that it is sown against the will of Nature, it scorches the land and causes the soil actually to deteriorate in quality.

Flax of Egypt, Gaul, and Italy.

II. Flax is chiefly grown in sandy soils, and with a single ploughing. No other plant grows more quickly: it is sown in spring and plucked in summer, and owing to this also it does damage to the land. Nevertheless, one might forgive Egypt for growing it to enable her to import the merchandise of Arabia and India. Really? And are the Gallic provinces also assessed on such revenue as this? And is it not enough that they have the mountains separating them from the sea, and that on the side of the ocean they are bounded by an actual vacuum,[a] as the term is? The Cadurci, Caleti, Ruteni, Bituriges, and the Morini who are believed to be the remotest of mankind, in fact the whole of the Gallic provinces, weave sailcloth, and indeed by this time so do even our enemies across the Rhine, and linen is the showiest dress-material known to their womankind. This reminds us of the fact recorded by Varro that it is a clan-custom in the family of the Serrani for the women not to wear linen dresses. In Germany the women carry on this manufacture in caves dug underground;[b] and similarly also in the Alia district of Italy between the Po and the Ticino, where the linen wins the prize as the third best in Europe, that of Saetabis being first, as the second prize is won by the linens of Retovium

vicina[1] Alianis capessunt Retovina et in Aemilia via Faventina. candore Alianis semper crudis Faventina praeferuntur, Retovinis tenuitas summa densitasque, candor qui[2] Faventinis, sed lanugo nulla, quod apud alios gratiam, apud alios offensionem habet. nervositas filo aequalior paene quam araneis tinnitusque cum dente libeat experiri; ideo duplex quam ceteris pretium.

10 Et ab his Hispania citerior habet splendorem lini praecipua torrentis in quo politur natura, qui adluit Tarraconem; et tenuitas mira ibi primum carbasis repertis. non dudum ex eadem Hispania Zoelicum venit in Italiam plagis utilissimum; civitas ea Gallaeciae et oceano propinqua. est sua gloria et Cumano in Campania ad piscium et alitum capturam,
11 eadem et plagis materia: neque enim minores cunctis animalibus insidias quam nobismet ipsis lino tendimus. sed Cumanae plagae concidunt apro saetas et vel[3] ferri aciem vincunt, vidimusque iam tantae tenuitatis ut anulum hominis cum epidromis transirent, uno portante multitudinem qua saltus cingeretur.[4] nec id maxume mirum, sed singula earum stamina centeno quinquageno filo constare, sicut paulo ante Fulvio[5] Lupo qui in praefectura Aegypti obiit.

[1] vicina? *Mayhoff*: in vicino.
[2] *Sillig*: candoraeque *cdd. pler.*: candorque *Vat. Lat.* 3861, *m.* 2.
[3] *Mayhoff*: apros aetas ceu e *aut sim.*
[4] *Rackham*: cingerentur.
[5] Fulvio? *ex inscr. Mayhoff*: Iulio.

near the Alia district and Faenza on the Aemilian Road. The Faenza linens are preferred for whiteness to those of Alia, which are always unbleached, but those of Retovium are supremely fine in texture and substance and are as white as the Faventia, but have no nap, which quality counts in their favour with some people but puts off others. This flax makes a tough thread having a quality almost more uniform than that of a spider's web, and giving a twang when you choose to test it with your teeth; consequently it is twice the price of the other kinds.

Flax of Spain and Campania for nets.

And after these it is Hither Spain that has a linen of special lustre, due to the outstanding quality of a stream that washes the city of Tarragon, in the waters of which it is dressed; also its fineness is marvellous, Tarragon being the place where cambrics were first invented. From the same province of Spain Zoëla flax has recently been imported into Italy, a flax specially useful for hunting-nets; Zoëla is a city of Gallaecia near the Atlantic coast. The flax of Cumae in Campania also has a reputation of its own for nets for fishing and fowling, and it is also used as a material for making hunting-nets: in fact we use flax to lay no less insidious snares for the whole of the animal kingdom than for ourselves! But the Cumae nets will cut the bristles of a boar and even turn the edge of a steel knife; and we have seen before now netting of such fine texture that it could be passed through a man's ring, with running tackle and all, a single person carrying an amount of net sufficient to encircle a wood! Nor is this the most remarkable thing about it, but the fact that each string of these nettings consists of 150 threads, as recently made for Fulvius Lupus who died in the office of governor of Egypt.

12 mirentur hoc ignorantes in Agypti quondam regis quem Amasim vocant thorace in Rhodiorum insula Lindi in templo Minervae CCCLXV filis singula fila constare, quod se expertum nuperrime prodidit Mucianus ter cos., parvasque iam reliquias eius
13 superesse hoc[1] experientium iniuria. Italia et Paelignis etiamnum linis honorem habet, sed fullonum tantum in usu; nullum est candidius lanaeve similius, sicut in culcitis praecipuam gloriam Cadurci obtinent: Galliarum hoc et tomenta pariter inventum. Italiae quidem mos etiam nunc durat in appellatione stramenti. Aegyptio lino minimum firmitatis, plurimum
14 lucri. quattuor ibi genera: Taniticum, Pelusiacum, Buticum, Tentyriticum regionum nominibus in quibus nascuntur. superior pars Aegypti in Arabiam vergens gignit fruticem quem aliqui gossypion vocant, plures xylon et ideo lina inde facto xylina. parvus est similemque barbatae nucis fructum defert cuius ex interiore bombyce lanugo netur. nec ulla sunt cum candore molliora pexiorave. vestes inde sacer-
15 dotibus Aegypti gratissumae. quartum genus othoninum appellant; fit e palustri velut harundine, dumtaxat panicula eius. Asia e genista facit lina ad retia praecipue in piscando durantia, frutice made-

[1] hoc? *Mayhoff*: hac.

---

[a] *Stramentum*, straw strewn to sleep on: *cf.* our *paillasse*, 'bed of straw'.

This may surprise people who do not know that in a breastplate that belonged to a former king of Egypt named Amasis, preserved in the temple of Minerva at Lindus on the island of Rhodes, each thread consisted of 365 separate threads, a fact which Mucianus, who held the consulship three times quite lately, stated that he had proved to be true by investigation, adding that only small remnants of the breastplate now survive owing to the damage done by persons examining this quality. Italy also values the Pelignian flax as well, but only in its employment by fullers—no flax is more brilliantly white or more closely resembles wool; and similarly the flax grown at Cahors has a special reputation for mattresses: this use of it is an invention of the provinces of Gaul, as likewise is flock. As for Italy, the custom even now survives in the word [a] used for bedding. Egyptian flax is not at all strong, but it sells at a very good price. There are four kinds in that country, Tanitic, Pelusiac, Butic and Tentyritic, named from the districts where they grow. The upper part of Egypt, lying in the direction of Arabia, grows a bush which some people call cotton, but more often it is called by a Greek work meaning 'wood': hence the name *xylina* given to linens made of it. It is a small shrub, and from it hangs a fruit resembling a bearded nut, with an inner silky fibre from the down of which thread is spun. No kinds of thread are more brilliantly white or make a smoother fabric than this. Garments made of it are very popular with the priests of Egypt. A fourth kind is called othoninum; it is made from a sort of reed growing in marshes, but only from its tuft. Asia makes a thread out of broom, of which specially durable fishing-nets are

Egyptian flax.

facto x diebus, Aethiopes Indique e malis, Arabes e curcurbitis in arboribus, ut diximus, genitis.

16 III. Apud nos maturitas eius duobus argumentis intellegitur, intumescente semine aut colore flavescente. tum evolsum et in fasciculos manuales colligatum siccatur in sole pendens conversis superne radicibus uno die, mox quinque aliis contrariis in se fascium cacuminibus, ut semen in medium cadat. inter medicamina huic vis et in quodam rustico ac praedulci Italiae transpadanae cibo, sed iam pridem
17 sacrorum tantum, gratia. deinde post[1] messem triticiam virgae ipsae merguntur in aquam solibus tepefactam, pondere aliquo depressae, nulli enim levitas maior. maceratas indicio est membrana laxatior, iterumque inversae ut prius sole siccantur, mox arefactae in saxo tunduntur stuppario malleo. quod proximum cortici fuit, stuppa appellatur, deterioris lini, lucernarum fere luminibus aptior; et ipsa tamen pectitur ferreis aculeis[2] donec omnis
18 membrana decorticetur. medullae numerosior distinctio candore, mollitia; cortices quoque decussi clibanis et furnis praebent usum.[3] ars depectendi digerendique—iustum a quinquagenis fascium libris . . .[4] quinas denas carminari[5]—linumque nere et

[1] *Edd.*: post deinde.
[2] *Mayhoff*: crenis *Pintianus*: taeniis? *Ian*: aenis.
[3] corticesque (*pro* cortices quoque) decussi . . . usum *supra post* decorticetur *Mayhoff*.
[4] *Lacunam Rackham.*
[5] cortices . . . carminari *hic Ian*: *infra* post decorum est *codd.*

---

[a] The text seems defective, a plural noun having been lost.

made, the plant being soaked in water for ten days; the Ethiopians and Indians make thread from apples, and the Arabians from gourds that grow on trees, as we said. XII. 38.

Mode of preparing flax for weaving linen.

III. With us the ripeness of flax is ascertained by two indications, the swelling of the seed or its assuming a yellowish colour. It is then plucked up and tied together in little bundles each about the size of a handful, hung up in the sun to dry for one day with the roots turned upward, and then for five more days with the heads of the bundles turned inward towards each other so that the seed may fall into the middle. Linseed makes a potent medicine; it is also popular in a rustic porridge with an extremely sweet taste, made in Italy north of the Po, but now for a long time only used for sacrifices. When the wheat-harvest is over the actual stalks of the flax are plunged in water that has been left to get warm in the sun, and a weight is put on them to press them down, as flax floats very readily. The outer coat becoming looser is a sign that they are completely soaked, and they are again dried in the sun, turned head downwards as before, and afterwards when thoroughly dry they are pounded on a stone with a tow-hammer. The part that was nearest the skin is called oakum—it is flax of an inferior quality, and mostly more fit for lampwicks; nevertheless this too is combed with iron spikes until all the outer skin is scraped off. The pith has several grades of whiteness and softness, and the discarded skin is useful for heating ovens and furnaces. There is an art of combing out and separating flax: it is a fair amount for fifteen . . .[a] to be carded out from fifty pounds' weight of bundles; and spinning flax is a respectable occupation even for

viris decorum est; iterum deinde in filo politur,
inlisum crebro silici ex aqua, textumque rursus
tunditur clavis, semper iniuria melius.

19 IV. Inventum iam est etiam quod ignibus non
absumeretur. vivum id vocant, ardentesque in focis
conviviorum ex eo vidimus mappas sordibus exustis
splendescentes igni magis quam possent aquis.
regum inde funebres tunicae corporis favillam ab
reliquo separant cinere. nascitur in desertis adustis-
que Indiae locis, ubi non cadunt imbres, inter diras
serpentes, adsuescitque vivere ardendo, rarum inventu, difficile textu propter brevitatem; rufus de
20 cetero colos splendescit igni. cum inventum est,
aequat pretia excellentium margaritarum. vocatur
autem a Graecis ἀσβέστινον ex argumento naturae
suae. Anaxilaus auctor est linteo eo circumdatam
arborem surdis ictibus et qui non exaudiantur caedi.
ergo huic lino principatus in toto orbe. proximus
byssino, mulierum maxime deliciis circa Elim in
Achaia genito; quaternis denaris scripula eius
21 permutata quondam ut auri reperio. linteorum
lanugo, e velis navium maritimarum maxime, in
magno usu medicinae est, et cinis spodii vim habet.

men. Then it is polished in the thread a second time, after being soaked in water and repeatedly beaten out against a stone, and it is woven into a fabric and then again beaten with clubs, as it is always better for rough treatment.

Incombustible and other linens.

IV. Also a linen has now been invented that is incombustible. It is called 'live' linen, and I have seen napkins made of it glowing on the hearth at banquets and burnt more brilliantly clean by the fire than they could be by being washed in water. This linen is used for making shrouds for royalty which keep the ashes of the corpse separate from the rest of the pyre. The plant [a] grows in the deserts and sun-scorched regions of India where no rain falls, the haunts of deadly snakes, and it is habituated to living in burning heat; it is rarely found, and is difficult to weave into cloth because of its shortness; its colour is normally red but turns white by the action of fire. When any of it is found, it rivals the prices of exceptionally fine pearls. The Greek name for it is *asbestinon*,[b] derived from its peculiar property. Anaxilaus states that if this linen is wrapped round a tree it can be felled without the blows being heard, as it deadens their sound. Consequently this kind of linen holds the highest rank in the whole of the world. The next place belongs to a fabric made of fine flax grown in the neighbourhood of Elis in Achaia, and chiefly used for women's finery; I find that it formerly changed hands at the price of gold, four denarii for one twenty-fourth of an ounce. The nap of linen cloths, principally that obtained from the sails of sea-going ships, is much used as a medicine, and its ash has the efficacy of metal dross.

[a] It is really the mineral asbestos. [b] 'Inextinguishable.'

est et inter papavera genus quoddam quo candorem lintea praecipuum trahunt.

22 V. Temptatum est tingui linum quoque, ut vestium insaniam acciperet, in Alexandri Magni primum classibus Indo amne navigantis, cum duces eius ac praefecti certamine quodam variassent et insignia navium, stupueruntque litora flatu versicoloria pellente. velo[1] purpureo ad Actium cum M. Antonio Cleopatra venit eodemque fugit. hoc fuit imperatoriae navis insigne postea.[2]

23 VI. In theatris tenta[3] umbram fecere, quod primus omnium invenit Q. Catulus cum Capitolium dedicaret. carbasina deinde vela primus in theatro duxisse traditur Lentulus Spinther Apollinaribus ludis. mox Caesar dictator totum forum Romanum intexit viamque sacram ab domo sua et clivum usque in Capitolium, quod munere ipso gladiatorio mira-
24 bilius visum tradunt. deinde et sine ludis Marcellus Octavia Augusti sorore genitus in aedilitate sua avunculi XI consulatu a kal. Aug. velis forum inumbravit, ut salubrius litigantes consisterent, quantum mutati a[4] moribus Catonis censorii qui sternendum quoque forum muricibus censuerat! vela nuper et

[1] pellente vela. purpureo *Mayhoff*.
[2] postea *hic*? *Mayhoff*: *cum sqq. ceteri* (Po. R. ea *Sillig*).
[3] tenta? *Mayhoff* (extenta *Detlefsen*): spectant *Sillig*: tantum.
[4] *Mayhoff*: mutatis (mutati *cd. Par. Lat.* 6795).

[a] In order to discourage loitering there.

Among the poppies also there is a kind from which an outstanding material for bleaching linen is extracted.

V. An attempt has been made to dye even linen so as to adapt it for our mad extravagance in clothes. This was first done in the fleets of Alexander the Great when he was voyaging on the river Indus, his generals and captains having held a sort of competition even in the various colours of the ensigns of their ships; and the river banks gazed in astonishment as the breeze filled out the bunting with its shifting hues. Cleopatra had a purple sail when she came with Mark Antony to Actium, and with the same sail she fled. A purple sail was subsequently the distinguishing mark of the emperor's ship.

Dyed linen ensigns and sails.

VI. Linen cloths were used in the theatres as awnings, a plan first invented by Quintus Catulus when dedicating the Capitol. Next Lentulus Spinther is recorded to have been the first to stretch awnings of cambric in the theatre, at the games of Apollo. Soon afterwards Caesar when dictator stretched awnings over the whole of the Roman Forum, as well as the Sacred Way from his mansion, and the slope right up to the Capitol, a display recorded to have been thought more wonderful even than the show of gladiators which he gave. Next even when there was no display of games Marcellus the son of Augustus's sister Octavia, during his period of office as aedile, in the eleventh consulship of his uncle, from the first of August onward fixed awnings of sailcloth over the forum, so that those engaged in lawsuits might resort there under healthier conditions: what a change this was from the stern manners of Cato the ex-censor, who had expressed the view that even the forum ought to be paved with sharp pointed stones![a] Recently

Coloured awnings in theatres.

49–44 B.C.

23 B.C.

colore caeli, stellata, per rudentes iere etiam in
amphitheatris principis Neronis. rubent in cavis
aedium et muscum ab sole defendunt; cetero mansit
25 candori pertinax gratia. honor ei iam [1] et Troiano
bello—cur enim non et proeliis intersit ut naufragiis?
thoracibus lineis paucos tamen pugnasse testis est
Homerus. hinc fuisse et navium armamenta apud
eundem interpretantur eruditiores, quoniam, cum
σπαρτὰ dixit, significaverit sata.

26 VII. Sparti quidem usus multa post saecula coeptus
est, nec ante Poenorum arma quae primum Hispaniae
intulerunt. herba et haec, sponte nascens et quae
non queat seri, iuncusque proprie aridi soli, uni terrae
data [2] vitio: namque id malum telluris est, nec aliud
ibi seri aut nasci potest. in Africa exiguum et inutile
gignitur. Carthaginiensis Hispaniae citerioris portio,
nec haec tota sed quatenus parit, montes quoque
27 sparto operit. hinc strata rusticis eorum, hinc ignes
facesque, hinc calceamina et pastorum vestes;
animalibus noxium praeterquam cacuminum teneritate.
ad reliquos usus laboriose evellitur ocreatis
cruribus manuque textis manicis convoluta, osseis
iligneisve conamentis, nunc iam in hiemem iuxta,

[1] *Mayhoff*: honor etiam.
[2] *Mayhoff*: dato.

---

[a] A kind of broom, the botanists' *Stipa tenacissima*.

awnings actually of sky blue and spangled with stars have been stretched with ropes even in the emperor Nero's amphitheatres. Red awnings are used in the inner courts of houses and keep the sun off the moss growing there; but for other purposes white has remained persistently in favour. Moreover as early as the Trojan war linen already held a place of honour—for why should it not be present even in battles as it is in shipwrecks? Homer *Il.* II. 529, 830.
testifies that warriors, though only a few, fought in linen corslets. This material was also used for rigging ships, according to the same author as interpreted by the more learned scholars, who say that the word *sparta* used by Homer means 'sown'. *Il.* II. 135.

Fabrics of esparto.

VII. As a matter of fact the employment of esparto[a] began many generations later, and not before the first invasion of Spain by the Carthaginians. Esparto 237 B.C.
also is a plant, which is self-sown and cannot be grown from seed; strictly it is a rush, belonging to a dry soil, and all the blame for it attaches to the earth, for it is a curse of the land, and nothing else can be grown or can spring up there. In Africa it makes a small growth and is of no use. In the Cartagena section of Hither Spain, and not the whole of this but as far as this plant grows, even the mountains are covered with esparto grass. Country people there use it for bedding, for fuel and torches, for footwear and for shepherd's clothes; but it is unwholesome fodder for animals, except the tender growth at the tops. For other purposes it is pulled out of the ground, a laborious task for which gaiters are worn on the legs and the hands are wrapped in woven gauntlets, and levers of bone or holmoak are used; nowadays the work goes on nearly into winter, but it is done most

facillime tamen ab idibus Maiis in Iunias: hoc maturitatis tempus.

28 VIII. Volsum fascibus in acervo alligatum[1] biduo, tertio resolutum spargitur in sole siccaturque et rursus in fascibus redit sub tecta. postea maceratur, aqua marina optume, sed et dulci si marina desit, siccatumque sole iterum rigatur. si repente urgueat desiderium, perfusum calida in solio ac siccatum stans con-
29 pendium operae patitur.[2] hinc[3] autem tunditur ut fiat utile, praecipue in aquis marique invictum: in sicco praeferunt e cannabi funes; set spartum alitur etiam demersum, veluti natalium sitim pensans. est quidem eius natura interpolis, rursusque quam libeat
30 vetustum novo miscetur. verumtamen conplectatur animo qui volet miraculum aestumare quanto sit in usu omnibus terris navium armamentis, machinis aedificationum aliisque desideriis vitae. ad hos omnes usus quae sufficiant minus $\overline{\text{XXX}}$ passuum in latitudinem a litore Carthaginis Novae minusque $\overline{\text{C}}$ in longitudinem esse reperientur. longius vehi impendia prohibent.

31 IX. Iunco Graecos ad funes usos nomini credamus quo herbam eam appellant, postea palmarum foliis

[1] *Mayhoff*: animatum.
[2] patitur? (*cf.* XVIII 91) *Mayhoff*: fatetur.
[3] hinc? *Mayhoff*: hoc.

---

[a] Σχοῖνος (1) 'rush', (2) 'rope'.

easily between the middle of May and the middle of June, which is the season when the plant ripens.

Manufacture of esparto cloth.

VIII. When it has been plucked it is tied up in bundles in a heap for two days and on the third day untied and spread out in the sun and dried, and then it is done up in bundles again and put away under cover indoors. Afterwards it is laid to soak, preferably in sea water, but fresh water also will do if sea water is not available; and then it is dried in the sun and again moistened. If need for it suddenly becomes pressing, it is soaked in warm water in a tub and put to dry standing up, thus securing a saving of labour. After that it is pounded to make it serviceable, and it is of unrivalled utility, especially for use in water and in the sea, though on dry land they prefer ropes made of hemp; but esparto is actually nourished by being plunged in water, as if in compensation for the thirstiness of its origin. Its quality is indeed easily repaired, and however old a length of it may be it can be combined again with a new piece. Nevertheless one who wishes to understand the value of this marvellous plant must realize how much it is employed in all countries for the rigging of ships, for mechanical appliances used in building, and for other requirements of life. A sufficient quantity to serve all these purposes will be found to exist in a district on the coast of Cartagena that extends less than 100 miles along the shore and is less than 30 miles wide. The cost of carriage prohibits its being transported any considerable distance.

Early use of esparto for rope-making.

IX. We may take it on the evidence of the Greek word[a] for a rush that the Greeks used to employ that plant for making ropes; though it is well known that afterwards they used the leaves of palm trees

philuraque manifestum est. inde translatum a Poenis sparti usum perquam simile veri est.

32 X. Theophrastus auctor est esse bulbi genus circa ripas amnium nascens, cuius inter summum corticem eamque partem qua vescuntur esse laneam naturam ex qua inpilia vestesque quaedam conficiantur; sed neque regionem in qua id fiat nec quicquam diligentius praeterquam eriophoron id appellari in exemplaribus quae equidem invenerim tradit, neque omnino ullam mentionem habet sparti cuncta magna cura persecutus CCCXC[1] annis ante nos, ut iam et alio loco diximus, quo apparet post id temporis in usum venisse spartum.

33 XI. Et quoniam a miraculis rerum coepimus, sequemur eorum ordinem, in quibus vel maximum est aliquid nasci ac vivere sine ulla radice. tubera haec vocantur undique terra circumdata nullisque fibris nixa aut saltem capillamentis, nec utique extuberante loco in quo gignuntur aut rimas sentiente; neque ipsa terrae cohaerent, cortice etiam includuntur, ut plane nec terram esse possimus dicere neque aliud quam terrae
34 callum. siccis haec fere et sabulosis locis frutectosisque nascuntur. excedunt saepe magnitudinem mali cotonei, etiam librali pondere. duo eorum genera,

[1] *Hardouin*: CCCL *cd. Par. Lat.* 10318 (= *suppl. Lat.* 685): CCCXL.

---

[a] *Hist. plant.*, VII. 13. 8, the modern *Muscari comosum*, etc.
[b] It *is* mentioned in *Hist. Plant.*, I. 8.

and the inner bark of lime trees. It is extremely probable that the Carthaginians imported the use of esparto grass from Greece.

X. Theophrastus states that there is a kind of bulb [a] growing in the neighbourhood of river banks, which contains a woolly substance (between the outer skin and the edible part) that is used as a material for making felt slippers and certain articles of dress; but he does not state, at all events in the copies of his work that have come into my hands, either the region in which this manufacture goes on or any particulars in regard to it beyond the fact that the plant is called 'wool-bearing'; nor does he make any mention at all of esparto grass,[b] although he has given an extremely careful account of all plants at a date 390 years before our time (as we have also said already in another place); which shows that esparto grass XV.1. came into use after that date.

Truffles. XI. And now that we have made a beginning in treating of the marvels of nature, we shall proceed to take them in order, by far the greatest among them being that a plant should spring up and live without having any root. The growths referred to are called truffles; they are enveloped all round with earth and are not strengthened by any fibres or at least filaments, nor yet does the place they grow in show any protuberance or undergo cracks; and they themselves do not stick to the earth, and are actually enclosed in a skin, so that while we cannot say downright that they consist of earth, we cannot call them anything but a callosity of the earth. They usually grow in dry and sandy soils and in places covered with shrubs. They often exceed the size of a quince, even weighing as much as a pound. They are of two

harenosa dentibus inimica et altera sincera; distinguntur et colore, rufo nigroque et intus candido. laudatissuma Africae. crescant anne vitium id terrae—neque enim aliut intellegi potest—ea protinus globetur magnitudine qua futurum est, et vivant necne[1], non facile arbitror intellegi posse; putrescendi

35 enim ratio communis est cum ligno. Lartio Licinio praetorio viro iura reddenti in Hispania Carthagine paucis his annis scimus accidisse mordenti tuber ut deprehensus intus denarius primos dentes inflecteret, quo manifestum erit terrae naturam in se globari. quod certum est, ex his erunt quae nascantur et seri non possint.

36 XII. Simile est et quod in Cyrenaica provincia vocant misy, praecipuum suavitate odoris ac saporis, sed carnosius, et quod in Threcia iton et quod in Graecia ceraunion.

37 XIII. De tuberibus haec traduntur peculiariter: cum fuerint imbres autumnales ac tonitrua crebra, tunc nasci, et maxime[2] tonitribus, nec ultra annum durare, tenerruma autem verno esse. quibusdam locis accepta tantum riguis[3] feruntur, sicut Mytilenis negant nasci nisi exundatione fluminum invecto

[1] *Mayhoff*: ac ne *aut* anne.
[2] *Mayhoff*: maximume.
[3] *Pintianus*: acceptam turriguis *aut sim.* (accepta tamen irriguis? *Mayhoff*).

kinds, one gritty in texture and unkind to the teeth, and the other devoid of impurities; they also differ in their colour, which is red or black, and the inside is white. The African variety is the most highly spoken of. I do not think it can be easily ascertained whether they grow in size, or whether this blemish of the earth—for they cannot be understood as anything else—forms at once a ball of the size that it is going to be; nor whether they are alive or not, for they decay in the same way as wood does. We know for a fact that when Lartius Licinius, an official of praetorian rank, was serving as Minister of Justice at Cartagena in Spain a few years ago, he happened when biting a truffle to come on a denarius contained inside it, which bent his front teeth; this will clearly show that truffles are lumps of earthy substance balled together. One thing that is certain is that truffles will be found to belong to the class of things that spring up spontaneously and cannot be grown from seed.

Similar plants.

XII. There is also a similar plant the name of which in the province of Cyrene is *misy*, which has a remarkably sweet scent and flavour, but is more fleshy than the truffle; and one in Thrace called *iton*, and one in Greece, *ceraunion* or 'thunder-truffle'.

Particulars as to truffles.

XIII. Peculiarities reported about truffles are that they spring up when there have been spells of rain in autumn and repeated thunderstorms, and that thunderstorms bring them out particularly; that they do not last beyond a year; and that those in spring are the most delicate to eat. In some places acceptable truffles only grow in marshy places, for instance at Mytilene it is said that they only grow on ground flooded by the rivers, when the floods have

semine ab Tiaris: est autem is locus in quo plurima nascuntur. Asiae nobilissima circa Lampsacum et Alopeconnesum, Graeciae vero circa Elim.

38 XIV. Sunt et in fungorum genere Graecis dicti pezicae, qui sine radice aut pediculo nascuntur.

XV. Ab his proximum dicetur auctoritate clarissimum laserpicium, quod Graeci silphion vocant, in Cyrenaica provincia repertum, cuius sucum laser vocant, magnificum in usu medicamentisque[1] et ad
39 pondus argentei denarii repensum. multis iam annis in ea terra non invenitur, quoniam publicani qui pascua conducunt maius ita lucrum sentientes depopulantur pecorum pabulo. unus omnino caulis nostra memoria repertus Neroni principi missus est. si quando incidit pecus in spem nascentis,[2] hoc deprehenditur signo: ove cum comederit dormiente
40 protinus, capra sternuente. diuque iam non aliud ad nos invehitur laser quam quod in Perside aut Media et Armenia nascitur, large sed multo infra Cyrenaicum, id quoque adulteratum cummi aut sacopenio aut faba fracta, quo minus omittendum videtur C. Valerio M. Herennio cos. Cyrenis advecta Romam publice laserpicii pondo xxx, Caesarem vero dictatorem initio belli civilis inter aurum argentumque protulisse ex aerario laserpicii pondo MD.

[1] *an* usu vitae *vel* usu medico alimentisque? *Mayhoff.*
[2] in silphium nascens (*vel* in s. dum pascitur) *coni. Warmington. Fortasse* in caulem nascentis.

---

[a] Perhaps our 'alexanders', but more likely *Ferula tingitana* and *F. marmarica* (which still exist in N. Africa) and related species.

brought down seed from Tiara: that is the place where most grow. The most famous Asiatic truffles grow round Lampsacus and Alopeconnesus, and the most famous Greek ones in the district of Elis.

XIV. The fungus class also includes those called by the Greeks *pezicae*, which grow without root or stalk.

XV. Next after these we will speak about laser- *Silphium.* wort,[a] a remarkably important plant, the Greek name for which is *silphium*; it was originally found in the province of Cyrenaica. Its juice is called *laser*, and it takes an important place in general use and among drugs, and is sold for its weight in silver denarii. It has not been found in that country now for many years, because the tax-farmers who rent the pasturage strip it clean by grazing sheep on it, realizing that they make more profit in that way. Only a single stalk has been found there within our memory, which was sent to the Emperor Nero. If a grazing flock ever chances to come on a promising young shoot, this is detected by the indication that a sheep after eating it at once goes to sleep and a goat has a fit of sneezing. And for a long time now no laserwort has been imported to us except what grows in Persia or Media and Armenia, in abundant quantity but much inferior quality to that of Cyrenaica, and even so adulterated with gum, *sacopenium*, or with crushed beans; this makes it even more necessary for us not to omit to state the facts that in the consulship of Gaius Valerius and Marcus Herennius, 30 pounds of 93 B.C. laserwort plant was imported to Rome by the government, and that during the dictatorship of Caesar, at the beginning of the civil war he produced 49 B.C. out of the treasury together with gold and silver 1500 lbs. of laserwort plant.

41 Id apud auctores Graeciae certissimos[1] invenimus natum imbre piceo repente madefacta tellure circa Hesperidum hortos Syrtimque maiorem septem annis ante oppidum Cyrenarum, quod conditum est urbis nostrae anno CXLIII; vim autem illam per $\overline{\text{IV}}$
42 stadium Africae valuisse; in ea laserpicium gigni solitum, rem feram ac contumacem et, si coleretur, in deserta fugientem, radice multa crassaque, caule ferulaceo ac simili crassitudine. huius folia maspetum vocabant, apio maxime similia; semen erat folia-
43 ceum, folium ipsum vere deciduum. vesci pecora solita, primoque purgari, mox pinguescere carne mirabilem in modum iucunda. post folia amissa caule ipso et homines vescebantur modis omnibus[2] decocto, elixo assoque,[3] eorum quoque corpora XL primis diebus purgante. sucus duobus modis capiebatur, e radice atque caule, et haec duo erant nomina, ῥιζίας atque καυλίας, vilior illo ac putrescens. radici
44 cortex niger. ad mercis adulteria sucum ipsum in vasa coiectum admixto furfure subinde concutiendo ad maturitatem perducebant, ni ita fecissent, putrescentem. argumentum erat maturitatis colos siccitas-
45 que sudore finito. alii tradunt laserpicii radicem

[1] *Mayhoff*: euidentissimos *aut* ventissimos *aut* vetustissimos.
[2] modis (umhis, umhos, uiciis *aut sim. cdd.*) omnibus *hic Mayhoff*: *infra post* purgante.
[3] *Mayhoff*: assoque elixo.

---

[a] From the Greek words for 'root' and 'stalk'.

We find it stated in the most reliable authors of Greece that this plant first sprang up in the vicinity of the Gardens of the Hesperids and the Greater Syrtis after the ground had been suddenly soaked by a shower of rain the colour of pitch, seven years before the foundation of the town of Cyrenae, which was in the year of our city 143; that the effect of this rainfall extended over 500 miles of Africa; and that the laserwort plant grew widely in that country as an obstinate weed, and if cultivated, escaped into the desert; and that it has a large thick root and a stalk like that of fennel and equally thick. The leaves of this plant used to be called *maspetum*; they closely resembled parsley, and the seed was like a leaf, the actual leaf being shed off in spring. It used to be customary to pasture cattle on it; it first acted as a purgative, and then the beasts grew fat and produced meat of a marvellously agreeable quality. After the plant had shed its leaves the people themselves used to eat the actual stalk, cooked in all sorts of ways, boiled and roasted; with them also it operated as a purge for the first six weeks. The juice used to be obtained in two ways, from the root and from the stalk, and the two corresponding names for it were *rizias* and *caulias*,[a] the latter inferior to the former and liable to go bad. The root had a black rind. The juice itself was adulterated for trade purposes by being put into vessels with a mixture of bran added and then shaken up till it was brought into ripe condition; without this treatment it went bad. A proof of its being ripe was its colour and dryness, the damp juice having completely disappeared. Other accounts say that the plant had a root more than 18 inches long, and that at all events there was an

Provenance and uses of silphium.

611 B.C.

fuisse maiorem cubitali, tuber utique[1] in ea supra terram; hoc inciso profluere solitum sucum ceu lactis, supernato caule quem magydarim vocarunt; folia aurei coloris pro semine fuisse, cadentia a canis ortu austro flante; ex his laserpicium nasci solitum annuo spatio et radice et caule consummantibus sese. hi et circumfodi solitum prodidere, nec purgari pecora, sed aegra sanari aut protinus mori, quod in paucis accidere. Persico silphio prior opinio congruit.

46 XVI. Alterum genus eius est quod magydaris vocatur, tenerius et minus vehemens sine sucoque, quod circa Syriam nascitur, non proveniens in Cyrenaica regione; gignitur et in Parnaso monte copiosum quibusdam laserpicium vocantibus: per quae omnia adulteratur rei saluberrimae utilissimaeque auctoritas. probatio sinceri prima in colore modice rufo et, cum frangatur, intus candido, mox tralucente gutta quaeque saliva celerrime liquescat. usus in multis medicaminibus.

47 XVII. Sunt etiamnum duo genera non nisi sordido nota volgo, cum quaestu multum polleant. in primis

[1] *Sic? Mayhoff*: tuberque *aut* tubertique.

[a] This is asafoetida (*scorodosma foetida*).

excrescence on it protruding above the surface of the ground; that when an incision was made in this, a juice resembling milk would flow out; and that there was a stalk growing above the excrescence which they called *magydaris*; that the plant had leaves of a golden colour which served as seed, being shed after the rise of the Dogstar when a south wind was blowing, and that out of these fallen leaves shoots of laserwort used to spring, both root and stalk making full growth in the space of a year. These authors also stated that it was customary to dig round the roots of the plant; and that it did not act as a purge with cattle, but if they were ailing it cured them, or else they died at once, the latter not happening in many cases. The former view corresponds with the Persian variety of silphium.

Varieties of laserwort.

XVI. There is another kind of laserwort called *magydaris*,[a] which is gentler and less violent in its effects, and has no juice; this grows in the neighbourhood of Syria, not being found in the Cyrenaica region. Also there is a plant growing in great abundance on Mount Parnassus that is called laserwort plant by some persons. All these varieties are used for adulteration, bringing discredit on a very salutary and useful commodity. The first test of the genuine article is in the colour, which is reddish, and white inside when the mass is broken; and the next test is if the juice that drips out is transparent and melts very quickly in saliva. It is employed as an ingredient in a great many medicaments.

Varieties used for dyeing, wool-dressing, food and scent.

XVII. There are also two kinds that are known only to the avaricious herd, as they are very profitable articles of trade. First comes madder, which is

rubia tinguendis lanis et coriis necessaria: laudatissima Italica et maxime suburbana, et omnes paene provinciae scatent ea. sponte provenit seriturque similitudine erviliae, verum spinosis foliis [1] et caule. geniculatus hic est quinis circa articulos in orbe foliis. semen eius . . .[2] rubra [3] est. quos in medicina usus
48 habeat dicemus suo loco. XVIII. At quae vocatur radicula lavandis demum lanis sucum habet, mirum quantum conferens candori mollitiaeque. nascitur sativa ubique, sed sponte praecipua in Asia Syriaque, saxosis et asperis locis, trans Euphraten tamen laudatissuma, caule ferulaceo, tenui et ipso, cibis indigenarum expetito aut [4] unguentis, quicquid sit cum quo decoquatur, folio oleae. struthion Graeci vocant. floret aestate, grata aspectu, verum sine odore, spinosa et caule lanuginoso [5]. semen ei nullum, radix magna, quae conciditur ad quem dictum est usum.

49 XIX. Ab his superest reverti ad hortorum curam, et suapte natura memorandam et quoniam antiquitas nihil prius mirata est quam Hesperidum hortos ac regum Adonidis et Alcinoi, itemque pensiles, sive illos Semiramis sive Assyriae rex Syrus [6] fecit, de quorum

[1] foliis *add. Mayhoff*.
[2] ⟨rubrum, postremo nigrum, radix⟩ *Mayhoff coll. Diosc.*
[3] *Urlichs*: rubia.
[4] *Rackham*: et.
[5] *Edd.*: lanuginis.
[6] *Ian* (regina Nitocris *Urlichs*): Cyrus (reagin syriis *cd. Par. Lat.* 10318).

---

[a] The MSS. are defective here. The words inserted, as omitted by a copyist's error, are from Dioscorides.
[b] Perhaps *Reseda luteola*, 'dyers' rocket', though *radicula* is nowhere mentioned as supplying a dye.
[c] *I.e.* kitchen gardens.

indispensable for dyeing woollens and leather; the most highly esteemed is the Italian, and especially that grown in the neighbourhood of Rome, and almost all the provinces teem with it. It grows of itself, but a variety like chickling vetch, but with prickly leaves and stalk, is also grown from seed. This plant has a jointed stem, with five leaves arranged in a circle round each joint. The seed is red and finally turns black, and the root red.[a] Its medicinal properties we shall state in their XXIV. 94.
proper place. XVIII. But the plant called the rootlet [b] has a juice that is only used for washing woollens, contributing in a remarkable degree to their whiteness and softness. It can be grown anywhere under cultivation, but an outstanding self-sown variety occurs in Asia and Syria, on rocky and rugged ground, though the most highly esteemed grows beyond the Euphrates. Its stalk being slender resembles fennel; and it is much sought after by the natives to supply articles of food or perfumes, according to the ingredients with which it is boiled down. It has the leaf of an olive. The Greek name of this plant is 'little sparrow'. It flowers *Soapwort.*
in summer, and the blossom is pretty to look at but has no scent. It is a thorny plant, with a stalk covered with down. It has no seed, but a large root, which is cut up for the purpose mentioned.

The pleasures of a kitchen-garden.

XIX. It remains to return from these plants to the cultivation of gardens [c], a subject recommended to our notice both by its own intrinsic nature and by the fact that antiquity gave its highest admiration to the garden of the Hesperids and of the kings Adonis and Alcinous, and also to hanging gardens, whether those constructed by Semiramis or by Syrus King of

50 opere alio volumine dicemus. Romani quidem reges
ipsi coluere; quippe etiam Superbus nuntium illum
saevum atque sanguinarium filio remisit ex horto. in
XII tabulis legum nostrarum nusquam nominatur villa,
semper in significatione ea hortus, in horti vero heredium; quam ob rem comitata est et religio quaedam,
hortoque et foro tantum contra invidentium effascina-
tiones dicari videmus in remedio saturica signa,
quamquam hortos tutelae Veneris adsignante Plauto.
iam quidem hortorum nomine in ipsa urbe delicias
51 agros villasque possident. primus hoc instituit
Athenis Epicurus otii magister; usque ad eum moris
non fuerat in oppidis habitari rura.

Romae quidem per se hortus ager pauperis erat;
52 ex horto plebei macellum, quanto innocentiore victu!
mergi enim, credo, in profunda satius est et ostrearum
genera naufragio exquiri, aves ultra Phasim amnem
peti ne fabuloso quidem terrore tutas, immo sic
pretiosiores, alias in Numidia Aethiopiaeque in
sepulchris aucupari, aut pugnare cum feris mandique
capientem quod mandat alius. at, Hercules, quam
vilia haec, quam parata voluptati satietatique, nisi

---

[a] Pliny does not return to the subject in the *Natural History*.
[b] See § 169 below.
[c] Not in any extant play.
[d] In order to get pearls.
[e] *Phasianae*, pheasants, from *Phasis*, the Rion.
[f] The reference is to the sorceries of Medea and the exploits of Jason and the Argonauts in Colchis.
[g] Guinea-fowls.
[h] These birds would be ruffs. Cf. X. 74, 132.

Assyria, about whose work we shall speak [a] in another volume. The kings of Rome indeed cultivated their gardens with their own hands; in fact it was from his garden that even Tarquin the Proud sent that cruel and bloodthirsty message to his son.[b] In our Laws of the Twelve Tables the word 'farm' never occurs —the word 'garden' is always used in that sense, while a garden is denoted by 'family estate'. Consequently even a certain sense of sanctity attached to a garden, and only in a garden and in the Forum do we see statues of Satyrs dedicated as a charm against the sorcery of the envious, although Plautus speaks [c] of gardens as being under the guardianship of Venus. Nowadays indeed under the name of gardens people possess the luxury of regular farms and country houses actually within the city. This practice was first introduced at Athens by that connoisseur of luxurious ease, Epicurus; down to his day the custom had not existed of having country dwellings in towns.

Value of a kitchen-garden for food and luxury.

At Rome at all events a garden was in itself a poor man's farm; the lower classes got their market-supplies from a garden—how much more harmless their fare was then! It gives more satisfaction, forsooth, to dive into the depth of the sea and seek for the various sorts of oysters [d] at the cost of a shipwreck, and to fetch birds [e] from beyond the river Rion, birds which not even legendary terrors [f] can protect—in fact these actually make them more prized! or to go fowling for other birds [g] in Numidia and among the tombs of Ethiopia,[h] or to fight with wild beasts, and, in hunting for game for someone else to devour, to be devoured oneself! But I protest, how little does garden produce cost, how adequate it is for

53 eadem quae ubique indignatio occurreret! ferendum sane fuerit exquisita nasci poma, alia sapore, alia magnitudine, alia monstro pauperibus interdicta, inveterari vina saccisque castrari, nec cuiquam adeo longam esse vitam ut non ante se genita potet, e frugibus quoque quondam alicam[1] sibi excogitasse luxuriam, ac medulla tantum earum superque pistrinarum operibus et caelaturis vivere, alio pane procerum, alio volgi, tot generibus usque ad infimam plebem
54 descendente annona[2]: etiamne in herbis discrimen inventum est, opesque differentiam fecere in cibo etiam uno asse venali? in his quoque aliqua sibi nasci tribus negant, caule in tantum saginato ut pauperis mensa non capiat. silvestres fecerat natura corrudas, ut passim quisque demeteret: ecce altiles spectantur asparagi, et Ravenna ternos libris rependit. heu prodigia ventris! mirum esset non licere pecori
55 carduis vesci, non licet plebei! aquae quoque separantur, et ipsa naturae elementa vi pecuniae discreta sunt. hi nives, illi glaciem potant, poenasque montium in voluptatem gulae vertunt. servatur rigor[3]

[1] *Mayhoff coll.* XVIII. 109, 112: alitum.
[2] *Budaeus*: anima.
[3] *Mayhoff*: algor *edd. vett.*: liquor *Urlichs, Detlefsen*: ligora *aut* ligura.

---

[a] *I.e.* fancy rolls and pastry.
[b] Cardoons. See pp. 518–519.

pleasure and for plenty, did we not meet with the same scandal in this as in everything else! We could no doubt have tolerated that choice fruits forbidden to the poor because of their flavour or their size or their portentous shape should be grown, that wines should be kept to mature with age and robbed of their virility by being passed through strainers, and that nobody should live so long as not to be able to drink vintages older than himself, and that luxury should also have long ago devised for itself a malted porridge made from the crops and should live only on the marrow of the grain, as well as on the elaborations and modellings [a] of the bakers' shops—one kind of bread for my lords and another for the common herd, the yearly produce graded in so many classes right down to the lowest of the low: but have distinctions been discovered even in herbs, and has wealth established grades even in articles of food that sell for a single copper? The ordinary public declares that even among vegetables some kinds are grown that are not for them, even a kale being fattened up to such a size that there is not room for it on a poor man's table. Nature had made asparagus to grow wild, for anybody to gather at random; but lo and behold! now we see a cultivated variety, and Ravenna produces heads weighing three to a pound. Alas for the monstrosities of gluttony! It would surprise us if cattle were not allowed to feed on thistles, but thistles [b] are forbidden to the lower orders! Even the water-supply is divided into classes, and the power of money has made distinctions in the very elements. Some people drink snow, others ice, and turn what is the curse of mountain regions into pleasure for their appetite. Coolness is stored up

Luxury of water-supply; luxurious food.

aestibus excogitaturque ut alienis mensibus nix algeat. decocunt alii aquas, mox et illas hiemant. nihil utique homini sic quomodo rerum naturae placet.
56 etiamne herba aliqua diviti tantum pascetur[1]? nemo Sacros Aventinosque montes et iratae plebis secessus circumspexerit? macellum[2] certe aequabit quos pecunia separaverit. itaque, Hercules, nullum quam[3] macelli vectigal maius fuit Romae clamore plebis incusantis apud omnes principes donec remissum est portorium mercis huius, conpertumque non aliter quaestuosius censum haberi aut tutius ac minore fortunae iure: cum credatur pensio ea pauperrumis,[4] in solo sponsor est et sub die reditus superficiesque caelo quocumque gaudens.

57 Hortorum Cato praedicat caules: hinc primum agricolas[5] aestumabant prisci, et sic statim faciebant iudicium, nequam esse in domo matrem familias—etenim haec cura feminae dicebatur—ubi indiligens esset extra hortus: quippe e carnario aut macello vivendum esse. nec caules ut nunc maxime probabant, damnantes pulmentaria quae egerent alio pulmentario: id erat oleo parcere, nam gari desideria
58 etiam in exprobratione erant. horti maxime place-

[1] pascetur? *Mayhoff*: nascitur *Caesarius*: pascitur.
[2] *Mayhoff*: mox enim.
[3] quam *add.*? *Mayhoff*.
[4] *Mayhoff*: pauperum is.
[5] agricolas? *Mayhoff*: agricolae.

---

[a] Made especially from mackerel.

against the hot weather, and plans are devised to keep snow cold for the months that are strangers to it. Other people first boil their water and then bring even that to a winter temperature. Assuredly mankind wants nothing to be as nature likes to have it. Shall even a particular kind of plant be reared to serve only the rich man's table? Can nobody have been warned by the Sacred Mount or the Aventine Hill, and the secessions of the angry Commons? Doubtless the provision-market will level up persons whom money divides into classes. And so, I vow, no impost at Rome bulked larger than the market dues in the outcry of the common people, who denounced them before all the chiefs of state until the tax on this commodity was remitted, and it was discovered that there was no method of rating that was more productive or safer and less governed by chance: as this payment is trusted to the poorest, the surety is in the soil, and the revenues lie in open daylight, just as does the surface of their land, rejoicing in the sky whatever be its aspect. B.C. 494 *and* 449.

Cato sings the praises of garden cabbages; people in old days used to estimate farmers by their garden-produce and thus at once to give a verdict that there was a bad mistress in the house where the garden outside, which used to be called the woman's responsibility, was neglected, as it meant having to depend on the butcher or the market for victuals. Nor did people approve very highly of vegetables as they do now, since they condemned delicacies that require another delicacy to help them down. This meant economizing oil, since it was actually counted as a reproach to need a rich sauce[a]. Those products of the garden were most in favour which needed no

Early economy in vegetables. *R.R.* CLVI. 1.

bant quae non egerent igni parcerentque ligno, expedita res et parata semper, unde et acetaria appellantur, facilia concoqui nec oneratura sensus[1] cibo, et quae minime accenderent desiderium. pars eorum ad condimenta pertinens fatetur domi versuram fieri solitam, atque non Indicum piper quaesitum
59 quaeque trans maria petimus. iam in fenestris suis plebs urbana imagine[2] hortorum cotidiana oculis rura praebebant, antequam praefigi prospectus omnes coegit multitudinis innumerae saeva latrocinatio. quamobrem sit aliquis et his honos, neve auctoritatem rebus vilitas adimat, cum praesertim etiam cognomina procerum inde nata videamus, Lactucinosque in Valeria familia non puduisse appellari, et contingat aliqua gratia operae curaeque nostrae Vergilio quoque confesso quam sit difficile verborum honorem tam parvis perhibere.

60 XX. Hortos villae iungendos non est dubium riguosque maxime habendos, si contingat, praefluo amne, si minus, e puteo rota organisve pneumaticis vel tollenonum haustu rigatos. solum proscindendum a favonio in autumnum praeparantibus post XIV dies iterandumque ante brumam. octo iugerum operis palari[3] iustum est, fimum tres pedes alte cum terra

[1] *Mayhoff*: sensu. [2] *Mayhoff*: in imagine. [3] *V.l.* parari.

[a] Possibly an allusion to *Georg.* IV. 6: *In tenui labor, at tenuis non gloria;* though actually Virgil applies these words to bees.

fire for cooking and saved fuel, and which were a resource in store and always ready; whence their name of salads, easy to digest and not calculated to overload the senses with food, and least adapted to stimulate the appetite. The fact that one set of herbs is devoted to seasoning shows that it used to be customary to do one's borrowing at home, and that there was no demand for Indian pepper and the luxuries that we import from overseas. Indeed the lower classes in the city used to give their eyes a daily view of country scenes by means of imitation gardens in their windows, before the time when atrocious burglaries in countless numbers compelled them to bar out all the view with shutters. Therefore let vegetables also have their meed of honour and do not let things be robbed of respect by the fact of their being common, especially as we see that vegetables have supplied even the names of great families, and a branch of the Valerian family were not ashamed to bear the surname Lettuce. Moreover some gratitude may attach to our labour and research on the ground that Virgil [a] also confessed how difficult it is to provide such small matters with dignified appellations.

XX. There is no doubt that it is proper to have gardens adjoining the farm-house, and that they should be irrigated preferably by a river flowing past them, if it so happens, or if not, be supplied with water from a well by means of a wheel or windmills, or ladled up by swing-beams. The soil should be broken up in preparation for autumn a fortnight after the west wind sets in, and gone over again before midwinter. It will take eight men to dig over an acre of land, mix dung with the soil to a

Laying out of garden ground.

misceri, areis distingui easque resupinis pulvinorum toris, ambiri singulas tramitum sulcis qua detur accessus homini scatebrisque decursus.

XXI. In hortis nascentium alia bulbo commendantur, alia capite, alia caule, alia folio, alia utroque, alia semine, alia cartilagine, alia carne, aut[1] utroque, alia cortice aut cute et cartilagine, alia tunicis carnosis.

61 XXII. Aliorum fructus in terra est, aliorum et extra, aliorum non nisi extra. quaedam iacent crescuntque, ut cucurbita et cucumis; eadem pendent, quamquam graviora multo etiam iis quae in arboribus gignuntur, sed cucumis cartilagine et carne constat, cucurbita cortice et cartilagine; cortex huic
62 uni maturitate transit in lignum. terra conduntur raphani napique et rapa, atque alio modo inulae, siser, pastinacae. quaedam vocabimus ferulacea, ut anetum, malvas; namque tradunt auctores in Arabia[2] malvas septumo mense arborescere bacu-
63 lorumque usum praebere. exemplo est arbor malvae in Mauretania Lixi oppidi aestuario, ubi Hesperidum horti fuisse produntur, cc passibus ab oceano iuxta delubrum Herculis antiquius Gaditano, ut ferunt: ipsa altitudinis pedum xx, crassitudinis quam circumplecti nemo possit. in simili genere habebitur et cannabis. nec non et carnosa aliqua appella-

[1] *Mayhoff*: carnea.
[2] [in Arabia] *Mayhoff coll. Theophr.* (in Arabia *fictum ex* mabia = malua).

---

[a] *Siser* may be the parsnip. *Pastinaca* originally denoted the carrot, but came to include also the parsnip.
[b] Mallow has no relation to any other plants in this chapter.

depth of three feet, mark it out in plots and border these with sloping rounded banks, and surround each plot with a furrowed path to afford access for a man and a channel for irrigation.

Garden plants, their various values.

XXI. Some plants growing in gardens are valued for their bulb, others for their head, others for their stalk, others for their leaf, others for both, others for their seed, others for their cartilage, others for their flesh, or for both, others for their husk or skin and cartilage, others for their fleshy outer coats.

Their various structures and habits.

XXII. Some plants produce their fruits in the earth, others outside as well, others only outside. Some grow lying on the ground, for instance gourds and cucumbers; these also grow in a hanging position, though they are much heavier even than fruits that grow on trees, but the cucumber is composed of cartilage and flesh and the gourd of rind and cartilage; the gourd is the only fruit whose rind when ripe changes into a woody substance. Radishes, navews and turnips are hidden in the earth, and so in a different way are elecampane, skirret and parsnips [a]. Some plants we shall call of the fennel class, for instance dill and mallow [b]; for authorities report that in Arabia mallows grow into trees in seven months, and serve as walking-sticks. There is an instance of a mallow-tree on the estuary of the town of Lixus in Mauretania, the place where the Gardens of the Hesperids are said to have been situated; it grows 200 yards from the ocean, near a shrine of Hercules which is said to be older than the one at Cadiz; the tree itself is 20 ft. high, and so large round that nobody could span it with his arms. Hemp will also be placed in a similar class. Moreover there are also some plants to which we shall give the name

bimus, ut spongeas in umore pratorum enascentes. fungorum enim callum in ligni arborumque natura diximus et alio genere tuberum paulo ante.

64 XXIII. Cartilaginum generis extraque terram est cucumis, mira voluptate Tiberio principi expetitus; nullo quippe non die contigit ei, pensiles eorum hortos promoventibus in solem rotis olitoribus rursusque hibernis diebus intra specularium munimenta revocantibus. quin et lacte mulso semine eorum biduo macerato apud antiquos Graeciae auctores scriptum

65 est seri oportere, ut dulciores fiant. crescunt qua coguntur forma; in Italia virides et quam minimi, in provinciis quam maximi et cerini aut nigri placent. copiosissimi Africae, grandissimi Moesiae. cum magnitudine excessere, pepones vocantur. vivunt hausti in stomacho in posterum diem nec perfici queunt in cibis, non insalubres tamen plurimum. natura oleum odere mire, nec minus aquas diligunt;

66 desecti quoque ad eas modice distantes adrepunt, contra oleum refugiunt aut, si quid obstet vel si pendeant, curvantur intorquenturque; id vel una

of 'fleshy', for instance the spongy plants that grow in water-meadows. As to the tough flesh of funguses, we have mentioned it already in treating the nature of timber and of trees, and in the case of another class, that of truffles, a short time ago. XVI. 31, XIX. 33 sqq.

Cartilaginous vegetables: the cucumber.

XXIII. Belonging to the class of cartilaginous plants and growing on the surface of the ground is the cucumber, a delicacy for which the emperor Tiberius had a remarkable partiality; in fact there was never a day on which he was not supplied with it, as his kitchen-gardeners had cucumber beds mounted on wheels which they moved out into the sun and then on wintry days withdrew under the cover of frames glazed with transparent stone. Moreover it is actually stated in the writings of early Greek authors that cucumber seed should be soaked for two days in milk mixed with honey before it is sown, in order to make the cucumbers sweeter. They grow in any shape they are forced to take; in Italy green ones of the smallest possible size are popular, but the provinces like the largest ones possible, and of the colour of wax or else dark. African cucumbers are the most prolific, and those of Moesia the largest. When they are exceptionally big they are called pumpkins. Cucumbers when swallowed remain in the stomach till the next day and cannot be digested with the rest of one's food, but nevertheless they are not extremely unwholesome. They have by nature a remarkable repugnance for oil, and an equal fondness for water; even when they have been cut from the stem, they creep towards water a moderate distance away, but on the contrary they retreat from oil, or if something is in their way or if they are hanging up, they grow curved and twisted. This

nocte deprehenditur, si vas cum aqua subiciatur, a quattuor digitorum intervallo descendentibus ante posterum diem, at si oleum eodem modo adsit,[1] in hamos curvatis. iidem in fistulam flore demisso mira
67 longitudine crescunt. ecce cum maxime nova forma eorum in Campania provenit mali cotonei effigie. forte primo natum ita audio unum, mox semine ex illo genus factum; melopeponas vocant. non pendent hi sed humi rotundantur, colore aureo. mirum in his praeter figuram coloremque et odorem quod maturitatem adepti quamquam non
68 pendentes statim a pediculo recedunt. Columella suum tradit commentum ut toto anno contingant, fruticem rubi quam vastissimum in apricum locum transferre et recidere duum digitorum relicta stirpe circa vernum aequinoctium; ita in medulla rubi semine cucumeris insito terra minuta fimoque circumaggeratas resistere frigori radices. cucumerum Graeci tria genera fecere, Laconicum, Scytalicum, Boeotium; ex his tantum Laconicum aqua gaudere. sunt qui herba nomine quae vocatur culix adtrita semen eorum maceratum seri iubeant, ut sine semine nascantur.

69 XXIV. Similis et cucurbitis natura, dumtaxat in nascendo: aeque hiemem odere, amant rigua ac

[1] *Rackham* (*vel* <subiectum> sit): sit.

may be observed to take place even in a single night, because if a vessel with water is put underneath them they descend towards it a hand's breadth before the next morning, but if oil is similarly near they will be found curved into crooked shapes. Also if their flower is passed down into a tube they grow to a remarkable length. Curious to say, just recently a new form of cucumber has been produced in Campania, shaped like a quince. I am told that first one grew in this shape by accident, and that later a variety was established grown from seed obtained from this one; it is called apple-pumpkin. Cucumbers of this kind do not hang from the plant but grow of a round shape lying on the ground; they have a golden colour. A remarkable thing about them, beside their shape, colour and smell, is that when they have ripened, although they are not hanging down they at once separate from the stalk. Columella gives a plan XI.
of his own for getting a supply of cucumbers all the year round—to transplant the largest blackberry bush available to a warm, sunny place, and about the spring equinox to cut it back, leaving a stump two inches long; and then to insert a cucumber seed in the pith of the bramble and bank up fine earth and manure round the roots, so that they may withstand the cold. The Greeks have produced three kinds of cucumbers, the Spartan, the Scytalic and the Boeotian; of these it is said that only the Spartan variety is fond of water. Some people tell us to steep cucumber seed in the plant called *culix* pounded up before sowing it, which will produce a cucumber having no seed.

Gourds: varieties and modes of growing.

XXIV. The gourd is also of a similar nature, at all events in its manner of growing: it has an equal aversion for cold and is equally fond of water and

fimum. seruntur ambo semine in terra sesquipedali
fossura, inter aequinoctium vernum et solstitium,
Parilibus tamen aptissime. aliqui malunt ex kal.
Mart. cucurbitas et nonis cucumes et per Quinquatrus serere, simili modo reptantibus flagellis
scandentes per parietum aspera in tectum usque
natura sublimitatis avida. vires sine adminiculo
standi non sunt, velocitas pernix, levi umbra camaras
70 ac pergulas operiens. inde haec prima duo genera,
camararium et plebeium quod humi crescit[1]; in
priore mire tenui pediculo libratur pondus immobile
aurae. cucurbita quoque omni modo fastigiatur,
vaginis maxime vitilibus, contecta[2] in eas postquam
defloruit, crescitque qua cogitur forma, plerumque[3]
draconis intorti figura. libertate vero pensili concessa iam visa est IX pedum longitudinis. particulatim
cucumis floret, sibi ipse superflorescens, et sicciores
locos patitur, candida lanugine obductus, magisque
dum crescit.

71 Cucurbitarum numerosior usus, et primus caulis in
cibo, atque ex eo in totum natura diversa: nuper in
balnearum usum venere urceolorum vice, iam pridem
vero etiam cadorum ad vina condenda. cortex vdirii

[1] *Mayhoff*: crevit *cd. Vat. Lat.* 3861: credi *rell.*
[2] *Rackham*: contexta *aut* coniecta.
[3] *Mayhoff*: plerumque et.

[a] A festival held on April 21 in celebration of the founding of Rome.
[b] March 19–23.

manure. Both gourds and cucumbers are grown from seed sown in a hole dug in the ground eighteen inches deep, between the spring equinox and midsummer, but most suitably on the day of the Parilia.[a] Some people however prefer to start sowing gourds on March 1 and cucumbers on March 7, and to go on through the Feast of Minerva.[b] These two plants both climb upward with shoots creeping over the rough surface of walls right up to the roof, as their nature is very fond of height. They have not the strength to stand without supports, but they shoot up at a rapid pace, covering vaulted roofs and trellises with a light shade. Owing to this they fall into these two primary classes, the roof-gourd and the common gourd which grows on the ground; in the former class a remarkably thin stalk has hanging from it a heavy fruit which a breeze cannot move. The gourd as well as the cucumber is made to grow in all sorts of long shapes, mostly by means of sheathes of plaited wicker, in which it is enclosed after it has shed its blossom, and it grows in any shape it is compelled to take, usually in the form of a coiled serpent. But if allowed to hang free it has before now been seen three yards long. The cucumber makes blossoms one by one, one flowering on the top of the other, and it can do with rather dry situations; it is covered with white down, especially when it is growing.

Various uses of gourds.

There are a larger number of ways of using gourds. To begin with, the stalk is an article of food. The part after the stalk is of an entirely different nature; gourds have recently come to be used instead of jugs in bath-rooms, and they have long been actually employed as jars for storing wine. The rind of gourd while it is green is thin, but all the same it is

tener, deraditur nihilominus in cibis[1], saluber ac lenis pluribus modis, ex his tamen qui perfici humano ventre
72 non queant sed[2] intumescant. semina quae proxima a[3] collo fuerunt proceras pariunt; item ab imis, sed non comparandas supra dictis; quae in medio rotundas, quae in lateribus crassas brevioresque. siccantur in umbra et, cum libeat serere, in aqua
73 macerantur. cibis, quo longiores tenuioresque, eo[4] et gratiores, et ob id salubriores quae pendendo crevere; minimumque seminis tales habent, duritia eius in cibis gratiam terminante. eas quae semini serventur ante hiemem praecidi non est mos; postea
74 fumo siccantur condendis hortensiorum seminibus rusticae supellectili. inventa est ratio qua cibis quoque servarentur—eodemque modo cucumis—usque ad alios paene proventus; et id quidem muria fit, sed et scrobe opaco in loco harena substrato fenoque sicco operto[5] ac deinde terra virides servari tradunt. sunt et silvestres in utroque genere et omnibus fere hortensiis; sed et his medica tantum natura est, quam ob rem differentur in sua volumina.

75 XXV. Reliqua cartilaginum naturae terra occultantur omnia. in quibus de rapis abunde dixisse potera-

[1] cibis cibus *cdd.*: *del.* cibus *cd. Vat. Lat.* 3861, *m.* 2.
[2] *Rackham*: sed non.
[3] a *add*? *Mayhoff.*
[4] eo *add.*? *Mayhoff.*
[5] *Mayhoff*: opertis.

scraped off when they are served as food; and although it is healthy and agreeable in a variety of ways, it is nevertheless one of the rinds that cannot be digested by the human stomach, but swell up. The seeds that were nearest the neck of the plant produce long gourds, and so do those next to the bottom, though the gourds grown from them are not comparable with those mentioned above; the seeds in the middle grow into round gourds, and those at the sides into thick and shorter ones. The seeds are dried in the shade, and when they are wanted for sowing they are steeped in water. The longer and thinner gourds are, the more agreeable they are for food, and consequently those which have been left to grow hanging are more wholesome; and this kind contain fewest seeds, the hardness of which limits their agreeableness as an article of diet. Gourds kept for seed are not usually cut before winter; after cutting they are dried in smoke for storing seeds of garden plants—the farm's stock in store. A plan has been invented by which they are preserved for food also—and the same in the case of cucumbers—to last almost until the next crops are available. This method employs brine; but it is reported that gourds can also be kept green in a trench dug in a shady place and floored with sand and covered over with dry hay and then with earth. There are also wild varieties of both cucumbers and gourds, as is the case with almost all garden plants; but these also only possess medicinal properties, and therefore they will be deferred to the Books devoted to them. xx. 3; 13.

Underground cartilaginous plants. Turnips and navew.

XXV. The remaining plants of a cartilaginous nature are all hidden in the ground. Among these, we might appear to have already spoken amply 126 ff.

mus videri, nisi medici masculini sexus facerent in his rotunda, latiora vero et concava feminini, praestantiora suavitate et ad condendum [1] faciliora; saepius sata transeunt in marem. idem naporum quattuor [2] genera fecere, Corinthium, Cleonaeum, Liothasium,
76 Boeotium, quod et [3] per se viride dixerunt. ex his in amplitudinem adolescit Corinthium, nuda fere radice; solum enim hoc genus superne tendit, non ut cetera in terram. Liothasium quidam Thracium appellant, frigorum patientissimum. at Boeotium dulce est, rotunditate etiam brevi notabile, neque ut Cleonaeum praelongum. in totum quidem quorum levia folia ipsi quoque dulciores, quorum scabra et angulosa et
77 horrida amariores. est praeterea genus silvestre cuius folia sunt erucae similia. palma Romae Amiterninis datur, dein Nursinis, tertia nostratibus. cetera de satu eorum in rapis dicta sunt.

78 XXVI. Cortice et cartilagine constant raphani, multisque eorum cortex crassior etiam quam quibusdam arborum. amaritudo plurima illis est et pro crassitudine corticis. cetera quoque aliquando lignosa.
79 et vis mira colligendi spiritum laxandique ructum; ob

[1] *V.l.* condiendum.
[2] *Pintianus*: quinque.
[3] *Dalec.*: et quod.

---

[a] But Theophrastus, *H.P.* VII, 4, 2 seems to show that all the following *napi* are really radishes.

about the turnip, were it not that medical men class the round plants in this group as being of the male sex and the more spread out and curved ones as female, the latter being superior in sweetness and easier to store; though after being repeatedly sown they turn into male plants. The same authorities have made four classes of navews,[a] the Corinthian, Cleonaean, Liothasian and Boeotian, the last also called merely the green turnip. Of these the Corinthian turnip grows to a very large size, with its root almost bare, for only this kind grows upward, not down into the ground as the others do. The Liothasian kind is by some called Thracian navew; it stands cold extremely well. The Boeotian navew is sweet, and also is remarkable for its short round shape, not being elongated like the Cleonaean variety. In fact, generally speaking, navews the leaves of which are smooth also themselves have a sweeter taste, and those with rough and angular and bristly leaves are more bitter. There is also a wild kind the leaves of which resemble colewort. At Rome the prize is given to the turnips of San Vettorino, and next to those of Norcia, and the third place to the local variety. The rest of the facts about growing navews have been stated in the passage dealing with turnips. XVIII. 129.

Radishes: their properties and varieties

XXVI. Radishes consist of an outer skin and a cartilage, and with many of them the skin is even thicker than the bark of some kinds of trees. They have an extremely pungent flavour, which varies in proportion to the thickness of the skin. The other parts as well are sometimes of a woody substance. They have a remarkable power of causing flatulence and eructation; consequently

id cibus inliberalis, utique si proxume olus mandatur, si vero ipse cum olivis druppis, rarior ructus fit minusque faetidus. Aegypto mire celebratur olei propter fertilitatem quod e semine eius faciunt. hoc maxime cupiunt serere, si liceat, quoniam et quaestus plus quam e frumento et minus tributi est nullumque ibi
80 copiosius oleum. genera raphani Graeci fecere tria foliorum differentia, crispi atque levis et tertium silvestre; atque huic levia quidem folia sed breviora ac rotunda copiosaque ac fruticosa; sapor autem asper et medicamenti instar ad eliciendas alvos. et in prioribus tamen differentia a[1] semine, quoniam aliqua
81 peius, aliqua admodum exiguum ferunt: haec vitia non cadunt nisi in crispa folia. nostri alia fecere genera: Algidense a loco, longum atque tralucidum, alterum rapi figura quod vocant Syriacum, suavissimum fere ac tenerrimum hiemisque patiens praecipue. verum[2] tamen ex Syria non pridem advectum apparet, quoniam apud auctores non reperitur; id
82 autem toto hieme durat. etiamnum unum silvestre Graeci cerain vocant, Pontici armon, alii leucen, nostri armoraciam, fronde copiosius quam corpore. in

[1] a *add. Hardouin.*
[2] praecipue. verum *Mayhoff*: praecipuum.

---

[a] Or 'crisped-leaf'. If so, it would be a cabbage (Greek ῥάφανος) confused with a radish (Greek ῥαφανίς).
[b] Horse-radish though *cerais* is properly wild radish.

they are a vulgar article of diet, at all events if cabbage is eaten immediately after them, though if the radish itself is eaten with half-ripe olives, the eructation caused is less frequent and less offensive. In Egypt the radish is held in remarkable esteem because it produces oil, which they make from its seed. The people are very fond of sowing radish seed if opportunity offers, because they make more profit from it than from corn and have a smaller duty to pay on it, and because no plant there yields a larger supply of oil. The Greeks have made three kinds of radish, distinguished by difference of the leaves—the wrinkled [a] radish, the smooth radish and third the wild kind; though the last has smooth leaves, they are shorter and round, and numerous and bushy; the taste of this radish is however rough, and it acts like a drug with a purgative effect. Among the kinds mentioned before however there is also a difference arising from the seed, since some produce an inferior seed and some an extremely small one; but these defects only apply to the wrinkled-leaf variety. Our own people have made other classes—the Monte Compatri radish, named from its locality, a long and semi-transparent radish, and another shaped like a turnip which they call Syrian radish, about the sweetest and most tender of any, and exceptionally able to stand the winter. It appears however to have been imported from Syria only lately, since it is not found mentioned in the authorities; still, it lasts through the whole of the winter. There is also one wild variety [b], called by the Greeks *cerais*, in the Pontus country *armos*, or by other people *leuce*, and by our nation *armoracia*; this radish grows more leaves than root. But in testing

omnibus autem probandis maxime spectantur caules; inmitium enim rotundiores crassioresque sunt ac longis canalibus, folia ipsa crispiora[1] et angulis horrida.

83 Seri vult raphanus terra soluta, umida; fimum odit palea contentus: frigore adeo gaudet ut in Germania infantium puerorum magnitudinem aequet. seritur post id. Feb. ut vernus sit, iterumque circa Vulcanalia, quae satio melior; multi et Martio et Aprili serunt et Septembri. incipiente incremento confert alterna folia circumobruere, ipsos vero adcumulare, nam qui extra terram emersit durus fit atque fungo-
84 sus. Aristomachus detrahi folia per hiemem iubet et ne lacunae stagnent accumulari; ita in aestate[2] grandescere. quidam prodidere, si palo adacto caverna palea insternatur sex digitorum altitudine, deinde inseratur semen[3] fimumque et terra congeratur, ad magnitudinem scrobis crescere. praecipue tamen salsis aluntur; itaque etiam talibus aquis rigantur, et in Aegypto nitro sparguntur, ubi sunt
85 suavitate praecipui. in totum quoque salsugine amaritudo eorum eximitur fiuntque coctis similes; namque et cocti dulcescunt et in naporum vicem transeunt.

[1] crispiora (*vel* hirsutiora)? *Mayhoff*: tristiora.
[2] *cd. Par. Lat.* 6797 (ἐν τῷ θέρει *Theophr.*): aestatem *rell.*
[3] *Rackham*: deinde in semen.

the value of all kinds of radishes most attention is given to the stems, as those of a harsh flavour have stems that are rounded and thicker and grooved with long channels, and the leaves themselves are more crinkled and have prickly corners.

Cultivation of radishes.

The radish likes to be sown in loose, damp soil. It dislikes dung and is content with a dressing of chaff; and it is so fond of cold that in Germany it grows as big as a baby child. Radish for the spring crop is sown after February 13, and the second sowing, which is a better crop, is about the Festival of Vulcan;[a] but many also sow it in March and April and in September. When it begins to make growth, it pays to bank up every other leaf on each plant and to earth up the roots themselves, as a root that projects above the ground becomes hard and full of holes. Aristomachus advises stripping off the leaves during winter, and piling up earth round the plants to prevent muddy puddles forming round them; and he says that this will make them grow a good size in summer. Some authors have stated that if a hole is made by driving in a stake and covered at the bottom with chaff to a depth of six inches, and a seed is sown in it and dung and earth are heaped on it, a radish grows to the size of the hole. All the same they find saltish soils specially nourishing, and so they are even watered with salt water, and in Egypt, where they are remarkable for sweetness, they are sprinkled with soda. Also brackishness has the effect of entirely removing their pungency, and making them like radishes that have been boiled, inasmuch as boiling a radish sweetens it and turns it into something like a navew.

[a] August 23–30.

Crudos medici suadent ad colligenda acria viscerum cum sale dandos esse, atque ita vomitionibus prae-
86 parant meatum. tradunt et praecordiis necessarium hunc sucum, quando φθειρίασιν cordi intus inhaerentem non alio potuisse depelli conpertum sit in Aegypto regibus corpora mortuorum ad scrutandos morbos insecantibus. atque, ut est Graeca vanitas, fertur in templo Apollinis Delphis adeo ceteris cibis praelatus raphanus ut ex auro dedicaretur, beta ex argento,
87 rapum ex plumbo. scires non ibi genitum M'. Curium imperatorem, quem ab hostium legatis aurum repudiaturo adferentibus rapum torrentem in foco inventum annales nostri prodidere. scripsit et Moschion Graecus unum de raphano volumen. utilissimi in cibis hiberno tempore existimantur, iidemque dentibus semper inimici, quoniam adterant: ebora certe poliunt. odium iis cum vite maximum, refugitque iuxta satos.

88 XXVII. Lignosiora sunt reliqua in cartilaginum genere a nobis posita, mirumque omnibus vehementiam saporis esse. ex his pastinacae unum genus agreste sponte provenit, alterum

---

[a] Pediculosis or Morbus pediculosus. It is doubtful what disease was denoted by this term. Modern medicine uses it of the pathological symptoms due to the presence of lice on the body.

[b] Including carrot.

Medical men recommend giving raw radishes with salt for the purpose of concentrating the crude humours of the bowels, and they use this mixture to act as an emetic. They also say that radish juice is an essential specific for disease of the diaphragm, inasmuch as in Egypt, when the kings ordered *post mortem* dissections to be made for the purpose of research into the nature of diseases, it was discovered that this was the only dose that was capable of removing *phtheiriasis* [a] attacking the internal parts of the heart. Also it is said that the radish was rated so far above all other articles of food that, such is the frivolity of the Greeks, in the temple of Apollo at Delphi, a radish modelled in gold was dedicated as a votive offering, though only a silver beetroot and a turnip of lead. You might be sure that Manius Curius was not a native of Delphi, the general who is recorded in our annals to have been found by the enemy's envoys roasting a turnip at the fire, when they came bringing the gold which he was going indignantly to refuse. Also the Greek author Moschion wrote a whole volume about the radish. Radishes are considered an extremely valuable article of food in winter time, though at the same time people think them to be always bad for the teeth, because they wear them down; at all events they can be used for polishing ivory. There is a great antipathy between radishes and vines, which shrink away from radishes planted near them.

Medicinal use of radishes.

Value set on the radish.

XXVII. The rest of the plants that we have placed in the cartilaginous class are of a woodier substance, and it is noticeable that they all have an extremely pungent taste. Among these there is one wild kind of parsnip that grows of its own accord, and another

Varieties of parsnip. [b]

Graeciae seritur radice vel semine vere primo vel autumno, ut Hygino placet, Februario, Augusto,
89 Septembri, Octobri, solo quam altissume refosso. annicula utilis esse incipit, bima utilior, gratior autumno patinisque maxime, et sic quoque virus intractabile illi est. hibiscum a pastinaca gracilitate distat, damnatum in cibis, sed medicinae utile. est et quartum genus in eadem similitudine pastinacae quam nostri Gallicam vocant, Graeci vero daucon, cuius genera etiam quattuor fecere, inter medicamenta dicendum.

90 XXVIII. Siser et ipsum Tiberius princeps nobilitavit flagitans omnibus annis e Germania. Gelduba appellatur castellum Rheno inpositum ubi generositas praecipua, ex quo apparet frigidis locis convenire. inest longitudine nervus qui decoctis extrahitur, amaritudinis tamen magna parte relicta, quae mulso in cibis temperata etiam in gratiam vertitur. nervus idem et pastinacae maiori, dumtaxat anniculae. siseris satus mensibus Februario, Martio, Aprili, Augusto, Septembri, Octobri.

91 XXIX. Brevior his est et torosior amariorque inula, per se stomacho inimicissuma, eadem dulcibus mixtis

---

[a] The wild carrot.
[b] Some authorities identify the *siser* with the parsnip.

kind belonging to Greece that is grown from a root or from seed set at the beginning of spring or else in autumn, according to Hyginus, in February or in August or September or October, the ground having been dug over as deeply as possible. A root only a year old begins to be serviceable, but a two year old plant is more valuable; it is more agreeable in autumn, and especially for boiling in saucepans, and even so it has a pungency that cannot be got rid of. The marsh-mallow differs from the parsnip in being of a more slender shape; it is condemned as an article of diet, but is useful for medical purposes. There is also a fourth kind of plant that bears the same resemblance to a parsnip, which our people call the Gallic parsnip, but the Greeks, who have subdivided it also into four classes, call *daucos* [a]; this will have to be mentioned among the medicinal plants. XXV. 110.

Skirret.

XXVIII. The skirret [b] also has been advertised by the emperor Tiberius's requisitioning an annual supply of it from Germany. There is a castle on the Rhine called Gelb where a specially fine kind of skirret grows, showing that cold localities suit it. It contains a core running through its whole length, which is drawn out when it has been boiled, though nevertheless a great part of its bitterness remains, which when it is used as a food is modified by adding wine sweetened with honey, and is actually turned into an attraction. The larger parsnip also contains a core of the same kind, though only when it is a year old. The time for sowing skirret is in the months of February, March, April, August, September and October.

Elecampane.

XXIX. Elecampane is shorter and more substantial than the roots described, and also more bitter; eaten by itself it disagrees violently with the stomach, but

saluberrima. pluribus modis austeritate victa gratiam invenit: namque et in pollinem tunditur arida liquidoque dulci temperatur, et decocta posca aut adservata, vel macerata pluribus modis, et tunc mixta defruto aut subacta melle uvisve passis aut pinguibus
92 caryotis. alio rursus modo cotoneis malis vel sorbis aut prunis, aliquando pipere aut thymo variata defectus praecipue stomachi excitat, inlustrata maxime Iuliae Augustae cotidiano cibo. supervacuum eius semen, quoniam oculis ex radice excisis ut harundo seritur, et haec autem et siser et pastinaca utroque tempore, vere et autumno, magnis seminum intervallis, inula ne minus quam ternorum pedum, quoniam spatiose fruticat. siser transferre melius.
93 XXX. Proxima hinc est bulborum natura, quos Cato in primis serendos praecipit celebrans Megaricos. verum nobilissima est scilla, quamquam medicamini nata exacuendoque aceto; nec ulli amplitudo maior, sicuti nec vis asperior. duo genera medicae, masculum[1] albis foliis, femineum[2] nigris; et tertium genus est cibis gratum, Epimenidu vocatur, angustius folio
94 ac minus aspero. seminis plurimum omnibus; celerius tamen proveniunt satae bulbis circa latera natis; et ut

[1] masculae *Mayhoff* (mascule *cd. Par. Lat.* 10318).
[2] *Rackham*: femine (*cd. Par. Lat.* 10318) *aut* femina (feminae *Mayhoff*).

---

[a] Esculent bulbs of the onion class are meant.

it is very wholesome when blended with sweet things. There are several ways of overcoming its acridity and rendering it agreeable: it is dried and pounded into flour and seasoned with some sweet juice, or it is boiled or kept in soak in vinegar and water, or steeped in various ways, and then mixed with boiled down grape-juice or flavoured with honey or raisins or juicy dates. Another method again is to flavour it with quinces or sorbs or plums, and occasionally with pepper or thyme, making it a tonic particularly salutary for a weak digestion; it has become specially stimulating from having been the daily diet of Julia the daughter of Augustus. Its seed is superfluous, as it is propagated like a reed, from eyes cut out of the root; it also, like the skirret and the parsnip, is planted at either season, spring or autumn, with large spaces left between the plants—for elecampane not less than a yard, because it throws out shoots over a wide space. Skirret is better transplanted.

Bulbs: squill, arum and other varieties.

XXX. Next after these in natural properties are the bulbs[a], which Cato particularly recommends for cultivation, specially praising the Megarian kind. But the most famous bulb is the squill, although it naturally serves as a drug and is used for increasing the sourness of vinegar; and no other bulb is of larger size, just as also no other has a more powerful pungency. There are two kinds used for medicine, the male squill with white leaves and the female squill with dark leaves; and there is also a third kind, agreeable as an article of diet, called Epimenides's squill—this has a narrower leaf with a less pungent taste. All produce a very large quantity of seed, though they come up more quickly if grown from the bulbs that shoot out round their sides; and to make

R.R. VIII. 2.

crescant, folia quae sunt his ampla deflexa circa obruuntur; ita sucum omnem in se trahunt capita. sponte nascuntur copiosissimae [1] in Baliaribus Ebusoque insulis ac per Hispanias. unum de eis volumen condidit Pythagoras philosophus, colligens medicas
95 vires, quas proximo reddemus libro. reliqua genera bulborum differunt colore, magnitudine, suavitate, quippe cum quidam crudi mandantur, ut in Cherroneso Taurica; post hos in Africa nati maxime laudantur, mox Apuli. genera Graeci haec fecere: bolbinen, setanion, opitiona, cyica, aegilopa, sisyrinchion; in hoc mirum imas eius radices crescere hieme, verno autem, cum apparuerit viola, minui has, contra
96 ipsum deinde [2] bulbum pinguescere. est inter genera et quod in Aegypto aron vocant, scillae proximum amplitudine, foliis lapatho,[3] caule recto duum cubitorum baculi crassitudine, radice mollioris naturae,
97 quae estur et cruda. effodiuntur bulbi ante ver, aut deteriores illico fiunt—signum maturitatis est folia inarescentia ab imo; viridioresque [4] improbant, item longos ac parvos, contra rubicundis rotundioribusque laus et grandissimis. amaritudo plerisque in vertice est, media eorum dulcia. bulbos non nasci nisi e

[1] *Mayhoff*: copiosissime.
[2] *Sic? Mayhoff*: minuthac *aut* minus ut hac (*aut alia*) contrahi tunc deinde *cdd.*
[3] *Rackham*: lapathi.
[4] *Sic? Mayhoff*: vetustioresque.

them grow bigger, the leaves, which in this plant are of a large size, are bent down in a circle round them and covered with soil, so causing the heads to draw all the juice into themselves. They grow wild in very large quantities in the Balearic Islands and Iviza, and throughout the Spanish provinces. The philosopher Pythagoras wrote a whole book about them, including an account of their medicinal properties, which we shall record in the next Volume. XX. 102 sqq.
The remaining kinds of bulbs differ in colour and size and in flavour, some being eaten raw, for instance in the Crimea; next after these the ones that grow in Africa are most highly spoken of, and then those of Apulia. The Greeks have distinguished the following kinds—*bolbine*, *setanion*, *opition*, *cyix*, *aegilops* and *sisyrinchion*; the last possesses the remarkable *Barbary nut.*
property that its bottom roots grow in winter, but in the spring-time, when the violet has appeared, these diminish while the actual bulb, on the other hand, afterwards begins to swell out. Among the varieties of bulb there is also the one that in Egypt they call the *arum*, which is very near to the squill in size and *Cuckoo-pint.*
to the sorrel in foliage, with a straight stalk a yard long of the thickness of a walking-stick, and a root of softer substance, which can even be eaten raw. Bulbs are dug up before the beginning of spring, or else they at once go off in quality; it is a sign that they are ripe when the leaves become dry at the lower end. The rather green ones are disapproved of, as also are the long and the small ones, whereas those of a reddish colour and rounder shape are praised, as also are those of the largest size. Usually their top has a bitter taste and the middle parts are sweet. Previous writers have stated that bulbs only grow

semine priores tradiderunt, sed in Praenestinis campis sponte nascuntur, ac sine modo etiam in Remorum arvis.

98 XXXI. Hortensiis omnibus fere singulae radices,
ut raphano, betae, apio, malvae; amplissima autem
lapatho, ut quae descendat ad tria cubita—silvestri
minor—et umida, effossa quoque diu vivit. quibusdam tamen capillatae, ut apio, malvae, quibusdam
surculosae, ut ocimo, aliis carnosae, ut betae aut
magis etiamnum croco, aliquis ex cortice et carne
constant, ut raphano, rapis, quorundam geniculatae
99 sunt, ut graminis. quae rectam non habent radicem
statim plurimis nituntur capillamentis, ut atriplex et
blitum; scilla autem et bulbi et cepae et alium non
nisi in rectum radicantur. sponte nascentium quaedam numerosiora sunt radice quam folio, ut spalax,
100 perdicium, crocum. florent confertim [1] serpullum,
habrotonum, napi, raphani, menta, ruta. et cetera
quidem, cum coepere, deflorescunt, ocimum autem
particulatim et ab imo incipit, qua de causa diutissime
floret. hoc et in heliotropio herba evenit. flos aliis
candidus, aliis luteus, aliis purpureus. folia cadunt a
cacuminibus origano, inulae et aliquando rutae
iniuria laesae. maxime concava sunt cepae, getio.

[1] confertim e *Theophr. Bodaeus* : cum fraxino.

---

[a] *Apium* also includes celery, and often means that plant.

[b] Meadow saffron? *Perdicium* would be *Polygonum maritimum*.

from seed, but as a matter of fact they spring up of themselves in the plains near Palestrina, and also in unlimited quantity in the country round Reims.

Varieties of root, leaf and flower.

XXXI. Nearly all kitchen-garden plants have only a single root, for instance radish, beet, parsley,[a] mallow. Sorrel has the largest root, going as far as a yard and a half into the ground (the root of the wild sorrel is smaller), and its root is full of sap, and lives a long time even after being dug up. In some of these plants, however, for instance parsley and mallow, the root is fibrous, in some, for instance basil, woody, in others fleshy, as in beet or still more in saffron, and with some, for instance radish and turnip, the roots consist of rind and flesh, and the roots of some, for instance hay-grass, are jointed. Those which have not a straight root support themselves immediately with a great many hairy fibres, for instance orage and blite; but squill and the bulbs and onion and garlic only throw out straight roots. Some of the plants that grow self-sown have more root than leaf, for instance *spalax*,[b] partridge-plant and crocus. Wild thyme, southernwood, navews, radishes, mint and rue blossom all in a bunch. All other plants shed their blossom all at once as soon as they have begun to do so, but basil does so gradually, starting from the bottom, and consequently it flowers for a very long time. This also happens in the case of the heliotrope. Some plants have a white flower, others yellow and others purple. Wild marjoram and elecampane shed their leaves from the top down, and so sometimes does rue when it has been damaged by an accident. The onion and the *getion*-leek have especially hollow leaves.

101 XXXII. Alium cepasque inter deos in iureiurando habet Aegyptus. cepae genera apud Graecos Sarda, Samothracia, Alsidena, setania, schista, Ascalonia ab oppido Iudaeae nominata. omnibus corpus totum pingui tunicarum cartilagine [1], omnibus etiam odor lacrimosus et praecipue Cypriis, minime Cnidiis. e
102 cunctis setania minima, excepta Tusculana, sed dulcis; schista autem et Ascalonia condiuntur.[2] schistam hieme cum coma sua relincunt, vere folia detrahunt et alia subnascuntur isdem divisuris, unde et nomen. hoc exemplo reliquis quoque generibus detrahi iubent, ut in capita crescant potius quam in semen. et
103 Ascaloniarum propria natura: etenim velut steriles sunt ab radice, et ob id semine seri illas, non deponi iussere Graeci, praeterea serius, circa ver, at [3] cum germinent, transferri; ita crassescere et properare cum [4] praeteriti temporis pensitatione. festinandum autem in iis est, quoniam maturae celeriter putrescunt. si deponantur, caulem emittunt [5] et semen,
104 ipsaeque evanescunt. est et colorum differentia: in Isso enim et Sardibus candidissimae proveniunt. sunt in honore et Creticae, de quibus dubitant an eaedem sint quae Ascaloniae, quoniam satis capita

[1] omnibus . . . cartilagine *hic?* *Mayhoff*: *post* Cnidiis *codd.*
[2] *V.l.* conduntur (*cf.* 105).
[3] *Mayhoff*: a *vel* aut.
[4] *Mayhoff*: cum properare.
[5] *Caesarius*: mittunt.

[a] Perhaps the shallot.

Varieties of onion.

XXXII. In Egypt people swear by garlic and onions as deities in taking an oath. Among the Greeks the varieties of onion are the Sardinian, Samothracian, Alsidenian, setanian, the split onion, and the Ascalon onion [a], named from a town in Judaea. In all these the body consists entirely of coats of greasy cartilage; also they all have a smell which makes one's eyes water, especially the Cyprus onions, but least of all those of Cnidos. The smallest of all except the Tuscany onion is the setanian, though it has a sweet taste; but the split onion and the Ascalon onion need flavouring. The split onion is left with its leaves on in winter, these being pulled off in spring, and others grow in their place at the same divisions, from which these onions get their name. This has suggested the recommendation to strip the other kinds also of their leaves, so as to make them grow to heads rather than run to seed. Ascalon onions also have a peculiar nature, being in a manner sterile at the root, and consequently the Greeks have advised growing them from seed and not planting them, and moreover sowing them rather late, about spring-time, but transplanting them when they are in bud; this method, they say, causes them to fill out and grow quickly, making up for the time lost. But in their case haste is necessary, because when ripe they quickly go rotten. If grown from roots they throw out a stalk and run to seed, and the bulb withers away. There is also a difference of colours, the whitest onions growing at Issus and at Sardis. Those of Crete are also esteemed, though the question is raised whether they are identical with the Ascalon variety, because when grown from seed they make large heads but run to stalk and seed when

crassescunt, depositis caulis et semen; distant sapore
105 tantum dulci. apud nos duo prima genera: unum condimentariae, quam illi getion, nostri pallacanam vocant, seritur mensibus Martio, Aprili, Maio, alterum capitatae quae ab aequinoctio autumni vel a favonio. genera eius austeritatis ordine: Africana, Gallica, Tusculana, Ascalonia, Amiternina. optima autem quae rotundissima, item rufa acrior quam candida, et sicca quam viridis, et cruda quam cocta
106 sicut [1] quam condita. seritur Amiternina frigidis et umidis locis, et sola alii modo capite, reliquae semine proximaque aestate nullum semen emittunt sed caput tantum quod increscit; [2] sequenti autem anno permutata ratione semen gignitur, caput ipsum corrumpitur. ergo omnibus annis separatim semen cepae causa seritur, separatim cepa seminis. servantur autem
107 optime in paleis. getium paene sine capite est, cervicis tantum longae et ideo totum in fronde, saepiusque resecatur ut porrum; ideo et illud serunt, non deponunt. cetero cepas ter fosso seri iubent extirpatis radicibus herbarum, in iugera denas libras, intermisceri satureiam, quoniam melius proveniat,

[1] *Mayhoff coll. Diosc.* II 180: sicca.
[2] *Dalec.*: inarescit.

planted; they only differ from the Ascalon onions in their sweet flavour. In our country we have two principal varieties, one the kind of onion used for seasoning, the Greek name for which is *getion*-leek and the Latin 'pallacana', which is sown in March, April or May, and the other the onion with a head, which is sown after the autumn equinox or when the west wind has begun to blow in the springtime. The varieties of the latter, in order of their degrees of pungency, are the African, the Gallic, and those of Tusculum, Ascalon and Amiternae. Those of the roundest shape are the best; also a red onion is more pungent than a white one, or a dry one than one still fresh, and a raw one than one that has been cooked, and also than one that has been kept in store. The Amiternum kind is grown in cold and damp places, and is the only one that grows with a head only, like garlic, all other varieties being grown from seed and next summer producing no seed but only a head which goes on growing in size; but in the following year just the contrary, seed is produced but the actual head goes rotten. Consequently every year there are two separate processes, seed being sown to produce onions and onions planted for seed. Onions keep best stored in chaff. The scallion has hardly any head at all, only a long neck, and consequently it all goes to leaf, and it is cut back several times, like common leek; consequently it also is grown from seed, not by planting. In addition, they recommend digging over the ground three times and weeding out the plant-roots before sowing onions; and using ten pounds of seed to the acre, with savory mixed in, as the onions come up better; and moreover stubbing and hoeing the

Storage and cultivation of onions.

runcari praeterea et sariri, si non saepius, quater. Ascaloniam mense Februario serunt nostri. semen ceparum nigrescere incipientium[1] antequam inarescat[2] metunt.

108 XXXIII. Et de porro in hac cognatione dici conveniat, praesertim cum sectivo auctoritatem nuper fecerit princeps Nero vocis gratia ex oleo statis mensum omnium diebus nihilque aliud ac ne panem[3] quidem vescendo. seritur semine ab aequinoctio autumno, si sectivum facere libuit, densius. in
109 eadem area secatur donec deficiat; stercoraturque semper, si nutritur in capita, antequam secetur. cum increvit, in aliam aream transfertur summis foliis leviter recisis ante medullam et capitibus retractis tunicis[4] extremis. antiqui silice vel testa[5] subiecta capita dilatabant—hoc item in bulbis; nunc sarculo leviter convelluntur radices, ut delum-
110 batae alant neque distrahant. insigne quod, cum fimo laetoque solo gaudeat, rigua odit; et tamen proprietate quadam soli constant: laudatissimum[6] Aegypto, mox Ostiae atque Ariciae. sectivi duo genera: herbaceum folio, incisuris eius evidentibus, quo utuntur medicamentarii, alterum genus flavidioris

[1] *Rackham*: incipiens autem.
[2] *Detlefsen*: marcescant.
[3] *Sillig*: pane.
[4] *Rackham*: tunicisve.
[5] *Salmasius*: tecta.
[6] *Mayhoff*: laudatissimus in.

ground four times, if not more. Our farmers sow the Ascalon onion in February. The seed of onions is harvested when they begin to turn black, before they get dry.

Leek: its cultivation; its varieties.

XXXIII. It may also be suitable to mention the leek in this family of plants, especially as importance has recently been given to the chive by the emperor Nero, who on certain fixed days of every month always ate chives preserved in oil, and nothing else, not even bread, for the sake of his voice. It is grown from seed sown just after the autumnal equinox; if it is for the purpose of chives, it must be sown rather thickly. It goes on being cut in the same bed till it gives out; and if it is being grown to make heads it is always well manured before it is cut. When it is fully grown, it is moved to another bed, after having the points of the leaves above the central part carefully trimmed off and the tips of the coats drawn back from the heads. Growers in former times used to broaden out the heads by putting them under a stone or a potsherd, and the same with bulbs as well; but now the practice is gently to pull the roots loose with a hoe, so that being bent they may feed the plant and not draw it apart. It is a remarkable fact that although the leek likes manure and a rich soil, it hates damp places. Nevertheless there is a connexion between the varieties and some peculiarity of the soil: the most highly esteemed kind belongs to Egypt, and the next to Ostia and to La Riccia. There are two kinds of chive; one with grass-green leaves, with distinct markings on them—this is the chive used by druggists—and another kind with leaves of a yellower colour and rounder in shape, on which the

folii rotundiorisque, levioribus incisuris. fama est Melam equestris ordinis, reum ex procuratione a Tiberio principe accersitum, in summa desperatione suco porri ad trium denariorum argenteorum pondus hausto confestim expirasse sine cruciatu. ampliorem[1] modum negant noxium esse.

111 XXXIV. Alium ad multa ruris praecipue medicamenta prodesse creditur. tenuissimis et quae separantur in[2] universum velatur membranis, mox pluribus coagmentatur nucleis, et his separatim vestitis, asperi saporis; quo pluris nuclei fuere hoc est asperius. taedium huic quoque halitu, ut cepis, nullum tamen
112 cocti.[3] generum differentia in tempore—praecox maturescit LX diebus—tum et[4] in magnitudine. ulpicum quoque in hoc genere Graeci appellavere alium Cyprium, alii ἀντισκόροδον, praecipue Africae celebratum inter pulmentaria ruris, grandius alio; tritum in oleo et aceto mirum quantum increscit spuma. quidam ulpicum et alium in plano seri vetant castellatimque grumulis inponi distantibus inter se pedes ternos iubent; inter grana digiti IIII[5] interesse debent; simul atque tria folia eruperint, sariri:
113 grandescunt quo saepius sariuntur. maturescentium caules depressi in terram obruuntur: ita cavetur ne

[1] at minorem? *Mayhoff*.
[2] *Edd.*: et quae spernantur *aut* sperantur.
[3] cocti? *Mayhoff*: cocto? *Warmington*: coctis.
[4] tum et? *Mayhoff*: tamen.
[5] IIII *add. Sillig.*

[a] Perhaps the Latin should be altered to give 'But a smaller dose'.

markings are less prominent. There is a story that a member of the Order of Knights named Mela, when recalled from a deputy-governorship by the emperor Tiberius to be impeached for maladministration, in extreme despair swallowed a dose of leek-juice weighing three denarii in silver, and immediately expired without suffering any pain. A larger dose [a] is said to have no injurious effect.

XXXIV. Garlic is believed to be serviceable for making a number of medicaments, especially those used in the country. It is enveloped in very fine skins in entirely separate layers, and then consists of several kernels in a cluster, each of these also having a coat of its own; it has a pungent flavour, and the more kernels there were the more pungent it is. Garlic as well as onions gives an offensive smell to the breath, though when boiled it causes no smell. The difference between the various kinds consists in the time they take to ripen—the early kind ripens in 60 days—and also in their size. Ulpicum also comes in this class, the plant called by the Greeks Cyprian garlic, or by others antiscorodon; it holds a high rank among the dishes of the country people, particularly in Africa, and it is larger than garlic; when beaten up in oil and vinegar it swells up in foam to a surprising size. Some people say that ulpicum and garlic must not be planted in level ground, and advise placing it in little mounds a yard apart like a chain of forts; there must be a space of four inches between the grains, and as soon as three leaves have broken out the plants must be hoed over: they grow larger the oftener they are hoed. When they begin to ripen, their stalks are pressed down into the earth and

Garlic: its medicinal value.

in frondem luxurient. in frigidis utilius vere seri quam autumno. cetero, ut odore careant, omnia haec iubentur seri cum luna sub terra sit, colligi cum in coitu. sine his Menander e Graecis auctor est alium edentibus, si radicem betae in pruna tostam supere-
114 derint, odorem extingui. sunt qui et alium et ulpicum inter Compitalia ac Saturnalia seri aptissime putent. alium et semine provenit, sed tarde; primo enim anno porri crassitudinem capite efficit, sequenti dividitur, tertio consummatur; pulchriusque tale existimant quidam. in semen exire non debet, sed intorqueri caules satus gratia, ut caput validius fiat.
115 quod si diutius alium cepamque inveterare libeat, aqua salsa tepida capita unguenda sunt; ita diuturniora fient melioraque usui, at[1] in satu sterilia. alii contenti sunt primo super prunam[2] suspendisse abundeque ita profici arbitrantur ne germinent, quod facere alium cepamque extra terram quoque certum est et cauliculo aucto[3] evanescere. aliqui et alium palea
116 servari optime putant. alium est et in arvis sponte nascens—alum vocant—quod adversus improbitatem alitum depascentium semina coctum, ne renasci possit,

[1] *Rackham*: et.
[2] prunam? *coll.* § 113 *etc. Mayhoff*: prunas.
[3] aucto *quid. ap. Gelen.*: acto.

[a] May 2 and December 17.

covered up: this prevents their making too lush foliage. In cold soils it pays better to plant in the spring than in autumn. Moreover with all of these plants, to prevent their having an objectionable smell, it is advised to plant them when the moon is below the horizon and to gather them when it is in conjunction. The Greek writer Menander states that people eating garlic without taking these precautions can neutralize the smell by eating after it a beetroot roasted on the hot coals. Some people think that the best time for planting both garlic and ulpicum is between the Feast of the Crossways and the Feast of Saturn.[a] Garlic can also be grown from seed, but it is a slow process, as the head only makes the size of a leek in the first year and divides into cloves in the second year, making full growth in the third year; and some people think that this variety of garlic is a finer kind. It must not be allowed to run to seed, but the stalks must be twisted up for purposes of propagation, so that it may form a stronger head. But if garlic or onions are wanted to keep for some time, their heads should be soaked in warm salt water; that will make them last longer and will render them better for use, though barren in seeding. Others are content to begin by hanging them up over burning coal, and think that this expedient is quite sufficient to prevent their sprouting, which it is well known that garlic and onions do even when out of the ground, and after enlarging their small stalk they wither away. Also some people think that garlic keeps best when stored in chaff. There is also another garlic called alum that grows self-sown in the fields, which, after having been boiled to prevent its shooting up again, is scattered

Growing and storing garlic.

abicitur, statimque quae devoravere aves stupentes et, si paulum commorere, sopitae manu capiuntur.[1] est et silvestre quod ursinum vocant, odore simili,[2] capite praetenui, foliis grandibus.

117 XXXV. In horto satorum celerrime nascuntur ocimum, blitum, napus, eruca—tertio enim die erumpunt; anetum quarto, lactuca quinto, raphanus x, sexto cucumis, cucurbita et septimo [3]—prior cucumis—, nasturtium, sinapi quinto, beta aestate sexto, hieme decimo, atriplex octavo, cepae XVIX aut XX, gethyum X aut duodecimo; contumacius coriandrum, cunila quidem et origanum post XXX diem, omnium autem difficillime apium; XL enim die cum celerrime,
118 maiore ex parte L [4] emergit. aliquid et seminum aetas confert, quoniam recentia maturius gignunt in porro, gethyo, cucumi, cucurbita, ex vetere autem celerius proveniunt apium, beta, cardamum, cunila, origanum, coriandrum. mirum in betae semine, non enim totum [5] eodem anno gignit, sed aliquid sequente, aliquid et tertio; itaque ex copia seminis modice nascitur. quaedam anno tantum suo pariunt, quaedam saepius, sicut apium, porrum, gethyum; haec enim semel sata pluribus annis restibili fertilitate proveniunt.

[1] manu capiuntur *hic Rackham* : *ante* et . . . sopitae.
[2] *Dalec.* : odor est mili *aut* odore mili.
[3] *Sic ? e Theophr. Mayhoff* : raphanus sexto cucumis cucurbita septimo.
[4] L *add. e Theophr. Hermolaus.*
[5] *E Theophr. Caesarius* : tota.

---

[a] In Latin arithmetic 3 is called the third number after 1 (*tertio die* = the day after to-morrow), and this applies to all the numbers here.
[b] *Nasturtium* is cress, not our 'nasturtium'.

about as a protection against the ravages of birds that eat up the seeds, and the birds that swallow it at once become stupefied, and if you wait a little, go completely unconscious and can be caught by hand. There is also a wild kind called bear's garlic, with a similar smell, which has a very small head and large leaves.

Other kitchen-garden plants grown from seed.

XXXV. Of kitchen-garden plants the quickest to grow are basil, blite, navew and rocket; these break out of the ground two [a] days after they are sown. Dill comes up in 3 days, lettuce 4, radish 9, cucumber 5, gourd even 6—cucumber is earlier—, cress [b] and mustard 4, summer beet 5, winter beet 9, orage 7, onions 18 or 19, long onion 9 or 11; coriander is more obstinate, and indeed cunila [c] and wild marjoram do not come up before 30 days, but the most difficult of all is parsley, for it comes up in 39 days at the quickest, and in the majority of cases in 49 days. Something also depends on the age of the seed, as fresh seed comes up more quickly in the case of leek, long onion, cucumber and gourd, but parsley, beet, cress, cunila, wild marjoram and coriander grow more quickly from old seed. There is a curious thing about beet seed that the whole of it does not germinate in the same year but some only in the year following, and some even two years later; and consequently a quantity of seed only produces a moderate crop. Some plants only produce seed in the same year as they are planted, but some more often, for instance parsley, leek and long onion, as these when once sown retain their fertility and come up several years running.

[c] *I.e.* savory.

119 XXXVI. Semina plurimis rotunda, aliquis oblonga, paucis foliacia et lata, ut atriplici, quibusdam angusta et canaliculata, ut cumino. differunt et colore nigro, candidiore, item duritia surculacea. in folliculo sunt raphanis, sinapi, rapo; nudum semen est coriandri, aneti, feniculi, cumini, cortice obductum bliti, betae,
120 atriplicis, ocimi, at lactucis in lanugine. nihil ocimo fecundius; cum maledictis ac probris serendum praecipiunt ut laetius proveniat; sato pavitur terra. et cuminum[1] qui serunt precantur ne exeat. quae in cortice sunt difficillime inarescunt, maximeque ocimum, et ideo siccantur omnia ac fiunt[2] fecunda. utique meliora nascuntur acervatim sato semine quam sparso; ita certe porrum et apium serunt in laciniis colligatum, apium etiam paxillo caverna facta ac fimo
121 ingesto. nascuntur autem omnia aut semine aut avolsione, quaedam et[3] semine et surculo ut ruta, origanum, ocimum—praecidunt enim et hoc, cum pervenit ad palmum altitudinis—, quaedam et semine et radice, ut cepa, alium, bulbi et si quorum radices anniferorum[4] relinquuntur. eorum vero quae a radice nascuntur radix diuturna et fruticosa est, ut bulbi, gethyi, scillae. fruticant alia et non capitata, ut
122 apium et beta. caule reciso fere quidem omnia regerminant exceptis quae non scabrum caulem

[1] *Gelen.*: ad cacuminum.
[2] fiunt? (γίνεται *Theophr.*) *Mayhoff*: sunt.
[3] et *add. Rackham.*
[4] *Edd.*: radicem minimi ferorum.

---

[a] *anniferi*, sending up a new stalk every year.

XXXVI. The seeds of most plants are round, but those of some oblong; in a few they are foliated and broad, for instance orage, in some narrow and grooved, for instance cummin. They differ in colour as well, dark or lighter, and also in woody hardness. The seeds of radishes, mustard and turnip are contained in a pod; the seed of coriander, dill, fennel and cummin has no cover, that of blite, beet, orage and basil is covered with a skin, while that of lettuces is wrapped in down. No seed is more prolific than basil; they recommend sowing it with curses and imprecations to make it come up more abundantly; when it is sown the earth is rammed down. Also people sowing cummin pray for it not to come up. It is difficult for seeds contained in a pod to get dry, particularly basil, and consequently they are all dried artificially to make them fertile. In any case plants grow better when the seed is sown in heaps than when it is scattered; indeed it is on that principle that they sow leek and parsley tied up in strips of rag, and also before sowing parsley they make a hole with a dibble into which they put dung. All plants grow either from seed or from slips, or some both from seed and from cuttings, as rue, wild marjoram, basil—for people lop off the top of this plant too when it has reached the height of a palm; and some plants grow both from seed and from a root, as onion, garlic, bulbs, and the perennials [a] the roots of which stay alive. But with plants that grow from a root the root lives a long time and throws out shoots, for instance bulbs, long onions and squills. Others make shrubby growth and without heads, for instance parsley and beet. When the stalk is cut back, nearly all plants except those which have not got a rough stem throw out fresh shoots, indeed

Growing from seeds, slips and roots.

habent, et in usum vero ocimum, raphanus, lactuca; hanc etiam suaviorem putant a regerminatione. raphanus utique iucundior detractis foliis antequam decaulescat. hoc et in rapis; nam et eadem dereptis foliis cooperta terra crescunt durantque in aestatem.

123 XXXVII. Singula genera sunt ocimo, lapatho, blito, nasturtio, erucae, atriplici, coriandro, aneto; haec enim ubique eadem sunt neque aliud alio melius usquam. rutam furtivam tantum provenire fertilius putant sicut apes furtivas pessume. nascuntur autem etiam non sata mentastrum, nepete, intubum, puleium. contra plura genera sunt eorum quae diximus dice-

124 musque et in primis apio. id enim quod sponte in umidis nascitur helioselinum vocatur, uno folio nec hirsutum, rursus in siccis hipposelinum, pluribus foliis, simile helioselino; tertium est oreoselinum, cicutae foliis, radice tenui, semine aneti, minutiore tantum. et sativi autem differentiae in folio denso, crispo aut rariore et leviore, item caule tenuiore aut crassiore, et caulis aliorum candidus est, aliorum purpureus, aliorum varius.

125 XXXVIII. Lactucae Graeci tria fecere genera: unum lati caulis, adeo ut ostiola olitoria ex iis factitari

---

[a] Wild celery. In Theophrastus (*H.P.* VII, 6, 3), Pliny misread or misheard *μανόφυλλον* as *μονόφυλλον*.

basil, radish and lettuce put out new shoots that can be used; lettuce is thought to be even sweeter if grown from a fresh sprouting. Anyway radish is more agreeable when its leaves have been stripped off before it runs to stalk. The same is also true in the case of turnips, for they likewise if banked up with earth after the leaves have been pulled off go on growing and last into summer.

XXXVII. Basil, sorrel, spinach, cress, rocket, orage, coriander and dill are plants of which there is only one kind, as they are the same in every locality and no better in one place than another. It is a common belief that rue which you have stolen grows better, just as stolen bees are believed to do very badly. Wild mint, cat-mint, endive and pennyroyal spring up even without being sown. On the other hand plants which we have mentioned and are going to mention have several varieties, and particularly parsley. The parsley that grows wild in damp places has a Greek name meaning marsh-parsley [a]; it has a single leaf and is not of shaggy growth; again, the Greek name of another, a many-leaved parsley resembling marsh-parsley, but growing in dry places, is horse-parsley; a third kind is called mountain-parsley in Greek—it has the leaves of hemlock, a thin root, and seed like that of dill only smaller. Moreover cultivated parsley also has varieties in the leaf, which is bushy and crinkled or scantier and smoother, and also in the stalk, thinner or thicker, and in some plants the stalk is white, in others purple, in others mottled.

Varieties, etc., of kitchen-garden plants.

Celery.

Alexanders.

Parsley.

XXXVIII. The Greeks have distinguished three kinds of lettuce, one with so broad a stalk that it is said that the wicket-gates of kitchen gardens are

Varieties of lettuce.

prodiderint—folium his paulo maius herbaceo et angustissimum, ut alibi consumpto incremento—, alterum rotundi caulis, tertium sessile, quod Laconicum vocant. alii colore et tempore satus genera discrevere; esse enim nigras quarum semen mense Ianuario seratur, albas quarum Martio, rubentes quarum Aprili, et omnium earum plantas post binos menses
126 differri. diligentiores plura genera faciunt, purpureas, crispas, Cappadocicas, Graecas, levioris[1] has folii caulisque lati, praeterea longi et angusti, intubis similis; pessimum autem genus cum exprobratione amaritudinis appellavere πικρίδα. est etiamnum alia distinctio albae quae μηκωνὶς vocatur a copia lactis soporiferi, quamquam omnes somnum parere creduntur; apud antiquos Italiae hoc solum genus earum
127 fuit, et ideo lactucis nomen a lacte. purpuream maximae radicis Caecilianam vocant, rotundam vero ac minima radice, latis foliis, ἀστυτίδα, quidamque εὐνουχεῖον, quoniam haec maxime refragetur veneri. est quidem natura omnibus refrigeratrix et ideo aestate gratia. stomacho fastidium auferunt cibique
128 adpetentiam faciunt. divus certe Augustus[2] lactuca

[1] levioris? *e Colum. Mayhoff*: longioris.
[2] *Edd.*: certus *cdd.* (certe *cd. Vat. Lat.* 3861, *m.* 2: certe hac *cd. Par. Lat.* 10318.)

---

[a] According to Columella, named from Caecilius Metellus, who in 251 B.C. defeated the Carthaginian fleet at Palermo.

often made of them; these plants have leaves rather larger than those of the green garden-lettuce, and extremely narrow, the nutriment being apparently used up elsewhere; the second kind has a round stalk, and the third is a squat-growing plant, called the Spartan lettuce. Other people have classified lettuces by colour and season of sowing, saying that the black lettuce is the kind sown in January, the white in March and the red in April, and that all of these kinds can be transplanted at the end of two months. More precise authorities make a larger number of varieties, the purple, the crinkly, the Cappadocian, the Greek—the last with a smoother leaf and a broad stalk, and in addition the lettuce with a long and narrow leaf, which resembles endive; while the worst kind of all has been given the name in Greek of bitter lettuce, in condemnation of its bitter taste. There is moreover another variety of white lettuce the Greek name for which is poppy-lettuce, from its abundance of juice with a soporific property, although all the lettuces are believed to bring sleep; this was the only kind of lettuce in Italy in early times, which accounts for the Latin name for lettuce, derived from the Latin for milk. A purple lettuce with a very large root is called Caecilius's lettuce,[a] while a round one with a very small root and broad leaves is called in Greek the anti-aphrodisiac, or otherwise the eunuch's lettuce, because this kind is an extremely potent check to amorous propensities. Indeed they all have a cooling quality, and consequently are acceptable in summer. They relieve the stomach of distaste for food and promote appetite. At all events it is stated that the late lamented Augustus in

conservatus in aegritudine fertur prudentia Musae medici, cum prioris C. Aemili[1] religio nimia eam abnegaret, in tantum recepta commendatione ut servari etiam in alienos menses eas oxymeli tum repertum sit. sanguinem quoque augere creduntur.

Est etiamnum quae vocatur caprina lactuca de qua dicemus inter medicas; et ecce cum maxime coepit inrepere sativis admodum probata quae Cilicia vocatur, folio Cappadocicae, ni crispum latiusque esset.

129 XXXIX. Neque ex eodem genere possunt dici neque ex alio intubi, hiemis hi patientiores virusque praeferentes, sed caule non minus grati. seruntur ab aequinoctio verno, plantae eorum ultimo vere transferuntur. est et erraticum intubum quod in Aegypto cichorium vocant, de quo plura alias. inventum omnes thyrsos vel folia lactucarum prorogare urceis conditos et recentes in patinis coquere.
130 seruntur lactucae anno toto laetis et riguis stercoratisque, binis mensibus inter semen plantamque et maturitatem. legitimum tamen a bruma semen iacere, plantam favonio transferre, aut semen favonio, plantam aequinoctio verno. albae maxime hiemem
131 tolerant. umore omnia hortensia gaudent et stercore,

[1] *C. F. Hermann*: cameli.

an illness, thanks to the sagacity of his doctor, Musa, was cured by lettuce, which had been refused him by the excessive scruples of his previous doctor, Gaius Aemilius; this was such a good advertisement for lettuces that the method was then discovered of keeping them into the months when they are out of season, pickled in honey-vinegar. It is also believed that lettuces increase the blood-supply.

There is also a variety called the goat-lettuce of which we shall speak among drugs; and only quite XX. 58.
recently there has begun to be introduced among the cultivated lettuces a kind held in considerable esteem called the Cilician lettuce, which has the leaf of the Cappadocian kind, only crinkly and broader.

Other advice for kitchen-gardening.

XXXIX. Endive cannot be said to belong either to the same class of plant as lettuce or to another class, being better able to endure the winter and having more acridity of flavour; but its stalk is equally agreeable. It is sown after the spring equinox, and the seedlings are bedded out at the end of the spring. There is also a wild endive called in Egypt chicory, about which more will be said elsewhere. A method has been discovered of XX. 73, XXI. 88.
preserving all the stalks or leaves of lettuces by storing them in pots and boiling them in saucepans while fresh. Lettuces can be sown all the year round in favourable soil that is watered by streams and manured, with two months between sowing and bedding out and two between that and maturity. The regular plan, however, is to sow just after mid-winter and to bed out when the west wind sets in, or else to sow then and bed out at the spring equinox. White lettuce stands the winter best. All garden plants are fond of moisture and manure, especially lettuce,

praecipue lactucae et magis intubi; seri etiam radices inlitas fimo interest et repleri ablaqueatas[1] fimo.[2] quidam et aliter amplitudinem augent, recisis cum ad semipedem excreverint fimoque suillo recenti inlitis. candorem vero putant contingere iis[3] dumtaxat quae sint seminis albi, si harena de litore a primo incremento congeratur in medias atque increscentia folia contra ipsas[4] religentur.

132 XL. Beta hortensiorum levissima est. eius quoque a colore duo genera Graeci faciunt, nigrum et candidius, quod praeferunt—parcissumi seminis—appellantque Siculum; candoris sane discrimine praeferentes et lactucam. nostri betae genera vernum et autumnale faciunt a temporibus satus, quamquam et Iunio
133 seritur, transfertur autumno[5] planta. hae quoque et oblini fimo radices suas locumque similiter madidum amant. usus his et cum lenti ac faba, idemque qui oleris, et praecipuus ut lenitas excitetur acrimonia sinapis. medici nocentiorem quam olus esse iudicavere, quamobrem adpositas non nemini[6] degustare etiam religio est, ut validis potius in cibo sint. gemina
134 iis natura, et oleris et capite ipso exilientis bulbi.

[1] *Edd.*: ablaqueata.
[2] fimo? *Mayhoff*: humo.
[3] *Rackham*: his.
[4] *Edd.* (ipsa *Mayhoff*): ipso.
[5] *Mayhoff*: autem in.
[6] *V.l.* memini.

---

[a] The ancients ate only the leaves and not the root of beet.

and even more endive: indeed it pays to plant them with the roots smeared with dung and to loosen the ground round them and fill up with dung. Some use other means also of increasing their size, cutting them back when they have reached six inches high and giving them a dressing of fresh swine's dung. As for colour, it is thought that at all events lettuces grown from white seed can be blanched if as soon as they begin to grow sand from the sea-shore is heaped round them up to half their height and the leaves as they start sprouting are tied back against the plants themselves.

XL. Beet is the smoothest of the garden plants. *Beet.* The Greeks distinguish two kinds of beet also, according to the colour, black and whitish—they prefer the latter, which has a very scanty supply of seed, and call it Sicilian beet; indeed they prefer lettuce also with distinctive quality of whiteness. Our people distinguish two kinds of beet according to time of sowing, spring beet and autumn beet, although beet is also sown in June, and the plant transplanted in autumn. Beets also like even their roots to be smeared with dung, and have a similar liking for a damp place. Beets are also made into a salad with lentils and beans, and are dressed [a] in the same way as cabbages, the best way being to stimulate their insipidity with the bitterness of mustard. The doctors have pronounced beet to be more unwholesome than cabbage, on account of which there are persons who scruple even to taste beets when served at table; and consequently they are preferably an article of diet for people with strong digestions. Beets have a double structure, that of the cabbage, and, at the actual head of the root as it springs up, that of an onion. They

species summa in latitudine; ea contingit, ut in lactucis, cum coeperint colorem trahere inposito levi pondere. neque alii hortensiorum latitudo maior; in binos pedes aliquando se pandunt multum et soli natura conferente, siquidem in Circeiensi agro
135 amplissimae proveniunt. sunt qui betas punico malo florente optime seri existiment, transferri autem cum quinque foliorum esse coeperint; mira differentia (si vera est) candidis alvom elici, nigris inhiberi; et cum brassica corrumpatur in dolio vini sapor, eundem[1] betae foliis demersis restitui.

136 XLI. Olus caulesque, quibus nunc principatus hortorum, apud Graecos in honore fuisse non reperio, sed Cato brassicae miras canit laudes, quas in medicinae[2] loco reddemus. genera eius facit: extentis foliis, caule magno, alteram crispo folio, quam apiacam vocant, tertiam minutis caulibus, levem, teneram,
137 minimeque probat. brassica toto anno seritur, quoniam et toto secatur, utilissime tamen ab aequinoctio autumni; transferturque cum quinque foliorum est. cymam[a] a prima satione praestat proxima vere; hic est quidam ipsorum caulium delicatior teneriorque cauliculus, Apicii luxuriae et per eum Druso Caesari

[1] eūdem? *Mayhoff*: eodem *aut* odorem.
[2] medicinae? *Mayhoff*: medendi.

[a] Perhaps this was an accepted term for stale wine beginning to have a flavour like the taste of cabbage-water.
[b] See p. 514, n.

are most valued for width, which is secured, as in lettuces, by placing a light weight on them when they have begun to assume their colour. No other garden plant grows broader: occasionally beets spread out to two feet across, the nature of the soil also contributing a great deal to this, inasmuch as the widest spreading beets grow in the territory of Circeii. Some people think that beets are best sown when the pomegranate is in blossom, and transplanted when they have begun to make five leaves; and that by a remarkable difference (if this really exists) white beet acts as a purge and black beet as an astringent; and that when the flavour of wine in a cask is getting spoiled by 'cabbage',[a] it can be restored to what it was by plunging in some leaves of beet.

XLI. Cabbages and kales which now have preeminence in gardens, I do not find to have been held in honour among the Greeks; but Cato sings marvellous praises of the head of cabbage, which we shall repeat when we deal with medicine. He classifies cabbages as follows—a kind with the leaves wide open and a large stalk, another with a crinkly leaf, which is called celery-cabbage, and a third with very small stalks; the last is a smooth and tender cabbage, and he puts it lowest in value. Cabbage is sown all the year round, since it is also cut all the year round, but it pays best to sow it at the autumnal equinox; and it is transplanted when it has made five leaves. In the next spring after its first sowing it yields sprout-cabbage; this is a sort of small sprout from the actual cabbage stalks, of a more delicate and tender quality, though it was despised by the fastidious taste of Apicius[b] and owing to him by Drusus

Cabbages. *R.R.* CLVI. f. XX. 78 ff.

138 fastiditus, non sine castigatione Tiberii patris. post cymam ex eadem brassica contingunt aestivi autumnalesque cauliculi, mox hiberni, iterumque cymae, nullo aeque genere multifero, donec fertilitate sua consumatur. altera satio ab aequinoctio verno est, cuius planta extremo vere plantatur, ne prius cyma quam caule pariat; tertia circa solstitium, ex qua, si umidior locus est, aestate, si siccior, autumno plantatur. umor fimumque si defuere, maior saporis gratia est, si abundavere, laetior fertilitas. fimum asininum maxime convenit.

139 Est haec quoque res inter opera ganeae, quapropter non pigebit verbosius persequi. praecipuus fit caulis sapore ac magnitudine primum omnium si in repastinato seras, dein si terram fugientes cauliculos sequare terra adtollentesque[1] se proceritate luxuriosa exaggerando aliam accumules ita ne plus quam cacumen emineat. Tritianum hoc genus vocatur, bis
140 conputabili inpendio taedioque. cetera genera complura sunt: Cumanum sessile[2] folio, capite patulum; Aricinum altitudine non excelsius, folio numerosius quam[3] tenerius;[4] hoc utilissimum existimatur quia sub omnibus paene foliis fruticat cauliculis

[1] *C. F. W. Mueller*: tollentesque *aut* dolentesque.
[2] sessili *cd. Par. Lat.* 6795.
[3] *Edd.*: qm̄ *aut* quō *aut* quo *cdd.* (quoniam *cd. Tolet.*).
[4] *Mayhoff*: tenuius.

Caesar, not without reproof from his father Tiberius. After the sprout-cabbage from the same stalk we get summer and autumn sprouts, and then winter ones, and a second crop of sprout-cabbage, as no kind of plant is equally productive, until it gets exhausted by its own fertility. The second sowing begins at the spring equinox, and the seedling is bedded out at the end of spring, so that it may not bear in the sprout-cabbage stage before making cabbage-head; the third is about midsummer, and the produce of this is bedded out during the summer if the place is rather damp and in autumn if it is drier. It has a more agreeable taste if it has not had much moisture or manure, but makes a more abundant growth if they have been plentiful. Ass's dung makes the most suitable manure for it.

Growing cabbages is also one of the ways of supplying table luxuries, so it will not be out of place to pursue the subject at greater length. A way to produce a kale of outstanding flavour and size is if first of all you sow it in ground that has been dug, and next keep pace with the shoots breaking through the soil by earthing them up and when they begin to rise to a luxuriant height make another pile of earth against them by raising the bank so that not more than their head emerges. The kind so grown is called Tritian cabbage, and it may be estimated that it takes twice the usual outlay and trouble. There are quite a number of other varieties: Cumae cabbage, with its leaf close to the ground and a spreading head; La Riccia cabbage, no taller in height, with a leaf more plentiful than tender—this kind is considered extremely useful because underneath almost all the leaves it throws

peculiaribus; Pompeianum procerius caule ab radice tenui intra folia crassescit: rariora haec angustioraque, sed teneritas in dote est; frigora non tolerat, quibus etiam aluntur Bruttiani praegrandes foliis, caule
141 tenues, sapore acuti. Sabellico usque in admirationem crispa sunt folia quorum crassitudo caulem ipsum extenuet, sed dulcissimi perhibentur ex omnibus. nuper subiere Lacuturnenses ex convalle Aricina,[1] capite praegrandes, folio innumeri, alii in orbem conlecti,[2] alii in latitudinem torosi; nec plus ullis capitis post Tritianum, cui pedale aliquando con-
142 spicitur et cyma nullis serior. cuicumque autem generi pruinae plurimum suavitati[3] conferunt; sectis,[4] nisi obliquo vulnere defendatur medulla, plurimum nocent.[5] semini destinati non secantur. est etiam sua gratia numquam plantae habitum excedentibus;[6] ἁλμυρίδια vocant, quoniam nisi in maritumis non proveniunt. aiunt navigatione quoque longinqua virides adservari si statim desecti ita ne humum adtingant in cados olei quam proxime siccatos opturatosque condantur omni spiritu excluso.
143 sunt qui plantam in transferendo alga subdita pedicu-

[1] *Post* Aricina *gloss.* ubi quondam fuit lacus turrisque quae remanet *del. Urlichs.*
[2] *Mayhoff*: porrecti *edd. vett.*: correcti.
[3] suavitati? *coll.* § 182 *Mayhoff*: suavitatis.
[4] sectis? *Mayhoff* (*ipse* at): nec *cdd.* (et *cd. Par. Lat.* 6795).
[5] *Mayhoff*: nocet.
[6] *Sillig*: excellentibus.

---

[a] A note interpolated in the text here runs 'where formerly there was a lake, and a tower which still remains'.
[b] Perhaps sea-kale or sea-fennel.

out small sprouts of a peculiar kind; the Pompei cabbage is taller, and has a thin stalk near the root but grows thicker between the leaves, these being scantier and narrower, but their tenderness is a valuable quality. This cabbage cannot stand cold, which actually promotes the growth of Bruttian cabbages with their extremely large leaves, thin stalk and sharp taste. The Sabellian cabbage has leaves that are quite remarkably crisp and so thick as to exhaust the stalk itself, but these are said to be the sweetest of all the cabbages. There have recently come into notice the Lacuturna cabbages from the valley of La Riccia,[a] which have a very large head and leaves too many to count; some of these cabbages are bunched together into a circular shape and others bulge out broadwise; and no other cabbages make more head, not counting the Tritian kind, which is sometimes seen with a head measuring a foot across, and which sprouts as early as any other sort. But with any kind of cabbages hoarfrosts contribute a great deal to their sweetness, although a frost after the cabbages have been cut does the plants a great deal of damage, unless the pith is safeguarded by using a slanting cut. Cabbages intended for seed are not cut. A peculiarly attractive kind is one that never exceeds the size of a young plant; they call these *halmyridia*,[b] because they only grow on the sea-coast. They say that these keep green even on a long voyage if as soon as they are cut they are prevented from touching the earth by being put into oil-jars that have been dried just before and are bunged up so as to shut out all air. Some people think that the plant will mature more quickly if in the process of transplanting some sea-

lo nitrive triti quod tribus digitis capiatur celeriorem ad maturitatem fieri putent; sunt qui semen trifolii nitrumque simul tritum adspergant foliis. nitrum in coquendo etiam viriditatem custodit, ut et[1] Apiciana coctura, oleo ac sale priusquam coquantur maceratis.

144 est inter herbas genus inserendi praecisis germinibus et caulis in medullam semine ex aliis addito; hoc et in cucumere silvestri. nec non olus quoque silvestre est triumpho divi Iulii carminibus praecipue iocisque militaribus celebratum: alternis quippe versibus exprobravere lapsana se vixisse aput Dyrrachium, praemiorum parsimoniam cavillantes. est autem id cyma silvestris.

145 XLII. Omnium in hortis rerum lautissima cura asparagis. de origine eorum e[2] silvestribus corrudis[3] abunde dictum et quomodo eos iuberet Cato in harundinetis seri. est et aliud genus incultius asparago, mitius corruda, passim etiam in montibus nascens, refertis superioris Germaniae campis, non inficeto Ti. Caesaris dicto herbam ibi quandam nasci simillimam

146 asparago. nam quod in Neside Campaniae insula sponte nascitur longe optimum existimatur. hortensium seritur spongeis; est enim plurimae radicis altissumeque germinat. viret thyrso primum emi-

[1] ut et *Mayhoff*: ut in *coni. Dalec.*: aut.
[2] e *add. Mayhoff*: in *edd. vett.*
[3] *Mayhoff*: curis.

---

[a] A celebrated gourmet under Augustus and Tiberius, whose name is attached to a cookery book in ten volumes, still extant.

weed is placed under the foot-stalk, or else a pinch of pounded soda, as much as can be picked up with three fingers; and some have a plan of sprinkling the leaves with soda ground up with trefoil seed. Soda added in cooking also preserves the greenness of cabbages, as does also Apicius's [a] recipe for steeping them in oil and salt before they are boiled. There is a method of grafting vegetables by cutting short the shoots and inserting into the pith of the stalk seed obtained from other plants; this has even been done in the case of wild cucumber. There is also a kind of wild cabbage which has been made famous particularly by the songs and jests of the troops at the triumph of the late lamented Julius, as in capping verses they taunted him with having at the siege of Durazzo made them live on white charlock—this was a hit at the stinginess with which he rewarded their services. This is a wild cabbage sprout.

XLII. Of all cultivated vegetables asparagus needs the most delicate attention. Its origin from wild asparagus has been fully explained, and how Cato recommends growing it in reed-beds. There is also another kind less refined than garden asparagus but less pungent than the wild plant, which springs up in many places even in mountain districts; the plains of Upper Germany are full of it, the emperor Tiberius not ineptly remarking that in that country a plant very like asparagus grows as a weed. In fact the kind that grows wild in the island of Nisita off the coast of Campania is deemed far the best asparagus there is. Garden asparagus is grown from root-clumps, for it is a plant with a large amount of root and it buds very deep down. When the thin stem first shoots above ground the plant is green, and the shoot while

Asparagus.

XVI. 173.

R.R. CLXI

cante, qui caulem educens tempore ipso fastigatur[1]
147 in toros striatos.[2] potest et semine seri. nihil diligentius comprehendit Cato, novissimumque libri est, ut appareat rem[3] irrepentem[4] ac noviciam fuisse. locum subigi iubet umidum aut crassum, semipedali undique intervallo seri, ne calcetur, praeterea ad lineam grana bina aut terna paxillo demitti—videlicet
148 semine tum tantum serebantur—, id fieri secundum aequinoctium vernum, stercore satiari, crebro purgari, caveri ne cum herbis evellatur asparagus, primo anno stramento ab hieme protegi, vere aperiri, sariri, runcari, tertio incendi verno. quo maturius incensus est hoc melius provenit; itaque harundinetis maxime convenit quae festinant incendi. sariri iubet idem non antequam asparagus natus fuerit, ne in sariendo
149 radices vexentur; ex eo velli asparagum ab radice, nam si defringatur, stirpescere et intermori; velli donec in semen eat (id autem maturescere ad ver) incendique, ac rursus, cum apparuerit asparagus, sariri ac stercorari. ac post annos IX, cum iam vetus sit, digeri subacto stercoratoque, tum spongeis seri singulorum pedum intervallo. quin et ovillo fimo
150 nominatim uti, quoniam aliud herbas creet. nec

[1] *Mayhoff*: fastigatus est.
[2] *Mayhoff*: striatur *aut* striatus.
[3] rem *add. Mayhoff*.
[4] *Rackham*: repentem.

making a longer stalk simultaneously tops off into grooved protuberances. It can also be grown from seed. No subject included by Cato is treated more carefully, and it is the last topic of his book, showing that it was a novelty just creeping in. His advice is to dig over a place with a damp or heavy soil and sow the seeds six inches apart each way, so as to avoid treading on them; and moreover to put two or three seeds in each hole, made with a dibble along a line—obviously at that time asparagus was only grown from seed. He recommends doing this after the vernal equinox, using plenty of dung, frequently cleaning with the hoe, taking care not to pull up the asparagus with the weeds, in the first year protecting the plants against winter with straw, uncovering them in spring and hoeing and stubbing the ground; and setting fire to the plants in the third spring. The earlier asparagus is burnt off, the better it thrives, and consequently it is specially suitable for growing in reed-beds, which burn speedily. He also advises not hoeing the beds before the asparagus springs up, for fear of disturbing the roots in the process of hoeing; next plucking off the asparagus heads close to the root, because if they are broken off, the plant runs to stalk and dies off; going on plucking them till they run to seed (which begins to mature towards spring-time) and burning them off, and when the asparagus plants have appeared, hoeing them over again and manuring them. Nine years later, he says, when the plants are now old, they must be separated and the ground worked over and manured, and then they must be replanted with the tufts spaced out a foot apart. Moreover he expressly specifies using sheeps' dung, as other manure produces weeds. No

quicquam postea temptatum utilius apparuit nisi quod circa id. Feb. defosso semine acervatim parvulis scrobibus serunt, plurimum maceratum fimo; dein [1] nexis inter se radicibus spongeas factas post aequinoctium autumni disponunt pedalibus intervallis fer-
151 tilitate in denos annos durante. nullum gratius his solum quam Ravennatium hortorum indicavimus. corrudam—hunc enim intellego silvestrem asparagum, quem Graeci ὅρμινον aut μυάκανθον vocant aliisque nominibus—invenio nasci et arietis cornibus tunsis atque defossis.

152 XLIII. Poterant videri dicta omnia quae in pretio sunt, ni restaret res maximi quaestus non sine pudore dicenda. certum est quippe carduos apud Carthaginem magnam Cordubamque praecipue sestertium sena milia e parvis reddere areis,[2] quoniam portenta quoque terrarum in ganeam vertimus, serimusque
153 etiam ea quae refugiunt cunctae quadripedes. carduos ergo duobus modis, autumno planta et semine ante nonas Martias, plantaeque ex eo disponuntur ante id. Novemb. aut in locis frigidis circa favonium. stercorantur etiam, si dis placet,[3] laetiusque proveniunt. condiuntur quoque aceto melle diluto addita laseris radice et cumino,[4] ne quis dies sine carduo sit.

[1] ⟨biennio⟩ dein *C. F. W. Mueller* (serunt, per biennium macerant fimo? *coll. Palladio Mayhoff*).
[2] *Salmasius*: eis.
[3] displicet *cd. Vat. Lat.* 3861.
[4] *E Gargilio Mayhoff*: cumini (cumina *cd. Par. Lat.* 10318).

---

[a] This is the cardoon, out of which the modern artichoke has been developed.
[b] The middle of spring.

method of cultivation tried later has proved to be more useful, except that they now sow about February 13 by digging in the seed in heaps in little trenches, usually preparing the seed by soaking it in dung; as a result of this process the roots twine together and form tufts, which they plant out at spaces of a foot apart after the autumn equinox, the plants going on bearing for ten years. There is no soil that asparagus likes better than that of the kitchen-gardens at Ravenna, as we have pointed out. XVI. 173, XIX. 54. I find it stated that corruda (which I take to be a wild asparagus, called by the Greeks *horminos* or *myacanthos* as well as by other names) will also come up if pounded rams' horns are dug in as manure.

Thistles grown for the table.

XLIII. It might be thought that all the vegetables of value had now been mentioned, did not there still remain an extremely profitable article of trade, which must be mentioned not without a feeling of shame. The fact is it is well known that at Carthage and particularly at Cordova crops of thistles[a] yield a return of 6000 sesterces from small plots—since we turn even the monstrosities of the earth to purposes of gluttony, and actually grow vegetables which all four-footed beasts without exception shrink from touching. Thistles then we grow in two ways, from a slip planted in autumn and from seed sown before March 7, the seedlings from which are planted out before November 13, or in cold localities about the season[b] of the west wind. They are sometimes manured as well, if heaven so wills, and come up more abundantly. They are also preserved in honey diluted with vinegar, with the addition of laserwort root and cummin, so that there may be no day without thistles for dinner.

154 XLIV. Cetera in transcursu dici possunt. ocimum Parilibus optime seri ferunt, quidam et autumno, iubentque cum in hiemem seratur aceto semen perfundi. eruca quoque et nasturtium vel aestate vel hieme facillime nascuntur. eruca praecipue frigorum contemptrix diversae est quam lactuca naturae con-
155 citatrixque veneris; idcirco iungitur illi fere in cibis, ut nimio frigori par fervor inmixtus temperamentum aequet. nasturtium nomen accepit a narium tormento, et inde vigoris significatio [1] proverbio usurpavit id vocabulum veluti torporem excitantis. in Arabia mirae amplitudinis dicitur gigni.

156 XLV. Ruta quoque seritur favonio et ab aequinoctio autumni. odit hiemem et umorem ac fimum, apricis gaudet ac siccis terraque quam maxime lateraria; cinere vult nutriri, hic et semini miscetur ut careat urucis. auctoritas ei peculiaris aput antiquos fuit: invenio mulsum rutatum populo datum a Cornelio Cethego in consulatu collega Quinti Flaminini comitiis peractis. amicitia ei cum fico tanta ut [2] nusquam
157 laetior proveniat [3] quam sub hac arbore. seritur et surculo, melius in perforatam fabam indito, quae suco nutrit conprehendendo surculum. serit et se ipsa,

[1] significationem? *Rackham.*
[2] *Mayhoff*: tantum.
[3] *Edd.*: provenit.

---

[a] April 21.
[b] *Nasturtium* = 'nostril-tormenter', from *naris* and *torqueo.*
[c] Ἔσθιε κάρδαμον, 'eat some Cress', said to sluggish people.

XLIV. A cursory description can suffice for the rest of the plants. The best time for sowing basil is said to be at the Feast of Pales,[a] and some say in autumn also, advising that when it is sown for winter the seed should be moistened with vinegar. Also rocket and cress can be grown very easily either in summer or in winter. Rocket particularly thinks nothing of cold. Its properties are quite different from those of lettuce, and it acts as an aphrodisiac; consequently it is usually blended with lettuce in a salad, so that the excessive chilliness of the lettuce may be tempered and counter-balanced by being mingled with an equal amount of heat. Cress has got its Latin name[b] from the pain that it gives to the nostrils, and owing to this the sense of vigorousness has attached itself to that word in the current expression,[c] as denoting a stimulant. It is said to grow to a remarkably large size in Arabia. *Other plants for salad.*

XLV. Rue also is sown when the west wind blows in spring, and just after the autumn equinox. It hates cold weather, damp and dung, and likes sunny, dry places and a soil containing as much brick-clay as possible; it requires to be manured with ashes, which are also mixed with the seed to banish caterpillars. Rue was held in special importance in old times: I find that honied wine flavoured with rue was given to the public by Cornelius, Quintus Flamininus's colleague in the consulship, after the election had been concluded. Rue is so friendly with the fig that it grows better under this tree than anywhere else. It can also be grown from a slip, preferably inserted into a hole made in a bean, which holds the slip firmly and nourishes it with its juice. It also reproduces itself by layering, since if *Rue.* 323 B.C.

namque incurvato cacumine alicuius rami, cum attigit terram statim radicatur. eadem et ocimo natura, nisi quod difficilius arescit semen. ruta[1] runcatur non sine difficultate pruritivis ulceribus, ni munitis manibus id fiat oleove defensis. condiuntur autem et eius folia servanturque fasciculis.

158 XLVI. Ab aequinoctio verno seritur apium semine paulum in pila pulsato: crispius sic putant fieri aut si satum calcetur cylindro pedibusve. proprium ei quod colorem mutat. honos in Achaia coronare victores sacri certaminis Nemeae.

159 XLVII. Eodem tempore seritur menta planta vel, si nondum germinat, spongea. non[2] minus haec umido gaudet. aestate viret, hieme flavescit. genus eius silvestre mentastrum; ex hoc propagatur ut vitis, vel si inversi rami serantur. mentae nomen suavitas odoris aput Graecos mutavit, cum alioqui mintha vocaretur, unde veteres nostri nomen declinaverunt,
160 nunc autem coepit dici ἡδύοσμον. grata tomento,[3] mensas odore percurrit in rusticis dapibus. semel sata diutina aetate durat. congruit puleio, cuius natura in carnariis reflorescens saepius dicta est. haec quoque servantur simili genere, mentam dico puleiumque et nepetam. condimentorum tamen

[1] *Mayhoff*: sed ruta *Urlichs*: arescit sed durata.
[2] non *add. Hardouin* (mire *pro* minus? *Mayhoff*).
[3] *Mayhoff*: grato *aut* grato mento.

---

[a] *Apium* also includes celery, and indeed celery is really meant here.
[b] Especially peppermint.

the end of a branch curves over, when it touches the ground the plant at once strikes root. Basil also has the same properties, except that its seed dries with more difficulty. Stubbing rue is a process not without difficulty, because it causes itching ulcers, unless it is done with the hands protected by gloves or safeguarded by oiling. The leaves of rue are also preserved, being kept in bundles.

XLVI. Parsley [a] sowing begins at the vernal equinox, the seed being first gently pounded in a mortar: it is thought that the parsley is made crisper by this process, or if the seed is rolled or trodden into the earth after being sown. A peculiarity of parsley is that it changes its colour. In Achaia it has the distinction of providing the wreath worn by the winners of the sacred contest at Nemea. *Parsley (celery).*

XLVII. This is also the time for planting mint,[b] using a shoot, or if it is not yet making bud, a matted tuft. Mint is equally fond of damp ground. It is green in summer and turns yellow in winter. There is a wild kind of mint called mentastrum; this is propagated by layering, like a vine, or by planting stalks end downwards. The name of mint has been altered in Greece because of its sweet scent; it used to be called *mintha*, from which our ancestors derived the Latin name, but now it has begun to be called by a Greek word meaning 'sweet-scented'. It is agreeable for stuffing cushions, and pervades the tables with its scent at country banquets. One planting lasts for a long period. It is closely related to pennyroyal, which has the property which we have spoken of more than once of flowering when it is in a larder. These other herbs, I mean mint and also pennyroyal and catmint, are kept in the same kind of way. Yet *Mint, pennyroyal, cummin.* II. 108, XVIII. 227.

omnium[1] quae fastidiis . . .[2] cuminum amicissumum.
161 mum. nascitur in summa tellure vix haerens et in sublime tendens, in putribus et calidis maxime locis medio serendum vere. alterum eius genus silvestre quod rusticum vocant, alii Thebaicum, si tritum ex aqua potetur in dolore stomachi,[3] in Carpetania nostri orbis maxime laudatur, alioqui Aethiopico Africoque palma est; quidam huic[4] Aegyptium praeferunt.

162 XLVIII. Sed praecipue olusatrum mirae naturae est; hipposelinum Graeci vocant, alii zmyrnium. e lacrima caulis sui nascitur, seritur et radice. sucum eius qui colligunt murrae saporem habere dicunt,
163 auctorque est Theophrastus murra sata natum. hipposelinum veteres praeceperant in locis incultis, lapidosis iuxta maceriam seri—nunc et repastinato seritur et a favonio post aequinoctium autumnum—quippe cum capparis quoque seratur siccis maxime, area in defossum cavata ripisque undique circumstructis lapide; alias evagatur per agros et cogit solum sterilescere. floret aestate, viret usque ad vergiliarum occasum, sabulosis familiarissimum. vitia eius quod trans maria nascitur diximus inter peregrinos frutices.

[1] *Urlichs*: *alii alia* omnia.
[2] *Lacunam Urlichs*: ⟨amica sunt⟩ ? *Mayhoff*.
[3] stomachi ⟨prodest⟩ *edd.*
[4] *Edd.*: hoc.

[a] The verb has been lost in the Latin text.
[b] From Thebes in Egypt.
[c] Our alexanders.
[d] *Hist. Plant.* IX. i.

of all the seasonings which gratify [a] a fastidious taste, cummin is the most agreeable. It grows on the surface of the ground, hardly adhering to the soil and stretching upward, and it should be sown in the middle of spring, in crumbly and specially warm soils. Another kind of cummin is the wild variety called country cummin, or by other people Thebaic [b] cummin. For pounding up in water and using as a draught in cases of stomach-ache the most highly esteemed kind in our continent is that grown at Carpetania, though elsewhere the prize is awarded to Ethiopian and African cummin; however some prefer the Egyptian to the African.

Alexanders; caper.

XLVIII. A herb of exceptionally remarkable nature is black-herb,[c] the Greek name for which is horse-parsley, and which others call zmyrnium. It is reproduced from the gum that trickles from its own stalk, but it can also be grown from a root. The people who collect its juice say that it tastes like myrrh, and Theophrastus [d] states that it sprang first from sown myrrh seed. Old writers had recommended sowing horse-parsley in uncultivated stony ground near a garden wall; but at the present day it is sown in land that has been dug over and also after a west wind has followed the autumn equinox. The reason for the old plan was that the caper also is sown principally in dry places, after a plot has been hollowed out for deep digging and stone banks have been built all round it: otherwise it strays all over the fields and takes the fertility out of the soil. It blossoms in summer and continues green till the setting of the Pleiads; it is most at home in sandy soil. The bad qualities of the caper that grows over seas we have spoken of among the exotic shrubs. XIII. 127.

164 XLIX. Peregrinum et careum gentis suae nomine appellatum, culinis principale. in quacumque terra seri vult ratione eadem qua olusatrum, laudatissimum tamen in Caria, proximum Phrygia.

165 L. Ligusticum silvestre est in Liguriae suae montibus, seritur ubique; suavius sativum sed sine viribus. panacem aliqui vocant; Crateuas apud Graecos cunilam bubulam eo nomine appellat, ceteri vero conyzam, id est cunilaginem, thymbram vero quae sit cunila. haec aput nos habet vocabulum et aliud satureia dicta in condimentario genere. seritur mense Februario, origano aemula: nusquam utrumque additur, quippe similis effectus; sed cunilae Aegyptium origanum tantum praefertur.

166 LI. Peregrinum fuit et lepidium. seritur a favonio, dein, cum fruticavit, iuxta terram praeciditur, tunc runcatur stercoraturque. per biennium hoc postea, iisdem fruticibus, utuntur, si non saevitia hiemis ingruat, quando inpatientissimum est frigorum. exit et in cubitalem altitudinem, foliis lauri, sed mollioribus.[1] usus eius non sine lacte.

167 LII. Git pistrinis, anesum et anetum culinis et medicis nascuntur, sacopenium, quo laser adulteratur, et ipsum in hortis quidem, sed medicinae tantum.

[1] *Rackham* (mollibus *edd.*): mollius.

---

[a] Caria in Asia Minor.
[b] Elecampane, or fleabane.
[c] Roman coriander, or fennel-flower.

XLIX. The caraway is also an exotic, and bears a name derived from the country[a] it belongs to; it is chiefly for the kitchen. It will grow in any country if cultivated in the same way as black-herb, though the kind most highly spoken of grows in Caria, and the next best in Phrygia. *Caraway.*

L. Lovage grows wild in the mountains of its native Liguria, but is cultivated everywhere; the cultivated kind is sweeter but lacks strength. Some people call it *panax*, but the Greek writer Crateuas gives that name to cow-cunila, though all others call that *conyza*,[b] which is really cunilago, while real cunila they call *thymbra*. With us cunila has another name also, being called satureia and classed as a spice. It is sown in February; and it is a rival of wild marjoram, the two never being used as ingredients together, because they impart a similar flavour; but only the Egyptian wild marjoram is reckoned superior to cunila. *Lovage.* *Savory.* *Marjoram.*

LI. Pepperwort also was originally an exotic. It is sown after the spring west wind starts, and then, when it has begun to shoot, it is cut down close to the ground and afterwards hoed and manured. Subsequently the plant thus treated is serviceable for two years with the same shoots, provided it is not attacked by a severe winter, as it is very incapable of bearing cold. It grows to a height of as much as eighteen inches; it has the leaves of the bay-tree, but softer. It is always used mixed with milk. *Pepperwort.*

LII. Git[c] is grown for use in bakeries, anise and dill for the kitchen and for doctors; sacopenium, employed for adulterating laserwort, is also grown as a garden plant, but only for medicinal purposes. *Other kitchen plants and medicinal herbs.*

LIII. Sunt quaedam comitantia aliorum satus, ut papaver; namque cum brassica seritur ac porcillaca,
168 et eruca cum lactuca. papaveris sativi tria genera: candidum, cuius semen tostum in secunda mensa cum melle apud antiquos dabatur; hoc et panis rustici crustae inspergitur, adfuso ovo inhaerens, ubi inferiorem crustam apium gitque Cereali sapore condiunt. alterum genus est papaveris nigrum, cuius scapo inciso lacteus sucus excipitur. tertium genus rhoean
169 vocant Graeci, idem [1] nostri erraticum; sponte quidem, sed in arvis cum hordeo maxime nascitur, erucae simile, cubitali altitudine, flore rufo et protinus deciduo, unde et nomen a Graecis accepit. de reliquis generibus papaveris sponte nascentis dicemus in medicinae loco. fuisse autem in honore apud Romanos semper indicio est Tarquinius Superbus, qui legatis a filio missis decutiendo papavera in horto altissima sanguinarium illud responsum hac facti [2] ambage reddidit.

170 LIV. Rursus alio comitatu aequinoctio autumni seruntur coriandrum, anetum, atriplex, malva, lapathum, caerefolium, quod paederota Graeci vocant, et acerrimum sapore igneique effectus ac saluberrimum corpori sinapi, nulla cultura, melius tamen planta tralata: quin e diverso vix est sato semel eo liberare
171 locum, quoniam semen cadens protinus viret. usus

[1] idem (*vel* et)? *Mayhoff*: id.
[2] tacita? *coll. Livio Mayhoff.*

---

[a] The 'pomegranate poppy' (*Papaver hybridum*). The writer supposes the Greek name to be derived from ῥεῖν 'to flow'. The 'white' and 'black' (= pale and dark) poppies mentioned above are opium-poppies.

LIII. There are some plants that are sown in company with others, for instance the poppy, which is sown with cabbage and purslain, and rocket is sown with lettuce. There are three kinds of cultivated poppy: the white, the seed of which in old days used to be roasted and served with honey at second course; it is also sprinkled on the top crust of country loaves, an egg being poured on to make it stick, while celery and git are used to give the bottom crust a festival flavour. The second kind of poppy is the black poppy, from which a milky juice is obtained by making an incision in the stalk. The third kind i called by the Greeks *rhoeas* [a] and in our country wild poppy; it does indeed grow uncultivated, but chiefly in fields sown with barley; it resembles rocket, and grows eighteen inches high, with a red flower which falls very quickly, and which is the origin of its Greek name. We shall speak of the remaining kinds of self-sown poppy under the head of drugs. That the poppy has always been in favour at Rome is indicated by the story of Tarquinius the Proud, who knocked off the heads of the tallest poppies in his garden and by means of this unspoken rebus conveyed to the envoys sent to him by his son that sanguinary answer of his.

Poppy.

XX. 198.

LIV. Again there is another group of plants which are sown at the autumn equinox—coriander, dill, orage, mallow, sorrel, chervil, the Greek name for which is lad's love, and mustard, which with its pungent taste and fiery effect is extremely beneficial for the health. It grows entirely wild, though it is improved by being transplanted: but on the other hand when it has once been sown it is scarcely possible to get the place free of it, as the seed when it falls germinates at once.

Mustard and other autumn-sown herbs.

eius etiam pro pulmentario in patellis decocti[1] citra intellectum acrimoniae; cocuntur et folia, sicut reliquorum olerum. sunt autem trium generum: unum gracile, alterum simile rapi foliis, tertium erucae. semen optimum Aegyptium. Athenienses napy appellaverunt, alii thlaspi,[2] alii saurion.

172 LV. Serpyllo et sisymbrio montes plerique scatent, sicut Threciae; itaque[3] deferunt ex his avulsos ramos seruntque, item Sicyone ex suis montibus et Athenis ex Hymetto. simili modo et sisymbrium serunt, laetissimum nascitur in puteorum parietibus et circa piscinas ac stagna.

173 LVI. Reliqua sunt ferulacei generis, ceu feniculum anguibus, ut diximus, gratissimum, ad condienda plurima cum inaruit utile,[4] eique perquam similis thapsia, de qua diximus inter externos frutices, deinde utilissima funibus cannabis. seritur a favonio; quo densior est eo tenerior. semen eius, cum est maturum, ab aequinoctio autumni destringitur et sole aut vento aut fumo siccatur. ipsa cannabis vellitur post vindemiam ac lucubrationibus decorticata purgatur.
174 optima Alabandica, plagarum praecipue usibus. tria eius ibi genera: inprobatur cortici proximum aut

[1] *Rackham*: decocto.
[2] *Hardouin*: thapsi.
[3] *Mayhoff*: utaque *aut* utique *aut sim.*
[4] utile *add.* ? *Mayhoff*.

It is also used to make a relish, by being boiled down in saucepans till its sharp flavour ceases to be noticeable; also its leaves are boiled, like those of all other vegetables. There are three kinds of mustard plant, one of a slender shape, another with leaves like those of turnip, and the third with those of rocket. The best seed comes from Egypt. The Athenian word for mustard is *napy*, those of other dialects *thlaspi* and lizard-herb.

LV. Most mountains teem with thyme and wild mint, for instance the mountains of Thrace, and so people pluck off sprays of them there and bring them down to plant; and they do the same at Sicyon from mountains there and at Athens from Hymettus. Wild mint is also planted in a similar manner; it grows most abundantly on the walls of wells and round fishpools and ponds. *Thyme and wild or water-mint.*

LVI. There remain the garden plants of the fennel-giant class, for instance fennel, which snakes are very fond of, as we have said, and which when dried is useful for seasoning a great many dishes, and thapsia, which closely resembles it, of which we have spoken among foreign bushes, and then hemp, which is exceedingly useful for ropes. Hemp is sown when the spring west wind sets in; the closer it grows the thinner its stalks are. Its seed when ripe is stripped off after the autumn equinox and dried in the sun or wind or by the smoke of a fire. The hemp plant itself is plucked after the vintage, and peeling and cleaning it is a task done by candle light. The best is that of Arab-Hissar, which is specially used for making hunting-nets. Three classes of hemp are produced at that place: that nearest to the bark or the pith is considered of inferior value, while that *Fennel; hemp.* VIII. 99. XIII. 124.

medullae, laudatissima est e medio quae mesa vocatur. secunda Mylasea. quod ad proceritatem quidem attinet, Rosea agri Sabini arborum altitudinem aequat.
175 ferulae duo genera in peregrinis fruticibus diximus. semen eius in Italia cibus est; conditur quippe duratque in urceis vel anni spatio. duo ex[1] ea olera,[2] caules et racemi.[3] corymbian hanc vocant corymbosque quos condunt.[4]

176 LVII. Morbos hortensia quoque sentiunt sicut reliqua terra sata. namque et ocimum senectute degenerat in serpyllum, et sisymbrium in zmintham, et ex semine brassicae vetere rapa fiunt, atque invicem. et necatur cuminum haemodoro,[5] nisi repurgetur: est autem unicaule, radice bulbo simili, non nisi in gracili solo nascens. alius privatim cumini morbus scabies. et ocimum sub canis ortu pallescit. omnia vero
177 accessu mulieris menstrualis flavescunt. bestiolarum quoque genera innascuntur, napis pulices, raphano urucae et vermiculi, item lactucis et oleri, utrique hoc amplius limaces et cocleae, porro vero privata animalia quae facillime stercore iniecto capiuntur condentia in id se. ferro quoque non expedire tangi rutam, cunilam, mentam, ocimum auctor est Sabinus Tiro in libro κηπουρικῶν quem Maecenati dicavit.

[1] ex *add. Mayhoff.* [2] olera? *Mayhoff*: genera.
[3] [duo . . . racemi] *Urlichs.* [4] *Warmington*: condiunt.
[5] *αἱμοδώρῳ Detlefsen*: ab imo dorso *cdd.*: ab imo orto haemodoro *Warmington coll. Theophr.* H.P. VIII, 8, 5 *ὑποφυόμενον εὐθὺς ἐκ τῆς ῥίζης τῷ κυμίνῳ . . . τὸ αἱμόδωρον.*

from the middle, the Greek name for which is 'middles', is most highly esteemed. The second best hemp comes from Mylasa. As regards height, the hemp of Rosea in the Sabine territory grows as tall as a fruit-tree. The two kinds of fennel-giant have been mentioned above among exotic shrubs. XIII. 123.
In Italy its seed is an article of diet; in fact it is stored in pots and lasts for as much as a year. Two different parts of it are used as vegetables, the stalks and the branches. This fennel is called in Greek clump-fennel, and the parts that are stored, clumps.

Diseases of kitchen-garden plants.

LVII. Garden vegetables are also liable to disease, like the rest of the plants on earth. For instance basil degenerates with old age into wild-thyme and sisymbrium into mint, and old cabbage seed produces turnip, and so on. Also cummin is killed by broom-rape unless it is thoroughly cleaned: this is a plant with a single stalk and a root resembling a bulb, and it only grows in a thin soil. Another disease peculiar to cummin is scab. Also basil turns pale at the rising of the Dog-Star. All plants indeed turn yellow when a woman comes near them at her monthly period. Also various insects breed on garden plants—springtails in navews, caterpillars and maggots in radish, and also on lettuces and cabbage, both of which are more infested by slugs and snails than radish; and the leek has special insects of its own, which are easily caught by throwing dung on the plants, as they burrow into it. According to Sabinus Tiro in his book *On Gardening*, which he dedicated to Maecenas, it is also bad for rue, savory, mint or basil to come in contact with iron.

178 LVIII. Idem contra formicas, non minimum hortorum exitium si non sint rigui, remedium monstravit limum marinum aut cinerem opturandis earum foraminibus. sed efficacissime heliotropio herba necantur; quidam et aquam diluto latere crudo inimicam his
179 putant. naporum medicina ervi aliquid una seri, sicut olerum cicer, arcet enim urucas. quo si omisso enatae sint, remedio est absinthi sucus decocti inspersus vel sedi: genus hoc herbae quam alii ἀείζωον vocant,[1] dixi-
180 mus. semen olerum si suco eius madefactum seratur, olera nulli animalium obnoxia futura tradunt; in totum vero necari urucas si palo inponantur in hortis ossa capitis ex equino genere, feminae dumtaxat. adversus urucas et cancrum fluviatilem in medio horto suspensum auxiliari narrant; sunt qui sanguineis virgis tangant ea quae nolunt his obnoxia esse. infestant et culices riguos hortos, praecipue si sint arbusculae aliquae; hi galbano accenso fugantur.

181 Nam quod ad permutationem seminum attinet, quibusdam ex his firmitas maior est, ut coriandro, betae, porro, nasturtio, sinapi, erucae, cunilae et fere acribus; infirmiora autem sunt atriplici, ocimo, cucurbitae, cucumi, et aestiva omnia hibernis magis; minime autem durat[2] gethyum. sed ex his quae

[1] quam . . . vocant *hic Mayhoff*: *ante* genus.
[2] *Mayhoff*: durant minime autem.

LVIII. The same author has given an account of a remedy against ants, which are not the least destructive of pests in gardens not well supplied with water; the plan is to stop up the mouths of ant-holes with sea-slime or ashes. But the most effective thing for killing ants is the heliotrope plant; and some people also think that water in which an unbaked brick has been soaked is injurious to these insects. It protects navews to sow some bitter vetch with them, and similarly chick-pea for cabbages, as it keeps off caterpillars. If neglect of this precaution has led to the appearance of caterpillars, the remedy is to sprinkle them with a decoction of wormwood or of houseleek; we have mentioned this class of plant, which some call *immortel*. It is stated that if cabbage seed is soaked in the juice of houseleek before being sown, the cabbages will be immune from all kinds of insects; and it is said that caterpillars can be totally exterminated in gardens by fixing up on a stake the skull of an animal of the horse class, provided it is that of a female. There is also a story that a river crab hung up in the middle of a garden is a protection against caterpillars. Some people touch plants which they want to be immune from caterpillars with slips of blood-red cornel. Also gnats infest damp gardens, especially if there are any shrubs in them; these can be driven away by burning galbanum resin.

Protection against ants.

XVIII. 159.

In regard to the deterioration of seeds, some keep longer than others, for instance coriander, beet, leek, cress, mustard, rocket, savory and the pungent seeds generally; while the seeds of orage, basil, gourd and cucumber do not keep so well, and summer seeds in general are not so strong as winter ones. The least lasting is long-onion seed. Of these

Longevity of seeds.

sunt fortissima nullum ultra quadrimatum utile est, dumtaxat serendo; culinis et ultra tempestiva sunt.

182 LIX. Peculiaris medicina raphano, betae, rutae, cunilae in salsis aquis, quae et alioqui plurimum suavitati et fertilitati conferunt. ceteris dulcium aquarum rigua prosunt; utilissimae ex his quae frigidissimae et quae potu suavissimae, minus utiles e stagno et quas elices[1] inducunt quoniam herbarum semina invehunt. praecipue tamen imbres alunt, nam et bestiolas innascentes necant.

183 LX. Hortis[2] horae rigandi matutino atque vespera, ne infervescat aqua sole, ocimo tantum et meridie; nam etiam satum celerrime erumpere putant inter initia ferventi aqua aspersum. omnia autem tralata meliora grandioraque fiunt, maxime porri napique. in tralatione et medicina est, desinuntque sentire iniurias, ut gethyum, porrum, raphani, apium,
184 lactucae, rapa, cucumis. omnia autem fere silvestria sunt[3] et foliis minora et caulibus, suco acriora, sicut cunila, origanum, ruta. solum vero ex omnibus lapathum silvestre melius; hoc in sativis rumix vocatur, omnium quae seruntur nascunturque fortissimum.[4] tradunt certe semel satum durare nec vinci umquam,
185 aeternum[5] maxime iuxta aquas. usus[6] eius cum

[1] *Hermolaus*: silices *edd.*: ilices.
[2] *Sic? Mayhoff*: bestiolae . . . necantur. his.
[3] *Mayhoff*: fere sunt et silvestria.
[4] *Mayhoff*: fortissimum quae servantur *cd. Par. Lat.* 10318: *om. rell.*: nascuntur *cdd.* (nascitur *cd. Par. Lat.* 6797?).
[5] aeternum? *Mayhoff*: a terra.
[6] *Mayhoff* :aquam usus (aqua sucus *cd. Par. Lat.* 10318).

---

[a] See note [b] on § 185.

however which keep best none is of any use after four years, at all events for sowing; they are fit for kitchen use even beyond that period.

Directions for watering.

LIX. There is a curative property specially effective for radish, beet, rue and savory in salt water, which moreover also contributes a great deal to their sweetness and to their fertility. All other plants are benefited by being watered with fresh water, the most useful for the purpose being water from streams, which is extremely cool and very sweet to drink; water from a pond or brought by a conduit is not so useful, because it carries with it the seeds of weeds. However it is rain that nourishes plants best, as rain-water also kills insects that breed on them.

LX. For gardens the times for watering are in the morning and the evening, so that the water may not be heated by the sun. It only suits basil to water it at midday as well; for it is thought that this plant even when first sown will break out most rapidly if at the first stage it is watered with water that is warm. All plants grow better and larger when transplanted, most of all leeks and navews. Also transplanting has a medicinal effect, and such plants as long onion, leek, radishes, parsley, lettuces, turnip and cucumber cease to suffer from injuries when transplanted.[a] But almost all the wild varieties, for example savory, wild marjoram, rue, are smaller in leaf and stalk, and have a more acrid juice. Indeed sorrel is the only one of all the plants of which the wild variety is the better; the cultivated sorrel is called rumix, and it is the strongest of all the plants grown under cultivation or wild; at all events it is reported that when once it has been established it lasts on and is never overcome, and that it is specially everlasting when close to water.

Transplanting.

Use of wild plants.

tisana tantum in cibis: leniorem[1] gratioremque saporem praestat. silvestre ad multa medicamina utile est. (Adeoque nihil omisit cura ut carmine quoque conprehensum reperiam, fabis caprini fimi singulis cavatis si porri, erucae, lactucae, apii, intubi, nasturtii semina inclusa serantur, mire provenire. quae sunt et silvestria eadem sativis sicciora intelleguntur et acriora.)

186 LXI. Namque et sucorum saporumque dicenda differentia est, vel maior in his quam[2] in pomis. sunt autem acres cunilae, origani, nasturtii, sinapis, amari absinthii, centaurei, aquatiles cucumeris, cucurbitae, lactucae, acuti thymi, cunilaginis, acuti et odorati apii, aneti, feniculi. salsus tantum e saporibus non nascitur, aliquando extra insidit pulveris modo, et cicerculis tantum.

187 LXII. Atque ut intellegatur vana ceu plerumque vitae persuasio, panax piperis saporem reddit et magis etiam siliquastrum ob id piperitidis nomine accepto, libanotis odorem turis, zmyrnium murrae. de panace abunde dictum est. libanotis locis putribus et macris ac roscidis seritur; radicem habet olusatri, nihil ture differentem; usus eius post annum stomacho saluberrimus. quidam eam nomine alio rosmarinum

[1] *Mayhoff*: leviorem.
[2] quam *cdd.* (sicut *cd. Par. Lat.* 10318).

[a] Not known.
[b] The sentences in the parenthesis seem to come in better at the end of § 183.
[c] A variant reading gives 'the difference being even greater in the wild varieties, as it is in the case of fruits'.

It is only used for the table mixed with pearl-barley, which gives it a softer and more agreeable flavour. The wild variety supplies a number of drugs. (And so careful has research been to overlook nothing, that I actually find it stated in a poem [a] that if the seeds of leek, rocket, lettuce, parsley, endive and cress are planted enclosed in hollow pellets of goat's dung, each seed in a separate pellet, they come up wonderfully. With plants of which there is also a wild variety, the latter are thought to be more dry and acrid than the cultivated sort.[b])

LXI. Now we ought also to speak of the difference of the juices and flavours of herbs, this being even greater in their case than in fruits.[c] The juice of savory, wild marjoram, cress and mustard has an acrid taste; the juice of wormwood and centaury is bitter, that of cucumbers, gourds and lettuces watery; that of thyme and cunilago pungent; that of parsley, dill and fennel pungent and scented. The only flavour not found in plants is the taste of salt, though occasionally it is present as a sort of external layer, like a dust, and this only in the case of the chickling vetch. *Juices of herbs.*

LXII. And to show how unfounded, as so frequently, is the view ordinarily held, all-heal has the taste of pepper, and still more so has pepperwort, which consequently is called pepper-plant; and grass of Lebanon has the scent of frankincense, and alexanders that of myrrh. About all-heal enough has been said already. Libanotis grows in thin powdery soil, and in places where there is a heavy dew; it has the root of olusatrum, exactly like frankincense; when a year old it is extremely wholesome for the digestion. Some people call it by another name, *Flavours of herbs.* XII. 127. *Lecokia Cretica.*

188 appellant. zmyrnium olus seritur iisdem locis murramque radice resipit. eadem et siliquastro satio. reliqua a ceteris et odore et sapore differunt, ut anetum; tantaque est diversitas atque vis ut non solum aliud alio mutetur sed etiam in totum auferatur: apio eximunt coqui de obsoniis acetum, eodem cellarii in saccis odorem vino gravem.

189 Et hactenus hortensia dicta sint ciborum gratia dumtaxat. maximum quidem opus in iisdem naturae restat, quoniam proventus tantum adhuc summasque quasdam tractavimus, vera autem cuiusque natura non nisi medico effectu pernosci potest, opus ingens occultumque divinitatis et quo nullum reperiri possit maius. ne singulis id rebus contexeremus iusta fecit ratio, cum ad alios medendi desideria pertinerent, longis utriusque dilationibus futuris si miscuissemus. nunc suis quaeque partibus constabunt poteruntque a volentibus iungi.

rosemary. Alexanders is a garden herb that grows in the same places, and its root has the taste of myrrh. Pepperwort grows in the same way. The remaining plants are peculiar in both scent and taste, for example anise; and so great is their diversity and their potency that not only is one of them modified by another but it is entirely counteracted: cooks use parsley to remove the tang of vinegar from their dishes, and parsley enclosed in bags is also employed by butlers to rid wine of disagreeable odour.

Medical uses of plants follow.

And so far we have spoken about garden plants merely as providing articles of diet. There still remains indeed a most important operation of nature in the same department, inasmuch as hitherto we have only treated of their produce and given certain summary outlines; whereas the true nature of each plant can only be fully understood by studying its medicinal effect, that vast and recondite work of divine power, and the greatest subject that can possibly be found. Due regard for method has led us not to combine with each object in succession the question of its medicinal value, because a different set of people are concerned with the requirements of medical practice, and either topic would have met with long interruptions if we had mixed the two together. As it is, each subject will occupy its own section, and any who wish will be able to combine them.

INDEX OF PERSONS

(A few short biographical notes are added to supplement the information given in the text.)

INDEX OF PERSONS

INDEX OF PERSONS

Printed in Great Britain by Richard Clay (The Chaucer Press), Ltd., Bungay, Suffolk

THE LOEB CLASSICAL LIBRARY

VOLUMES ALREADY PUBLISHED

Latin Authors

Ammianus Marcellinus. Translated by J. C. Rolfe. 3 Vols.

Apuleius: The Golden Ass (Metamorphoses). W. Adlington (1566). Revised by S. Gaselee.

St. Augustine: City of God. 7 Vols. Vol. I. G. E. McCracken. Vol. II. W. M. Green. Vol. III. D. Wiesen. Vol. IV. P. Levine. Vol. V. E. M. Sanford and W. M. Green. Vol. VI. W. C. Greene.

St. Augustine, Confessions of. W. Watts (1631). 2 Vols.

St. Augustine, Select Letters. J. H. Baxter.

Ausonius. H. G. Evelyn White. 2 Vols.

Bede. J. E. King. 2 Vols.

Boethius: Tracts and De Consolatione Philosophiae. Rev. H. F. Stewart and E. K. Rand.

Caesar: Alexandrian, African and Spanish Wars. A. G. Way.

Caesar: Civil Wars. A. G. Peskett.

Caesar: Gallic War. H. J. Edwards.

Cato: De Re Rustica; Varro: De Re Rustica. H. B. Ash and W. D. Hooper.

Catullus. F. W. Cornish; Tibullus. J. B. Postgate; Pervigilium Veneris. J. W. Mackail.

Celsus: De Medicina. W. G. Spencer. 3 Vols.

Cicero: Brutus, and Orator. G. L. Hendrickson and H. M. Hubbell.

[Cicero]: Ad Herennium. H. Caplan.

Cicero: De Oratore, etc. 2 Vols. Vol. I. De Oratore, Books I. and II. E. W. Sutton and H. Rackham. Vol. II. De Oratore, Book III. De Fato; Paradoxa Stoicorum; De Partitione Oratoria. H. Rackham.

Cicero: De Finibus. H. Rackham.

Cicero: De Inventione, etc. H. M. Hubbell.

Cicero: De Natura Deorum and Academica. H. Rackham.

Cicero: De Officiis. Walter Miller.

Cicero: De Republica and De Legibus: Somnium Scipionis. Clinton W. Keyes.

Cicero: De Senectute, De Amicitia, De Divinatione. W. A. Falconer.

Cicero: In Catilinam, Pro Flacco, Pro Murena, Pro Sulla. Louis E. Lord.

Cicero: Letters to Atticus. E. O. Winstedt. 3 Vols.

Cicero: Letters to His Friends. W. Glynn Williams. 3 Vols.

Cicero: Philippics. W. C. A. Ker.

Cicero: Pro Archia Post Reditum, De Domo, De Haruspicum Responsis, Pro Plancio. N. H. Watts.

Cicero: Pro Caecina, Pro Lege Manilia, Pro Cluentio, Pro Rabirio. H. Grose Hodge.

Cicero: Pro Caelio, De Provinciis Consularibus, Pro Balbo. R. Gardner.

Cicero: Pro Milone, In Pisonem, Pro Scauro, Pro Fonteio, Pro Rabirio Postumo, Pro Marcello, Pro Ligario, Pro Rege Deiotaro. N. H. Watts.

Cicero: Pro Quinctio, Pro Roscio Amerino, Pro Roscio Comoedo, Contra Rullum. J. H. Freese.

Cicero: Pro Sestio, In Vatinium. R. Gardner.

Cicero: Tusculan Disputations. J. E. King.

Cicero: Verrine Orations. L. H. G. Greenwood. 2 Vols.

Claudian. M. Platnauer. 2 Vols.

Columella: De Re Rustica. De Arboribus. H. B. Ash, E. S. Forster and E. Heffner. 3 Vols.

Curtius, Q.: History of Alexander. J. C. Rolfe. 2 Vols.

Florus. E. S. Forster; and Cornelius Nepos. J. C. Rolfe.

Frontinus: Stratagems and Aqueducts. C. E. Bennett and M. B. McElwain.

Fronto: Correspondence. C. R. Haines. 2 Vols.

Gellius, J. C. Rolfe. 3 Vols.

Horace: Odes and Epodes. C. E. Bennett.

Horace: Satires, Epistles, Ars Poetica. H. R. Fairclough.

Jerome: Selected Letters. F. A. Wright.

Juvenal and Persius. G. G. Ramsay.

Livy. B. O. Foster, F. G. Moore, Evan T. Sage, and A. C. Schlesinger and R. M. Geer (General Index). 14 Vols.

Lucan. J. D. Duff.

Lucretius. W. H. D. Rouse.

Martial. W. C. A. Ker. 2 Vols.

Minor Latin Poets: from Publilius Syrus to Rutilius Namatianus, including Grattius, Calpurnius Siculus, Nemesianus, Avianus, and others with "Aetna" and the "Phoenix." J. Wight Duff and Arnold M. Duff.

Ovid: The Art of Love and Other Poems. J. H. Mozley.

Ovid: Fasti. Sir James G. Frazer.
Ovid: Heroides and Amores. Grant Showerman.
Ovid: Metamorphoses. F. J. Miller. 2 Vols.
Ovid: Tristia and Ex Ponto. A. L. Wheeler.
Persius. Cf. Juvenal.
Petronius. M. Heseltine; Seneca; Apocolocyntosis. W. H. D. Rouse.
Phaedrus and Babrius (Greek). B. E. Perry.
Plautus. Paul Nixon. 5 Vols.
Pliny: Letters, Panegyricus. Betty Radice. 2 Vols.
Pliny: Natural History. Vols. I.–V. and IX. H. Rackham. VI.–VIII. W. H. S. Jones. X. D. E. Eichholz. 10 Vols.
Propertius. H. E. Butler.
Prudentius. H. J. Thomson. 2 Vols.
Quintilian. H. E. Butler. 4 Vols.
Remains of Old Latin. E. H. Warmington. 4 Vols. Vol. I. (Ennius and Caecilius.) Vol. II. (Livius, Naevius, Pacuvius, Accius.) Vol. III. (Lucilius and Laws of XII Tables.) Vol. IV. (Archaic Inscriptions.)
Sallust. J. C. Rolfe.
Scriptores Historiae Augustae. D. Magie. 3 Vols.
Seneca: Apocolocyntosis. Cf. Petronius.
Seneca: Epistulae Morales. R. M. Gummere. 3 Vols.
Seneca: Moral Essays. J. W. Basore. 3 Vols.
Seneca: Tragedies. F. J. Miller. 2 Vols.
Seneca: Naturales Quaestiones. T. H. Corcoran. 2 Vols.
Sidonius: Poems and Letters. W. B. Anderson. 2 Vols.
Silius Italicus. J. D. Duff. 2 Vols.
Statius. J. H. Mozley. 2 Vols.
Suetonius. J. C. Rolfe. 2 Vols.
Tacitus: Dialogus. Sir Wm. Peterson. Agricola and Germania. Maurice Hutton.
Tacitus: Histories and Annals. C. H. Moore and J. Jackson. 4 Vols.
Terence. John Sargeaunt. 2 Vols.
Tertullian: Apologia and De Spectaculis. T. R. Glover. Minucius Felix. G. H. Rendall.
Valerius Flaccus. J. H. Mozley.
Varro: De Lingua Latina. R. G. Kent. 2 Vols.
Velleius Paterculus and Res Gestae Divi Augusti. F. W. Shipley.
Virgil. H. R. Fairclough. 2 Vols.
Vitruvius: De Architectura. F. Granger. 2 Vols.

Greek Authors

Achilles Tatius. S. Gaselee.

Aelian: On the Nature of Animals. A. F. Scholfield. 3 Vols.

Aeneas Tacticus, Asclepiodotus and Onasander. The Illinois Greek Club.

Aeschines. C. D. Adams.

Aeschylus. H. Weir Smyth. 2 Vols.

Alciphron, Aelian, Philostratus: Letters. A. R. Benner and F. H. Fobes.

Andocides, Antiphon, Cf. Minor Attic Orators.

Apollodorus. Sir James G. Frazer. 2 Vols.

Apollonius Rhodius. R. C. Seaton.

The Apostolic Fathers. Kirsopp Lake. 2 Vols.

Appian: Roman History. Horace White. 4 Vols.

Aratus. Cf. Callimachus.

Aristophanes. Benjamin Bickley Rogers. 3 Vols. Verse trans.

Aristotle: Art of Rhetoric. J. H. Freese.

Aristotle: Athenian Constitution, Eudemian Ethics, Vices and Virtues. H. Rackham.

Aristotle: Generation of Animals. A. L. Peck.

Aristotle: Historia Animalium. A. L. Peck. Vols. I.–II.

Aristotle: Metaphysics. H. Tredennick. 2 Vols.

Aristotle: Meteorologica. H. D. P. Lee.

Aristotle: Minor Works. W. S. Hett. On Colours, On Things Heard, On Physiognomies, On Plants, On Marvellous Things Heard, Mechanical Problems, On Indivisible Lines, On Situations and Names of Winds, On Melissus, Xenophanes, and Gorgias.

Aristotle: Nicomachean Ethics. H. Rackham.

Aristotle: Oeconomica and Magna Moralia. G. C. Armstrong; (with Metaphysics, Vol. II.).

Aristotle: On the Heavens. W. K. C. Guthrie.

Aristotle: On the Soul. Parva Naturalia. On Breath. W. S. Hett.

Aristotle: Categories, On Interpretation, Prior Analytics. H. P. Cooke and H. Tredennick.

Aristotle: Posterior Analytics, Topics. H. Tredennick and E. S. Forster.

Aristotle: On Sophistical Refutations.
On Coming to be and Passing Away, On the Cosmos. E. S. Forster and D. J. Furley.

Aristotle: Parts of Animals. A. L. Peck; Motion and Progression of Animals. E. S. Forster.

ARISTOTLE: PHYSICS. Rev. P Wicksteed and F. M. Cornford. 2 Vols.

ARISTOTLE: POETICS and LONGINUS. W. Hamilton Fyfe; DEMETRIUS ON STYLE. W. Rhys Roberts.

ARISTOTLE: POLITICS. H. Rackham.

ARISTOTLE: PROBLEMS. W. S. Hett. 2 Vols.

ARISTOTLE: RHETORICA AD ALEXANDRUM (with PROBLEMS. Vol. II). H. Rackham.

ARRIAN: HISTORY OF ALEXANDER and INDICA. Rev. E. Iliffe Robson. 2 Vols.

ATHENAEUS: DEIPNOSOPHISTAE. C. B. GULICK. 7 Vols.

BABRIUS AND PHAEDRUS (Latin). B. E. Perry.

ST. BASIL: LETTERS. R. J. Deferrari. 4 Vols.

CALLIMACHUS: FRAGMENTS. C. A. Trypanis.

CALLIMACHUS, Hymns and Epigrams, and LYCOPHRON. A. W. Mair; ARATUS. G. R. MAIR.

CLEMENT OF ALEXANDRIA. Rev. G. W. Butterworth.

COLLUTHUS. Cf. OPPIAN.

DAPHNIS AND CHLOE. Thornley's Translation revised by J. M. Edmonds: and PARTHENIUS. S. Gaselee.

DEMOSTHENES I.: OLYNTHIACS, PHILIPPICS and MINOR ORATIONS. I.–XVII. AND XX. J. H. Vince.

DEMOSTHENES II.: DE CORONA and DE FALSA LEGATIONE. C. A. Vince and J. H. Vince.

DEMOSTHENES III.: MEIDIAS, ANDROTION, ARISTOCRATES, TIMOCRATES and ARISTOGEITON, I. AND II. J. H. Vince.

DEMOSTHENES IV.–VI: PRIVATE ORATIONS and IN NEAERAM. A. T. Murray.

DEMOSTHENES VII.: FUNERAL SPEECH, EROTIC ESSAY, EXORDIA and LETTERS. N. W. and N. J. DeWitt.

DIO CASSIUS: ROMAN HISTORY. E. Cary. 9 Vols.

DIO CHRYSOSTOM. J. W. Cohoon and H. Lamar Crosby. 5 Vols.

DIODORUS SICULUS. 12 Vols. Vols. I.–VI. C. H. Oldfather. Vol. VII. C. L. Sherman. Vol. VIII. C. B. Welles. Vols. IX. and X. R. M. Geer. Vol. XI. F. Walton. Vol. XII. F. Walton. General Index. R. M. Geer.

DIOGENES LAERTIUS. R. D. Hicks. 2 Vols.

DIONYSIUS OF HALICARNASSUS: ROMAN ANTIQUITIES. Spelman's translation revised by E. Cary. 7 Vols.

EPICTETUS. W. A. Oldfather. 2 Vols.

EURIPIDES. A. S. Way. 4 Vols. Verse trans.

EUSEBIUS: ECCLESIASTICAL HISTORY. Kirsopp Lake and J. E. L. Oulton. 2 Vols.

GALEN: ON THE NATURAL FACULTIES. A. J. Brock.

THE GREEK ANTHOLOGY. W. R. Paton. 5 Vols.

Greek Elegy and Iambus with the Anacreontea. J. M. Edmonds. 2 Vols.

The Greek Bucolic Poets (Theocritus, Bion, Moschus). J. M. Edmonds.

Greek Mathematical Works. Ivor Thomas. 2 Vols.

Herodes. Cf. Theophrastus: Characters.

Herodian. C. R. Whittaker. 2 Vols.

Herodotus. A. D. Godley. 4 Vols.

Hesiod and The Homeric Hymns. H. G. Evelyn White.

Hippocrates and the Fragments of Heracleitus. W. H. S. Jones and E. T. Withington. 4 Vols.

Homer: Iliad. A. T. Murray. 2 Vols.

Homer: Odyssey. A. T. Murray. 2 Vols.

Isaeus. E. W. Forster.

Isocrates. George Norlin and LaRue Van Hook. 3 Vols.

[St. John Damascene]: Barlaam and Ioasaph. Rev. G. R. Woodward, Harold Mattingly and D. M. Lang.

Josephus. 9 Vols. Vols. I.–IV.; H. Thackeray. Vol. V.; H. Thackeray and R. Marcus. Vols. VI.–VII.; R. Marcus. Vol. VIII.; R. Marcus and Allen Wikgren. Vol. IX. L. H. Feldman.

Julian. Wilmer Cave Wright. 3 Vols.

Libanius. A. F. Norman. Vol. I.

Lucian. 8 Vols. Vols. I.–V. A. M. Harmon. Vol. VI. K. Kilburn. Vols. VII.–VIII. M. D. Macleod.

Lycophron. Cf. Callimachus.

Lyra Graeca. J. M. Edmonds. 3 Vols.

Lysias. W. R. M. Lamb.

Manetho. W. G. Waddell: Ptolemy: Tetrabiblos. F. E. Robbins.

Marcus Aurelius. C. R. Haines.

Menander. F. G. Allinson.

Minor Attic Orators (Antiphon, Andocides, Lycurgus, Demades, Dinarchus, Hyperides). K. J. Maidment and J. O. Burtt. 2 Vols.

Nonnos: Dionysiaca. W. H. D. Rouse. 3 Vols.

Oppian, Colluthus, Tryphiodorus. A. W. Mair.

Papyri. Non-Literary Selections. A. S. Hunt and C. C. Edgar. 2 Vols. Literary Selections (Poetry). D. L. Page.

Parthenius. Cf. Daphnis and Chloe.

Pausanias: Description of Greece. W. H. S. Jones. 4 Vols. and Companion Vol. arranged by R. E. Wycherley.

Philo. 10 Vols. Vols. I.–V.; F. H. Colson and Rev. G. H. Whitaker. Vols. VI.–IX.; F. H. Colson. Vol. X. F. H. Colson and the Rev. J. W. Earp.

PHILO: two supplementary Vols. (*Translation only.*) Ralph Marcus.

PHILOSTRATUS: THE LIFE OF APOLLONIUS OF TYANA. F. C. Conybeare. 2 Vols.

PHILOSTRATUS: IMAGINES; CALLISTRATUS: DESCRIPTIONS. A. Fairbanks.

PHILOSTRATUS and EUNAPIUS: LIVES OF THE SOPHISTS. Wilmer Cave Wright.

PINDAR. Sir J. E. Sandys.

PLATO: CHARMIDES, ALCIBIADES, HIPPARCHUS, THE LOVERS, THEAGES, MINOS and EPINOMIS. W. R. M. Lamb.

PLATO: CRATYLUS, PARMENIDES, GREATER HIPPIAS, LESSER HIPPIAS. H. N. Fowler.

PLATO: EUTHYPHRO, APOLOGY, CRITO, PHAEDO, PHAEDRUS. H. N. Fowler.

PLATO: LACHES, PROTAGORAS, MENO, EUTHYDEMUS. W. R. M. Lamb.

PLATO: LAWS. Rev. R. G. Bury. 2 Vols.

PLATO: LYSIS, SYMPOSIUM, GORGIAS. W. R. M. Lamb.

PLATO: REPUBLIC. Paul Shorey. 2 Vols.

PLATO: STATESMAN, PHILEBUS. H. N. Fowler; ION. W. R. M. Lamb.

PLATO: THEAETETUS and SOPHIST. H. N. Fowler.

PLATO: TIMAEUS, CRITIAS, CLITOPHO, MENEXENUS, EPISTULAE. Rev. R. G. Bury.

PLOTINUS: A. H. Armstrong. Vols. I.–III.

PLUTARCH: MORALIA. 16 Vols. Vols. I.–V. F. C. Babbitt. Vol. VI. W. C. Helmbold. Vols. VII. and XIV. P. H. De Lacy and B. Einarson. Vol. VIII. P. A. Clement and H. B. Hoffleit. Vol. IX. E. L. Minar, Jr., F. H. Sandbach, W. C. Helmbold. Vol. X. H. N. Fowler. Vol. XI. L. Pearson and F. H. Sandbach. Vol. XII. H. Cherniss and W. C. Helmbold. Vol. XV. F. H. Sandbach.

PLUTARCH: THE PARALLEL LIVES. B. Perrin. 11 Vols.

POLYBIUS. W. R. Paton. 6 Vols.

PROCOPIUS: HISTORY OF THE WARS. H. B. Dewing. 7 Vols.

PTOLEMY: TETRABIBLOS. Cf. MANETHO.

QUINTUS SMYRNAEUS. A. S. Way. Verse trans.

SEXTUS EMPIRICUS. Rev. R. G. Bury. 4 Vols.

SOPHOCLES. F. Storr. 2 Vols. Verse trans.

STRABO: GEOGRAPHY. Horace L. Jones. 8 Vols.

THEOPHRASTUS: CHARACTERS. J. M. Edmonds. HERODES, etc. A. D. Knox

THEOPHRASTUS: ENQUIRY INTO PLANTS. Sir Arthur Hort, Bart. 2 Vols.

THUCYDIDES. C. F. Smith. 4 Vols.

TRYPHIODORUS. Cf. OPPIAN.
XENOPHON: CYROPAEDIA. Walter Miller. 2 Vols.
XENOPHON: HELLENICA. C. L. Brownson. 2 Vols.
XENOPHON: ANABASIS. C. L. Brownson.
XENOPHON: MEMORABILIA AND OECONOMICUS. E. C. Marchant. SYMPOSIUM AND APOLOGY. O. J. Todd.
XENOPHON: SCRIPTA MINORA. E. C. Marchant and G. W. Bowersock.

IN PREPARATION

Greek Authors

ARISTIDES: ORATIONS. C. A. Behr.
MUSAEUS: HERO AND LEANDER. T. Gelzer and C. H. WHITMAN.
THEOPHRASTUS: DE CAUSIS PLANTARUM. G. K. K. Link and B. Einarson.

Latin Authors

ASCONIUS: COMMENTARIES ON CICERO'S ORATIONS. G. W. Bowersock.
BENEDICT: THE RULE. P. Meyvaert.
JUSTIN–TROGUS. R. Moss.
MANILIUS. G. P. Goold.

DESCRIPTIVE PROSPECTUS ON APPLICATION

London **WILLIAM HEINEMANN LTD**
Cambridge, Mass. **HARVARD UNIVERSITY PRESS**